MUSIC,
POWER,
AND POLITICS

MUSIC, POWER, AND POLITICS

Edited by Annie J. Randall

ROUTLEDGE
NEW YORK AND LONDON

Johns Hopkins University Press has generously given permission to reprint Michael Eldridge's essay, "There Goes the Transnational Neighborhood: Calypso Buys a Bungalow," from *Callaloo* 25:2 (2002).

Published in 2005 by
Routledge
270 Madison Avenue
New York, NY 10016

Published in Great Britain by
Routledge
2 Park Square
Milton Park, Abingdon
Oxon OX14 4RN U.K.
www.routledge.co.uk

Routledge is an imprint of the Taylor & Francis Group.
Printed in the United States of America on acid free paper.

Library of Congress Cataloging-in-Publication Data

Music, power, and politics / edited by Annie J. Randall.
   p. cm.
  Includes bibliographical references and index.
  ISBN 0-415-94364-7 (hb : alk. paper)
  1. Popular music–Social aspects. 2. Folk music—Social aspects.
I. Randall, Annie Janeiro.
  ML3470.M893 2004
  780'.9—dc22

                                         2004001365

Contents

Acknowledgments

I am grateful to the British Forum for Ethnomusicology which, with the generous support of the British Academy, sponsored the society's annual meeting in 2001 (London, UK). Its theme of "Music and Power" provided the cornerstone for this volume; twelve of the thirteen essays here were presented as conference papers for that meeting. The additional essay, by Michael Eldridge, was presented as a paper at the 2001 annual meeting of the Society for American Music (Port of Spain, Trinidad). Dr. Laudan Nooshin, the principal organizer of the BFE meeting and head of the program committee (that included Henry Stobart, Rachel Harris, and Maria Mendonça), is owed a huge debt of gratitude for her vision in coordinating this extremely stimulating conference. I thank also Sue Ramus and the team of student helpers from Brunel University who assisted Dr. Nooshin with local arrangements. I warmly thank each of the BFE and SAM participants who accepted my invitation to contribute their research to this volume; it has been very gratifying to correspond with this particular group of committed scholars for the past two and a half years.

Thanks are due to those at Bucknell University who provided departmental and institutional support at various stages of this project: Vice President and Provost Stephen Bowen, Vice President for Academic Affairs, Jim Rice, and Music Department Chair, Bill Kenny. For their help in finding materials and preparing them for publication I thank Laurel Evans, Janet Clapp, and Debra Balducci of Bucknell, Jocelyne Rubinetti of Drew University's library, and my research assistant, Megan Rancier.

I completed most of the manuscript's preparation in 2002–03 while researching Italian political music of the Fascist *ventennio*, first in Rome and then at Columbia University's Italian Academy for Advanced Studies in America. Though my work on that subject will appear in a future volume, it is deeply connected to the subject matter of this one; I therefore thank the Italian Academy, its director, Professor David Freedberg, and the Fellows for their collegial support during the very fruitful period of my fellowship in New York. In the same vein I acknowledge Dario Massimi of Rome's Gramsci Institute and the archivists at the Istituto Ernesto de Martino, Sesto Fiorentino. I am also grateful for insights gained during conversations about this project with Suzanne Cuzick (New York University), Martha Mockus (SUNY, Stony Brook), Ellie Hisama (CUNY Graduate Center and Brooklyn College), Steven Feld and Alison Leitch (University of New Mexico), Silvana Patriarca (Fordham University), Carla Cappetti (City College of New York), Pellegrino D'Acierno (Hofstra University), and Lella Gandini (American Academy in Rome).

I fondly acknowledge my friends Jewel, Benny, and Viola in Cincinnati, and singing companions in Lewisburg—Emek, Bernardo, Karen, Dan, Paula, Jim, Gianna, and Barney—who share my enthusiasm for political music in general and Italian resistance songs in particular. Thanks always to my mother for her love, encouragement, and revolutionary spirit.

Annie J. Randall

Introduction

This book traces the operations of power—social, economic, and political—through the medium of music and through discourses about music. None of the authors makes a claim for the power of music *itself* to persuade, coerce, resist, or suppress; rather, they address the uses to which music is put, the controls placed on it, and discursive treatments of it. Guiding these investigations through a variety of historical and cultural contexts are the theories of Gramsci, Adorno, Foucault, Baudrillard, and Attali; indeed, the volume could be viewed as a set of case studies based on these scholars' theories.

Several themes run through the book, and the chapters can be grouped accordingly. Jelena Jovanović's "The Power of Recently Revitalized Serbian Rural Folk Music in Urban Settings" and Sharon Meredith's "Barbadian *Tuk* Music—A Fusion of Musical Cultures" might be read together as investigations of music that assert racial or ethnic identity against the homogenizing tendencies of the nation-state. Jovanović's chapter also relates to Bennett Hogg's "Who's Listening?"; both examine the operations of power through music in territories of the former Yugoslavia, although Hogg concentrates on the use of modern electronic technologies while Jovanović examines the recovery of ancient rural folk singing traditions. Singing traditions are also the topic of Grant Olwage's "Discipline and Choralism: The Birth of Musical Colonialism," which views choral instruction methods through a Foucauldian lens.

Intersections of electronic technology, music, and gender inform Helen Reddington's "Hands Off My Instrument!"—a discussion of women in punk during the Thatcher era in England. Her essay, if read alongside Edward Larkey's "Fighting for the Right (to) Party? Discursive Negotiations of Power in Preunification East German Popular Music," a treatment of rock music in preunification East Germany, yields many points of similarity and contrast; while the time period is the same and the genre of music is similar, the issues faced by the musicians in negotiating their positions vis-à-vis radio stations and the recording industry could not have been more different. Equally stark contrasts of another kind can be found between Larkey's essay and Britta Sweers' "The Power to Influence Minds: German Folk Music during the Nazi Era and After." Only fifty years separate the eras, but in that time eastern Germany had passed from Nazism to Communism and one form of extreme government control of music to another. Geography also ties together two essays with Caribbean themes; both Eldridge's "There Goes the Transnational Neighborhood: Calypso Buys a Bungalow" and Meredith's "Barbadian *Tuk* Music—A Fusion of Musical Cultures" focus on the uses of West Indian musical genres as tools of identity in late colonial and postcolonial time frames.

The theme of music in totalitarian contexts links Sweers' essay with Keith Howard's "Dancing for the Eternal President," a study of modern-day Korean mass dancing in public, government-sponsored spectacles. Government use of individual pieces of iconic music for purposes of historical self-fashioning is a theme connecting Hon-Lun Yang's "The Making of a National Musical Icon: Xian Xinghai and his *Yellow River Cantata*," a treatment of Maoist China's musical showpiece, and Annie Randall's essay on a U.S. patriotic standard, "A Censorship of Forgetting: Origins and Origin Myths of 'Battle Hymn of the Republic.'" Both Randall's chapter and Hellier-Tinoco's "Power Needs Names: Hegemony, Folklorization, and the *Viejitos* Dance of Michoacán, Mexico" discuss at some length the role of "objective" academic methodologies in establishing and maintaining power structures; while Randall looks at historical musicology and class, Hellier-Tinoco centers her study on the sociological practices of categorization and its role in hegemonic folkorization processes.

Laudan Nooshin's "Subversion and Countersubversion: Power, Control, and Meaning in the New Iranian Pop Music," a discussion of Western-style pop music in a context of contemporary Middle Eastern religious fundamentalism, is the only chapter to address music and religion explicitly. Olwage's treatment of choralism, however, implicates the Anglican Church in its discussion of colonial discipline, while Randall identifies the suppression of religious fundamentalism in U.S. history as an important element of her argument regarding "Battle Hymn's" origin myth.

Though the time frame of topics covered in this book span, roughly, a period of one hundred and fifty years (from c. 1850 to 2000), dozens more could be filled with investigations of music, power, and politics in earlier eras. Similarly, each geographical area represented in this volume could generate its own set of essays on the operations of power through music. Genre too could be used as an organizing principle for yet other volumes; preceding the word "music" in the book's title, any number of terms such as "pop," "orchestral," "band," "choral," "jazz," "pedagogical," or "patriotic" could serve as qualifiers. In other words, the topic is certainly not new nor is it confined to any particular area of music; however, surprisingly little has been written on it in any systematic or theoretically coherent way from within the disciplines of musicology and ethnomusicology. The chapters—while written mostly by ethnomusicologists—embrace the work of the twentieth century's most prominent cultural theorists and represent a synthesis of ideas from the fields of sociology, philosophy, musicology, ethnomusicology, and cultural studies. This volume is intended to introduce readers to this synthesis and to provide points of departure for further research on the diverse topics presented here.

We invite readers to visit our website at **http://www.musicpowerpolitics.com**. There we have posted musical excerpts and illustrations to accompany several of the book's chapters. The site will be updated periodically and will include additional material as it becomes available.

A.J.R.
Lewisburg, PA
2004

CHAPTER 1

A Censorship of Forgetting: Origins and Origin Myths of "Battle Hymn of the Republic"

Annie J. Randall

Immediately following the events of September 11, 2001, the song "God Bless America" was everywhere.[1] Everyone, it seemed, was singing it— from senators on the capitol steps to traders at the New York Stock Exchange to ordinary citizens who kept candlelight vigils outside the White House. Other patriotic standards dominated the airwaves; we heard nonstop over radio, television, and the Internet "Amber Waves of Grain," "America," and of course, "The Star Spangled Banner." For a televised memorial moderated by Oprah Winfrey at Yankee Stadium days after September 11, "Battle Hymn of the Republic" was also performed.[2] The promise of "Battle Hymn's" avenging Christ figure, to loose "the fateful lightning of his terrible swift sword" and to "crush the serpent with his heel," seemed particularly suited to the moment.

The irony seemed overwhelming: the 1862 song that we were singing in response to a terrorist attack was itself, in an earlier version, a celebration of a terrorist (see figs 1.1 and 1.2). The "John Brown Song" commemorated the radical abolitionist Brown's bloodiest act—the 1859 armed takeover of a military installation at Harper's Ferry, Virginia—by which Brown intended to spark a massive revolt among millions of slaves throughout the South (see fig. 1.3).[3] Hoping to extract more than irony from this unusual moment, I began to think about "Battle Hymn's" well-known origin myth: a narrative that frames author Julia Ward Howe's moment of poetic inspiration as an expression of Northern resolve to wage civil war to preserve the union. I thought also about the "John Brown Song" (hereafter called "John Brown's Body") and its less well known origins as a fundamentalist camp meeting

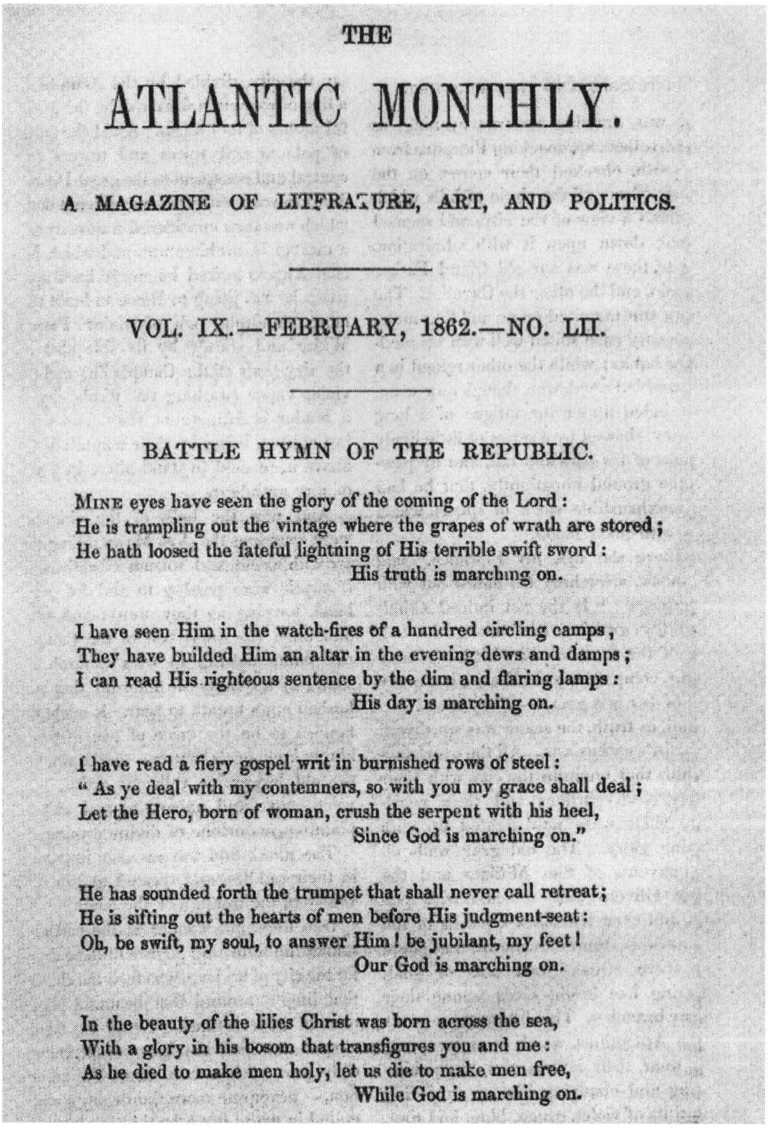

THE

ATLANTIC MONTHLY.

A MAGAZINE OF LITERATURE, ART, AND POLITICS.

VOL. IX.—FEBRUARY, 1862.—NO. LII.

BATTLE HYMN OF THE REPUBLIC.

MINE eyes have seen the glory of the coming of the Lord :
He is trampling out the vintage where the grapes of wrath are stored ;
He hath loosed the fateful lightning of His terrible swift sword :
    His truth is marching on.

I have seen Him in the watch-fires of a hundred circling camps,
They have builded Him an altar in the evening dews and damps ;
I can read His righteous sentence by the dim and flaring lamps :
    His day is marching on.

I have read a fiery gospel writ in burnished rows of steel :
" As ye deal with my contemners, so with you my grace shall deal ;
Let the Hero, born of woman, crush the serpent with his heel,
    Since God is marching on."

He has sounded forth the trumpet that shall never call retreat ;
He is sifting out the hearts of men before His judgment-seat :
Oh, be swift, my soul, to answer Him ! be jubilant, my feet !
    Our God is marching on.

In the beauty of the lilies Christ was born across the sea,
With a glory in his bosom that transfigures you and me :
As he died to make men holy, let us die to make men free,
    While God is marching on.

Figure 1.1. Julia Ward Howe's "Battle Hymn of the Republic" as it appeared in the *Atlantic Monthly* in 1862.

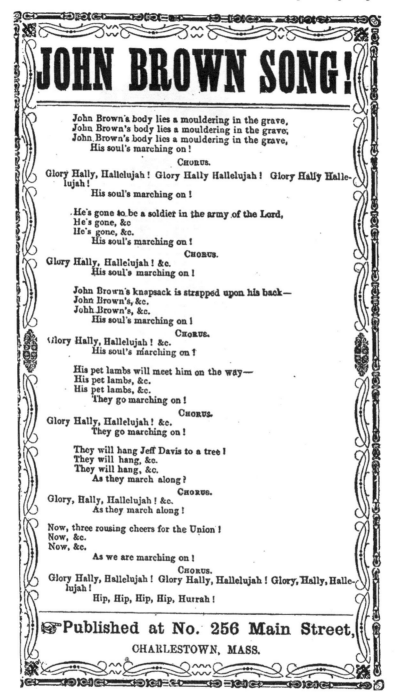

Figure 1.2. "Battle Hymn's" predecessor, the first printed copy of "John Brown Song," 1861 broadside.

Figure 1.3. "The Tragic Prelude. John Brown." Mural by John Steuart Curry in the State Capitol of Topeka, Kansas, c. 1937–1942 (Courtesy of Kansas State Historical Society.)

hymn of the 1850s, "Say Brothers, Will You Meet Us."[4] Multiple authors, most of them anonymous, borrowed this tune, gave it new texts, and used it to hail Brown's terrorist war to abolish the centuries-long practice of slavery in America.[5] Would we have sung "Battle Hymn" in response to September 11, or could we have sung it so innocently had its origins in American terrorism and religious fundamentalism not been sanitized by its origin myth? Surely, it was the *myth*, with its simple message of a divinely ordained national mission in which good triumphed over evil and God repulsed the devil, that made the vengeful song seem appropriate.

I take Roland Barthes' ideas on the function of myth as a starting point for this discussion of "Battle Hymn's" origins and its origin myth:

> Myth deprives the object of which it speaks of all History. In it, History evaporates. It is a kind of ideal servant: it prepares all things, brings them, lays them out, the master arrives, it silently disappears: all that is left for one to do is to enjoy this beautiful object without wondering where it comes from.... [T]his felicitous figure ... removes from sight ... all soiling traces of origin.[6]

Following Barthes, my questions in this chapter concern "Battle Hymn's" "soiling traces." Who has identified them as such? Why has the ideal servant removed them? Who is the master? We observe the servant in action at the time of "Battle Hymn's" publication in 1862 and earlier during the 1861 surge in its predecessor's popularity. Working back to the prewar source of both songs, "Say Brothers Will You Meet Us," we glimpse him one final time. In tracking the servant's activities I hope to show the means by which "Battle Hymn's" myth fosters a kind of civic amnesia, or a censorship of forgetting, that prevents critical engagement with themes of radicalism and religious fundamentalism in United States history. [7]

NAILING DOWN THE COFFIN WITH "THE SONG THAT WROTE ITSELF"[8] (1862)

In mythologizing Howe's text, the ideal servant lays out a series of historical erasures, blanks, and selectively remembered facts concerning the author and the poem's creation, publication, and dissemination. While most historical sources mention that Howe's "Battle Hymn" took its tune from a Union Army marching song known as "John Brown's Body," they fail to note the dozens of Brown-centered versions in circulation before and after the *Atlantic Monthly* published Howe's version in February 1862 and its still earlier source, "Say Brothers."[9] As early as "Battle Hymn's" first publication, its prewar, fundamentalist genesis was already disappearing from view: the *Atlantic Monthly* did not print the signature chorus, "Glory! Glory! Hallelujah!"—which is without doubt "Battle Hymn's" most explicit link with camp meetings. Also rarely mentioned is the Northern government's role in elevating Howe's version to the status of a national standard and the stake it had in doing so: soon after its publication in the *Atlantic*, it was reprinted in thousands of Union Army songbooks and became the de facto "official version" for newly conscripted troops in the war against the South.[10] Indeed, its allusive casting of a good North against an evil South, a Northern God against a Southern devil, and a divinely ordained Federalism against an aberrational, secessionist government provided clearly defined images for a hymn that functioned, as its title implies, as a battle cry. More importantly, it excised the issue of slavery from the text. While removing all direct references to John Brown and slavery, Howe's version replaces the uneven meter of "John Brown's Body" with a strict, seven-foot metrical pattern. In the academically disciplined realm of Howe's iambic heptameter, it is hard to imagine that, to the same tune, the raucous, provocative, colorful line "We'll feed Jeff Davis sour apples 'til he gets the diarhee" ever existed.[11] Indeed, the "elevated," classical language served the government's purpose perfectly by supplanting politically contentious reminders of John Brown and his terrorist acts with images of transcendence and eternal righteousness.

In stark contrast to "Battle Hymn," in which the words "slave," "slavery," and "bondage," never appear, most versions of "John Brown's Body" feature explicit antislavery or anti-South images. For instance, in 1861 the Massachusetts Volunteers sang: "They will hang Jeff Davis from a tree (x3)/As they march along,"[12] while Sojourner Truth's text reads, "See there above the center, where the flag is waving bright,/We are going out of slavery; we're bound for freedom's light;/We mean to show Jeff Davis how the Africans can fight,/As we go marching on!"[13] Ednah Dean Proctor's version commemorating the 1863 Emancipation Proclamation proclaims: "John Brown died on the scaffold for the slave!/Dark was the hour when we dug his hallowed grave;/Now God avenges the life he gladly gave,/Freedom reigns today!"[14] Despite the apotheosis of Howe's Brown-free version in official government spectacles and publications, increasingly explicit Brown-centered texts continued to proliferate, effectively galvanizing abolitionist sentiment; they reflected and helped shape public opinion regarding the slave economy's role in the conflict between North and South.[15]

The connection between abolitionist agitation and Northern war aims was not something Washington wanted to play up; rather, they wanted to downplay it while emphasizing preservation of the Union as the North's primary goal. Threat of abolition inflamed a situation still thought to be salvageable without recourse to a protracted war; President Lincoln, as late as March 1861 (just one month before the outbreak of war), was committed to upholding slavery in the states where it existed.[16] If the government's attempts to turn attention from slavery had been difficult before Brown's raid, it was virtually impossible after. Brown's extremism had captured the nation's attention and, as the many versions of the song suggest, its imagination as well.[17] Sung by countless army regiments, played by military and civilian brass bands across the North, and even performed around the parlor piano in middle class homes, "John Brown's Body" was embedded in public consciousness. It took strong government advocacy and the propagation of a powerful origin myth to move "the cult figure" Brown to the margins of public discourse.[18]

The key element in "Battle Hymn's" origin myth is Julia Ward Howe herself (see fig. 1.4). The packaging of her text as the product of divine revelation relies heavily on the removal of her authorial hand but also on her virtuous presence as a representation of the nobly intentioned North. The myth is usually presented in the form of the following narrative: having sung a version of "John Brown's Body" early in the day on November 18, 1861, along with Union troops who were marching outside her carriage, Howe returned to her Washington, DC hotel with the tune still in her ears. Her traveling companion had suggested, "Why do you not write some good words for that stirring tune?"[19] With the notion for a new text thus implanted by Reverend James Freeman Clarke, she recalled that, "I awoke in the gray of morning twilight; and as I lay waiting for the dawn, the long

Figure 1.4. Julia Ward Howe, c. 1862.

lines of the desired poem began to twine themselves in my mind. ... [W]ith a sudden effort, I sprang out of bed, and found in the dimness an old stump of a pen. ... I scrawled the verses almost without looking at the paper."[20]

Endless retellings of Howe's memoir craft an image of the author as a divine conduit: We read in an account of 1925 that Howe "heard the voice of the nation speaking through her lips," and in another of 1942 that "the words flashed into her consciousness as though telegraphed there by some outside force."[21] And in 1979, "So easily the words had come to Mrs. Howe! Had God himself inspired her?"[22] Even more mysteriously, an article of 1956 claims that "Battle Hymn" was "the song that wrote itself."[23] While Howe's own memoir reads as a fairly standard, late-nineteenth-century romanticization of a moment's inspiration, in the hands of later writers we seem to enter the realm of miracle, trance, or spirit possession. By these means, Howe's agency is removed.

Viewing Howe as a conduit serves to squelch questions about her own political orientation, and by extension, the immediate political context of "Battle Hymn." Though the excerpt mentioned above from her memoir is cited frequently as proof of her conduit role (after all, she herself seems to deny full authorial credit), other parts of her memoirs that point clearly to her political interest and agency are left out. Rarely quoted, for instance, are the passages stating that she actually had met John Brown and that her husband, Samuel Gridley Howe, was one of the "Secret Six" who funded Brown's raid on Harper's Ferry.[24] Were these not-so-secret facts the reason Mrs. Howe's name was left off the February 1862 publication?[25] Would these details linking her closely to the world of politics, radical abolitionism, and John Brown himself have compromised her necessary blankness and the text's transcendent aura? As one objective of the origin myth is to remove the soiling trace of John Brown, it would undermine this purpose completely to consider, as one author speculates, that Howe may have even visualized John Brown as the vengeful figure tearing through the landscape with his terrible swift sword.[26]

RADICALISM IN A SMALLER FONT, FUNDAMENTALISM UNDER FOOT (1861–1862)

Howe's version was not the only attempt to move John Brown from the center to the margin. Almost at the same time her text appeared in the *Atlantic Monthly*, Oliver Ditson's piano–vocal score had changed the title of "John Brown's Body" to "Glory Hallelujah" and offered the name Ellsworth (reported to be "a protegé of President Lincoln who was shot dead while pulling down a Confederate flag at Alexandria, Virginia")[27] as an alternative to John Brown. Perhaps in recognition of the ubiquity of the John Brown version, Ditson did not attempt to erase Brown completely from the text; rather his name appears in a smaller font directly below Ellsworth's (see fig. 1.5). The singer is thus offered a clear, partisan choice between the soldier Ellsworth's defense of the Union and the abolitionist Brown's crusade against slavery. (See Appendix for full Ditson text.)[28]

The hymn "Say Brothers Will You Meet Us" (see fig. 1.6) is rarely acknowledged as the source of the tune for "Glory Hallelujah," "John Brown's Body," and "Battle Hymn of the Republic."[29] Having circulated throughout the 1850s in Methodist hymnals and via oral transmission in religious camp meetings,[30] "Say Brothers" was readily parodied by the troops stationed at Fort Warren, Boston Harbor, Massachusetts for whom the hymn had been a favorite. (See website [http://www.musicpowerpolitics.com] for audio file.) In the months following the war's outbreak in April 1861, Massachusetts soldiers replaced the text "Say Brothers will you meet us" with "John Brown's body lies a-mould'ring in the grave" and transformed the hymn's tranquil lilt to a rowdy march.

The text of "Say Brothers" reads: "Say, brothers, will you meet us/Say, brothers, will you meet us,/Say, brothers, will you meet us,/On Canaan's happy shore. CHORUS: Glory, glory, hallelujah,/Glory, glory, hallelujah,/Glory, glory, hallelujah,/For ever, evermore. 2. By the grace of God we'll meet you (x3)/Where parting is no more./CHORUS. 3. Jesus lives and reigns forever (x3), On Canaan's happy shore./CHORUS."

Figure 1.5. "Glory Hallelujah," Oliver Ditson publisher, 1862. (Courtesy Rare Book, Manuscript, and Special Collection Library, Duke University.)

Comparison of "Say Brothers Will You Meet Us" and "John Brown's Body" reveals much more than a simple change of text. The music's meter, while usually notated as 4/4 for both songs, is a true 4/4 in "Say Brothers" but a martial 2/4 in "John Brown's Body." The duple of the march is the most radically different musical element of "John Brown's Body." Contributing to the change in affect from hymn to march are the new, heavily accented, eleven-syllable lines of the march's verses; trampled underfoot are the relaxed, legato, seven-syllable lines and occasionally slurred dotted quarter-eighth note figures of "Say Brothers."[31] Even though the "Glory, hallelujah" refrain remains ostensibly unchanged, it too undergoes a transformation as explicit as the country's change from peace to inevitable war: its fourth line, sung now in march rhythm and changed from "for ever, ever more" to "His soul's marching on" or "As we go marching on," signals an irreversible fall from grace, from heaven to earth, from the eternal to the temporal. The words "Glory, glory, hallelujah," though the same in both songs, now glorify diametrically opposed states:

Figure 1.6. "Say Brothers Will You Meet Us," as printed in *Songs of Zion*, American Tract Society, 1864.

eternal peace in the case of "Say Brothers" and war in the case of "John Brown's Body." It should be added here that Howe's version seems to resolve the opposites by bringing God himself onto the battlefield: it is implied from the final lines of her third, fourth, and fifth verses ("God is marching on") that the eternal and temporal realms have fused in this moment of holy war.

Given the unmistakable images of holy war conjured up by Howe's verses, it seems counterintuituve to distance "Battle Hymn" from "Say Brothers" and the world of the highly emotional religious camp meetings that spawned it; indeed, "Battle Hymn" invokes a "fiery gospel," "[God's] righteous sentence," and other images that would seem to connect it to the world of circuit riders, revivalist preaching, and ecstatic worship. Yet the origin myth tells us that its classical meter, "elevated" language, biblical allusions, and Howe's own patrician status emanated from Northern "high" church culture while the "low" culture, Southern origins of the camp meeting song are barely mentioned. The usually unchallenged claim that "Battle Hymn's" text is superior to earlier versions asserts a specifically Northern institutional superiority and serves to divert interest from its allegedly inferior, Southern progenitor, "Say Brothers," and the fundamentalist culture from which it sprang.

REGARDING THE SERVANT REGARDING CAMP MEETINGS

In exploring the culture of mid-nineteenth-century frontier camp meetings where "Say Brothers" most likely originated, we enter the world of the working-class poor whose musical activities have not, to date, received sustained or systematic musicological attention. Musicological tools, both conceptual and analytical, to explore music created under such conditions are in short supply; most professional training in musicology focuses on the written or printed score, and assumes musical expertise or a degree of literacy among the historical actors who would have performed the music. Camp meetings, then, represent a methodological minefield: there are few conventional musical artifacts, most "performers" were musically illiterate, and religious ecstasy was the vehicle of improvised text/music production.[32] In the absence of tools to recast the problem in different terms, rich sites of musical activity remain hidden from historical view and are, consequently, forgotten. Confusion over the authorship of "Say Brothers" illuminates a dimension of this problem and suggests that we are, perhaps, not asking the right questions of such material.

Studies of nineteenth-century American music consistently label "Say Brothers" as a "camp meeting hymn" but fudge with equal consistency on the issue of its authorship.[33] Some sources, assuming sole authorship, cite William Steffe as composer.[34] Others hedge with the words "adapted by" or "attributed to" William Steffe.[35] We might ask: Does the term "camp meeting hymn" simply indicate the location of the hymn's performance or does it signal special circumstances surrounding its creation?[36] Does the presumption of a sole author or composer prevent exploration of the possibility that a song may have had several creators or might have resulted from group improvisation? On what evidence is the attribution to Steffe made? From what sources was the tune adapted? Is an attribution of "anonymous" accurate when nontraditional evidence—such as first-person accounts of musical practices at camp meetings—suggests that multiple creators may have crafted "Say Brothers" over a period of time extending over the course of several camp meetings, months apart?[37]

In itself, yet another unattributed or misattributed nineteenth-century hymn tune would not be cause for alarm; along with the broad nature of hymnody's sources, the irregularity of nineteenth-century publication practices makes this a common occurrence.[38] But this is no ordinary hymn tune: it is known throughout the world, has inspired countless *contrafacta*, has been a centerpiece of practically every U.S. protest movement of the twentieth century from women's suffrage to Vietnam, and has taken on iconic significance in film, television, and theatrical productions.[39] Its acknowledged status as both a national treasure and, indeed, a national monument comparable to the Statue of Liberty in recognizability makes it especially puzzling that this hymn's origins have failed to attract rigorous scholarly attention and have not sparked critical examinations of musicology's methodologies—methodologies that have, to date, failed to provide more than superficial historical context for this important song.

Perhaps the "soiling trace" of the working class accounts for this; the persistent *déclassé* stigma attached to music research about the working class has meant that their oral traditions remain relatively untouched by professional musicologists.[40] In some sense this could be regarded as a blessing in disguise because, according to Hubbs, the scholarly gaze often reproduces and extends the ignorance it intends to address by failing to question its underlying assumptions of musical quality and aesthetic value. Such assumptions saturate every aspect of advanced music scholarship and work to deny artistic and historic value to products oral tradition. Indeed, the musical culture of religious camp meetings is far removed from the "high" church ethos attached to Howe's "Battle Hymn," and was characterized by ecstatic, improvisatory practices that are consistently marginalized in document-based, composer-centric musicology.

Specialists in nineteenth-century American religious history describe camp meeting music as the creative product of participants who, when seized by the spirit of a particular sermon or prayer, would take lines from a preacher's text as a point of departure for a short, simple melody. The melody was either borrowed from a preexisting tune or made up on the spot. The line would be sung repeatedly, changing slightly each time, and shaped gradually into a stanza that could be learned easily by others and memorized quickly.[41] "Say Brothers," with its short, repetitious text, may well be the result of such a process; if so, then it was printed in Methodist hymnals *retrospectively* after circulating for months or even years via oral transmission.[42] Many hymns originating as spontaneous group expressions of religious sentiment were later collected, adapted, and arranged by *compilers* such as William Steffe. The collection and arrangement of camp meeting hymns subjected the pieces to a process of *normalization*: metrically "raggedy," melodically "irregular" songs produced by participants would be "arranged" according to metrical, rhythmic, melodic, and formal norms of nineteenth-century hymnody; "irregularities" were smoothed over or excised in favor of the homogeneous sound that characterized most mid- to late-nineteenth-century hymnals.[43] Nevertheless, it is still possible to discern in the normalized versions the varied social, ethnic, and musical backgrounds of participants that shaped the character of camp meeting hymns.

Participants from Anglo–Irish, African American, and German ancestry brought their music with them to camp meetings and shared favorite tunes from their various traditions. This variety accounts for many hymns' marked resemblance to African American spirituals or Anglo–Irish traditional tunes. Two speculations regarding the origin of "Say Brothers" take into account the broad array of musics that circulated typically in camp meetings. Boyd Stutler states that the melody was adapted by Methodist Charles Wesley from a British sailor chantey that, in turn, derived from a pre-1700 Swedish drinking song,[44] while W. E. B. DuBois and C. A. Browne suggest that the tune may have originated in antebellum African American communities.[45] Such free mixing of music from several sources was a constant element in camp meeting worship;[46] also typical were the songs' unusual mode of circulation and transformation via ecstatic group dynamics which were accompanied by constant, sometimes violent, physical movement.

Spontaneous physical manifestations of God's presence in the participants' bodies during acts of confession, conviction, salvation, and conversion were among the camp meetings' most distinctive features; alongside reports of highly theatrical preaching and ceaseless music-making exist vivid recollections of these manifestations or "bodily exercises." Such first-person accounts of the seemingly chaotic atmosphere in which hymns like "Say Brothers" were born have caused some to characterize the camp meeting as an "extended emotional orgy."[47] Numerous preachers' diaries and participants' letters report that the central activity of conversion of sinners was marked by the dramatic falling to the ground of dozens to hundreds of people at a time. While falling was the most common of the camp meetings' so-called bodily exercises, the process of conversion was also marked by dancing, barking, running, rolling, and the "jerks." Ellen Eslinger writes, "A person captured by the jerks would shake, or jerk rapidly. As the head snapped back and forth, sometimes so rapidly that the person's facial features appeared blurred, a quick cry or yelp might be uttered."[48] Other accounts describe the unique soundscape of the meetings:

> Some people were crying for mercy; some shouting redeeming grace; and others collected in numberless small circles of twelve or twenty singing hymns.... [S]inners [were] dropping down on every hand, shrieking, groaning, crying for mercy.... Some singing and shouting, clapping their hands, hugging and even kissing, laughing ... the noise was like the roar of Niagara.... Some of the people were singing, while others were shouting vociferously. Confusion reigned.... [S]ometimes almost all the serious people were praying at once, each with his own voice. In the meeting house, sung six songs at once."[49]

Such uncontrolled musical activities could not have been more different from the closely scripted hymn singing practices of the "high" church; similarly, the singers' relative freedom from rigid social hierarchies represented yet another stark contrast between the practices of camp meetings and those of contemporaneous religious institutions. Indeed, the singing and its unique circumstances would seem to have mirrored exactly the ideal of *communitas* and reversal of status that characterized the camp meetings; albeit temporarily, participants enjoyed equal standing with one another and practiced an inclusiveness that was otherwise unknown in antebellum American life.[50] Salvation was possible for all regardless of social status and without intermediaries such as priests, bishops, cardinals or the institutions they represented; children, adults, blacks, whites, men, women took part in the drama of conversion and could equally expect to experience God's manifestation.[51]

Interestingly, Mrs. Howe is also thought to have experienced some sort of possession by an external, spiritual force as she composed the text for "Battle Hymn." Yet it is hard to imagine two more contrasting sites of divine inspiration—the wide, open spaces of the frontier camp meeting and the confines of a Washington DC hotel room—or two more contrasting and differently privileged tropes of holy manifestation.

RESISTING THE MIRACULOUS EVAPORATION

While lamenting what Barthes calls "the miraculous evaporation of history"[52] via acts of exscription that bleach soiling traces from the American past, I also celebrate the countless *contrafacta* that have kept alive both the oppositional spirit of "John Brown's Body" and the oral tradition that spawned "Say Brothers." Every new version that challenges government policy—such as those created by suffragists in the 1890s, labor activists in the 1910s, and anti-Vietnam war protesters in the 1960s—reclaims the melody's heritage as a vehicle of popular protest and recalls the pivotal role of radical resistance at crucial points in U.S. history. "The Movement's Moving On" (1965), for instance, links the abolitionism of the 1860s to the civil rights movement of the 1960s while alluding to anti-Vietnam war sentiment and economic justice issues:

> Mine eyes have seen injustice in each city, town, and state/Your jails are filled with black men and your courts are white with hate/And with every bid for freedom someone whispers to us, "Wait."/That's why we keep marching on./CHORUS: Move on over or we'll move on over you (x3)/And the movement's moving on. 2. You conspire to keep us silent in the field and in the slum/You promise us the vote and sing us, "We Shall Overcome,"/But John Brown knew what freedom was and died to win us some/That's why we keep marching on. CHORUS. 3. Your dove of peace with bloody beak sinks talons in a child/You bend the olive branch to make a bow, then with a smile/You string it with the lynch rope you've been hiding all the while/That's why we keep marching on. 6. Many noble dreams are dreamed by small and voiceless men/Many noble deeds are done the righteous to defend/We're here today, John Brown, to say we'll triumph in the end/That's why we keep marching on.[53]

Such versions constitute conscious acts of remembering that, in effect, counter "Battle Hymn's" myth and the censorship of forgetting it fosters.

Appendix

"Glory Hallelujah" (Boston: Oliver Ditson, 1861–1862)

Ellsworth's [John Brown's] body lies a mould'ring in the grave (x3)/His soul is marching on!/CHORUS: Glory! Glory! Hallelujah! (x3)/His soul is marching on. 2. The stars of Heaven are looking kindly down (x3)/On the grave of poor Ellsworth [old John Brown]! CHORUS. 3. He's gone to be a soldier in the army of the Lord! (x3)/His soul is marching on! CHORUS. 4. Ellsworth's [John Brown's] knapsack is strapped upon his back (x3)/His soul is marching on. CHORUS. 5. His pet lambs will meet him on the way (x3)/And they'll go marching on. CHORUS. 6. They will hang Jeff Davis to a tree (x3)/As they march along. CHORUS. 7. Let's give three good rousing cheers for the union (x3)/As we're marching on. CHORUS.

Notes

A version of this paper was presented at the April 2001 meeting of the British Forum for Ethnomusicology (BFE) in London, England. I presented a version with a different focus at the March 2002 meeting of the Society for American Music (SAM) in Lexington, Kentucky. The change in focus was due entirely to the events now known simply as "9/11." The BFE meeting spawned its own wonderful parody of "Battle Hymn" (in response to Adam Kuper's keynote address) which demonstrated the tune's seemingly infinite capacity to adapt and express resistance to authority. The SAM presentation generated probing questions and thoughtful suggestions from Karen Ahlquist, Susan Cook, Peter Burkholder, Anne Dhu McLucas, Adrienne Fried Block, Naomi André, and Stephen Baur. I am grateful to members of both societies for their very helpful comments. Special thanks to Richard Crawford and Olivia Bloechl for their responses to the final version.

1. On the morning of September 11, 2001, a terrorist group of Islamic fundamentalists hijacked four commercial airplanes with the intention of crashing them into government and financial landmarks in New York City and Washington, DC. Three of the planes reached their targets: the World Trade Center's twin towers and the Pentagon, causing thousands of deaths. The fourth, presumed to be headed for the White House, crashed in a field in south central Pennsylvania. The attack sparked domestic and international crises that, at the time of this writing in mid-2004, were still unfolding.

2. CNN broadcast "Prayer for America" on Sunday, September 23, 2001. I thank Jenny Johnson for her insights regarding this event's use of music.

3. Born into a religious family in Connecticut in 1800, John Brown carried on his family's tradition of abolitionist activism by assisting escaped slaves through the Underground Railroad and the League of Gileadites. In May 1856, Brown was involved in the highly publicized slaying of five proslavery settlers in the contested state of Kansas (whose status as a slave or free state was to be determined by a vote of its residents). His continued antislavery activities were funded by wealthy New England abolitionists—the Secret Six—who raised hundreds of thousands of dollars for Brown's increasingly violent acts. Assisted by twenty-one men, Brown failed in his October 1859 attempt to take over the federal arsenal at Harper's Ferry, Virginia, and in December of the same year was hanged for murder, treason, and intent to incite slave rebellion.

4. Throughout this chapter I refer to the c. 1860 song that begins "John Brown's body lies a-mould'rin' in the grave" as "John Brown's Body." The same text was known variously as "The John Brown Song" or "John Brown."

5. Camp meetings, which drew participants from wide geographical areas, developed along the Kentucky frontier c. 1800 as part of the evangelical movement known as the "Second Great Awakening." Held in forest groves where participants would camp in their own tents for a number of days, the meetings flourished in the first half of the nineteenth century—growing from about four hundred known meetings in 1811 to almost a thousand in 1820 (Lorenz, 22). Itinerant preachers, mostly Methodist, were known as "circuit riders" and devoted themselves to the task of public conversion and salvation of sinners. See Brown (1992), Bruce (1974), Lorenz (1980), and Eslinger (1999).

6. Roland Barthes, *Mythologies* (New York: Hill and Wang, 1972), 151.

7. Peter Dreier and Dick Flacks make a similar point in "Patriotism's Secret History," *The Nation* (June 3, 2002): 39–42.

8. The subheading alludes to two sources: Edmund Clarence Steadman's paean to Brown, quoted in C. A. Browne (revised by Willard Heaps), *The Story of Our National Ballads* (New York: Thomas Y. Crowell Co., 1960), 141, and Louise Hall Tharp's "The Song that Wrote Itself," *American Heritage* 8 (December 1956): 10–13, 100–101. Steadman's verse reads, "Each drop from old Brown's life veins,/Like the red gore of the dragon,/May spring up a vengeful fury, hissing/Through your slave-worn lands!/And old Brown,/Osawatomie Brown,/May trouble you more than ever, when/You've nailed his coffin down!"

9. Many sources, however, describe in scrupulous detail the coincidence that a foot soldier by the name of John Brown happened to be a member of the Massachusetts regiment that first created the text known as "John Brown's Body."

10. See Richards and Elliott, *Julia Ward Howe*, 92; and Browne (rev. Heaps), *National Ballads*, 188. Songsheet or "broadside" versions were especially popular because they could be printed and distributed quickly and cheaply. A good example is the broadside of Howe's "Battle Hymn" produced by the Supervisory Committee for Recruiting of Colored Regiments under

the direction of Major General George Stearns. For a reproduction see the Library of Congress's "America Singing: Nineteenth-Century Song Sheets" section of the American Memory project at www.loc.gov (accessed 6/1/04).

11. See Boyd Stutler, "John Brown's Body," *Civil War History* 4 (1958): 254. Jefferson Davis was the president of the Confederacy.

12. Full text reproduced in George Kimball, "Origin of the John Brown Song," *New England Magazine*, new series 1 (1890): 373.

13. Regiments of African American soldiers sang verses adapted from Truth's version. Suzanne Pullon Fitch and Roseann M. Mandziuk, *Sojourner Truth as Orator: Wit, Story, and Song* (Westport, Conn.: Greenwood Press, 1997), 221–22. This same text is often attributed to Captain Lindley Miller and was published under his name as a broadside by the Supervisory Committee for Recruiting Colored Regiments.

14. Proctor's full text appears in Vicki Eaklor's comprehensive *American Antislavery Songs: A Collection and Analysis* (New York: Greenwood, 1988), 504.

15. Three other contemporaneous versions are reproduced in Eaklor (1988): William Lloyd Garrison's "Our National Visitation," 90; L. H.'s "The Massachusetts John Brown Song," 500; and Caroline A. Robbins'"On the Conquest of Atlanta by the Union Troops," 512. All three were originally published in Garrison's abolitionist newspaper *The Liberator*. Stutler found sixty-five separate pieces of sheet music on the John Brown–Glory Hallelujah theme in addition to countless variants in war-era penny song sheets and pocket songsters (Stutler 258).

16. A concise account of the negotiations between North and South during the immediate prewar period can be found in Peter N. Carroll and David W. Noble, *The Free and the Unfree: A New History of the United States* (New York: Penguin, 1988), 208.

17. Brown's spirit and image permeated popular culture in the years following his first widely publicized terrorist act in 1856 to the extent that a Broadway play, "Osawatomie Brown," lauded his exploits. Numerous poems with Brown as their subject appeared in newspapers and magazines during the same period. Paul Finkelman, ed., *His Soul Goes Marching On: Responses to John Brown and the Harpers Ferry Raid* (Charlottesville: University Press of Virginia, 1995), 5, 41–66.

18. Finkelman refers to Brown as a "cult figure" in *His Soul Goes Marching On*, 5.

19. This line of dialogue is reproduced in several sources. See, for instance, Deborah Pickman Clifford, *Mine Eyes Have Seen the Glory: A Biography of Julia Ward Howe,* (Boston, Mass.: Little, Brown and Co., 1979), 144. Writing before the publication of Howe's memoirs, Kimball (1890) speculated that President Lincoln himself had made the suggestion to Howe to write a new text.

20. Julia Ward Howe quoted in Gary Williams, *Hungry Heart: The Literary Emergence of Julia Ward Howe* (Amherst: University of Massachusetts Press, 1999), 208.

21. Laura Richards and Maud Howe Elliott., *Julia Ward Howe 1819–1910* (Boston and New York: Houghton Mifflin Co., The Riverside Press, Cambridge, 1925), 91; Helen P. Hostetter, "'Sing It Again!' 'Glory, Glory, Hallelujah!' The Romance of a Great American Patriotic Hymn," *Etude* 60 (May 1942): 338; Alexander Woollcott, "She Sounded Forth the Trumpet," *The Reader's Digest* 40 (May 1942): 49.

22. Clifford, *Mine Eyes*, 144.

23. Tharp, "The Song that Wrote Itself," 10.

24. For instance, see Richards and Elliott, *Julia Ward Howe*, 75–76, 87.

25. Howe was an established author who, by 1862, had published collections of poetry and a play; few, if any, of these were published anonymously. See Clifford, *Mine Eyes*, for a complete list of Howe's publications, 299.

26. Browne (rev. Heaps), *National Ballads*, 170.

27. Stutler, "John Brown's Body," 255. Stutler reminds us that the *New York Tribune* was actually the first to publish Howe's text in its January 14, 1862, edition. *Atlantic Monthly,* however, held the copyright.

28. The entire score can be viewed at the Digital Scriptorium of Duke University's Rare Book, Manuscript, and Special Collections Library, available at http://scriptorium.lib.duke.edu/sheet-music/ (accessed 6/1/04). Four additional stanzas appear in the Ditson edition, none of which mention either Ellsworth or Brown. The additional stanza's chorus reflects the country's new political divisions: "Glory! Glory! Glory for the North!/Glory to the soldiers she is sending forth!/Glory! Glory! Glory for the North!/They'll conquer as they go." Stutler, "John Brown's Body," 260, gives April 1862 as the date for the Ditson edition while the Duke Scrip-

torium gives the year of publication as 1861. It is likely that Ditson's copyright was issued officially in 1862, months after the music was offered for sale.

29. Articles in the popular press such as those cited above (Hostetter 1942, Woollcott 1942, and Tharp 1956) include no references to "Say Brothers" or camp meetings.

30. George Kimball, a member of the Massachusetts regiment that created the *contrafactum* "John Brown's Body" from "Say Brothers," describes the process by which the troops came to know the camp meeting hymn and the circumstances surrounding the creation of the new text. Kimball, 371.

31. The first three lines of "Say Brothers'" four-line stanzas are seven (or eight) syllables long while all stanzas conclude with a six-syllable line, resulting in a 7,7,7,6 (or 8,8,8,6) form. The chorus follows the same pattern: 8,8,8,6. The busier surface of "John Brown's Body" is reflected in the 11,11,11,6 pattern of the stanzas. Howe's version is busier still; she expands the number of syllables per line to 14 or 15, yielding a comparatively frenzied 15,15,15,6 form.

32. A document-based approach will miss the story completely. For example, J. Heywood Alexander's *To Stretch Our Ears: A Documentary History of America's Music* (New York: W.W. Norton and Co., 2002), 210, mentions neither "John Brown's Body" nor "Say Brothers."

33. For instance, Crawford states that Howe's poem was "sung to a Methodist hymn tune of the late 1850s.... Like many enduring American songs, this one was made by several hands—poet, composer, arranger—some of them unknown." "John Brown's Body" is not mentioned. Richard Crawford, *An Introduction to America's Music* (New York: W. W. Norton and Co., 2001), 162.

34. See William Ward, ed., *The American Bicentennial Songbook*, vol. 1 (New York: Charles Hansen, 1975), 236.

35. See Jon Finson, *The Voices That Are Gone: Themes in Nineteenth-Century American Popular Song* (New York: Oxford University Press, 1994), n. 6, 124.

36. Hamm cites both "John Brown's Body" and "Say Brothers" as "Battle Hymn's" predecessors, but does not elaborate on the authorship implications of the term "camp-meeting hymn." Charles Hamm, *Music in the New World* (New York: W. W. Norton and Co., 1983), 245–46.

37. Browne (rev. Heaps)'s account is particularly confusing: He states that "Say Brothers" was a "Methodist hymn tune, originally composed by William Steffe in 1855. As a camp-meeting song, it had become popular with Negro churches and fire companies of Charleston, South Carolina ... Steffe's tune was sung by a group of Negro girls at Shady Hole, Georgia, during Sherman's March to the Sea, when a Federal band struck up the well-known tune, and may therefore have been adapted by him from a Negro folk song." C. A. Browne (revised by Willard Heaps), *The Story of Our National Ballads* (New York: Thomas Y. Crowell Co., 1960), 174. Why, then, call it "Steffe's tune"?

38. Such practices may be the source of contradictions found in Albert Christ-Janer, Charles W. Hughes, and Charles Sprague Smith's *American Hymns Old and New* (New York: Columbia University Press, 1980): Steffe is cited as composer of "Say Brothers" in volume 1 (p. 286), while in volume 2 (p. 558) we read that Steffe "may have composed or adapted the tune." Though the authors note that the tune served as the source for "Battle Hymn of the Republic," "John Brown's Body" is not mentioned.

39. To note just a few of the twentieth-century versions: Frances Weed Campbell's "Battle Hymn of the Suffragists" (1890), Ralph Chaplin's labor anthem, "Solidarity Forever" (1915), Wilson and Smith's Vietnam ballad, "Battle Hymn of Lieutenant Calley" (1971). Wolff mentions three additional suffragist settings of 1884 (Wolff, 8–9). Denisoff quotes part of another labor movement version, "Battle Hymn of '48" (Denisoff, 116–17). Hon-Lun Yang reports that a version of "Battle Hymn" was even adapted by protesters during Beijing's Tiananmen Square demonstrations in 1989 (personal correspondence). Stutler lists a number of adaptations by French, German, and British troops in World Wars I and II (Stutler, 260).

40. Nadine Hubbs advanced this argument in response to points raised by Susan Cook in her paper, "Private Sphere, Public Skin: Towards a Prehistory of Cher" at the Society for Ethnomusicology's annual meeting (Detroit, 2001).

41. A number of authors (Bruce, Sims, Hulan, Soderwall, Eslinger) describe this process. See, for example, Ellen Jane Lorenz, *Glory, Hallelujah! The Story of the Camp Meeting Spiritual* (Nashville, Tenn.: Parthenon Press, 1980), 43. For a contemporaneous account, see "The Early Camp-Meeting Song Writers" (n.a.) *Methodist Quarterly Review* (July 1859): 407.

42. See *Methodist Quarterly Review* (July 1859): 413.

43. It is this smoothness and regularity that has caused some to assume that these hymns were *composed* when, in fact, they were retrofitted, so to speak.
44. The song related "the misadventures of a sailor in Limping Lotta's saloon" (Stutler, 260).
45. This possibility, linking "Say Brothers" to the African-American spiritual tradition, invites new interpretations: its images could be read as veiled references to deliverance from slavery. Given the ever-increasing social and political tensions over the issue of slavery during the antebellum period, there seems good circumstantial evidence to support such interpretations. See above, note 36. See also W. E. B. DuBois (edited with introduction by David Roediger), *John Brown* (New York: The Modern Library, 2001), 224; and Charles Eugene Claghorn, *Battle Hymn: The Story Behind 'The Battle Hymn of the Republic'* (New York: Hymn Society of America, 1974), 7.
46. See Eileen Southern, *The Music of Black America* (New York: W.W. Norton, 1997), 82–89. See also Lorenz, Soderwall, Hulan, Eslinger, and Bruce.
47. Dickson D. Bruce, *And They All Sang Hallelujah: Plain Folk Camp-Meeting Religion 1800–1845* (Knoxville: University of Tennessee Press, 1974), 53.
48. Ellen Eslinger, *Citizens of Zion: The Social Origins of Camp Meeting Revivalism* (Knoxville: University of Tennessee Press, 1999), 222.
49. Eslinger, *Citizens of Zion*, 227.
50. Eslinger, *Citizens of Zion*, 225–40.
51. This is not to suggest naively that race, class, and gender divisions were erased in the antebellum camp meeting; they were, however, markedly less rigid than in American society at large. Members of all groups not only participated in the meetings but also assumed leadership roles as preachers or preachers' assistants.
52. Barthes, *Mythologies*, 151.
53. "The Movement's Moving On" by Len Chandler appears in Pete Seeger and Bob Reiser, eds., *Everybody Says Freedom: A History of the Civil Rights Movement in Songs and Pictures* (New York: W.W. Norton, 1989), 216.

Bibliography

Alexander, J. Heywood. *To Stretch Our Ears: A Documentary History of America's Music*. New York: W. W. Norton and Co., 2002.

Barthes, Roland. *Mythologies*. Selected and translated from the French by Annette Lavers. New York: Hill and Wang, 1972.

Baur, Stephen. "Music, Morals, and Social Management: Mendelssohn in Post–Civil War America." *American Music* 19 (2001): 64–130.

Bowman, Kent A. *Voices of Combat: A Century of Liberty and War Songs, 1765–1865*. New York: Greenwood Press, 1987.

Brown, Kenneth O. *Holy Ground: A Study of the American Camp Meeting*. New York: Garland, 1992.

Browne, C. A. Revised by Willard Heaps. *The Story of Our National Ballads*. New York: Thomas Y. Crowell Co., 1960.

Bruce, Dickson D. *And They All Sang Hallelujah: Plain Folk Camp-Meeting Religion 1800–1845*. Knoxville: University of Tennessee Press, 1974.

Carroll, Peter N., and David W. Noble. *The Free and the Unfree: A New History of the United States*. New York: Penguin, 1988.

Chaplin, Ralph. *Wobbly: The Rough and Tumble Story of an American Radical*. University of Chicago Press, 1948.

Christ-Janer, Albert, and Charles W. Hughes, and Carleton Sprague Smith. *American Hymns Old and New*. 2 vols. New York: Columbia University Press, 1980.

Claghorn, Charles Eugene. *Battle Hymn: The Story Behind 'The Battle Hymn of the Republic.'* New York: Hymn Society of America, 1974.

Clifford, Deborah Pickman. *Mine Eyes Have Seen the Glory: A Biography of Julia Ward Howe*. Boston: Little, Brown and Co., 1979.

Crawford, Richard. *An Introduction to America's Music*. New York: W. W. Norton and Co., 2001.

Denisoff, R. Serge. *Great Day Coming: Folk Music and the American Left*. Urbana: University of Illinois Press, 1971.

Dreier, Peter, and Dick Flacks. "Patriotism's Secret History." *The Nation* (June 3, 2002), 39–42.

DuBois, W. E. B. Edited with introduction by David Roediger. *John Brown*. New York: The Modern Library, 2001.

Eaklor, Vicki. *American Antislavery Songs: A Collection and Analysis*. New York: Greenwood, 1988.

"Early Camp-Meeting Song Writers, The." *Methodist Quarterly Review* (July 1859): 401–13. n. a.

Eslinger, Ellen. *Citizens of Zion: The Social Origins of Camp Meeting Revivalism*. Knoxville: University of Tennessee Press, 1999.

Finkelman, Paul, ed. *His Soul Goes Marching On: Responses to John Brown and the Harpers Ferry Raid*. Charlottesville: University Press of Virginia, 1995.

Finson, Jon W. *The Voices That Are Gone: Themes in Nineteenth-Century American Popular Song*. New York: Oxford University Press, 1994.

Fitch, Suzanne Pullon, and Roseann M. Mandziuk. *Sojourner Truth as Orator: Wit, Story, and Song*. Westport, Conn.: Greenwood Press, 1997.

Grant, Mary H. *Private Woman, Public Person: An Account of the Life of Julia Ward Howe from 1819 to 1868*. Brooklyn, N.Y.: Carlson Publishing Inc., 1994.

Hamm, Charles. *Music in the New World*. New York: W. W. Norton and Co., 1983.

Hostetter, Helen P. "'Sing It Again!' 'Glory, Glory, Hallelujah!' The Romance of a Great American Patriotic Hymn." *Etude* 60 (May 1942): 294, 338.

Howe, Julia Ward. *Reminiscences, 1819–1899*. Boston: Houghton, Mifflin and Co., 1899.

Hugh, Brent. "Texts Sung to the Tune of 'Battle Hymn of the Republic' and 'John Brown's Body.'" Site maintained by Prof. Hugh through Missouri Western State College Department of Music. 2001. Available at www.mwsc.edu/~bhugh/john-brown2.html (accessed 6/1/04).

Hulan, Richard Huffman. "Camp-Meeting Spiritual Folksongs: Legacy of the 'Great Revival in the West.'" PhD diss., University of Texas at Austin, 1978.

I. W. W. Songs: To Fan the Flames of Discontent. Nineteenth ed. New York: I.W.W. Publishing Bureau, 1923.

Kimball, George. "Origin of the John Brown Song." *New England Magazine*, new series 1 (1890): 371–76.

Lorenz, Ellen Jane. *Glory, Hallelujah! The Story of the Camp Meeting Spiritual*. Nashville: Parthenon Press, 1980.

MacIntyre, John J. *The Composer of the Battle Hymn of the Republic*. New York: self-published, 1917.

Richards, Laura, and Maud Howe Elliott. *Julia Ward Howe: 1819–1910*. Boston and New York: Houghton Mifflin Co., The Riverside Press, Cambridge, 1925.

Seeger, Pete, and Bob Reiser. *Everybody Says Freedom: A History of the Civil Rights Movement in Songs and Pictures*. New York: W.W. Norton and Co., 1989.

Sims, John Norman. "The Hymnody of the Camp Meeting Tradition." PhD diss., Union Theological Seminary, New York, 1960.

Sing Out: *The Folk Song Magazine* 36 (November–December 1991/January 1992): 10–11.

Soderwall, Lorin Harris. "The Rhetoric of the Methodist Camp Meeting Movement 1800–1850." PhD diss., University of Southern California, 1971.

Southern, Eileen. *The Music of Black Americans: A History*. New York: W.W. Norton and Co., 1997.

———. *Readings in Black American Music*. New York: W.W. Norton and Co., 1971.

Spaeth, Sigmund. *A History of Popular Music in America*. New York: Random House, 1948.

Stutler, Boyd. "John Brown's Body." *Civil War History* 4 (1958): 251–60.

Tharp, Louise Hall. "The Song That Wrote Itself." *American Heritage* 8 (December 1956): 10–13, 100–101.

Ward, William, ed. *The American Bicentennial Songbook*, vol. 1 (1770–1870s). New York: Charles Hansen, 1975.

Williams, Gary. *Hungry Heart: The Literary Emergence of Julia Ward Howe*. Amherst: University of Massachusetts Press, 1999.

Wilson, Julian, and James M. Smith. "Battle Hymn of Lt. Calley." 1971. Available at www.fortunecity.com/tinpan/parton/2/mylai2.html (accessed 6/1/04).

Woolf, Francie. *Give the Ballot to the Mothers: Songs of the Suffragists, A History in Song*. Springfield, Mo.: Denlinger's Publishers Ltd., 1998.

Woollcott, Alexander. "She Sounded Forth the Trumpet." *The Reader's Digest* 40 (May 1942): 49–50.

Zinn, Howard. *A People's History of the United States: 1942–Present*. New York: Harper Collins, 2003.

CHAPTER 2

Discipline and Choralism:
The Birth of Musical Colonialism

Grant Olwage

Discipline is its own type of ceremony.[1]

In the winter of 1863 a choir of "Fingoes and Hottentots" caused quite a
stir in the small Cape colonial city of Grahamstown. One of the first performances by a black choir in the Cape's second city, it was no everyday concert,
and "the *elite* of the musical inhabitants" accordingly turned out in their
curious droves. Equally extraordinary was the lengthy review that appeared
in *The Grahamstown Journal*, the Cape's largest circulating paper. Less
music criticism than social commentary, it discoursed on what slightly
later would be called the "Native Question." The performance illustrated
"several facts of social importance ... each of which would constitute a
fertile theme for the metaphysician, or the student in moral philosophy."
In the event, the report concerned itself with the more immediate, practical lessons to be drawn:

> First is demonstrated a truth of no ordinary importance, at a
> moment when the *taming* of our savage neighbors is looked upon
> by many as an utter impossibility, namely, the capacity of these
> savages for *civilization*. Next, we are struck by the fact that music
> has been able in a few short weeks to *subdue* and *discipline* natures
> so wild and intractable that moral teaching, law, and even our holy
> religion itself have laboured for years to conquer them with but
> very inadequate success.[2]

For the record, the program was packed with staples of the Victorian choral repertory. The review, as I mentioned though, was not so much concerned with the choir's performance as with the effect that practices of choir singing had on its black members. In short, the utility of choralism was its civilizing potential, where civilizing, as my italics above indicate, was synonymous with disciplining.

The white rhetoric of civilizing–disciplining had a particular urgency to it in 1860s Grahamstown; the political stability of the eastern Cape "frontier" remained elusive, with periodic warfare continuing into the late 1870s. In the most real—and for the white colonist, important—sense, civilizing the black population was a large-scale exercise in governmentality, paving the way, went the argument, for Pax Britannica.[3] The *Journal* summed up the concert as bearing witness to that Victorian commonplace, the "power of music to 'calm the savage breast.'" But the concert's "unprecedented success" was attributed to more than just "music." Specifically, "credit belong[ed] to Mr. Curwen's tonic sol-fa system of [sic] having thus far brought the savage within the pale of civilization." From this piece of settler social commentary I want to draw one point: Practices of colonialism had their testing grounds in the metropolis. If choralism, and especially the Victorian brand founded on the sol-fa method and notation, was to offer a bulwark against the "irruption of the Kafir hordes," it was only because of its reputed success in averting a revolution of the masses "at home."[4]

THE CLASSES OF 1848

Revolutionary events in France resonated loudly across the Channel. Noisily, in fact, as the music educator, John Hullah, disapprovingly observed of the Chartist riots of 1848: "Popular outbreaks result in a considerable increase in the noise and dirt of the world."[5] Hullah had enlisted as a "special Constable" during the London riots of 1848, a tamer British version of the French scenario during which workers agitated for various "rights." His biographer wife relates how his politics and professional activities converged at the time: "The birth of his aversion to Radicalism was always referred back to that period of his life when the beat of his *bâton* would have produced quite other sounds than those which usually followed its timely flourishes."[6] Whether Hullah's "Conservative tendencies" surfaced in the wake of a choir's vocal "disobediences" is a question that must hang enticingly in the air. Whatever the case, the conflation of what Althusser would distinguish as the "repressive" and "ideological" "state apparatuses" in the life-story of the most celebrated music educator at mid-century is typical of how the "governing classes" constructed choralism, often quite explicitly, as a "discipline."[7] Indeed, much has been written about the institutional genealogy of choralism as a discipline in Victorian England.[8] Briefly, I'll offer one further instance of this mode of "history telling" before trying to move beyond it.

Hullah is remembered for a number of initiatives, one of which was the mass sight-singing classes that began in early 1841 at Exeter Hall, the British headquarters of diverse philanthropic endeavors.[9] His singing subjects were always clearly, if generically, identified—"the lower orders," "the poorer classes"[10]—and the singing classes were no less part of the discourse of their government. Generally intended for the "improvement" of the working classes, they aimed specifically to foster "industry" and "national feeling."[11] By the end of the year, it was estimated that at least fifty thousand working-class children alone were singing from notes,[12] a spectacular success that quickly brought choralism to the attention of a number of eminent Victorian "liberals."

The Christian Socialist leader and education reformer Frederick Denison Maurice was one of these. His influential "philosophy" of working-class education, *Learning and Working* (1855), I suggest, was indebted to Hullah's example.[13] The political context of Maurice's work was the French revolution of 1848. But the moral was for England: "The whole country must look for its blessings through the elevation of its Working Class, that we must all sink if that is not raised. We have never dreamed that that class could be benefited, by losing its working character, by acquiring habits of ease or self-indulgence. We have rather thought that *all* must learn the dignity of labour and the blessings of self-restraint."[14]

The stakes for a "union of Learning with manual Work" were high, the "freedom, order, civilization of England" (x) was in the balance. In working out this union, Maurice took inspiration from Hullah's classes, which he praised as "beyond comparison the most successful" of "all experiments in English education" (102). And if the "higher classes had made [music] a mere amusement or gratification," for "the working people it [had to] be more than that." In their "appetite for musical cravings," Maurice detected "the cravings for *freedom* and *order*," which he took to be "the end of all education" (109).

"Freedom," and choral singing as freedom, was conceived as ideology in the classical Marxist sense.[15] "Order," by contrast, did not work as a strategy of obfuscation. Rather, in bringing universal "Law" into a relationship of correspondence with the "rules" of various educational subjects, "the detection of [the pupil's] false concords, and the punishment of them," for example, was "part of his initiation into the principals of order," "ordinances which [were] fixed for a whole society and [could not] be transgressed by any one" (114–15). The disciplinary value of choralism in particular, it seemed, was crucial in this regard. Hullah was eulogized as "a pioneer in a great moral revolution; upon the success of which it may depend in no slight degree whether a revolution of another kind shall be averted from our land."[16]

Donald E. Hall has shown that the Christian Socialist involvement in working-class education was born of the fear of workers' discontent, of the Chartist "monster." Their program of "Politics for the People," accordingly, was not envisaged as radical social or political reform, but as a program of containment, of what has frequently been called "internal colonialism."[17] Clearly, early Victorian choralism, as the example of Hullah shows, slotted into that program, and this has been long realized. But social histories of the disciplinary nature of choralism have, paradoxically, worked to erase the musical object of their analysis. Surely, the power of choralism as a discipline must have depended less on institutional affiliations and vague Victorian rhetoric, and rather on how it worked in practice?[18] To refocus attention on the practices of choralism, I cast my net wide in offering three somewhat disparate readings of choralism as a disciplinary technique: (1) an example of the ancillary, organizational apparatus that proliferated around the singing, (2) two aspects of choral performance practice, and (3) some thoughts on "choral music itself." All were crucial aspects of Victorian choral culture, of musicking that would be employed in the colonization of South Africa.

THE WORK OF THE CERTIFICATE

The discourse of "industry" was seldom far from rationalizing Victorian choralism. Not for nothing can its immediate ancestry be traced to places of labor. Singing instruction had been introduced in "charity schools" more than a century before moves to make it a component of Victorian elementary education were set in motion, and the pay-off for the children, for their benefactors' charity, was training for an artisan's apprenticeship.[19] For the northern county weavers of Lancashire and Yorkshire and the manufacturers of Norfolk, choralism had long been the "chief rational form of amusement." Hullah's hope that a new genre of choral "Labour Songs" would "inspire cheerful views of industry" among Britain's working classes was nothing new then.[20]

In Victorian officialese, leisure, including choralism, was called "rational recreation," the purpose of which, as Hugh Cunningham has suggested, was to "re-create a person for the more serious business of life, work."[21] It was also a kind of "illusion:" Maurice formulated the relationship of working-class education and choralism to industry as "rest in the midst of toil, even while it demanded from them toil of another kind."[22] Singing, then, had to be reworked to approximate work. One group of music educators who took this task on board were the "tonic sol-faists"; the notation and singing method under whose banner they worked would eventually become the preferred method of elementary music instruction in the Victorian world. But this was in the future.

In 1852, the Tonic Sol-fa Association announced the innovation of awarding a music "certificate" to those who had passed through its music literacy course. The motivations for the initiative were many, but one had to do with the format of Hullah's mass sight-singing classes, where little control over individual singers was possible. Even in the more circumscribed arena of the school classroom, noted the association's house journal, *The Tonic Sol-fa Reporter*, the teacher could not always give attention to the individual pupil. It was thus proposed "that each member of a class should determine to teach himself. It cannot be too soon or too well understood that *class-teaching is only an aid to self-teaching*." In the sol-faists' bid to restructure popular choral education, the certificate became the incentive to "personal effort."[23] It also brought choralism more securely within the Victorian ideology of self-improvement through work that was immortalized in Samuel Smiles' best-selling *Self-Help*.[24] Of course, there was a moral implicit in the rhetoric of "self-culture," which *The Reporter* did not fail to draw: "The Tonic Sol-fa movement [would] be judged, not by the inattentive and careless, but by its certificated members." "[I]dleness and inattention," conversely, hindered "progress" (89).[25]

The certificate involved the sol-faist in more than a narrative of personal progress: "The amount of individual effort and self-cultivation which it ha[d] called forth [would tell] wonderfully on the general progress and good singing of the class itself" (95). In other words, a trained singing body in the singular would improve the economy of the choral body as a whole. This insight was central to Foucault's analysis of the disciplines, which, he argued, produced "the docile body" only as a means to its incorporation in an "efficient machine" of larger dimensions. He illustrated the point with the example of the military machine: "The soldier whose body had been trained to function part by part for particular operations must in turn form an element in a mechanism at another level.... The body is constituted as a part of a multi-segmentary machine."[26] Probably the most potent idea of disciplinarity in the nineteenth century, the factory-army, the "work-force," became the single most common metaphor through which the Victorian choir was imagined.[27]

As Foucault has shown, at the heart of all disciplinary systems functions a "small penal mechanism" that enjoys a judicial privilege with its own laws, offences, forms of judgment, and punishment (177–78). Its overall effect is to normalize, which it achieves through, amongst other operations, "hierarchizing" (183). This was a basic premise of the sol-fa certificate. In every town the "certificated pupils" were encouraged to form themselves into an "'upper class,' or 'association of Tonic Sol-faers.'" No one was to be admitted to this club who could not show "a certificate within the cover of his music book" (*Reporter* 1853–1854: 96). The very designation "upper class" functioned as a penalizing exclusion not only of the uncertificated, but of those members of the working classes who had not internalized the message of social betterment through self-improvement. *The Reporter* moralized the relationship between work, certificate, and punishment as follows: "It will be esteemed a discredit for one who has passed through a course under an able teacher not to possess it" (89). In the hierarchizing work of the certificate, then, rank served as both reward and punishment (Foucault 1979:181), congratulating the disciplined singer–worker as it penalized idleness. One certificate, though, was soon insufficient reward–punishment, and in 1858 a graded series of certificates was introduced: elementary, intermediate, and advanced—the last leaving no doubt as to the progress achieved. The hierarchizing principle implicit from the outset in the certificate idea had become fully elaborated in the examining machinery of popular Victorian music education.[28]

Finally, the certificate not only distributed pupils according to rank, but also exercised over them constant pressure to conform (Foucault 1979, 183). In a parallel initiative to the threefold elaboration of the certificate idea, *The Standard Course* (1858) formalized sol-fa instruction as a highly structured set of "lessons and exercises" divided into a series of progressive "steps." The steps were defined as "a certain stage of the pupil's progress at which he is expected to stop and examine himself ... enabl[ing] all the members of a class to march together,—to keep step."[29] *The Standard Course* and awards, then, standardized; all involved in the quest for "the magic pieces of paper," as Ernest Walker later called the certificates, were compelled to conform.[30] This, in the end, was the grand aim of Victorian reform movements, of the disciplines. Sol-fa did not just style itself as a reform movement, it operated as one.[31]

MEANWHILE, IN THE COLONY ...

Just prior to the disciplining effects of choralism that *The Grahamstown Journal* had noted in the performance of the "Fingoes and Hottentots," the paper ran a series of reports explaining what tonic sol-fa was all about. The concluding article emphasized that sol-fa's success was due "not to its simplicity and comprehensiveness solely," but also to the disciplinary nature of its organizational setup:

> The success of the army depends as much on the skill of the commander as the proficiency of the corps; and undoubtedly a person endowed with Mr. Curwen's skill as a General could accom-

plish wonders with any system or code of discipline; but Mr. Curwen seems to have been aware that the powers of generalship are not delegated to every man; and having introduced a system of notation adapted to the humblest capacities, he found it necessary to establish a code of discipline which in itself might supply any short-comings on the part of persons who might find the duties of teacher pressed upon them.[32]

The "code of discipline" incorporated sol-fa's entire operational paraphernalia, which included the practices of the certificate: "Mr. Curwen subjects them to individual examination by authorized teachers; and a certificate of the student having satisfactorily passed the ordeal of such examination, is the only passport to the next course of lessons." To cap his colonial apology for sol-fa, the writer gave as example of its disciplining efficacy the performances of the "Kafir choir." By the end of the century, a sixth of all black pupils at African's largest mission institution, Lovedale, in the eastern Cape, were being examined for and awarded sol-fa certificates.[33]

VOICE CULTURE AND BODIES REAL AND METAPHORICAL

Like the certificate, Victorian choral performance practice was structured to work in fulfillment of the work ethic and the imperatives of the disciplines. Its combined practices were significantly called "voice culture," involving the singing subject in the cultivation of her own voice and so bringing her within the ambit of civilization; in the nineteenth century, "culture" retained its etymological sense of cultivation as work and was synonymous with civilization.[34] The work of voice culture as labor, though, will interest me less here. I want rather to pursue another of the disciplinary ideals for choralism: the fostering of national unity, "the utterance of one harmonious voice."[35]

In an example of what Richard Sennett famously called "the fall of public man," the Victorians seemed to fear the sound of their own voices.[36] Such a claim at least became common in differentiating between different vocal modes, between communal singing and individual speechifying:

> In the one case, they feel instinctively the impossibility of pitching their voices, or timing their syllables, *so as not to be heard individually*; while, in the other, the determined note, its tune and its time preconcerted, *absorbs all individual effort*. A speaker, be the crowd what it may, never loses the sound of his own voice; a singer in a chorus, though conscious of producing a sound, is often unable to distinguish it himself.[37]

Much later, in an article on "The Discipline of Choral Singing," Sir John Stainer spoke similarly of choristers "sink[ing] their individuality in the choral body:" "The man or woman or child who is perhaps rather self-willed and masterful in ordinary life, drops all this frame of mind at the choral practice.... Men and women who are petty tyrants elsewhere have to become mild as sheep."[38] Choralism felicitously was premised on a denial of (vocal) self; the individual, as Stainer noted, became a subject.

Stainer went on to suggest that "this doctrine of the suppression of self-interest for the benefit of the many [was] one of the key-stones of Christian ethics."[39] He might have added that it was a cornerstone of the Christian Socialist program of control. According to Hall, while "the English national 'body' appear[ed] hopelessly fragmented ... into warring bod*ies*," the Christian Socialists attempted to reunify the national social body in "a project of (re)metaphorization whereby lower-class identity was effectively rewritten and subsumed."[40] Indeed, from the outset, the new rational recreations, and choralism in particular, had been promoted for their class-bridging potential.[41] Not to push the analogy too far, but the choral body, in which the chorister's voice was first refashioned and then absorbed in a sonic unity, functioned as a metaphor par excellence for the idealized social body.

In the mission to remake the British voice, the choirmaster was guided by the voice training manual, a genre of literature that came into its own in the 1870s, proliferated in the decades immediately before and after 1900, and completed the Victorian reform of choral singing into a fully-fledged disciplinary regime.[42] Thus the epigram to the choral trainer in Novello's popular series of music primers—a quote from Ruskin—directed that "[e]very child should be taught from its youth to govern its voice."[43]

Recall that in the choral community, individuality was anathema; an ethics that choral aesthetics translated as the "art of blending": "In choirs many singers make great efforts to hear their own voices, whereas the secret of successful choral singing is the blending. Such a singer is obliged to pervert his natural production to make the tone stand apart. He would be more benefit to himself and the choir if his voice merged so well in the body of tone that he could not hear himself."[44]

The natural voice here was, paradoxically, not the pre-cultivated voice but the trained voice. This was a standard claim, a ploy to naturalize what I call the "bourgeois voice"—"that kind of sound which satisfies the educated ear"[45]—while presenting what one might call the "anachronistic voice"—variously that of the child, worker, or black South African—as unruly, body parts to be disciplined.[46] Another trainer thus held that "very *few* children sing *naturally* until they have been *trained* to do so."[47] The "perverted" chorister, then, was reneging on his training, backsliding into the unnaturalness of the anachronistic voice, at the same time that the conspicuousness of his vocal self(ish)ness subverted the choral ethic. There was, however, a corrective for this: "soft-singing."

The directive to sing softly was ubiquitous in choral voice training. All practicing was to be done *piano* and the voice-in-training was forbidden to exceed this dynamic until late in its cultivation.[48] The specific utilities of soft-singing were many: It preserved the young voice from damage, the trained adult voice from regression, and prevented intonation problems. It was also the antithesis of the uncultivated, anachronistic voice, correcting the "coarse, harsh, and shouting production of tone," as it produced "good tone" for choral blending.[49] Soft-singing was a microdisciplinary technique through which the voice was normalized as bourgeois, through which the anachronistic "rough voice" was remade.

The invention of roughness was, as Pierre Bourdieu has said, a "distinction of taste" as a matter of class.[50] It was also a pathologizing of class, a justification for reforming the anachronistic voice. It was in the name of this project that L. E. Sterner related the musical odyssey of a group of coal miners' children, "brought up in the slums and rough environment of poorly paid, ignorant working people." Prior to Sterner's intervention, their collective voice was "harsh, ugly, noisy, meaningless." After, it became "so refined and excellent that they would sing without accompaniment, with delicate and perfect harmonies." In vanquishing the rough voice, the "seeds of gentility were sown."[51] Sterner's "Ethics of Singing for Children" shows not just that the voice had been yoked to the moral terrain in which middle-class Victorian discourse operated, but that in the fortunes of the voice lay even the promise of upward mobility.[52]

How, more precisely, was soft-singing an exercise in control? First, from the individual chorister it demanded a total control of the body, almost unparalleled in the world of leisure. Hence, a subgenre concerned entirely with "vocal physiology," and often coauthored by medical science, followed in the wake of the popular voice trainer. For the trained singer, diverse anatomical parts, visible and invisible, from buttocks to tongue, were given very precise instructions of where they should be and what they should be doing. This practiced body was required in the name of, amongst others, "breath control," or "breath management," a prerequisite of tonal beauty, which in turn was best practiced by singing softly—and vice versa.[53] Second, it was in soft-singing that the choral body's sonic self was most easily surveillanced. If soft-singing maximized the possibilities for "correct" tone and blending, it also functioned as an aural panopticism in which any "wrong" tone—shouting, forcing, penetrating—was immediately audible.[54] Soft-singing, then, operated not only to produce a docile-body, both of the individual chorister and of the choir, but also, and this is an aspect of Foucault's analysis of the disciplines that is often overlooked, to improve the economy of those bodies. For the disciplines produced a relation of "docility-utility," increasing the forces of the body in terms of efficiency while diminishing those same forces in terms of obedience.[55] Soft-singing (con)formed voices so that they would work within choralism's uniform sound ideal.

It was with the same objective in mind that voice culture focussed with particular zeal on "register." Specifically, it was the phenomenon of the "break" that gave anxiety: "In some voices there is a marked difference between the lower range of sounds and the upper range, and there must of necessity be a point at which they meet. Here, in the untrained voice, a sudden change takes place, forming the so-called 'break of the voice.'"[56] The absence of homogeneity within the individual voice gave as much offense as the individual who disturbed the uniformity of the choral voice, and for this reason "one of the great aims of voice-training [was] to blend the upper and lower registers together, that no 'break' whatever [could] possibly be detected."[57] Overcoming this schizovocality involved yet more work, a series of exercises: "First of all, sustained notes are practiced; then the scales, both being sung *downwards*, until the registers of the voice are apparently blended into one. Then we take five notes below the break, five notes above the break, and five notes with the break in the middle. These are sung in turn *up and down* as softly as possible."[58]

The disciplining work that these exercises performed was to impose homogeneity on the individual voice. For ultimately, one singer with "two separate voices" was incapable of "blending;" the voice had to be "graded symmetrically like a string of pearls; at no point having, as it were, an uneven pearl or one off colour."[59]

AND THE CAPE'S "COLORED" VOICES?

A report on "Music at Lovedale" for a Scottish music magazine began with some "context": at "this small Scottish colony planted in the heart of Kaffraria," "some eight hundred native boys and girls [were] daily having instilled into them the precepts of Christianity, the doctrine of work, and the arts of civilization." The gist of the article was that "choral music [was] decidedly the strong feature of the place"; exactly whether it instilled Christianity, work, or civilization was left to the reader to decide. But there were problems. The voices, for example, lacked "roundness and resonance," offering "an indifferent display" that somewhat puzzled the writer, given that the choristers had been "brought under more civilising influences." Whatever the reason, the reader was informed that attention was being devoted to "voice production and deportment."[60]

HYMN-TIME

"But you had been stripped of some of your old vesture/By Monk, or another. Now you wore no frill,/And at first you startled me. But I knew you still,/Though I missed the minim's waver,/And the dotted quaver."[61]

Thomas Hardy's "Apostrophe to an Old Psalm Tune" is a lament of the early to mid-Victorian reform of church choralism, and for the tunes it had re-formed. It is hardly surprising that he wrote of the reforms in the context of the history of nineteenth-century British costume. In the same way that pre-Victorian tunes, if they survived, were "corrected" in their Victorian reception—a practice exemplified for Hardy in William Henry Monk's *Hymns Ancient and Modern*—so, in domesticating the pre-Victorian gentleman as a middle-class persona, the Victorians had stripped him of ornament and color to refashion him in black frock-coat and suit.[62] As the vocal bodies of the Victorian choral community were being trained, so, I want to argue, the body of music they were most likely to sing was a disciplined repertoire. Tunes, and larger works, often underwent wholesale compositional reform. Taking Hardy's lead, I will explore one instance of its rhythmic disciplining.[63]

One of the projects of the early Victorian church music reforms was the rediscovery of "ancient" tunes, beginning with those of the Reformation. OLD HUNDREDTH, popularly sung to the words "All people that on earth do dwell," was one of these. It was singular for not needing any of the reformers' special pleading for its revival, having an uninterrupted performance history since it first appeared in Britain in the early 1560s, and becoming for the Victorians a "national tune" that topped barrel organ play-lists.[64] As a mark of its popularity, it became the subject of a history. Part a chronicle of OLD HUNDREDTH's various incarnations in Britain, William Henry Havergal's history of the tune was also an argument for the restoration of the tune's "authentic" self, for "the past" would give evidence of "true" and "corrupt" versions.[65] Victorian hymnal editors and congregations, however, subscribed only partially to Havergal's prescriptions, and in several respects the forms OLD HUNDREDTH assumed in nineteenth-century Britain ran counter to the well-known findings of Victorian textual criticism.

How Havergal arrived at the "standard form" of OLD HUNDREDTH (see fig. 2.1), the "true English version of the tune" (16, 14), is an exemplary case of how the present intrudes in quests for "the past." Briefly, his model was not, as one might expect, the earliest known published version, but rather the version that appeared in its first printings in Britain (12–16). John Day, the editor of the first British musical psalters, however, had not shared Havergal's bent for authenticity, and varied, or "corrupted,"

Figure 2.1. Havergal's "standard" Old Hundredth.

OLD HUNDREDTH in subsequent editions (17–19). Indeed, "the early editors," bemoaned Havergal, "were not at all choice in selecting authentic copies of the Old Hundredth Psalm Tune. They seem to have printed, almost at random, first one version and then another" (20). Havergal's insistence on one "correct" tune was itself a disciplinary act, an early, small-scale precursor of "the critical edition" project. That his standard, in addition, was a rhythmically corrected tune is clear if we compare it to its earliest appearance. The first extant OLD HUNDREDTH, which appeared in a Genevan psalter, is identical to Figure 2.1, "with the exception," noted Havergal, "of the second and third notes of the last strain being minims instead of semibreves." In standardizing the tune, the original was "slightly modified, so as to equalize the time of all its strains," with the happy result that the "symmetry of the tune thus modelled [was] remarkably beautiful": "Each of its four strains comprise[d] four long and four short notes, uniformly but peculiarly disposed" (16–17). In short, Havergal's textual criticism was guided by contemporary aesthetic ideals that favored uniformity.[66]

By contrast, if many of the pre-1600 psalter versions were rhythmically more "complex," another tendency had been to reduce the notes to the same value as in Figure 2.2. Here, the ideal of rhythmic sameness reached its limit: 32 successive minims.[67] Rhythm had become homogenized in the most spectacularly banal manner.[68] It was this form of OLD HUNDREDTH, perhaps even more than Havergal's standard, that became the norm in Victorian Britain; while both often found their way into the various editions of *Hymns A&M*, its closest competitor in late Victorian Britain, Sankey's *Sacred Songs and Solos*, preferred the equal-note version. To extrapolate, on the basis of one tune, that Victorian choral music in general was a large-

Figure 2.2. The "equal-note" Old Hundredth.

scale compositional project in the disciplining of "music," is a claim that space won't allow me to substantiate here. As a compensatory gesture, though, the reception of Victorian choral music in twentieth-century histories of the nineteenth century will, I think, illustrate the point.

If we substitute "convention" for "discipline," then apologists for Western art have apparently cultivated an aversion to the hymn-tune and popular choral music since the nineteenth century. It was sometime during that century, we are told, that the imperative to originality become paramount, remaining central to our musicological creed until quite recently. Susan McClary thus writes that in the twentieth century we have "interpret[ed] reliance on convention as betraying a lack of imagination.... [T]he individualistic artist or critic shuns [it] with disdain and seeks value in those moves that escape the coercion of convention."[69] More than a century earlier, Stainer had labeled this ideology "Romanticism": "that 'frame of mind' which desires to assert itself, to announce its freedom from restraint, or even to set itself up in opposition to the rules and regulations accepted by the many ... a rebellion of the natural against the artificial; of the spontaneous against the conventional."[70]

Romanticism, then, as it has popularly come to be known, was the antithesis of the ethico-aesthetics of Victorian choralism: flaunting its communality, reacting against its disciplined music.

Histories of the nineteenth century as the "Age of Romanticism" have accordingly protested loudly against Victorian choralism, British and South African, in silencing it.[71] Already at the start of the twentieth century, when England's own historians were starting to narrate their country's musical rebirth (a.k.a., the "English Musical Renaissance"), the specter was raised of the "inferior composer of the quasi-clerical order," "a peculiarly Anglo-Saxon product" whose "bad religious music" had "deluged" the country for two hundred years.[72] Similarly, reflecting on the Victorian past, Rosa Newmarch spoke of "the monotonous manufacture of choral works," "the 'oratorio industry' "; the language of industrialization registered the standardizing of Victorian Britain's compositional output.[73] In canonizing the music of the English Musical Renaissance and the Romantic century as nonconventional, another disciplinary project has been under way.

AND IN THE CAPE ...

The idea of Victorian choral music, and especially its rhythm, as disciplined music has lived on in the reception of Victorian choral composition in South African music histories. Described as "stolid" and "square," the rhythm and meter of Victorian hymnody have, so the story goes, functioned as a "corset" or "strait-jacket" to the black choral composer's musical imagination.[74] A much cited instance of this is the transcription-arrangement of Ntsikana Gaba's "Great Hymn" (c.1820) made by the Lovedale-based composer, John Knox Bokwe, later in the nineteenth-century. Probably originally sung to precolonial Xhosa music, the notated tune bears the marks not only of the vagaries of the transcriptive act, but also of the deformative operations of the intervention, "arranged by."[75] For Bokwe, arranging meant providing a four-part homophonic harmonization that he had learnt from mainstream Victorian hymnody and used in his own compositions. The result was an awkward hybrid about which I wish to point out just one thing. Victorian hymn-tune harmony operated ideally within a particular metric-rhythmic framework, and this is apparent, quite visually, even in only the single melodic line of Figure 2.3.

If not what, then where harmony is implied is obvious: at the regulating "tempo" marking the melody goes into equal-note rhythm. By contrast, the musical "freedom" of m. 1, as the "ad lib" and more varied rhythms suggest, was conceived as harmony-less, as later, harmonized versions confirm. Needless to say, the equal-note section was not a feature of Xhosa musicking. It was, as we have seen in the case of OLD HUNDREDTH, a standard of Victorian hymn-tune composition—one that continued its regulating work in the colonies.

THE "BLACK PERIL" AND EXHIBITING CHORALISM AT THE CAPE

Equal notes, blending, the certificate—each in itself, perhaps, not too significant. But combined with other practices, a discipline "as complete as that of the national army" was born.[76] As I have too briefly suggested, all these practices found a home in the Colony, more particularly in the foreign mission to the eastern Cape. Moreover, as the review with which I began this chapter reveals, they were practiced within a similar discourse of "subdue and discipline"; the difference was that choralism's working-class subjects were now the mission's black converts. Of course, the black reception of metropolitan choralism is another story. "Mimicry," we know, bears within it the possibility of ambivalence, and what Homi K. Bhabha has

Figure 2.3. John Knox Bowke's "arrangement-transcription" of Ntsikana Gaba's "Great Hymn." *Christian Express* (May 1879): 15; staff transcripton from tonic sol-fa.

called the "deferral of syntax," "a specific *colonial* temporality and textuality of that space between enunciation and address" was very much in operation in the refracted colonial order of things choral.[77] But neither should we disavow the colonizer's avowals, their narrative of domination. Rather than rehearsing, in a parallel story, how the mission incorporated choralism within the practices of industry and discourses of social harmony, I want to explore how black choralism became a discipline of ceremony, how it exhibited discipline in the Cape.

In colonial South Africa, the black menace to white power went by many names. One was simply "the Black Peril." A refrain in the debate on the Native Question, the Peril irrupted periodically in the pre-Union colonies, reaching a climax in the discursive outbreak of 1911 to 1912, where it popularly signified black rape of white women. Widely regarded, even then, as a product of sensational colonial journalism, the Peril registered doubly: psychopolitically—articulating some of the most basic of the colonists' fears, feeding from and into the newly ascendant ideology of "segregation."[78] As Gareth Cornwell has put it: "The political scandal of the Black Peril [was] the subjection of a women of the dominant race to the power of a man of the subordinate race; the penetration of a white vagina by a black penis [was] an act of insurrection."[79] The myth of mass rape, then, was a symptom of a more general white fear of losing control. It was a scenario astutely analyzed in the eponymous novel, *The Black Peril* (1912). The crux of the Native Question, it suggested, was not which of either segregation or sociopolitical equality would be the better "solution," but that there existed the haunting possibility of a radical reversal in the relations of power: a future South Africa would no longer be "a white man's country" but "a veritable black man's land," "the great Black Peril that threatened the ultimate subjugation of the two races [that is, English and Dutch-Afrikaans speaking whites] by the coloured peoples was the real shadow that hung over the land."[80]

Inevitably, the Peril attracted the attention of the South African mission, ever a keen interlocutor on all matters black. This time, though, missionary intervention was more than usually self-interest. Not simply a black mark on the missionary record, the Peril posed fundamental questions as to the validity of its enterprise, of its disciplining mission. Missionary reaction was swift. A commission of inquiry was established to investigate the "so-called Black Peril," and its finding, conveyed to the General Missionary Conference of South Africa, held in Cape Town in 1912, and to the public at large, was that there was no Peril. The debunking report received some press, but more effective as damage-control, I suggest, were the series of choral concerts and the missionary exhibition organized to coincide with the conference.

The exhibition was the first of its kind in South Africa and the choir singing of an unprecedented scale; for the few musical events, the always cash-strapped mission had dispatched over three hundred black choristers, from at least three different missions in different parts of the country, to the capital by "special train."[81] Clearly, a massive exercise in mission public relations was under way. As impressive was its audacity. While Cape Town was the legislative and intellectual center of early-twentieth-century South Africa, the city was somewhat removed from the lived realities of everyday South African "race relations." The *Handbook and Programme* to the exhibition suggested that "the inhabitants of the Cape Peninsula [had] not much first-hand acquaintance with the native and his environment."[82] Even more, given the topicality of the Peril, it was particularly daring to send hundreds of black males into the white "mother city"; the eastern Cape missions had put together a two-hundred-voice strong male choir. The pay-off, though, was extensive publicity for the mission and the largest audiences the city hall had ever accommodated.[83] For the Cape Town public, however, black choralism held potentially nothing more than the novelty value of the exotic. It had, thus, to be made to "mean" for a specifically white Capetonian audience, to deliver unambiguously the message of the disciplining mission. In part, this was achieved through the manner in which the choral performances related to the exhibition. Briefly, then, I want to discuss the exhibition itself.

Compared to the metropolitan exhibitions, the Cape Town exhibition was small in scale, occupying a single, though large hall.[84] A spectator moving anticlockwise about the hall would have witnessed the following: the first half consisted of several living ethnological exhibits, with various "ethnic" peoples in "characteristic" settings, which were interspersed with displays of "native crafts." Having reached the halfway point, and turning back toward the entrance, the spectator then passed a series of stalls, exhibiting and selling the products of the mission industrial school, which showed "in what directions the native has been changed and uplifted by Christian missions."[85] The plan of the exhibition, then, told a familiar, nineteenth-century evolutionary tale. Indeed, it was billed as "a complete historical, ethnological and cultural exhibit of the native races of South Africa in relation to the white man."[86] But in elaborating the rider—"in relation to the white man"—the Cape Town exhibition offered a twist to that tale. While the civilizing plot of the metropolitan colonial exhibition had the white bourgeois self as hero of the story,[87] the (end)point of the Cape Town exhibition was the mission-educated black. It was a point *The Cape Times* seemed to have got when it moralized the exhibition as "an opportunity for ocular demonstration of mission work": "The object lesson afforded by the Bushmen in their cave at the one end of the scale, and the skilled workmanship displayed by natives trained in industrial institutions at the other end, is one effective answer to those who doubt or deny the use of mission."[88] In the context of the Peril, the utility of the mission was to display the civilized black as a model, working, disciplined citizen.[89]

This is precisely what the black choirs did—they displayed discipline. For, as Foucault maintained, discipline imposes a principle of compulsory visibility, and possesses, accordingly, "it[s] own type of ceremony."[90] The choral exhibition of discipline, moreover, was crucial. For the romance of the exotic proved a powerful distraction. It was not the industrial products, but the Bushmen and "native curiosities" that caught the public and press's eye. To trump these exoticisms with the mission's message of discipline was the choirs' allotted role.

All of this was minutely scripted. The relationship of the choirs to the exhibition, for a start, was circumscribed both physically and temporally. Usually, the exhibition was open only during the afternoon and evening. After having witnessed at the exhibition hall the transformation of savage to civilized black wrought by the mission, spectators attended, as a crowning confirmation, the nightly choral performance of discipline in the city hall; evolutionary time had been collapsed into a day's outing. For the spectator attending only the evening meetings, the narrative of progress was no less on show. Bioscope screenings of "characteristic scenes from native life" provided a counterpoint to the choirs, and the chair of the event, whether mayor, missionary, or liberal politician, introduced the black singers as "a tribute to the missionary enterprise."[91] In addition, the opportunity for misreading black choralism, of being lured by manifest exoticisms, was downplayed. Unlike the "African Choir" on tour in the United Kingdom in the early 1890s, for example, no pseudoprimitive mise-en-scène was enacted for Cape Town; there was no neo-traditional costume, no precolonial songs were programmed.[92] These fed into a tradition of exoticism in ethnological show business that played to the British publics' and science's ideas about "race,"[93] but did not suit the mission's message in and for South Africa. Rather, if the choirs were to act as a popular public refutation of the Black Peril, which so imperiled the mission's own existence, they had to be exemplars of the work of civilizing–disciplining. The plan seems to have worked. As a *Cape Times* leader summed up the week's events: "The visit of these 300 native singers has been something of a revelation to the public of Cape Town, no less on account of their admirable *behaviour* than on the score of their vocal performances. They commended the cause of missions, and provided an argument for them which appealed to many people much more than addresses and reports."[94]

The mission breathed a sigh of relief: "there is cause for deep thankfulness on account of the impression that ha[s] been left behind in the Mother City. One feels confident that many misunderstandings have been removed."[95] The performance of missionary politics, it seems, was most successfully propagated through the power of black choral performance.

Notes

My thanks to Christine Lucia for reading this chapter in other guises. I am obliged to mention that this research would probably not have been possible without Rhodes University's generous funding of my doctoral studies.

1. After Michel Foucault, *Discipline and Punish: The Birth of the Prison*, trans. Alan Sheridan (London: Peregrine, 1979), 188.
2. "Music and Civilization," *The Grahamstown Journal* (September 4, 1863), emphasis added.
3. For a "popular" history of the eastern Cape, see Noël Mostert, *Frontiers: The Epic of South Africa's Creation and the Tragedy of the Xhosa People* (London: Pimlico, 1993).
4. The editor of the *Journal*, Robert Godlonton, is best remembered for his narrative of the Sixth Frontier War, *The Irruption of the Kafir Hordes* (Cape Town: Struik, 1965 [1835]). Histories of colonialism have increasingly begun to trace the practices and discourses of everyday colonization not simply to their genesis in the metropolis but to their genesis as strategies of domination there. The work of the Chicago-based anthropologists Jean and John L. Comaroff has been particularly influential in this regard; see especially their study of evangelical colonialism, *Of Revelation and Revolution* (Chicago: University of Chicago Press, 1991 and 1997).
5. Quoted in Frances Hullah, *Life of John Hullah* (London: Longmans, Green, and Co., 1886), 54.
6. Hullah, *Life of John Hullah*, 54.
7. Louis Althusser, "Ideology and Ideological State Apparatuses (Notes Towards an Investigation)," *Lenin and Philosophy and Other Essays*, trans. Ben Brewster (London: NLB, 1971), 121–73.
8. See, for example, Dave Russell, *Popular Music in England, 1840–1914: A Social History* (Manchester: Manchester University Press, 1997; 2nd ed.); and E. D. Mackerness, *A Social History of English Music* (London: Routledge and Kegan Paul, 1964), esp. chaps. 4 and 5.
9. For an account of Hullah's educational work, see Gordon Cox, *A History of Music Education in England, 1872–1928* (Aldershot: Scholar, 1993), chaps. 2 and 3.
10. Somewhat misleadingly, I gloss Victorian choralism as a working-class activity in this chapter. While little research has been done on the social base of Victorian choralism, Dave Russell suggests that its membership was probably drawn from the "respectable lower classes"— that is, the lower-middle and skilled working classes; *Popular Music in England*, chap. 10. In Victorian dominant representations, however, popular choralism was typically a working-class activity, clearly pointing to whom its disciplinary practices were intended to subject.
11. James Kay-Shuttleworth, "Prefatory Minute of the Committee of Council on Education," reprinted in John Hullah, *Wilhelm's Method of Teaching Singing, Adapted to English Use* (London: John W. Parker, 1841), 4.
12. Bernarr Rainbow, *The Land without Music: Musical Education in England, 1800–1860, and Its Continental Antecedents* (London: Novello, 1967), 125.
13. Hullah gave classes at Maurice's Working Men's College around mid-century, and was involved with another of the leading Christian Socialists, the preacher–writer Charles Kingsley; see Cox, *A History of Music Education*, 12–14.
14. Frederick Denison Maurice, *Learning and Working* (Cambridge: Macmillan & Co., 1855), vii.
15. "I have spoken of men as spiritual beings. I have only justified the musical education on the ground that it arouses men, shut up in the dreariest mechanical employments, even sunk in moral debasement, to a feeling of their spiritual existence, to the consciousness of belonging to another economy than that which is conversant with the making or selling of commodities. I have supposed freedom and order to be impossible for men except as they come to understand that there is this higher economy for them; that they are not enclosed within the boundaries of the lower" (123). Marx and his thoughts on these matters were, of course, circulating in London at the time.
16. Frederick Denison Maurice, "Queen's College, London: Its Objects and Method," *Introductory Lectures, Delivered at Queen's College, London* (London: John W. Parker, 1849), 14.
17. Donald E. Hall, "On the Making and Unmaking of Monsters: Christian Socialism, Muscular Christianity, and the Metaphorization of Class Conflict," *Muscular Christianity: Embodying the Victorian Age*, ed. Donald E. Hall (Cambridge: Cambridge University Press, 1994), 52–54.
18. This is true even of (former chorister) John Potter's *Vocal Authority*, a work that throughout

strains to read a diverse range of singing styles as social process. In the chapter on Victorian choralism, though, Potter repeats the cliché that "singing as discipline [was] at the very root of Victorian church music and, by extension at the heart of the nascent national education system," but fails to ground the insight in an analysis of the micro-practices of choralism; *Vocal Authority: Singing Style and Ideology* (Cambridge: Cambridge University Press, 1998), 81.

19. See Nicholas Temperley, *The Music of the English Parish Church*, vol. 1 (Cambridge: Cambridge University Press, 1979), 101–105; and Eric Hopkins, *A Social History of the English Working Classes, 1815–1945* (London: Edward Arnold, 1979), 70.

20. Hullah, *Wilhelm's Method of Teaching Singing*, 3, 8.

21. Hugh Cunningham, "Leisure and Popular Culture," *The Cambridge Social History of Britain, 1750–1950*, vol. 2, *People and Their Environment*, ed. F .M. L. Thompson (Cambridge: Cambridge University Press, 1990), 296.

22. Maurice, *Learning and Working*, 99.

23. "Certificates of Proficiency," *The Tonic Sol-fa Reporter, and Magazine of Vocal Music for the People* (1853–1854), 89.

24. Samuel Smiles, *Self-Help, with Illustrations of Character and Conduct* (London, 1859), esp. chap. 2.

25. E. P. Thompson gives a good account of the resonances between the Protestant moralizing and capitalist disciplining of work-time in industrial Britain; "Time, Work-Discipline, and Industrial Capitalism," *Past and Present* 38 (1967), 56–97.

26. Foucault, *Discipline and Punish*, 164. By now it will be clear that I intend to "read" Victorian choralism as a Foucauldian discipline. In so doing, I suppose I assume Foucault's "theoretical" understanding of the workings of power—at least in this chapter. I note, however, that critiques of his model of power have underestimated the place of "resistance" in especially his later work. In the essay "The Subject and Power," for example, Foucault concludes that "between a relationship of power and a strategy of struggle there is a reciprocal appeal, a perpetual linking and a perpetual reversal. . . . The consequence of this instability is the ability to decipher the same events and the same transformations either from inside the history of struggle or from the standpoint of the power relationship"; *Critical Inquiry* 8 (1982), 794. My reading of choralism here is written from the latter, now somewhat unfashionable, side. Elsewhere, I switch sides; see "Music and Post/Colonialism: The Dialectics of Choral Culture on a South African Frontier" (PhD diss., Rhodes University, 2003), chaps. 5 and 6.

27. One example of each, courtesy of *The Reporter*: the conductor's task was "to play as it were on the vocal machine before him;" (April 1878), 85; and a good choral performance was likened to "the light and easy manoeuvring of a crack regiment perfect in accoutrement and accurate in discipline;" (Feb. 1876), 35.

28. Graded musical examinations, especially the British-based ABRSM and Trinity, are familiar to most of the world touched by British imperialism. But at mid-nineteenth century, the sol-fa certificates were a novelty, and the scale of examining unequalled; by the time of the sol-fa jubilee in 1891, over half a million certificates had been awarded; see John Spencer Curwen, *The Story of Tonic Sol-fa* (London: J. Curwen & Sons, 1891; 10th ed.), 11.

29. John Curwen, *The Standard Course of Lessons and Exercises in the Tonic Sol-fa Method of Teaching Music* (London: J. Curwen & Sons, 1896 [1858]; 12th ed.), v.

30. Ernest Walker, *A History of Music in England* (Oxford: Clarendon Press, 1906), 335.

31. For sol-fa's institutional affiliations with other Victorian reform movements, especially the foreign mission, and its lower middle-class and upper working-class social base, see my "Music and Post/Colonialism: The Dialectics of Choral Culture," chaps. 1–3.

32. Henry W. Bidwell, "Musical Education," *The Grahamstown Journal* (May 1, May 8, and May 19, 1863).

33. "Examination in Music," *The Christian Express* (October 1895), 160.

34. Robert J. C. Young, *Colonial Desire: Hybridity in Theory, Culture, and Race* (London: Routledge, 1995), 31.

35. Kay-Shuttleworth, "Prefatory Minute," 4.

36. Richard Sennett, *The Fall of Public Man* (New York: Alfred A. Knopf, 1977). The founder of tonic sol-fa, John Curwen, observed that there were "many who dreaded to hear their own *speaking* voice, but [were] glad to join in a singing tone, and so hide themselves in the mass

of unison around them"; *Music in Worship and Other Papers on People's Psalmody* (London: Tonic Sol-fa Agency, 1871), 7.

37. John Hullah, *The Duty and Advantage of Learning to Sing* (London: John W. Parker, 1846), 9.
38. John Stainer, "The Discipline of Choral Singing," *The Musical Herald* (July 1897), 204.
39. Stainer, "The Discipline of Choral Singing," 204.
40. Hall, "On the Making and Unmaking of Monsters," 49.
41. Russell, *Popular Music in England*, 287.
42. Victorian choral performance practice has fared even worse than Victorian choralism in general in attracting the academy's attention. A trawl through Clive Brown, *Classical and Romantic Performance Practice, 1750–1900* (Oxford: Oxford University Press, 1999); Howard Meyer Brown and Stanley Sadie, eds., *The New Grove Handbooks in Music Performance Practice: Music after 1600* (London: Macmillan, 1989); Roland Jackson, *Performance Practice, Medieval to Contemporary: A Bibliographic Guide* (New York and London: Garland, 1988); and the *Performance Practice Review* for 1988 to 1997 yield only absences in the research space that nineteenth-century choral performance should occupy.
43. James Bates, *Voice Culture for Children: A Practical Primer on the Cultivation of Young Voices, with Exercises for the Use of Schools, Choirs, Solo-Boys, Etc.* (London: Novello and Co., 1907).
44. James A. Birch, *The Voice-Trainer: Practical Hints and Exercises for Solo-Singers, Conductors, Choralists, and Voice-Training Classes* (London: J. Curwen & Sons, n.d. [1893]), 4.
45. Birch, *The Voice-Trainer*, 3.
46. The phrase is adapted from Anne McClintock's "anachronistic space": the discursive space employed by dominant Victorian ideology to signify what was "prehistoric, atavistic, and irrational, inherently out of place in the historical time of modernity," and into which various "others" were projected in disavowal; *Imperial Leather: Race, Gender, and Sexuality in the Colonial Context* (New York and London: Routledge, 1995), 40–41.
47. T. Maskell Hardy, *How to Train Children's Voices* (London: J. Curwen & Sons, 1910 [1899]; 5th ed.), 2.
48. Hardy, *How to Train Children's Voices*, 2; and A. Madeley Richardson, *Choir Training Based on Voice Production* (London: Vincent, n.d. [c.1900]), 29.
49. Hardy, *How to Train Children's Voices*, 4.
50. Pierre Bourdieu, *Distinction: A Social Critique of the Judgment of Taste*, trans. Richard Nice (Cambridge, Mass.: Harvard University Press, 1984).
51. Lawrence E. Sterner, "The Ethics of Singing for Children," *School Music Review* (February 1895), 160–61.
52. In accordance with the dominant discourse in which the voice of gentility was gentle, James Bates issued a caveat to the motto "manners makyth man:" "children should be taught early in life to realise that the very best behaviour will not atone for a rough repellant voice;" *Voice Culture for Children*, 7.
53. Hardy, *How to Train Children's Voices*, 39.
54. Bates, *Voice Culture for Children*, 13.
55. Foucault, *Discipline and Punish*, 137–38.
56. Birch, *The Voice-Trainer*, 7.
57. Hardy, *How to Train Children's Voices*, 16.
58. Ernest Newton, "Purity in the Art of Singing," *School Music Review* (February 1896), 172.
59. Birch, *The Voice-Trainer*, 8.
60. J[ames] A[itken], "Music at Lovedale," *The Musical Age* (August 1899), 183–84.
61. Thomas Hardy, *The Complete Poetical Works of Thomas Hardy*, vol. 2, ed. Samuel Hynes (Oxford: Clarendon Press, 1984), 163.
62. See Leonore Davidoff and Catherine Hall, *Family Fortunes: Men and Women of the English Middle Class, 1780–1850* (London: Hutchinson, 1987), 410–12.
63. For an extended discussion of the Victorian disciplining of hymn-tunes, see my "Music and Post/Colonialism: The Dialectics of Choral Culture," chap. 4.
64. John Spencer Curwen, *Studies in Worship Music, Chiefly as Regards Congregational History*, 1st series (London: J. Curwen & Sons, 1888; 2nd ed.), 270; and Temperley, *The Music of the English Parish Church*, 236.
65. William Henry Havergal, *A History of the Old Hundredth Psalm Tune* (New York: Mason Bros, 1854).
66. Elsewhere, I have suggested that the currency of a poetics of uniformity in Victorian church

music composition owed much to the rise of an aesthetics of the "masculine sublime" in Britain; "Hym(n)ing: Music and Masculinity in the Early Victorian Church," *Nineteenth-Century British Music Studies*, vol. 3, eds. Peter Horton and Bennett Zon (Aldershot: Ashgate, 2003), 21–44.

67. Performance is, of course, not always faithful to the written source. Barlines, pauses, or simply the organ may have indicated the lengthening of a phrase end or even beginning. But the equal-note version altered more than the first and final notes of OLD HUNDREDTH's phrases. Its popularity in print, moreover, suggests a performance tradition.

68. Havergal noted that the same was true of OLD HUNDREDTH's harmonization: "The harmony which used to be set to the tune, was far more varied and elaborate than any which is now used. Hardly a company of singers can now be found who sing the tune, as to its harmony, in more than one way; whereas, our forefathers were accustomed to harmonize and sing it in many ways." "The ordinary mode in which the tune is now harmonized in England, has been justly censured for its monotonous effect ... The old masters studiously avoided such sameness" (37–9).

69. Susan McClary, *Conventional Wisdom: The Content of Musical Form* (Berkeley and Los Angeles: University of California Press, 2000), 3.

70. John Stainer, *Music in Its Relation to the Intellect and the Emotions* (London: Novello, Ewer and Co., 1892) 38, 41–2.

71. I explore some of the reasons for the ex-scription of Victorian choralism from histories of both British and black South African musics in two introductory chapters in "Music and Post/Colonialism: The Dialectics of Choral Culture." When Carl Dahlhaus wrote that "no-one had a burden to bear because Beethoven wielded authority in music," he obviously did not have the historiographic misfortunes of Victorian choralism in mind; *Foundations of Music History*, trans. J. B. Robinson (Cambridge: Cambridge University Press, 1983), 9. Despite the reputed musicological winds of change, some things, it seems, stay the same: John Butt's chapters on choralism in the recent *Cambridge History of Nineteenth-Century Music* continue to marginalize the Victorians in the name of the canon; see "Choral Music" and "Choral Culture and the Regeneration of the Organ," *The Cambridge History of Nineteenth-Century Music*, ed. Jim Samson (Cambridge: Cambridge University Press, 2001), 213–36, and 522–43.

72. Walker, *A History of Music in England*, 349.

73. Rosa Newmarch, *Henry J. Wood* (London & New York: John Lane, 1904), 14–16.

74. As the corollary to the well-known "invention of African rhythm," Martin Scherzinger has dubbed this analytical metaphorics the "dubious invention of rhythmic simplicity in the West." See "Review: Veit Erlmann, *Music, Modernity, and the Global Imagination: South Africa and the West*," *Journal of the Royal Musical Association* 126, 1 (2001): 131.

75. For discussions of Ntsikana and the hymn, see Dave Dargie, "The Music of Ntsikana," *South African Journal of Musicology* 2 (1982), 7–28; and Veit Erlmann, *Music, Modernity, and the Global Imagination: South Africa and the West* (New York: Oxford University Press, 1999), chap. 5.

76. Henry W. Bidwell speaking about tonic sol-fa choralism in the eastern Cape Colony; "Musical Education," *The Grahamstown Journal* (29 May 1863).

77. Homi K. Bhabha, *The Location of Culture* (London and New York: Routledge, 1994), 95.

78. The mission's inquiry into the "so-called Black Peril" found, among other things, that (1) assaults on black women were much higher than on white women, (2) a white woman was safer from assault in South Africa than in England, and (3) assaults by white males were underreported, in part due to the prevalence of "concubinage." See *Report of the Proceedings of the Fourth General Missionary Conference of South Africa, Cape Town, July 3–9, 1912* (Cape Town: Townshend, Taylor and Snashall, 1912), 80–90. My account of the Peril is drawn in part from D. G. N. Cornwell, "Ambiguous Contagion: The Discourse of Race in South African English Writing, 1890–1930" (PhD diss., Rhodes University, 1995), chap. 3, section 3.

   Briefly, "segregation" refers to a specific political ideology that emerged around the turn of the century, and not to the petty practices of segregation that had always been part of colonial South African life. Associated with "liberal," English-speaking thinkers, it was later to be appropriated for the idea of apartheid. Typically contrasted to "assimilation," the policy of the Cape government from about mid-nineteenth century on, which it is said to have superceded, segregation is also often regarded as the antithesis of the mission's "civilizing mission," which in turn is facilely conflated with assimilation. The missionary archive, *pace* most histories of South African racial politics and thought, makes clear that the civilizing mission was a far more malleable idea. Certainly, the mission circa 1910, and well before, was no less implicated in the rise of segregationist thought than it was interested with the business of civilizing. For standard accounts of the rise of segregationist thought, though ones that neglect the evidence of the mission, see Saul Dubow, "Race, Civilization, and Culture: The Elaboration of Segregationist Discourse in the Inter-War Years," *The Politics of Race, Class, and Nationalism in Twentieth-Century South Africa,* eds. Shula Marks and Stanley Trapido (London and New York: Longman, 1987), 71–94; and Paul Rich, *White Power and the Liberal Conscience: Racial Segregation and South African Liberalism, 1921–1960* (Johannesburg: Ravan Press, 1984).

79. Cornwell, "Ambiguous Contagion," 107.

80. George Webb Hardy, *The Black Peril* (London: Holden & Hardingham, n.d. [1912]), 135–38, 142.

81. "Visit of Native Choirs to Cape Town," *The Christian Express* (August 1912), 135.

82. *Handbook and Programme of the South African Missionary Exhibition, July 2–9, 1912* (Cape Town: Cape Times Printers, 1912), 3.

83. "Missionaries in Council," *The Cape Times* (July 11, 1912), 6.

84. For a discussion of the colonial and missionary exhibitions in late-nineteenth-century Britain, see Annie E. Coombes, *Reinventing Africa: Museums, Material Culture, and Popular Imagination in Late Victorian and Edwardian England* (New Haven and London: Yale University Press, 1994), chaps. 4, 5, and 8.

85. "The Missionary Exhibition," *The Cape Times* (July 8, 1912), 8.

86. "Missionary Exhibition," *The Cape Argus* (June 29, 1912), 9.

87. See Raymond Corbey, "Ethnographic Showcases, 1870–1930," *Cultural Anthropology* 8, 3 (1993), 340–41, 359.

88. "Missionaries in Council," 6.

89. The participation of prominent members of the mission-educated black elite is a case in point. John L. Dube, for one, was quite aware that he, like the other exhibits, had been sent to Cape Town as "a curiosity of what the native people could do." Nonetheless, he took the stage to assure white audiences that, with a mission education that had taught him, amongst others, "discipline," he was not the perpetrator of the Peril; "The Natives," *The Cape Argus* (July 4, 1912), 7.

90. Foucault, *Discipline and Punish*, 187–88.

91. *Proceedings of the Fourth General Missionary Conference*, 126; and "Missionary Enterprise," *The Cape Times* (July 2, 1912).

92. For the African Choir's metropolitan performances, see Erlmann, *Music, Modernity, and the Global Imagination*, chap. 4. The mission had registered its disapproval of the African Choir's costume, regarding "the old barbarian dress, a dress none of [the choristers] ever wore at home, [as] physically and morally dangerous"; "The African Choir," *The Christian Express* (November 1891), 170.

The "large and varied repertoire" of the Peril choirs, which changed for every concert, was described as "native, adapted, and European"; "Missionaries in Council," 6. From the programs printed in the daily press, "European" meant white-composed music in English; "adapted," for example, meant Stainer in Xhosa translation; and "native" signified not precolonial music, but primarily choral music newly written by a mission-educated, black composer.

93. See Bernth Lindfors, ed., *Africans on Stage: Studies in Ethnological Show Business* (Bloomington: Indiana University Press, 1999).

94. "Missionaries in Council," 6; also "Missions and Natives," *The Cape Argus* (July 2, 1912), 8.

95. "Visit of Native Choirs to Cape Town," 135.

CHAPTER 3

Power Needs Names: Hegemony, Folklorization, and the *Viejitos* Dance of Michoacán, Mexico

Ruth Hellier-Tinoco

AN UNMISTAKABLE ICON

A line of masked "old men" treads falteringly across the stage, accompanied by the rhythmic strumming of a *vihuela* and the melodic strains of a violin. All the performers are costumed in white cotten shirts and trousers, covered with bright ponchos, heads topped with wide-brimmed straw hats. Rainbow-colored ribbons hang from the dancers' hats tumbling over the white *ixtle* hair of the carved, wooden masks. The striking image is unmistakable: This is *La Danza de los Viejitos*—the Dance of the Old Men, of Lake Pátzcuaro, Michoacán, Mexico. It is performed by local musicians and dancers from Jarácuaro, not as part of local village celebrations, but at state-organized "folkloric" events and in hotels and restaurants for regional, national, and international tourists. State governmental and tourist literature refers to it as "folklore" and places it in unambiguous contexts that label it as *P'urhépecha*[1] and "indigenous" and "from Lake Pátzcuaro, Michoacán." In the Lake Pátzcuaro region postcards, mugs, t-shirts and other tourist items display the iconic image of the masked old-man dancers and musicians, confirming and perpetuating the notion that the *Viejitos* Dance is an essential element of "Mexican folklore." Meanwhile in the heart of Mexico City, inside the ornate, art deco concert hall of the Palacio de Bellas Artes, the *Viejitos* Dance is also performed, by highly trained professional dancers and musicians of the *Ballet Folklórico Nacional de México*, the National Folklore Ballet of Mexico. As an accepted part of the repertoire of dance and music items carefully chosen to represent key peoples and regions of Mexico, the *Viejitos* Dance fulfils its role as a signifier of *P'urhépecha* and, by indexation, "indigenous" identity.

Perhaps all this appears to be innocuous enough; after all, it is simply entertainment, a common feature of governmental and tourist strategies in many regions of the world. I suggest, however, that there is a problem with this situation and with the way in which a demarcated and objectified set of practices, often music and dance, are classified as "folklore" and "folkloric" and used in performance contexts specifically linked with promoting regional and national identity—and tourism. Practices are intrinsically and often inextricably connected to people, particularly in dance and music contexts where notions of embodiment are clearly essential to notions of signification. It is in this realm that "folklore" may be considered to be a power technique or "power in action" (Foucault 1982: 219). In Mexico there is an indexical correlation between "folklore" and "indigenous peoples."[2] Such classification and classificatory processes are part of a complex web of power relations in which there is a romantic valorization of artistic practice of the diverse peoples labelled as "indigenous,"[3] while the people themselves continue to live in marginalized and repressed situations. The predominance of a romantic, idealistic, "folkloric" image of such peoples is diffused and perpetuated through the use of music and dance as tools of control.

As this problem is complex and multifaceted , this chapter can only examine one tiny part of this dense web. Recognizing that an understanding of contemporary contexts can only come from an examination of the past, the aim of this chapter is to plot and analyze the emergence and establishment of the *Viejitos* Dance of Lake Pátzcuaro as "folklore," and to interrogate practices and actions of the past.

POST-REVOLUTION MEXICO

In order to make sense of the events and actions surrounding the emergence of the *Viejitos* Dance, it is necessary to provide a brief historical and political context. After the dictatorship of Porfirio Díaz, from 1876 until 1911, the Mexican Revolutionary civil wars of 1910 to 1920 brought a bloody and chaotic period of struggle for control. When the warring stage of the revolution came to an end the revolutionary regimes sought desperately for techniques and policies that would unite the country, which was then a disparate and diverse patchwork of peoples, to create a single, unified nation. This was a complex period of Mexican history, full of ideological and political contradictions. Socioeconomic reform and transformation were key features of the new regime, whose objectives of political and economic stability through capitalism and modernization were viewed as possible only through integration of the rural and rural-"indigenous populations. A diverse range of policies and technologies were implemented to formulate and create a nationalist, unified country, many of which established a link between culture and political power (see Bartra 1989, Rowe and Schelling 1991, García Canclini 1993, and Knight 1990, 1994a, 1994b). Prominent within these technologies were those that may be described as hegemonic folklorization processes, in which certain practices were promoted as "folklore." One such practice was the *Viejitos* Dance of Lake Pátzcuaro, Michoacán.

FOLKLORIZATION IN ACTION

It is useful at this stage to provide a brief overview of some of the key events and figures in the emergence of the *Viejitos* Dance as folklore, which will enable us to gain insight into how folklorization processes operated.[4] In the early 1920s, a young man named Nicolás Bartolo Juárez, a *P'urhépecha* campesino[5] from the Lake Pátzcuaro island village of Jarácuaro, was taken to Mexico City in order to teach the *Viejitos* Dance to a group of student teachers for a performance event laid on for a delegation of Chilean officials. Subsequently, performances of the *Viejitos* Dance and other "cuadros costumbristas"[6]—scenes of traditional customs—were given at the Teatro Sintético del Murciélago, also in Mexico City, and again directed by Bartolo Juárez. In order to contextualize these performances of the *Viejitos* Dance, it is necessary to understand that prior to these performances in Mexico City, many forms of masked *Viejo*[7] dances had existed in the Lake Pátzcuaro and upland region of Michoacán,[8] usually performed in villages as informal entertainment and as part of ritual celebrations for the Christmas and New Year period.

With regard to the performances in Mexico City, it is particularly relevant to note that alongside the *Viejitos* Dance, other "customs" were "performed" or represented on stage. For example, the nationwide ceremony of *Noche de Muertos* ("night of the dead") was "performed," in a specific version from the Lake Pátzcuaro island village of Janitzio. This is highly significant in that it is not a music or dance performance, yet the promotion of this event of Janitzio has also played a major role in configurations and frameworks of "indigenousness" and "folklore," alongside the *Viejitos* Dance.

In 1930 an elaborate event entitled *Hamarándecua*, a *P'urhépecha* term meaning "customs," took place in Mexico City. This theatrical presentation of Michoacán customs included not only the *Viejitos* Dance (directed by Bartolo Juárez) and a representation of *Noche de Muertos* in Janitzio, but also a market scene and a wedding. Presenting the *Viejitos* Dance in this context not only continued to "fix" this version of the dance, but also established it as a part of *P'urhépecha* everyday life in a "folkloric" context. Three other performances in the 1930s also stand out for their promotion of the *Viejitos* Dance as "folklore." Two of these took place in Mexico City and placed the *Viejitos* Dance within a national context, alongside other music and dance pieces from diverse regions of Mexico. The first of these, in 1935, was an event entitled *Noche Mexicana* ("Mexican night"), which took place on Lake Chapultepec, with the *Viejitos* Dance again directed by Bartolo Juárez. The second, in 1937, took place in the sumptuous and significant Palacio de Bellas Artes, in a series of performances entitled *Danzas Auténticas Mexicanas* ("authentic Mexican dances"). It is notable that performers for this event came from the presumed villages of origin of the dances. The third notable event took place not in Mexico but in San Antonio, Texas, to an audience of Mexicans abroad as an unequivocal tool for reinforcing a unified Mexican national identity. "Authentic" *P'urhépecha* musicians and dancers were officially "sent" by the governor of Michoacán as part of celebrations for the *Día de la Raza* in 1938. A newspaper article makes it clear that the *Viejitos* Dance was, by this stage, established in Mexico as an essential element of Mexican identity, making particular links with "indigenous peoples" as inherent in the formula ("Será Ejecutada" 1938). What is important to note is that in each of these contexts, the *Viejitos* Dance was presented within performance frameworks as an "authentic" and "representative" artistic practice of the *P'urhépecha* people, establishing the dance as "folklore" through processes that may be regarded as folklorization.

As institutions and individuals were involved in these processes, it is useful to briefly mention key figures and institutions. Two men who played a major role were Francisco Domínguez and Rubén M. Campos. Both men were ethnomusicologists[9] and composers who worked for the SEP, the Secretariat of Public Education. In the early 1920s, Domínguez undertook fieldwork for the SEP in the Michoacán region, and in 1923 he organized a staged "folklore" event in the *P'urhépecha* highland town of Paracho, attended by local inhabitants and, more significantly, Michoacán government officials and dignitaries. Campos was an invited guest. Both men visited the tiny island of Jarácuaro, where they interviewed members of the Bartolo Juárez family whose reputation as accomplished musicians in the European "classical" tradition was already known to them; and both men subsequently included compositions and data about this family in publications (Campos 1928, Domínguez 1925, 1941). What is notable is the way in which the Bartolo Juárez family was presented as accomplished musicians, with clear abilities for ensemble playing (as a string quartet) and whose repertoire included music by composers such as Beethoven and Mozart. They were highly skilled in reading, notating, and composing music, and in particular the youngest son, Nicolás, was singled out for his well developed abilities. However, it was not this competent and skilled musicianship that was promoted in a national arena. When both Domínguez and Campos were on the island, they were witness to some form of performance of a *Viejitos* Dance, which would most likely have been an informal Christmas and New Year celebration around the houses and streets and in the atrium of the church. It was this dance, rather than the string quartet, that was subsequently appropriated and used for "outside" presentation, with Nicolás being invited to take the role of teacher and transmitter.

It is also notable that government officials were involved in promoting the events in which the *Viejitos* Dance was presented. For example, as governor of Michoacán, Lázaro Cárdenas was involved with *Hamarándecua*, and later, when he was president of the republic, his wife sponsored the event *Danzas Auténticas Mexicanas*. State institutions were the organizing bodies of the events, with the SEP in particular playing a major role. Publications also played a key role in formulating, establishing, and promoting the classification of "folklore," mostly through journals and books published through the SEP, with some articles specifically focused upon the Lake Pátzcuaro region, and in particular Janitzio (see González 1925, 1928a, and 1928b).

HOW ARE HUMAN BEINGS MADE SUBJECTS?

Having sketched out some of the key events, individuals, and institutions that played a part in establishing the *Viejitos* Dance as "folklore," we can move now to an analysis that reveals the power relations inherent in such processes, demonstrating the consequences and implications of these early events for subsequent decades of the twentieth century—and indeed for current contexts. In order to proceed with an analysis, we may usefully draw on the work of Michel Foucault, who has used the notion of "subjection" to describe a particular form of power relations that do not revolve around relations of dominance or exploitation, but rather focus on "aspects of a field of power farthest removed from the direct application of force. That dimension of power relations is where the identity of individuals and groups is at stake, and where order in its broadest meaning is taking form. This is the realm in which culture and power are most closely intertwined" (see Rabinow 1986: 260). The key question: how are human beings made subjects? provides a central focus for this examination (Foucault 1982: 212) and seeks to understand processes that have taken place that imply or instigate power relations. Foucault suggests that there are two meanings of the word "subject": in the first, the individual is subject to someone else by control and dependence, and in the second, the individual is tied to his/her own identity or self-knowledge.[10]

What I am proposing is that through the classification of "folklore" in relation to the *Viejitos* Dance, three "sets" of peoples were, and are, made subject to a certain form of control that acts at a governmental level, taking place through hegemonic processes. The three "sets" of people are first, the musicians and dancers of the *Viejitos* Dance, second, those classified as *P'urhépecha* peoples, and third, those classified as indigenous peoples of Mexico. A key process in terms of using folklore as a power mechanism involves classification. There is no doubt that classification is intrinsically linked with the exercising of power, for such a process involves deciding whom or what shall be included. As Foucault has noted, "there is nothing more tentative ... than the process of establishing an order among things" (1970: xix). However, establishing an order was indeed necessary for the postrevolution regimes, for as Gerard Kubik has noted, "one can only control what has been defined clearly, and what cannot be nailed down cannot be controlled" (1994: 33). Classification was a central tool for revolutionary ideologies and policies in which state control was paramount; the *Viejitos* Dance and other artistic practices form part of the context in which hegemonic power relations developed. Two specific "categories" are essential to form an understanding of the way in which using the *Viejitos* Dance may be interpreted as a form of implementing power techniques. These are "indigenous" and "folklore." While neither is a subset of the other, the two are inextricably linked, with large areas of overlap. Categorization of music, dance practices, and, by indexation, people as "folkloric" was deemed useful and necessary for creating a new national order, for mobilizing the masses, for integrating the rural "indigenous" peoples and paradoxically for unification and stratification. The concept and category of "folklore" became a crucial politicocultural term, encompassing rural "indigenous" practices and peoples throughout Mexico. The idea of "folklore" as a political tool has been examined by numerous scholars from a range of fields (see Harker 1985, Blacking 1987, Feld 1988, Mendoza 1998, Mendoza-Walker 1994, Poole 1990, García Canclini 1993).[11] They have demonstrated how governments and institutions are necessarily implicated in the promotion and manipulation of "folklore" as a tool for purposes linked with identity-construction, unification, and nationalization, and as such how it is it intrinsically connected with control and power relations. With regard to a specifically Latin American context, William Rowe and Victor Schelling have made a general examination of the way in which cultural actions come to be called folklore, particularly in terms of integrating rural populations into a modernist state for the development of a capitalist economy (1991: 5). In particular, they have examined "peasant handicrafts" as a form of folklore. My aim is to expand on these issues in two important aspects. First, my argument focuses on an ethnic distinction as opposed to the class distinction that Rowe and Schelling propose, and examines the way in which the "indigenous" rural populations were implicated through "folklore." Second, with a music/dance practice at the center of my study, folklore is embodied; hence, people are implicated in a much more direct way than is the case with handicrafts, through the inclusion of human bodies as objects.

INDIGENISMO AS A FORMULA FOR CONTROL

Before progressing to a discussion of folklore in the Mexican context, we must focus briefly on the concept of "indigenous," for this is crucial to notions of folklore as a technology of power in relation to the microcontext of the *Viejitos* Dance and to the macrocontext of folklore in Mexico. Prior to the arrival of the Spaniards in the early sixteenth century, the populations inhabiting the landmass of Mexico were ethnically diverse, encompassing a range of cultures, languages, and peoples. After the "conquest," although huge numbers of people were killed, displaced, or subjugated, a pattern of resistance emerged in which lifestyles and languages were maintained within a caste context. As a whole, these people were classified as *indios* ("Indians"), with specific names given to each "group," usually in relation to language. From independence in 1821 until the revolution of 1910, such forms of classification continued. As the revolutionary civil wars drew to a close, the population of Mexico still included diverse groups or communities of peoples. Over fifty indigenous languages existed (and still exist), the names of these languages used to classify not only those who spoke the language, but also those who lived in the same location and followed similar cultural patterns, but did not speak the language.[12] After the warring stage of the revolution, the revolutionary regimes saw the need to integrate the "indigenous" peoples and the rural population who were seen as obstacles to the progress of the nation (see Morris 1999: 375).[13] Regarding the complexities of classification in relation to both an "indigenous" identity and a "rural" identity, it must be understood that divergent positions were, and are, intrinsic to this context, with some governmental officials and scholars propounding views that regarded the "indigenous" peoples as distinct along racial lines, whereas others made a distinction along class lines (see Anderson 1970, Knight 1990, Bigas Torres 1990, García Mora 1997).

One of the most important movements in postrevolution Mexico was that of *indigenismo-mestizaje*.[14] While the ideology has parallels with movements in other Latin American countries, it should be understood here in the uniqueness of the Mexican context. *Mestizaje* involved the idea of transformation of the population into a "mixed" and therefore authentically Mexican nation, thus requiring the transformation of each indigenous individual to become mestizo. However, as Alan Knight has noted, the status of both indigenous and mestizo in Mexico was of a highly subjective nature, for it depended on "a range of perceived characteristics, rather than on any immutable and innate attributes" (1990: 74). After four centuries of miscegenation, any racial strains had become thoroughly mixed, and divisions were therefore ethnic, rather than racial. While *mestizaje* sought to "whiten" and mix the peoples, *indigenismo* placed an emphasis on romanticizing and valorizing certain aspects of indigenous cultures and peoples as a way of formulating and constructing an authentic Mexican nation.

SUBJECTION THROUGH HEGEMONIC PROCESSES

Here then is the essential paradox of the nationalizing processes of the 1920s and '30s. Integration and unification were key features, yet these were to be implemented through processes that necessarily implied and required reification and classification. How could an indigenous person become *mestizo* unless these categories were defined and therefore reified? As Knight has described, such classification involved imposition from outside: "Postrevolutionary *indigenismo* thus represented yet another non-Indian formulation of the 'Indian problem'; it was another white/mestizo construct.... [I]t involved the imposition of ideas, categories, and policies from outside. The Indians themselves were the objects not the authors, of *indigenismo*" (1990: 94–95).

Intrinsically connected with the formulation of *indigenismo* was the process of folklorization. As a tool of integration, "indigenous symbols were nationalized, establishing the indigenous people as part of the national folk culture" (Dawson 1998: 298, see also Knight 1990: 82, García Canclini 1993: 43). Creating the national folk culture involved processes of hegemonic folklorization, utilising and reifying practices such as the *Viejitos* Dance. Steven Feld has described the process of hegemonic folklorization as one in which dominating outside parties legitimate condensed, simplified, or commodified displays; invoke, promote, and cherish them as official and authentic custom; and at the same time misunderstand, ignore, or suppress the real creative forces and expressive meanings that animate them in the community (1988: 96). Such a description can be appropriately applied in relation to the *Viejitos* Dance, although the use of the term "dominating" tends to implicate obvious, asymmetrical power relations. I suggest that the way in which folklore operates, through subtle rather than obvious mechanisms, not only enables it to be useful for governmental control, but also reinforces the idea of "subjection" in which identity is formulated through processes far removed from the direct application of force.

Although Antonio Gramsci's concept of hegemony is now widely understood, it is worth reinforcing a particular attribute in relation to the Mexican context. As hegemony involves "initiatives and activities which form the apparatus of the political and cultural hegemony of the ruling classes" (Gramsci 1982: 258), it is clearly crucial to an understanding of 1920s and '30s Mexico; despite the socialist rhetoric of the revolutionary rulers, a hegemonic class, with middle class intellectuals as leaders, was in control. As Nestor García Canclini has noted, "No hegemonic class can wield its power and its ideology with total arbitrariness, solely from above downward; it needs the advance of the whole society, particularly in its historically progressive stage" (1993: 46). In order to achieve the advance of the whole society through hegemonic processes, populism—the idea of the people as controlling political power—was deployed. With populism, the need to gain the loyalty of the masses became a program that, at an imaginary level, placed the masses—the people—at the center of the nation and the state (Rowe and Schelling 1991: 9). This is key to understanding how "folklore" could operate so successfully, for crucial to folklore is the idea that people, in this case the "indigenous" masses, could be seen to be at the center of the nation.[15]

So when the *Viejitos* Dance was performed in Mexico City, it was the notion of "indigenous" at the center of the nation that was represented and proclaimed. This became all the more potent in performances, such as in the Palacio de Bellas Artes in 1937, when "authentic" dancers and musicians participated. It is this connection that provides the intricate and inextricable link between *indigenismo* and folklore, for it was the promotion of certain artistic and cultural practices, with the *Viejitos* Dance as an example that was essential to providing tangible, embodied examples of *indigenismo*. The process of performing the *Viejitos* Dance in the Palacio de Bellas Artes enabled and encouraged indigenous musicians and dancers to participate and, quite literally, take center stage. However, this took place only within controlled spaces, carefully organized by the ruling class and therefore subject to a network of power relations that was controlled and manipulated principally by the state.[16]

INDIVIDUALS AND INSTITUTIONS

In order to further understand the complex processes that enabled this network to develop, I will return briefly to a topic raised here earlier: the involvement of individuals and institutions in the processes. As Foucault has noted: "Let us not deceive ourselves; if we speak of the structures or the mechanisms of power, it is only insofar as we suppose that certain persons exercise power over others" (1982: 217). Foucault's call for an interrogation of the emergence of certain "disciplines" in order to understand their role in the formulation of power relations focuses on the social sciences and their study of human beings; through a mode of objectification, he contends that human beings are made subjects. Clearly, anthropology, ethnology, and ethnomusicology are centered on taking human beings as their subjects, and in postrevolution Mexico, it was these disciplines that were particularly important as tools in governmental strategies linked with promoting *indigenismo*. Indeed, in relation to postrevolutionary Mexico, Knight has described how "it was therefore the task of skilled and sympathetic intellectuals, ethnographers and anthropologists above all, to 'forge ... an Indian soul'" (Gamio 1960 [1916] Knight 1990: 94–95). In relation to the *Viejitos* Dance, it was Domínguez and Campos, both intellectuals and ethnomusicologists, who played major roles in collecting, re-presenting and promoting the dance within specific frameworks of performance and in publication. Although an examination of the connections between knowledge and power are not possible within the confines of this chapter, it is worthwhile highlighting the way in which intellectuals and scholars are implicated in a power technique that involves the capturing and production of "knowledge" (see Nietzsche 1967 and Foucault 1977a).[17]

ESSENTIALIZATION, OPPOSITION, AND REPRESENTATION

Returning to the key question of how human beings are made subjects, we must consider the implications and consequences of the folklorization processes, both in the microcontext of the *Viejitos* Dance and the macrocontext of postrevolution Mexico. One area of subjection involves a complex network in which identities and peoples are essentialized, partially through the invocation of a series of binaries. The paradoxical implications of creating unity through "dividing practices" should be evident here. By setting the *Viejitos* Dance apart and labeling it as "folklore," a sense of division and otherness is created and a chain reaction is set in motion that establishes attributes of both the practice and the people. So, for example, folklore is placed in opposition to art, authentic opposes inauthentic, traditional (backward-looking) opposes modern. As Rowe and Schelling have pointed out, "A vocabulary which places the high against the low, and so on, is obviously hierarchical, and in a historical sense has reinforced the hegemonic controls exercized by bourgeois ruling classes.... One set of classifications ... tends to be used as a totalising explanatory device for a text or texts, on the tacit assumption that other binaries will fall in behind it" (1991: 194). Despite the revolutionary regimes' efforts to break out of the former racist paradigms, by continuing to utilize the same language and terms, they remained in a hierarchical mode, so that "reversals of categories end up as utopian gestures (or alibis, in fact) on the part of the intellectual" (1991: 194). The consequences of this classification process included the paradoxical effect of establishing a panindigenous/rural category, with implications of unified form, features, and stylistic attributes. Categorising the *Viejitos* Dance as "folklore" enabled an implication of unity with other peoples/forms, therefore containing the practice and making full use of any signifying features, thus maintaining divisions between ruling and nonruling classes. Such classifications denied the internal diversity of each group, whose cultural practices not only differed from region to region, but also from village to village. By imposing "convenient" labels, diversity could be controlled.

Clearly, the concepts of intervention, appropriation, normalization, and legitimization are part of this framework where unequal power relations are implicit (see Wishnant 1983, Stekert 1993). There is no need to rerun the discussions of the late twentieth century surrounding representation (see Marcus and Fisher 1986, Clifford and Marcus 1986, Dornfeld 1992), except to say that representation is highly charged with aspects of power relations, relating to "who has the power to represent who" (Kirchenblatt-Gimblett 1992: 303). Scholars have recognized that the power to represent, and indeed the power to consume, other cultures is a form of dominance related to aspects of knowledge. The way in which the *Viejitos* Dance was used in the public domain in postrevolution Mexico provides a clear example of how one practice, linked to a specific place and peoples, was used to represent large sections of society, thus containing them within specific boundaries, in relation to both micro and macrocontexts, formulating and maintaining relations of subjection. This situation is made more potent through the use of dance and music practice, in which two levels of subjection are evident.

The first involves subjection through containment by taking and placing the *Viejitos* Dance, as representation of a "*P'urhépecha*" and "indigenous" identity within the frame of a performance event, regardless of who the performers are. The second involves the concept of embodiment in which performing identities are pitted against, or confused with, biological identities. Performers of the *Viejitos* Dance, from the Lake Pátzcuaro region, were subject to receiving an imposed identity, through their embodiment as "indigenous" performers of "folklore." So Nicolás Bartolo Juárez, the villager from Jarácuaro mentioned earlier who was taken to Mexico City to teach and perform the *Viejitos* Dance, was made subject to perceptions of his identity, embodied in and indexed through the notion of the *Viejitos*

Dance as "folklore." So too for the performers who participated in *Danzas Auténticas Mexicanas*. The sense in which these "indigenous" performers were quite literally given the opportunity to take center stage may be interpreted as a form of "disciplinary power" (Foucault 1997b: 170–77). The potency of this power comes from the fact that it is a power that seeks invisibility while the objects of power—those on whom it operates—are made the most visible. Although the staged performance events that are the focus of this discussion are far removed from the contexts of Foucault's research (e.g., prisons, mental asylums), nevertheless there are parallels to be drawn. Indeed, the recreational and entertainment contexts of the performance events make the disciplinary aspect appear far less obvious.

EIGHTY YEARS ON

Retrospectively critiquing policies and activities of the postrevolution period as technologies of power is not a new undertaking, for as Knight has noted, "it is neither difficult nor original to criticize, even to mock, [the] proselytizing efforts—as utopian, dogmatic, even authoritarian—... and the high-flown radical agenda of the 1930s [with it's] optimistic goals, bizarre innovations and dogmatic practices" (Knight 1994b: 415–16).[18] In relation to the broader geopolitical field of Latin America, Abril Trigo has described how "the difference between current Latin American studies and traditional [early twentieth century] Latin American thought is that the latter believed in the integrating capabilities of national literatures and art, while the former criticize them as apparatuses of power" (2000: 75).

Perhaps one of the better ways of making use of these interpretations and criticisms of the postrevolution period is in order to make sense of the present. Questions arise as to how far interpretations of power relations in postrevolution Mexico, with specific relation to uses of folklore, can be viewed as "beneficial" in the long term for those classified as "indigenous" and those who performed and participated in such activities. How does the concept of "folklore" function in Mexican society now and whose interests does it serve? The most obvious point to be made here is that eighty years after the *Viejitos* Dance was placed in a national arena under the label of "folklore," it is still placed in the same category and performed within similar contexts invoking similar patterns of oppositions. It is a classic example of the manipulation of "tradition" according to Henry Glassie's interpretation: "If tradition is a people's creation out of their own past, its character is not stasis but continuity; its opposite is not change but oppression, the intrusion of a power that thwarts the course of development. Oppressed people are made to do what others will have them to do" (1995:

396). Rowe and Schelling have described the long-lasting appeal of folk-lore in Mexico in connection with the persistence of populism as a force (1991: 9), and as populism is an activity of control used in hegemonic contexts, so the use of folklore must be interpreted as a tool of hegemonic control. As the idea of folklore has been promoted and perpetuated, so the "indigenous" peoples who are invoked through its implementation are confined to prescribed spaces and identities. Ethnicity is still reduced to external folkloristic forms, such as music, dance, and costume (Banks 1996: 158). Knight provides us with a succinct summary of contemporary contexts, describing how there is a "romantic valorization of 'Indian' arts and crafts, dance and music (witness the Ballet Folklórico). Yet there is a paradox at the heart of such policies. The Indians whose culture is valorized and whose emancipation is proclaimed find themselves once again in the position of reacting to an imposed ideology. Their reaction is utilitarian: they exploit whatever opportunities official *indigenismo* confers, even playing up to their exotic or romantic official image" (1990: 99–100).

Questions arise as to whether there is any form of resistance to this situation, or if indeed there are any perceptible benefits for those people whom I have suggested are in some ways subject to asymmetrical power relations through the categorization of "folklore" in general and through the *Viejitos* Dance specifically. Indeed, as Derek Sayer has suggested, ". . . state forms or enactments do not merely constrain. They may also empower and enable, often in differential ways. . . . Individuals and groups may creatively adapt and use the forms through which, on another level, they are confined and constrained (1994: 376). Knight's interpretation of a utilitarian response may usefully be applied in these contexts. For the musicians and dancers of the *Viejitos* Dance from Jarácuaro, this means accepting offers to perform, which brings financial remuneration—although often abysmally low—and a sense of personal and collective pride and status.[19] However, the asymmetrical power relations are evident, for those who perform the *Viejitos* Dance in hotels in Morelia, the state capital, are welcome in their performing capacity as "folkloric artefacts" who can act as a signifier for identity construction and as a draw for clients, yet these same individuals are unwelcome if they walk through the door of the hotel as visitors. Such a climate respects the "folkloric" identity but not the living, biological human being. This is how human beings are made subjects.

The *Viejitos* Dance as "folklore" is part of a web that is both complex and firmly rooted and that serves the big institutions of state tourism while continuing to maintain those people invoked by "folklore" in marginalized positions. While the government is seen to be proactive in providing spaces and stages for a diverse range of ethnic groups to display "colorful" parts of their cultures in "folklore" events, calls for action to redress problems of poverty, discrimination, and marginalization go unheeded. As in many global contexts, tourism plays a major role in the promotion of "folkloric" music, dance, and ritual. A recent event serves to provide an example. As noted earlier, the celebration of *Noche de Muertos* on the Lake Pátzcuaro island of Janitzio was "staged" and promoted in the 1920s in performance contexts with the *Viejitos* Dance. The framing of the celebration and the people of Janitzio as "indigenous" and "folkloric" was an essential element of this context. From the 1930s onward, tourists visited Janitzio for the celebration, increasing in numbers as the years passed, to approximately eighty thousand in 1995. In Hanover, Germany, at Expo 2000 the World Fair, the Mexican pavilion contained a representation of *Noche de Muertos* on Janitzio, carefully chosen for its potential to promote an exotic, "folkloric" otherness (see Hellier-Tinoco 2004). The *P'urhépecha* peoples of Lake Pátzcuaro, with whom this celebration and the *Viejitos* Dance is intrinsically linked, continue to be framed by outsiders, made subjects by both state and tourist institutions. "Folklore" as a concept in Mexico serves the interests of state and business, but not those who are the subjects of folklore.[20]

As for resistance, there are examples of resistance to this continued use of "folklore" by those who are the subjects of folklore. The musicians and dancers of Jarácuaro, who perform the *Viejitos* Dance in "folkloric" spaces, also participate with music and dances in local celebrations in their own village.[21] Local performances proliferate in villages and towns throughout Mexico, however, they are not classified as "folklore," for there is no outside presence—state official, anthropologist, or tourist—to invoke the relevance or to impose the category of "folklore."[22]

SUMMARY

Throughout this chapter, discussion has centered around one small part of a complex web of power relations—examining how the classificatory term "folklore" was utilized in postrevolution Mexico as a tool for hegemonic control. Central to the discourse is the idea that musicians and dancers and those implicated and indexed by the term "folklore" were made subjects through networks and webs of signification and indexation, particularly through a chain effect of oppositional attributes. The emergence and promotion of one specific dance/music practice from the Lake Pátzcuaro region of Michoacán, labelled the *Viejitos* Dance, was used as an example of how hegemonic folklorization processes were undertaken in postrevolution Mexico. Contemporary contexts demonstrate that the consequences of these classificatory processes include a continued romantic valorization of artistic practice of diverse ethnic communities of Mexico, while the people themselves continue to live in marginalized and repressed situations. The predominance of a romantic, idealistic, folkloric image of these peoples is diffused and perpetuated through the use of music and dance as tools of control. This microcontext must be viewed as part of a much larger discourse—at national and international levels—concerning perceptions of peoples and even nations, and imposed definitions and identities, which fundamentally influence relationships of control and subjection. Clearly the term "folklore" must not be taken as simple category, but instead should be interrogated and problematized as formulated and constructed within specific sociohistoric contexts, with sociopolitical objectives, and therefore as intrinsically connected with asymmetrical power relations. The use of "folklore" is essentially political by virtue of it being centered on the shaping and promotion of ideology. "Folklore" is still used as shorthand and a signifier of a chain of implications and perceived characteristics. The eternal paradox remains: Musicians and dancers are empowered to perform in public spaces, as a representation of "*P'urhépecha*" or "indigenous" identity, but only through frameworks that involve relations of subjection.

Notes

[See website for photos to accompany this chapter.]

1. *P'urhépecha* is the term used to categorize an ethnic "group" of "indigenous" peoples who live in an area of the state of Michoacán. The term *tarascan* was commonly used in the past, however *P'urhépecha* is now generally used. The implications of this change of classificatory terminology will not be discussed here.

2. Although all "indigenous" peoples and practices are classified as "folkloric," the converse is not true—that is, not all "folklore" is intrinsically linked with "indigenous" peoples.

3. As I discuss in this chapter, the term "indigenous" is an essentialist label for diverse ethnic peoples of Mexico. I make use of the term within quotation marks where past contexts have used the term, recognizing the major limitations and asymmetrical power relations inherent in the use of this term.

4. For detailed analysis see Hellier 2002.

5. "Campesino" was the term used to describe poor rural dwellers.

6. *Costumbrista* was a genre that was taking hold primarily in literary works, but was also in evidence in music/drama events. The central theme was the lives of the rural peasantry.

7. *Viejo* simply means old man, whereas the term *viejito* demonstrates a sense of endearment and fondness. Although *viejito* is sometimes translated as "little old man," the more common usage in Mexico is connected with endearment.

8. Masked "old men" dances are found not only in Mexico, but also in various regions of Latin America and in many other places in the world.

9. Although the term "ethnomusicology" did not exist during the period in question, I prefer to use it in relation to Domínguez and Campos because it most aptly encompasses the broad cultural focus within which their music research was situated.

10. The second part of this, the concept of being tied to one's own identity or self-knowledge, is highly relevant to the contexts discussed in this chapter, but unfortunately limitations of space necessitate its absence.

11. García Canclini's seminal text, *Transforming Modernity*, provides a thorough discussion of cultural power in the Mexican context, focusing mostly on handicrafts rather than music/dance practices.

12. The process of naming and classifying involved terms used by a particular group to label them-

selves as well as words imposed by others, often relating back to the period immediately after the arrival of the Spaniards.

13. Clearly, this is a simplistic explanation of what was an extraordinarily complex period of history. There is a debate as to whether the indigenous peoples were to be integrated or reintegrated (see Dawson 1998, Becker 1995, Bonfil 1970, Lomnitz-Adler 1992). While all indigenous peoples were classified as "rural," not all rural people were classified as "indigenous."

14. While *indigenismo* was not a new idea in Mexico, after the Revolution its formulation was different from previous manifestations.

15. For a thorough discussion of the notion of hegemony and power in relation to Mexican revolutionary state formation see Joseph and Nugent (1994).

16. I use the expression "the state" in full acceptance of Sayer's (from Abrams 1988) assertion that "the state" does not exist, but that the state is a *claim* that in its very name attempts to give unity, coherence, structure, and intentionality to what are in practice frequently disunited, fragmented attempts at domination. In this sense "the state" *is* an ideological project (rather than an agency that has such projects)" (1994: 371).

17. The author notes her own role in these processes and the potential for perpetuating asymmetrical power relations through her own work, however, the implications of this will not be discussed in this chapter.

18. For a discussion of the revolutionary regimes as a disinterested movement versus the revisionist interpretation of power-hungry careerists see, for example, Knight 1994b: 396.

19. This view is drawn from personal interviews with musicians and dancers of the Lake Pátzcuaro region.

20. Complex issues arise concerning economic benefits versus political and individual discrimination and marginalization.

21. For a discussion of the complexities of an event in Jarácuaro that takes place during the *Noche de Muertos* celebration, in which the Viejitos Dance is used to draw in visitors, see Hellier 2002.

22. This situation is clearly highly complex, but it is worth noting how scholarship has been complicit in perpetuating these frameworks, utilizing the term "folklore" in essentialist and ultimately meaningless, yet repressive contexts. In a macrocontext, for example, Bruno Nettl has described "Mexican folk song" as a "definable category" (1985: 4–5), while Gerard Béhague begins a brief analysis with the comment that "the most typical performance characteristics of Mexican folk music comprise . . ." (1973: 202), and then he goes on to list the characteristics.

References

Abrams, Philip. [1977] 1988. "Some Notes on the Difficulty of Studying the State." *Journal of Historical Sociology* 1(1):5–89.

Anderson, Charles. 1970. "The Concepts of Race and Class and the Explanation of Latin American Politics." In M. Morner, ed. *Race and Class in Latin America.* New York and London: Columbia University Press, 231–55.

Banks, Marcus. 1996. *Ethnicity: Anthropological Constructions.* London and New York: Routledge.

Bartra, Roger. 1989. "Culture and Political Power in Mexico." *Latin American Perspectives* 16, 2: 61–69.

Becker, Marjorie. 1995. *Setting the Virgin on Fire: Lázaro Cárdenas, Michoacán Campesinos, and the Redemption of the Mexican Revolution.* Berkeley: University of California Press.

Béhague, Gerard. 1973. "Latin American Folk Music." In B. Nettl, *Folk and Traditional Music of the Western Continents.* New Jersey: Prentice Hall, 179–206.

Bigas Torres, Sylvia. 1990. *La narrativa indigenista mexicana del siglo xx.* Guadalajara, México: Editorial Universidad de Guadalajara.

Blacking, John. 1987. *A Commonsense View of All Music: Reflections on Percy Grainger's Writings on Ethnomusicology and Music Education.* Cambridge: Cambridge University.

Bonfil Bantalla, Guillermo. 1970. "Del indigenismo de la revolución a la antropologíacrítica." In *De eso que llaman antropología mexicana.* Mexico.

Campos, Ruben M. 1928. *El Folklore y la Música Mexicana: Investigación acerca de la cultura musical en México.* México: la Secretaría de Educación Pública.

Clifford, James and George Marcus, eds. 1986, *Writing Culture: The Poetics and Politics of Ethnography*. Berkeley: University of California Press.

Dawson, Alexander S. 1998. "From Models for the Nation to Model Citizens: *Indigenismo* and the 'Revindication' of the Mexican Indian, 1920–40." *Journal of Latin American Studies* 30: 279–308.

Domínguez, Francisco. 1925. *Sones, Canciones y Corridos Michoacanos*. 3 vols. México: la Secretaría de Educación Pública.

———. 1941. *Álbum Musical de Michoacán*. México: la Secretaría de Educación Pública.

Dornfeld, Barry. 1992. "Representation and Authority in Ethnographic Film/Video: Reception." *Ethnomusicology* 36, 1: 95–98.

Dreyfus, H. and Paul Rabinow. 1982. *Michel Foucault: Beyond Structuralism and Hermeneutics*. Chicago: Harvester Press.

Esser, Janet Brody. 1984. *Máscaras Ceremoniales de los Tarascos de la Sierra de Michoacán*. México: Instituto Nacional de Indigenista, Series de Artes y Tradiciones Populares, number 2.

Feld, Steven. 1984. "Communication, Music, and Speech about Music." *Yearbook for Traditional Music* 16: 1–18.

———. 1988. "Aesthetics as Iconicity of Style, or 'Lift-up-over-Sounding': Getting into the Kaluli Groove." *Yearbook of Traditional Music* 20: 74–113.

Foucault, Michel. 1970. *The Order of Things: An Archaeology of the Human Sciences*. Trans. Alan Sheridan. New York: Pantheon.

———. 1977a. "Intellectuals and Power," in *Language, Counter-memory, Practice: Selected Essays and Interviews*. Ed. Donald F. Bouchard. Ithaca, N.Y.: Cornell University Press, 204–17.

———. 1977b. *Discipline and Punish: The Birth of the Prison*. Trans. Alan Sheridan. New York: Pantheon.

———. 1982. "The Subject and Power." In H. L. Dreyfus and P. Rabinow. *Michel Foucault: Beyond Structuralism and Hermeneutics*. Chicago: The Harvester Press, 208–26.

Friedlander, Judith. 1975. *Being Indian in Hueyapan: A Study of Forced Identity in Contemporary Mexico*. New York: St Martin's Press.

Gamio, Manuel. 1960 [1916]. *Forjando Patria*. Mexico City: Porrúa.

García Canclini, Néstor. 1993. *Transforming Modernity: Popular Culture in Mexico*. Austin: University of Texas Press.

García Mora, Carlos. 1997. "Etnias y lenguas en Charapan: Consideraciones Purepechistas." In C. Paredes Martínez, *Lengua y etnohistoria P'urépecha: Homenaje a Benedict Warren*. Morelia, Mexico: La Universidad Michoacana de San Nicolás de Hidalgo, 40–63.

Glassie, Henry. 1995. "Tradition." *Journal of American Folklore* 108 (430): 395–412.

González, Carlos. 1925. "La ceremonia de la ofrenda a los difuntos en el cementerio de la isla de Janitzio, la noche del primer de noviembre." *Ethnos* 3a. época: 11–16.

———. 1928a. "The Dance of the Moors—*La Danza de los Moros*." *Mexican Folkways* 4, 1: 31–36.

———. 1928b. "The day of the dead in Janitzio." *Mexican Folkways* 4, 1: 66–69.

Gramsci, Antonio. 1982 [1971]. *Selections from the Prison Notebooks of Antonio Gramsci*. Ed. and trans. Quintin Hoare and Geoffrey Smith. London: Lawrence and Wishart.

Harker, D. 1985. *Fakesong: The Manufacture of British 'Folksong' 1700 to the Present Day*. Milton Keynes, UK: Open University Press.

Hellier, Ruth. 2002. "Removing the Mask: the Viejitos Dance as political and ideological tool in post-revolution Mexico, 1920–1940." Ph.D. diss. University of Central England.

Hellier-Tinoco, Ruth. 2004. "Projections of Mexican-ness: Night of the Dead on the tiny island of Janitzio." Paper given at '*Nation or Notion?*' International Performance Studies Conference, University of Wales.

Joseph, Gilbert M. and Daniel Nugent, eds. 1994. *Everyday Forms of State Formation: Revolution and the Negotiation of Rule in Modern Mexico*. Durham and London: Duke University Press.

Kirshenblatt-Gimblett, Barbara and Edward M. Bruner. 1992. "Tourism." In R. Bauman, *Folklore, Cultural Performances, and Popular Entertainments*. New York and Oxford: Oxford University Press, 300–307.

Knight, Alan. 1990. "Racism, Revolution, and Indigenismo." In R. Graham, *The Idea of Race in Latin America*. Austin: University of Texas Press, 71–113.

———. 1994a. "Peasants into Patriots: Thoughts on the Making of the Mexican Nation." *Mexican Studies/Estudios Mexicanos* 10, 1: 135

———. 1994b. "Popular Culture and the Revolutionary State in Mexico, 1910–1940." *Hispanic American Historical Review* 74, 3: 393–444.

Kubik, Gerhard. 1994. "Ethnicity, Cultural Identity, and the Psychology of Culture Contact." In G. Béhague, ed. *Music and Black Ethnicity: The Caribbean and South America*. Miami: University of Miami, 17–46.

Lomnitz-Adler, Claudio. 1992. *Exits from the Labyrinth: Culture and Ideology in the Mexican National Space*. Berkeley: University of California Press.

Marcus, George E. and Michael M. J. Fischer. 1986. *Anthropology as Cultural Critique: An Experimental Moment in the Human Sciences*. Chicago: University of Chicago Press.

Mendoza, Z. S. 1998. "Defining Folklore: Mestizo and Indigenous Identities on the Move." *Bulletin of Latin American Research* 17, 2: 165–83.

———. 2000. *Shaping Society through Dance: Mestizo Ritual Performance in the Peruvian Andes*. Chicago: University of Chicago Press.

Mendoza-Walker, Z. 1994. "Contesting Identities through Dance: Mestizo Performance in the Southern Andes of Peru." *Repercussions: Critical Alternative Viewpoints in Music Scholarship* 3, 2: 50–80.

Montemayor, Carlos. 2000. "Chiapas: secunda retrospective." *La Jornada* 4. V. 2000.

Morris, Stephen D. 1999. "Reforming the Nation: Mexican Nationalism in Context." *Journal of Latin American Studies* 31: 363–97.

Nettl, Bruno. 1985. *The Western Impact on World Music Change, Adaptation and Survival*. New York: Schirmer Books.

Nietzsche, Friedrich. 1967. *On the Genealogy of Morals and Ecce Homo*, trans. Walter Kaufmann and R. J. Hollingdale. New York: Vintage.

Payne, Michael. 1997. *Reading Knowledge: An Introduction to Barthes, Foucault, and Althusser*. Oxford: Blackwell Publishers.

Poole, D. A. 1990. "Accommodation and Resistance in Andean Ritual Dance." *Drama Review* 34, 2: 98–126.

Rabinow, Paul. 1986. "Representations Are Social Facts: Modernity and Post-Modernity in Anthropology." In J. Clifford and G. Marcus (eds.) *Writing Culture: The Poetics and Politics of Ethnography*. California: University of California Press, 234–261.

Rhodes, Robin. 1999. "The Mexican Indigenous Rights Movement: The Life and Rights of the Nahua of the Puebla Sierra." *Sincronía* (An E-Journal of Culture Studies from the University of Guadalajara).

Rowe, W. and Schelling, V. 1991. *Memory and Modernity: Popular Culture in Latin America*. Verso: New York.

Sayer, Derek. 1994. "Everyday Form of State Formation: Some Dissident Remarks on "Hegemony." In G. Joseph, and D. Nugent, eds. *Everyday Forms of State Formation: Revolution and the Negotiation of Rule in Modern Mexico*. Durham and London: Duke University Press, 367–377.

Schechner, R. 1990. "Wayang Kulit in the Colonial Margin." *Drama Review* 34, 2: 25–61.

"Será Ejecutada la Danza de 'Los Viejitos' en S. Antonio, Texas, en la Fiesta de la Raza." *Heraldo Michoacano* 12. X. 1938.

Stekert, Ellen J. 1993. "Cents and Nonsense in the Urban Folksong Movement: 1930–66." In N. Rosenburg, *Transforming Tradition: Folk Music Revivals Examined*. Urbana: University of Illinois Press, 84–106.

Trigo, Abril. 2000. "Why Do I Do Cultural Studies?" *Journal of Latin American Cultural Studies* 9, 1: 73–93.

Wishnant, David. 1983. *All That Is Native and Fine: The Politics of Culture in an American Region*. Chapel Hill: University of North Carolina Press.

CHAPTER 4

The Power to Influence Minds: German Folk Music during the Nazi Era and After

Britta Sweers

Music associated with the term *Volksmusik* is viewed problematically in Germany today, and is marginalized largely because of its propagandistic uses during the Nazi era (1933–1945). I had always taken this marginal status for granted; neither I nor my friends had ever identified strongly with the various folk songs we had sung in kindergarten and school. Even though I was born and raised in Schleswig-Holstein, I had never felt deeply connected to its vernacular traditions because my parents were not native to this region.[1] With neither a strong personal connection to my region's music nor to the kitschy, Bavarian-Alpine images with which the highly popular *volkstümliche Musik* ("folkstyle music") is inseparably intertwined, a study of German traditional music seemed, for me, highly unlikely.

The impetus to explore my own German traditions emerged while I was researching the mid-twentieth-century transformation of English folk music.[2] During the course of that study, I encountered a situation that, at first, seemed similar to Germany's: A considerable portion of the English population after 1945 had rejected their country's traditional music. Wanting to pursue the topic in its German context, yet also wanting to avoid the political minefield connected to the difficult issue of German refugees in the post–World War II era,[3] I planned to do a private and, I thought, harmless research project on the general remnants of folk music in northern Germany. Yet upon talking informally to several older people, it quickly became obvious that it would be difficult to get beyond music associated with the events of the Nazi era.[4]

I too was affected by the music of that time (even though I was born a generation after the war, in 1969), a fact that became evident upon discussing the origin of the Christmas song "Es ist für uns eine Zeit angekommen" ("The time of advent has come") with my church choir. Its first verse reads, "Es ist für uns eine Zeit angekommen/Die bringt uns eine große Freud/Über's schneebedeckte Feld wandern wir/Durch die große weite Welt." (Literally translated as "A time has come for us/that brings us a great pleasure/Over the snow-covered field we walk/Through the big, wide world.") This song had been familiar to me from childhood on; however, only in the context of this research did I discover that it was originally a Swiss song, and that its Christian content had been neutralized by a new text in the 1930s in accordance with Nazi cultural doctrines to undermine the strong social influence of Christian churches.[5] When I shared this information with my church choir, the reactions were two-fold. One singer, a thirty-five-year-old mother, responded with confusion and searched the song's verses for any ideological implications, only to realize that it contained no overt devices from the Nazi era. Another singer, a former journalist and actor, just said, "So what?" Uninterested in the history of the song's textual change, she defended the pagan roots of her region's cultural traditions and insisted on celebrating the winter solstice with her family for fun, despite the irritation of several neighbors who, obviously, associated such pagan traditions with neo-Nazi ideology.[6]

The knowledge of the song's background left me with an uneasy feeling, and I started to wonder how, exactly, seemingly innocent folk music could have been imbued with such negative power that even two or three generations later, its traumatic impact could still be felt. This chapter explores folk music, in its original and altered forms, and the role it played within the totalitarian Nazi regime. I examine folk music's underlying concepts and their changing definition in selected contexts of the 1930s and '40s. Finally, the chapter considers the aftereffects of Nazi-era uses of folk music in postwar Germany. First, in order to provide orientation points that will help to place my informants' stories—that were, with regard to folk music, often fragmentary—in historical context,[7] I trace this topic's roots as presented in the literature on the history of German folk music.

ARTICULATING NATIONALISM THROUGH LEISURE ACTIVITIES: DIE JUGENDMUSIKBEWEGUNG

The idea of using folk music within organized movements and as a means of national expression predated the Nazis by several decades. The Nazis mainly adopted these practices, co-opted established social groups, and adapted the groups' activities to new political ends. Various organizations centered around German folk song such as the *Jugendmusikbewegung* ("youth music movement"), also known collectively as *Der Wandervogel* ("bird of passage"), were subject to this process.[8]

From the mid-nineteenth century on, German social and cultural life had been shaped increasingly by organized clubs, *Vereine*, and singing was a major component of the clubs' activities. In addition to societies that were founded explicitly for the purpose of singing, almost every *Verein*, from postal workers' clubs to physical exercise organizations, had its own singing group. The early *Wandervogel* (1896–1908) began in reaction to aspects of bourgeois life and music aesthetics and presented a counter-culture to the ubiquitous, harmony-singing *Männergesangsvereine* ("male choral societies") of the late-nineteenth century. They opposed formal-ized, bourgeois music education and strongly advocated amateur music making.[9] Dressed in fanciful folkloric outfits, the movement developed a richly varied repertoire (consisting of academic, drinking, nonsense, and folk songs) performed in unison or with relatively simple harmonies. *Der Wandervogel* also rediscovered long-forgotten repertoire, such as Catholic Christmas songs that had fallen into disuse after the Reformation; "Es kommt ein Schiff geladen" ("There comes a ship a-sailing"), which remains a favorite in contemporary church song repertoire still today, was among the revived material.[10]

The groups' activities were, for the most part, communal events with emphasis placed on hiking, camping, and singing. This organized social life was either completely taken over by the Nazis, as was evident with the *Finkensteiner Bund*, or forbidden, as happened to the somewhat anarchic, aristocratic, and antidemocratic groups like the *Nerother Wandervogel*. The *Jugendmusikbewegung* ended in its original form in 1933, while the *Männergesangsvereine* were, increasingly, incorporated into the organiza-tional structures of the Nazis.[11]

Concepts of the folk song in this period clearly resembled the theories of Johann Gottfried Herder and the Brothers Grimm, especially those concerned with its defining criteria.[12] Accordingly, folk song was still iden-tified as such chiefly by its oral, communal, and anonymously authored character (although the idea that folk song should reflect the mind of a community was becoming more important than anonymous authorship as a defining feature). Following Herder, Hans Breuer (1883–1918), editor of the major song book *Der Zupfgeigenhansl* (1908),[13] defined folk song as oral and old (with medieval origins) and excluded new compositions from his definition.[14] He maintained that folk song is not a fixed object, is subject to change over time, and addresses a variety of topics. The singer of folk song was idealized as a complete human being living in remote areas whose happy, perfect state was thought to be accessible through singing, and only during a short period of youth. This view amounted to a strong critique of modern bourgeois society that was anti-individualistic (hence the focus on communal activities) and also resulted in a hyper-Germanness.

While important collections of folk music appeared in German-speaking lands in the late-eighteenth and early-nineteenth centuries,[15] it was not until the second half of the nineteenth century that folk music became— similar to other European regions—a tool in music education and a means of enhancing feelings of national identity. The latter was particularly evident after the 1848 revolution and the formation of the German Empire in 1871. Yet the transformation from folk music's romanticized view toward nationalism became especially apparent in the decade before World War I. This can be seen in various editions of the best-selling *Zupfgeigenhansl*: The first edition (1908) disavowed sentimentality, yet displayed an extremely romantic view with the claim that "still today Freya who was said dead whispers from the hazel tree's leaf-robe."[16] Lamenting the disappearance of tradition and yearning for simplicity, the stated aim of this publication was to foster "love for the folk and reverence for its immortal works."[17] Its fourth edition (1910) promoted hiking as a "truly German custom, rooted strongly in native soil."[18]

Growing nationalism became more explicit in the seventh edition (1911), as evidenced by the remark that "if, from these songs, the young Wandervogel only get a sense of what constitutes Germanness, (i.e.) the awareness of belonging to a noble-minded folk, then quite a lot would have been gained."[19] Like the Greeks who "celebrated their Homer for centuries," it was held that Germans too had a (folk) tradition worthy of veneration. Complaining about the large number of those who mimicked superficial aspects of the tradition (such as traveling around as costumed bards and wandering knights), the ninth edition emphasized the nationalistic aspect of the folk repertoire; in the editor's view, singing was no mere leisure activity but had a deeper meaning and enhanced an awareness of what it meant to be German. Singing, therefore, facilitated the fulfillment of Germanness. The tenth edition noted an increase in the number of regional song books and judged that "the more tribal the character and particular the song book's features, the better; for the individual suits us Germans, and this is our particular strength."[20] In this 1913 edition, Breuer gloomily remarks that "new war sorrows, new national storm tides will spawn new folk songs as well."[21]

The first clear traces of an extreme nationalism are indeed evident here, and many students involved in the *Jugendmusikbewegung* later volunteered for military service in World War I; Breuer himself was killed in 1918. However, it is difficult to make any generalizations because the *Wandervogel* also displayed a strong pacifism.[22] Furthermore, these nationalist perspectives were not confined to Germany. Such sentiments were common throughout Europe at the time and were, for instance, embraced by English folk song collector Cecil Sharp, who, in advocating folk music in music education, claimed that "the study of the folk-song will also stimulate the growth of the feeling of patriotism.... The introduction of folk-songs into our schools will not only affect the musical life of England; it will tend also to arouse that love of country and pride of race, the absence of which we now deplore."[23]

FRITZ JÖDE AND WALTHER HENSEL'S CONCEPTS OF FOLK MUSIC

The different approaches of Fritz Jöde (1887–1970) and Walther Hensel (1887–1956), two major figures of the *Jugendmusikbewegung*, represent further important developments in changing concepts of folk music in early-twentieth-century Germany. Jöde founded the first state-subsidized youth music school in Berlin and was strongly involved in the modernization of the German musical education system. He advocated a system that focused on developing the individual skills of the students—an approach to pedagogy that was considered revolutionary at the time.[24] Jöde also supported singing outside of school and believed strongly in the benefits of communal musicianship. From 1925–1926 he organized open singing meetings in accordance with these beliefs and principles.[25] Questions of a song's age, mode of transmission, and breadth of distribution were obviously less important for Jöde than for the editors of *Zupfgeigenhansl*.[26] In Jöde's expanded view, the concept of folk music could include contemporary compositions, while the term "folk" (previously restricted to the rural or working classes) could apply equally to everyone. Though he focused on the role of the community, Jöde also emphasized the role of the individual in the performance and creation of folk song.

In contrast to Jöde, who dealt primarily with public music education, Walther Hensel (née Julius Janiczek) was much more focused on private music making in the home. Hensel's parents exposed him early to a vast folk song repertoire,[27] and, inspired by a school music teacher, he started to collect traditional songs that would later serve as the basis of the *Jugendmusikbewegung*'s songbooks and would also shape the contents of many post–World War II songbooks. After obtaining a PhD in philology, Hensel taught both German and French[28] and later became a singing instructor. In the years following the foundation of Czechoslovakia in 1918, he increasingly concentrated his efforts on folklore studies but by 1911 had already cofounded the German–Bohemian and the Moravian–Silesian branches of *Wandervogel*. Starting in 1923, he organized weeklong singing events in Finkenstein, and with the support of the

Finkensteiner Bund, he expanded his activities in Germany, Austria, Switzerland, Scandinavia, and the Netherlands.[29]

Hensel developed a rigid nationalistic view after the First World War and cofounded the *Böhmerlandbewegung* ("Bohemian movement").[30] Like Jöde, he emphasized the educational importance of singing, but displayed a more political, Germanist orientation (as was evident in his definition of folk song as exclusively German). For him, folk song's roots were to be traced to the sixteenth and seventeenth century German *Volkslied*, and for the first time, we observe the criterion of popularity (i.e., folk songs are music for the masses) promoted as a key defining feature of folk song. Issues of provenance and authenticity (establishing authorship or places and dates of origin) assumed less importance. Hensel emphasized the notion of an expressly German community or folk who were responsible and hardworking, unlike the so-called *Wochenbummler* ("week-dawdlers," or slackers) of the time.[31] Opposing democracy, capitalism, and the materialism of that era, Hensel strongly supported the idea of an authoritarian leadership. Singing folk songs was, according to Hensel, a civic duty, not a leisure-time activity; hence, his singing weeks at Finkenstein were extremely organized and controlled events. Arranging his extensive collection of folk songs hierarchically, Hensel distinguished six types of folk song ranging from the ideal, medieval *Edelvolkslieder* ("noble folk song") at the highest level, to imitative *Scheinvolkslied* ("mock folk song") at the lowest level. Hensel and his work remain controversial; although he was important in the development of school music education, he has often been criticized for his nationalistic attitudes.

After 1933, the two approaches formulated by Jöde and Hensel took off in different directions.[32] Several composers of Jöde's working groups like the *Musikantengilde* ("musicians' guild"), such as Heinrich Spitta, started to work for the *Hitlerjugend* ("Hitler Youth"), while Jöde's publisher, the Kallmeyer Verlag, became the *Hitlerjugend's* principal publisher after 1933. These associations with the *Hitlerjugend* were obviously formed in order to avoid complete isolation during the Nazi era; the musicians maintained the illusion that they would retain the freedom to distribute their own material and ideas. In reality, the *Musikantengilde*, although loyal to the principles of Weimar democracy and generally apolitical, turned out be too weak to offer open resistance and were assimilated by the Nazis.

The *Finkensteiner Bund* and its publisher, the Bärenreiter-Verlag, who first had strongly welcomed the Nazis, fell due to the support of the SA ("storm troops"), in disgrace after the Röhm Putsch in 1934, although the Bärenreiter-Verlag managed to maintain an independent profile during the Nazi era. After 1933, Hensel avoided publicity and eventually even lost contact with Finkenstein.

THE FOLK MUSIC CONCEPT AFTER 1933

During the Nazi regime, music was recognized as an important tool to organize and control the masses; folk music in particular became a focus of interest. Also during this period, the idea of what constituted folk music changed. Although the original tradition (typified by ballads, carols, and dances) was left basically unaltered, it was nevertheless expanded by other material, such as marching songs and new compositions. Indeed, such was the interest in music that various experts on German musical life between 1933 and 1945 agree that this time could almost be described as a "singing dictatorship."[33] As Werner Gerdes, a choir conductor in Braunschweig, remarked in 1942: "For us, any genetically healthy national comrade is musical enough to take up, within himself, simple melodic phrases, a sound harmony and a solid, powerful rhythm as acoustic phenomena of an inner attitude. . . . If all our dispositions are hereditarily healthy, there ought to be almost no unmusical German.[34]

This music was thought to express the inner human (and thus national) character. As Hermann Blume (composer of "Kamerad Horst Wessel" ["Comrade Horst Wessel"][35]) stated in 1933, "the national uprising of the German folk came from within the heart of the nation and finds its expression in the songs that are born out of it"—that is, the folk songs.[36] Likewise, he explained that his music was the product of his "feelings of deepest devotion to the folk rooted in his home soil of the Mark Brandenburg."[37] Folk music was openly recognized as a means of enhancing feelings of national(istic) German identity, as well as a tool to deepen the communal experience of mass events. As Wilhelm Ehmann, who had developed various theories of musical mass festivities, remarked in 1936: "Folk song is a piece of Weltanschauung. . . . The new musical attitude called 'Volkslied' is a communal way of life."[38] This perspective is also confirmed by Heinz Antholz, who experienced the Nazi era not only at school and university, but also as a soldier; he observed that music education had become a way of controlling and disciplining people, and incorporated a "gloomy desire for being doomed."[39]

Post-1933 conceptualizations of folk music include some of the above-mentioned criteria, yet with a slightly changed perspective:[40] Classical criteria were retained (such as the oral and anonymous character of folk music) and emphasis was still placed on the medieval era as a temporal point of origin. Yet, the issue of a song's mass appeal had become much more important; similar to Jöde, the term "folk" was now understood to include all classes, and folk song was brought to an anti-individualistic extreme through its interpretation as music for the masses. In addition to this change, folk song's purportedly inherent nationalism was taken to another extreme by restricting the notion of "everyone" or the "masses" only to those who met the Nazi criteria of Germanness. Similar to definitions proposed by Cecil Sharp in 1907,[41] yet with a stronger political edge, folk music and popular music in Germany were strictly separated: Folk song was distinguished from *Schlager* ("hits") of the 1920s and '30s, often originating in the United States.[42] Finally, folk song was understood as a tool—a means to be used for education. This clearly echoes the principles of the *Jugendmusikbewegung*, but with the crucial addition that art serves ideology.

By redefining folk music as a music for the masses and positing a strong nationalist component, the original conception was expanded to include "composed music"—propaganda and marching songs. The era between 1933 and 1945 indeed saw the emergence of numerous new songs that were perceived as folk music, alongside the ballads, carols, and dances from the original tradition.[43] This new material was made up of numerous *contrafacta* (folk songs with new texts; in several cases even taken over from the communist repertoire), simple marching songs, and a new song type with its own conventions.[44] Musically, this new song type did not borrow directly from folk song melodies, but was rather comprised of new melodies in folk style. Moving away from symmetrical structures, such as a-b-a forms, the composers of the *Hitlerjugend* partly fell back on the style of the previous *Jugendmusikbewegung*: Heinrich Spitta's songs, for instance, were characterized by the use of church modes (such as Dorian), short introductions, 9/8 meters (that became more complex in the 1940s), and catchy melodies made up of prime, octave, second intervals, and broken chords. However, in service to the value of anti-individualism, authors and composers were not publicly acknowledged by the authorities beyond obligatory mention in the songbooks, thus preserving the anonymous character of the classic folk tradition.

Textual themes of *Volksmusik* were extremely varied; the contents of marching songs and battle songs could be very specific (referring to actual events) or they could be largely metaphoric (using language of fate, fight, and sacrifice while never naming a particular enemy or event). Even after 1933, when Nazi ideology was dominant, the majority of the songs were of a more general character, and most did not propagate an obvious ideology. Surprisingly, these songs contained few overt references to racism. More striking, however, was the prominence of imagery drawn from mystic–religious Germanic and Scandinavian fire/light cults—cults promoted as a preferred alternative to Christianity. Richard Klopffleisch has demonstrated that 58 percent of the songs featured light/flame metaphors in the context of transfiguration, death, and redemption narratives.[45]

Due to its expanded definition, folk music's boundaries became extremely blurred, something that also became apparent during my interviews. Although my interviewees were able to make a distinction between folk songs (perceived as politically neutral) and the ideological marching music, they nevertheless seemed to remember marching songs as folk music more vividly than any other type of music, an impact that persists to the present day.

CHANGES IN PERFORMANCE CONTEXT

While the regime tried to deepen attachment to the *Heimaterde* ("native soil") by fostering local traditions, dialects, and music through so-called *Heimatabende* ("home evenings") (folkloric, evening gatherings that featured singing), another development concerning folk music was even more significant: Original folk material was now shifted into the new contexts of mass events, such as school festivities, and the activities of the two main Nazi youth organizations, the *Hitlerjugend* (HJ) and *Bund Deutscher Mädel* (BDM). The *Heimatabende* and these mass events, in tandem with political radio broadcasts, proved most effective in projecting propaganda into private households.

As Sybille Neumann has pointed out in her study of music education and school politics in the *Gau* (administrative district of) Hamburg,[46] attempts to influence the educational system in Germany began early in the Nazi era. Songs per se were seen as a central part of the Nazi education, and music education was meant to foster the development of "one folk" into a "culture-capable vast mass."[47] Folk song played a specific role, and only the most revered, centuries-old material was allowed in the curriculum. The repertoire of folk songs for school use was often tailored consciously to the students' gender; girls were, for instance, prepared by these songs for motherhood and, later, for their future role as soldiers' wives. Art music was accepted into the curriculum only if it was based on folk song.[48]

Post-1933 ideological changes were especially evident in new songbook editions, the increased number of mass events, and the development of new teaching curricula. Neumann notes that even though songbooks aimed at young people were seen as an ideal way to transmit ideology, new editions of old songbooks appeared slowly due to copyright protections of the older publications. For example, it was not until 1935 that a new, two-part songbook by Kurt Haefeker, *Unser Lied. Ein Sing- und Musizierbuch für die Jugend* ("Our song: A song and music book for young people") appeared in Hamburg's schools. It included only a few HJ songs, but two years later an appendix was published with twenty-four new songs.[49] Major changes became especially obvious in editions published during the war; children's songs were replaced by songs about war and soldiers. According to Neumann, instrumental music education was, obviously, little affected by these developments, apart from the increasing inclusion of marching songs in pedagogical literature.[50]

The effectiveness of these youth-oriented efforts is difficult to calculate, as it depended on the willingness of individual teachers to use the new material. Sebastian Spratte reports that mass events seemed to be the most effective vehicles for the politically focused music because, according to contemporary theories, during these events music was experienced emotionally, not intellectually.[51] The actual content of the material was only a small part of the focus of these manufactured, communal experiences; rather, their purpose was to foster unified thinking and feeling. As the regime's main targets were easily influenced children and teenagers, school activities, soon after 1933, featured a large number of communal activities, such as internal school honors, seasonal celebrations, and historical memorial days. The celebration of the summer solstice was specifically designated as a youth festivity.

Spratte also observes that these events were characterized by a clear structure that was always repeated: The ideal celebration included fixed elements—such as "The Führer's Greetings," a proclamation, a public oath—and concluded by singing the double anthem, the "Horst-Wessel-Song" and the actual national anthem. Music framed these elements and was seen to incite emotional responses; in the context of these participatory and communal events, music was supposed to go directly "to the heart" and played a significant role in creating the desired unity of thought. Spratte identified two major groups of songs that were favored in these settings: folk songs and newly composed material carrying nationalistic or ideological messages with a strong "we" character.[52] Communally sung folk songs, as confirmed by my informants, often remained unaltered and were used to forge cultural and national identification among the participants;[53] these songs were also seen as a strong enticement for people to participate in such events. By transferring folk material into new, communal contexts, the music took on new meanings and, indeed, became identified with these festivities.[54]

USES OF FOLK SONG IN YOUTH GROUPS AND AT KINDERGARTEN

The Nazis exercised complete control over the *Bund Deutscher Mädel* and the *Hitlerjugend*—youth groups in which participation was compulsory for young girls and boys, respectively, after 1939. In the case of these groups, it is especially obvious that the Nazis coopted the activities and structures—hiking, campfires, and singing—that were typical of preexisting communist youth groups and the *Jugendmusikbewegung*. Many of the HJ/BDM's activities closely resembled those of the earlier groups. Likewise, a major portion of the HJ/BDM's song material was adapted from preexisting sources. One third of the BDM songbook, *Wir Mädel singen* ("We girls sing"), was comprised of seasonal songs, while another large portion related to daily events. Popular canons such as "C-a-f-f-e-e," or well-known love songs like "Wenn alle Brünnlein fließen" ("when all little fountains are floating") were included as well.[55] By using these songs in the new contexts of early-morning drills, marching events, or in medleys alongside Nazi propaganda songs, the music took on a second, explicitly political layer of meaning— yet members of the BDM and HJ would still identify these songs as folk songs. Marching songs had the most lasting impact on participants not only because of their use in marching exercises, but also because they could be heard constantly, all over the cities. One informant (from Thuringia, born in 1920) who had been in the BDM could still recall, sixty years after the war, all the verses of the particularly eerie marching song "Es zittern die morschen Knochen" ("the brittle bones are trembling"). She described it as being imprinted on her memory forever, which exemplifies that such marching songs are remembered more vividly than other types of songs, even more than the songs performed at the folkloric *Heimatabende*.[56]

The same informant recalled that Thuringia's various regional *Gesangsvereine* ("choral societies"), each with a vast repertoire ranging from traditional songs to operetta, were not overtly forbidden by the Nazis but were subjected to new conditions such as compulsory membership in the NSDAP (National Socialist German Workers' Party). Party activities were often so time-consuming that there was little time left for anything else, hence, the music just silently disappeared and the harmless pastime of folk singing was replaced by political activities. Antholz reports a similar consequence of compulsory HJ marching exercises; they left almost no room for other activities which, in his case, prevented him from practicing and performing classical music.[57]

At the kindergarten level, one observes the insertion of propaganda and war songs alongside traditional children's songs such as "Hänschen klein" ("little Jack"). The songs of the pre-Nazi children's repertoire (except for canons) were increasingly attacked for their uselessness, and around 1934 explicitly political material began to replace it. In addition to playing NS games simulating plane attacks and war games (from 1940 on), songs glorifying Hitler, and war songs (such as the "Engeland(sic)-Lied" ["the England song"]) were performed.[58] Again, the Nazis adapted preexisting musical practices for their own use; they followed the nineteenth-century model in which patriotic songs about the Kaiser were part of the children's song repertoire. The Nazi era children's repertoire retained songs of the 1848 revolution and workers' movements, yet the origins of these songs were either suppressed or their melodies were given entirely new texts. Especially in the case of childrens' songs, informants remembered this music as folk song.

ATTEMPTS TO INVENT A NEW TRADITION: CHRISTMAS SONGS

In the context of the traditional Christmas repertoire, the Nazis did not succeed in co-opting preexisting musical practices. The Nazi regime had sought to reduce the strong influence of the churches (accordingly, church songs were increasingly excluded from the school music curriculum) and bourgeois nineteenth-century family culture. This was evident, musically, in the Party's attempts to change the strongest Christian seasonal tradition in Germany: Christmas. They attempted to secularize of Christian elements and institute new traditions and carols of a Germanic–pagan character.[59]

Often, lyrics were altered in order to blend Lutheran Germanism with the idea of being part of a chosen nationality. One example is the first verse of the song "Es ist ein Ros' entsprungen" ("lo how a rose e'er blooming"): Es ist ein Ros' entsprungen/Von einer Wurzel zart/Wie uns die Alten sungen/Von Jesse kam die Art ("Lo how a rose e'er blooming/from tender stem hath sprung/as the men of old have sung/of Jesse's lineage coming"). The subtlety of the change was the result of the multilayered meaning of the German expression *Art*: "Von Jesse kam die Art" ("of Jesse's lineage [*Art* = species] coming") was transformed to "von wunderbarer Art" ("of a wonderful kind") which, as Weber-Kellermann remarked, removed Christian agency and hinted at a heathen, natural magic.[60] The introductory example, "Es ist für uns eine Zeit angekommen," is an example of a *contrafactum*: Originally from Switzerland ("Unser Heiland Jesus Christ/der für uns Mensch geworden ist" ["our savior Jesus Christ/who was made man for us"]), it was performed by children dressed as the Three Kings as they walked from house to house on the sixth day of January. While the first line remained unchanged, the refrain's Christian context was secularized.

In contrast to the practice of subtly altering well-known lyrics, "Der Sunnenwendmann" ("the solstice man") illustrates Nazi attempts to overlay German–pagan elements onto the Christmas repertoire. In this song written by Martin Greif and composed by Ilse Lang, Odin, who rides a white horse and brings gifts for children, was intended as a substitute for Santa Claus. The text was, again, full of fire and light images drawn from traditional pagan stories. Attempts were made to promote songs celebrating St. Stephan's Day (December 26) because St. Stephan was the Christian counterpart of, among others, Balder, the German light-god. The horses associated with St. Stephan were linked not only to the horses in Balder's tale, but to the horses in the stable where Jesus was born, and was thought, therefore, to be a particularly credible addition to the seasonal repertoire.[61]

It was, however, hard to find a counterpart for the world famous "Stille Nacht, heilige Nacht" ("Silent Night, Holy Night")—a cornerstone of the Christian–German bourgeois tradition.[62] For example, "Hohe Nacht der klaren Sterne" ("sublime night of the clear stars") was set up as a counterpiece by poet Hans Baumann (who had written various pieces for the *Hitlerjugend*). It illustrates well the subtle differences between the original Christmas songs and the Nazi substitutes: Although the piece employs pagan elements such as fire, the green branch, and the tree, the text's poetic devices mask any specific historical or political references: (Verse one: "Sublime night of the clear stars/That stand like wide bridges/Over a deep distance/Over which our hearts move.")[63] Given our knowledge of the time in which the song was created, the second and third verses would seem to emphasize the mother-veneration supported by the Nazis, yet this is never explicit.

Although this song was a particular favorite during the Nazi era (and can still be found in some songbooks, even though its popularity declined after the war), the majority of the newly composed carols never gained wide acceptance. Generally speaking, and my informants indeed confirmed this, people simply refused to give up the religious Christmas tradition, especially when the course of the war started to change and the first cities were bombed.

POST-WAR CULTURAL CHANGES

Perhaps the most tragic impact of the Nazi era on musical life in Germany, and particularly Eastern Europe, was the near complete disappearance of Jewish music traditions from art music and numerous folk music traditions.[64] Other German regional traditions also began to vanish: The sociocultural situation after the Second World War was especially complicated due to the huge number of German refugees fleeing from eastern Europe. So-called *Heimatvereine* ("local history clubs") that fostered the revival of various regional traditions of the refugees from East Prussia, Pomerania, and Silesia formed quickly after the war, and cultural (song and dance) events were often dominated by strongly nationalistic (even right-wing) sentiments that were heavily laden with political import.[65] Moreover, families were split up and scattered all over Germany (members of one family could end up in Bavaria, the Rhine region, Schleswig-Holstein, and Eastern Germany); hence, it became even more difficult to continue or revive regional cultural traditions. The majority of the refugees (particularly those who had come to Germany as children) thus gave up their old traditions almost completely in order to integrate as quickly as possible and absorb many of the "indigenous" cultures.[66]

After the war, Nazi propaganda and marching songs were not only forbidden by the Allies, but were also reviled after having been forced upon the people during the final war years when the triumphal texts conveyed the opposite of what people actually experienced. The Nazi school repertoire was likewise rejected (although one informant recalled that some of the forbidden marching songs were still sung secretly by the older boys). Concerning the fostering of (local) traditional music after the war, my interviewees regarded this as of minor importance in their lives until the 1950s. It hence seemed that by the time the former traditions were taken up again in the postwar era, perceptions of folk music had been profoundly altered. The traditional material still existed but had lost much of its original meaning, even on a regional level.

Some dimensions of the postwar musical situation can be observed in the Blue Songbook from Schleswig-Holstein. Based on a songbook from 1927, its first edition came out in 1954. Traces of previous developments were still evident; the preface to the 1958 edition remarks, for instance, that "it is a songbook for Schleswig-Holstein. It has grown on the native soil and out of everything that it [*Heimat*] means to us, and, according to its character, declares its faith in the large community of all Germans."[67] Although it consciously left out songs against the former neighboring enemy Denmark, the early editions nevertheless still included a section called "Heimat, Volk, und Vaterland" ("home, folk, and fatherland") — an expression that would not be acceptable today because of its association with Nazi propaganda.

The first song listed in the Blue Songbook is the national anthem.[68] In 1952, the original first verse of the anthem as sung during the Nazi era ("Deutschland, Deutschland über alles" ["Germany, Germany over all"]) was replaced by the more neutral third verse ("Einigkeit und Recht und Freiheit" ["unity and righteousness and freedom"]) in West Germany. It seemed to allude, ironically, to the forced separation of Germany into east and west.[69] The book, with its distinctive blue cover, nevertheless indexes the anthem's melody with the words of the first, taboo verse—an editorial decision that was the controversial subject of heated discussions, yet also reflects the confusion caused by the introduction of the new verse.[70] It was followed by the anthem of Schleswig-Holstein and several songs by Heinrich Spitta, the *Hitlerjugend* composer, whose songs continued to be published in the postwar era. The contemporary political situation was also reflected in "Heilige Heimat, Land in Not" ("holy homeland, nation in distress") by Adolf Seifert, who is explicitly listed as a *Sudeten* German, an identification that harked back to the politically charged terminology of the Nazi era. The lasting impact of the Youth Music Movement is also evident as the book contains many songs of the *Jugendmusikbewegung* and of Fritz Jöde's collected material.

ESCAPISM AND REVIVAL

During the *Weltwirtschaftswunder* ("economic miracle") of the mid-1950s, the postwar generation (predominantly the working classes) seemed to drift into a kind of escapism. This was particularly evident in the so-called west German *Heimatfilm* (literally translated as "homeland movies") trend that presented sentimental films in idealized regional settings (preferably the Alps and the Black Forest, but also the Lüneburg Heath in northern Germany), combined with artificial, folksy elements.[71] Offering an escape from daily constraints, the films' major message—that everything "would be alright"—was particularly important for those who had experienced the war.[72]

Musically, the *Heimatfilm* phenomenon found its parallel in so-called *volkstümliche Musik* ("folk style music"), a commercial, deliberately folksy genre that relies on clichéd, romanticized images that were not characteristic of the original folk tradition (images such as untouched nature, Alpine mountain ranges, harvesting hay, and so on). For example, the gowns worn by *volkstümliche Musik* performers often bear little relation to actual traditional clothing, while *volkstümliche* texts present topics such as happy groundhogs and cows against idyllic, alpine pasture backdrops. Reacting to previous political abuse of the idea of tradition, the music and regional folk traditions were cleansed of any nationalistic context.

The West German folk revival that followed in the wake of the Anglo–American folk revival of the 1960s and 1970s went to the other extreme by taking on a strong edge of political and social criticism that left little room for folk romanticism. Partly associated with the "'68 generation" (the German political students' movement that also based their protest on, among many other issues, the Nazi background of their parent's generation), groups and performers such as Hannes Wader, Franz Josef Degenhardt, Liederjan, Zupfgeigenhansel, and Fiedel Michel built up a large repertoire of worker's songs, political material, and songs from as far back as the Peasants' Wars of 1525 and the 1848 Revolution.

Musically, these performers also deviated strongly from previous folk traditions. Similar to revival performers in other European countries, many Germans started out by imitating American, Irish, and Scottish musicians and developed an interest in their own music only later (as in the case of Fiedel Michel or Liederjan). In contrast to performers in other countries, however, German folk groups retained their connection to these musical models: A significant feature of the German folk/electric scene is the presence of German–Irish/Scottish groups or bands.[73] The major problem this revival movement faced was that the living, performing tradition was almost completely gone (with a few exceptions in the Alpine region that witnessed a kind of revival in the late 1980s as *Neue Volksmusik* ("new folk music"). Although the musicians could fall back on a broad range of German material, especially from the archive of folk music in Freiburg, these sources predominantly existed in written form. Recordings, especially of clearly distinguished performance practices, were scarce or difficult to access. As a consequence, and in clear contrast to *volkstümliche Musik* practices, groups continue to adapt Anglo–American performance styles, such as that of The Dubliners and Steeleye Span.

GAINING ACCESS TO A SUPPRESSED PAST

Postwar research on folk music during the Nazi era based on oral testimonies becomes increasingly difficult at the turn of the twenty-first century, as many witnesses who were adults during the 1930s and '40s are already dead. The majority of witnesses available presently were children or teenagers at that time (as were my own parents). As Spratte realized, the small number of contemporaneous, personal accounts from the Nazi era is the main problem in investigating such topics, despite the large range of contemporaneous written material that is now accessible.[74] Rather, one has to fall back on retrospective accounts (in the form of memoirs), which are often blurred by the trauma of war experiences or marred due to guilt-related repression triggered by the critical questions of postwar generations.[75] Yet, taken together, these testimonies can provide valuable information regarding the processes by which folk music became a powerful means of political influence.

Hence, the problem of gaining access to a suppressed past is complex, and a wide range of material must be considered in an effort to trace developments in the conceptualization and uses of folk music in the Nazi-era Germany. Although some developments can be seen clearly (such as the changes in the folk song concept), individual testimonies, experiences, and perspectives add layers of complexity (inevitably, when interviewing twenty witnesses, one will get twenty very different views) and make other developments difficult to analyze. For example, Spratte concluded that the execution of Nazi directives concerning music was not uniform and depended strongly on individual teachers who did not necessarily conform to the NSDAP and had the option to use neutral folk songs (e.g., seasonal material) exclusively.[76] Furthermore, school materials were not altered simultaneously,[77] and volumes such as the sea-shanty collection *Knurrhahn* ("Gurnard" ["the growling cock"], the marine songbook of the pilots' singing organization) from 1936 did not yet contain new ideological material.[78]

As several of my informants recalled, the number of festivities varied extremely and sometimes was limited to officially required events only. On the other hand, an informant from the heavily militarized town Gumbinnen/Gussew in former East Prussia recalled constant government presence; for instance, at school roll calls on Monday mornings, each child was required to recite one new quotation by a prominent Nazi.

The war itself and its disruptions of daily routines complicated the picture, especially with regard to children under the age of 10–12 years. For example, because of the heavy bombing of Hamburg in the summer of 1943 (during the firestorm on July 28, thirty to forty thousand inhabitants were killed), one informant (b. 1934) experienced little or no school until 1945. With many children evacuated to the countryside, plans for indoctrination became extremely difficult to control, or even to carry out, in that area. Yet, also here, accounts vary. Another informant (b. 1930) who had gone to school in Kiel, remarked that, despite school being cancelled, her *BDM* meetings were still held among the evacuated children.

Moreover, gaps in current musicological literature make it difficult to trace the activities of influential music figures from the Nazi era. For instance, the first edition of *Die Musik in Geschichte und Gegenwart* (also a major resource on German music), published between 1949 and 1976,[79] included many (often unnoticed) omissions in the commentary regarding events from the Nazi era. The 1959 article on Walther Hensel by Michael Komma avoids any critical comment.[80] Likewise, the 1965 article on Heinrich Spitta (written by Spitta himself)[81] contains large gaps concerning the composer's *Hitlerjugend* activities in the years from 1932 to 1939 and no commentary on his nationalistic beliefs. The supplements from 1973 and 1976 contain similar gaps and omissions.

SHADOWS OF THE PAST

Although the last type of music people seem to connect consciously with the Nazi era is folk music (as opposed to marching songs), its associations with the Nazi movement—both positive and negative—are nevertheless strong, a fact that attests to its powerful, subconscious operations. Many witnesses still express fond memories of the communal events they experienced during the folk singing/dancing evenings of the 1930s and '40s. Yet others, like the seventy-year-old informant from East Prussia, associate folk music with negative memories. This informant remembers that during the Stalingrad disaster of 1942–1943, many wounded soldiers were brought to the barracks of her hometown Gumbinnen/Gussew, close to the Russian border. On several evenings, the young girls were asked to sing (children's) folk songs for the entertainment of these soldiers, and she still associates the smell of decaying flesh and the feeling of frozen ears with these tunes.

Though the propaganda and marching songs were rejected in the postwar era, they were not completely forgotten. Tomi Ungerer, a graphic artist from Alsace, recalled that twenty to thirty years after the war, the music from that time still had a soothing effect on him when he was upset.[82] Even sixty years later, many of these songs are embedded in the musical memories of those who had been part of organizations such as BDM and HJ. This is confirmed by Antholz who, upon hearing the tune of "Alte Kameraden" ("old comrades," a Nazi-era marching song) in the 1990s, felt completely overwhelmed by war memories.[83] That this music and the memories it evokes still haunt many older Germans was confirmed by the informant from Gumbinnen/Gussew; she remarked that she often recognized many of the melodies she had sung in the 1930s and '40s on today's radio or TV (performed either instrumentally or with different words, of course). Obviously, the origin of the material is not widely known any longer. Several witnesses likewise reported a certain confusion concerning the tradition; those who were in kindergarten or at school during the Nazi era were not only wary of the subconscious effects of the wartime material, but also extremely unsure of the material they could still sing or pass on to their families.

Such wariness might be good in light of the strong emotions and sense of taboo that war-era songs tend to elicit. Yet although the younger postwar generations generally display strong suspicion of anything related to nationalism, they also experience a kind of helplessness in dealing with remnants of the Nazi era. Hence, any artifact from the period is treated as though it might contain an unexploded, ideological bomb from the past, as the reactions to the introductory Christmas song example amply demonstrate.

Notes

1. Schleswig-Holstein is Germany's northernmost federal state. My father (b. 1934) settled there with his parents who, for political reasons, left their home in Thuringia in 1938. My mother (b. 1938) came to the area as a refugee from East Prussia in 1945.
2. Britta Sweers, *Electric Folk in England—Musical and Sociocultural Aspects* (Diss. Hamburg 1999, Microfiche 2000).
3. A study of these traditional musics is always in danger of being connected with nationalist, right-wing issues with which many organizations of these dislocated populations have been associated.
4. Indeed, I was surprised that these interviewees, nearly fifty-six years after the end of the war, still recalled with precision a large number of propaganda and marching songs from that time in addition to various traditional songs. I also learned that many of the war generation associated the term "folk music" not only with old ballads or rural dances, but particularly with this propaganda and marching material along with newly composed songs from the 1930s and 1940s.

5. As Ingeborg Weber-Kellermann pointed out in *Das Buch der Weihnachtslieder*, 9th ed. (Mainz: Schott International, 1988), 318–19, the original verse 1 actually reads as follows: "Es ist für uns eine Zeit angekommen, es ist uns eine große Gnad,' Unser Heiland Jesus Christ, der für uns Mensch geworden ist." ("A time has come for us/ for us it is a great mercy/Our Savior Jesus Christ/who was made man for us.")

6. Neo-Nazis in particular still exalt these Germanic traditions that have been completely excluded from history school curricula since the end of the Second World War.

7. At this point (2002), interviews were still led on an informal level, based on written field notes, as several informants were extremely insecure about the recording situation and wanted to remain anonymous. I interviewed twelve people ages approximately sixty-five to eighty-two—all were basically relatives, parents, or grandparents of friends, as well as neighbors, as a relationship of personal trust was extremely important. Three interviews happened incidentally (for example, the one with the informant from Gumbinnen/Gussew occurred on a train trip from Rostock to Hamburg).

8. See Jürgen Frey and Kaarel Siniveer. *Eine Geschichte der Volksmusik* (Reinbek bei Hamburg: rororo, 1987) for a detailed account of this background, including the political developments of the nineteenth century and the history of the *Jugendmusikbewegung*.

9. The application of simple instruments such as sticks and tambourines ("*Orff* instruments") into the modern school music education stems from that era as well.

10. See Weber-Kellermann, *Das Buch der Weihnachtslieder*, chap. 6.

11. Frey/Siniveer, *Eine Geschichte der Volksmusik*, 173–77.

12. See Richard Klopffleisch, *Lieder der Hitlerjugend* (Frankfurt am Main: Peter Lang, 1997), for a comprehensive discussion of these concepts.

13. *Zupfgeige* is translated as "guitar."

14. See Richard Klopffleisch, *Lieder der Hitlerjugend*, 118–21.

15. For example, Johann Gottfried Herder's *Stimmen der Völker in Liedern: Volkslieder* (2 vols., 1779) and Arnim Brentano's *Des Knaben Wunderhorn* (1806/1808).

16. "Noch heute raunt die totgesprochene Freya aus dem Blättergewande der Haseln." Hans Breuer, ed. *Der Zupfgeigenhansl* (Leipzig: Hofmeister, 1908). This, as well all subsequent quotes of Breuer, are taken from the 10th edition, 1913.

17. "Liebe zum Volk und Ehrfurcht vor seinen unvergänglichen Werken." Breuer, *Der Zupfgeigenhansl*.

18. "eine fest in heimatlicher Erde wurzelnde treue deutsche Art." Breuer, *Der Zupfgeigenhansl*.

19. "Und wenn der junge Wandervogel aus diesen Liedern nichts weiter mitgenommen hätte als eine Ahnung dessen, was deutsch ist, das Bewußtsein, einem edel veranlagten Volke anzugehören, so wäre schon etliches gewonnen." Breuer, *Der Zupfgeigenhansl*.

20. "Jemehr Stammescharakter und Eigenart ein solches Singbuch hat, umso besser, denn uns Deutschen liegt das Individuelle, und das ist unsere besondere Kraft." Breuer, *Der Zupfgeigenhansl*.

21. "Neue Kriegsnöte, neue nationale Sturmfluten werden auch heute wieder neue Volkslieder emportreiben." Breuer, *Der Zupfgeigenhansl*.

22. Frey/Siniveer, *Eine Geschichte der Volksmusik*, 165.

23. Cecil Sharp, *English Folk-Song: Some Conclusions* (London: Simplin & Co., Novello & Co., 1907), 135–36.

24. Coming from a Hamburg-based shoemaker family, Fritz Jöde became a primary school teacher before studying musicology in Leipzig. He was appointed professor at the Academy of Church and Schoolmusic in Berlin in 1923. Despite early attempts in the 1880s, teachers in 1900 were still not specifically trained or even qualified. The music educational reform was stalled by the First World War, but was continued by Jöde after the war. Several of these reforms are still in place today.

25. Dismissed due to political reasons in 1935, Jöde went to Munich to work (obviously illegally) for the radio until 1938. Although he obtained a position at the Mozarteum in Salzburg in 1939 (when he joined the NSDAP [National Socialist German Workers' Party]), he yet again had to leave for political reasons in 1943 (when he left the Party again). In 1947, Jöde was appointed to the school music board in Hamburg, setting up the Office of School and Youth Music in 1951, when he was also appointed director of the department for music education at the newly founded School of Music in Hamburg. Although he retired in 1953, he remained active, especially in the teaching and promotion of folk song, until his death in 1970.

26. Klopffleisch, *Lieder der Hitlerjugend*, 121–24.

27. Walther Hensel came from a German–Moravian family, his father being a silk weaver and musician (a combination that was quite common in Bohemia) and his mother likewise distinguished by a vast folk song repertoire.

28. German academy for economy in Prague (1912–1919).

29. In 1925, Hensel became director of the youth music school in Dortmund and moved to Stuttgart in 1930. In 1941 he returned to Prague and took exile in Bavaria after 1945.

30. The "Bohemian Movement" was part of the nationalistic *Sudeten* German movement that had been formed in the newly founded Czechoslovakia in 1918. The extremely heterogeneous population comprised 28 percent Germans (basically living in the north, northwest, and southwest of Czechoslovakia) who had (unsuccessfully) tried to join German–Austria in November/December 1818 and subsequently became a strong anti-Czechoslovakian force (finally succeeding in 1938 when joining the German *Reich*).

31. Klopffleisch, *Lieder der Hitlerjugend*, 125–34. The term is a condescending description of those who rather enjoy their leisure time, instead of using it for further education, group activities, and so on.

32. See Klopffleisch, *Lieder der Hitlerjugend*, 109–11.

33. Anna-Christine Brade, "BDM-Identität zwischen Kampflied und Wiegenlied—eine Betrachtung des Repertoires im BDM-Liederbuch *Wir Mädel singen*," in *Lieder in Politik und Alltag des Nationalsozialismus*, eds. Gottfried Niedhardt and George Broderick (Frankfurt am Main: Peter Lang, 1999), 150.

34. "Für uns ist jeder erbgesunde Volksgenosse musikalisch genug, um einfache Melodiebögen, eine gesunde Harmonik sowie solide, kraftvolle Rhythmik als akustische Phänomene einer inneren Haltung in sich aufzunehmen.... Sind unser aller Anlagen erbmäßig gesund, so dürfte es unmusikalische deutsche Menschen so gut wie gar nicht geben." In Josef Wulf, *Musik im Dritten Reich. Eine Dokumentation* (Reinbek bei Hamburg rororo, 1966), 281.

35. After having been killed in his apartment, NSDAP (National Socialist German Workers' Party) member and SA leader Horst Wessel (1907–1930) was martyrized by the Nazis (historians agree that his death was also related to a quarrel in the procurer scene). His so-called "Horst-Wessel-Lied" ("Horst Wessel Song") became the (unofficial) second anthem, always sung in addition to the national anthem.

36. "die Nationale Erhebung des deutschen Volkes kam aus dem Herzen der Nation und findet Ausdruck in den Liedern, die aus ihr geboren werden." In Wulf, *Musik im Dritten Reich*, 79.

37. "In märkischer Heimaterde verwurzelten Empfinden tiefer Volksverbundenheit entsprungen." In Wulf, *Musik im Dritten Reich*, 80.

38. "Das Volkslied ist ein Stück Weltanschauung.... Die neue Musikgesinnung heißt 'Volkslied' als gemeinsame Lebenshaltung." In Brade, "BDM-Identität zwischen Kampflied und Wiegenlied," 150.

39. "düstere Lust am Untergang." Heinz Antholz. *Die (Musik-)Erziehung im Dritten Reich. Erinnerungen, Erfahrungen und Erkenntnisse eines Betroffenen* (Augsburg: Wißner, 1993), 86. Investigating his personal motivations rather than trying to defend himself, Antholz's autobiographical study on (music) education in the *Dritte Reich* offers one of the rare insights into the psychology of that era and serves as a reliable confirmation for the following observations. Thanks are due to Bernd Fröde for pointing out this source to me.

40. Klopffleisch, *Lieder der Hitlerjugend*, 134–41. Klopffleisch refers to authors who were active in the *Hitlerjugend*.

41. Sharp, *English Folk-Song— Some Conclusions*.

42. The relativity (or even double standards) of these concepts became obvious in the case of jazz music. As Antholz, *Die (Musik-) Erziehung im Dritten Reich*, 155, pointed out, although jazz was officially forbidden, the upper ranks of the Nazis (including parts of the SS) listened to this music and played it at parties.

43. See, for instance, Klopffleisch, *Lieder der Hitlerjugend*, for a detailed analysis of the material.

44. Klopffleisch, *Lieder der Hitlerjugend*, 184–212.

45. Klopffleisch, *Lieder der Hitlerjugend*, 203.

46. Originally an expression that described a tribal district in Germanic times, *Gau* became the term for an administrative district during the Nazi era.

47. "eine kulturfähige, breite Masse." Sybille Neumann, "Musikunterricht und Schulpolitik im "Gau Hamburg," in *Lieder in Politik und Alltag des Nationalsozialismus*, eds. Gottfried Niedhardt and George Broderick (Frankfurt am Main: Peter Lang, 1995), 146.

48. See Antholz, *Die (Musik-)Erziehung im Dritten Reich*, 110.
49. While HJ songs tended to change extremely quickly (they obviously wore off very fast), a school book could, at most, only be revised on a yearly basis. See Neumann, "Musikunterricht und Schulpolitik", 148–49.
50. Neumann, "Musikunterricht und Schulpolitik," 152.
51. Sebastian Spratte, "Die Schulfeier und Ihre Rolle im Erziehungssystem des Dritten Reiches," in *Lieder in Politik und Alltag des Nationalsozialismus*, eds. Gottfried Niedhardt and George Broderick (Frankfurt am Main: Peter Lang, 1999), 133–46. The article discusses school festivities and their function in the Nazi educational system.
52. Spratte, "Die Schulfeier," 139.
53. Solo performance was rejected as it was seen to undermine the communal ideology.
54. Spratte, "Die Schulfeier," 139.
55. Brade, "BDM-Identität zwischen Kampflied und Wiegenlied," 152–56.
56. See Antholz, *Die (Musik-)Erziehung im Dritten Reich*, 88, who basically equaled his memories of the *HJ* with these marching activities.
57. Antholz, *Die (Musik-)Erziehung im Dritten Reich*, 86.
58. See Günther Noll, "Kinderlied und Kindersingen in der NS-Zeit," in *Lieder in Politik und Alltag des Nationalsozialismus*, ed. Gottfried Niedhardt and George Broderick (Frankfurt am Main: Peter Lang, 1999), 115–29.
59. See Weber-Kellermann, *Das Buch der Weihnachtslieder*, ch. 7.
60. Weber-Kellermann, *Das Buch der Weihnachtslieder*, 307.
61. Balder also appears in a horse-healing tale in the so-called second *Spell from Merseburg* notated in medieval times.
62. Weber-Kellermann, *Das Buch der Weihnachtslieder*, 307–308. Author's own translation.
63. "Hohe Nacht der klaren Sterne/die wie weite Brücken stehn/über einer tiefen Ferne/drüber unsre Herzen ziehn." Author's own translation.
64. An example for this cultural gap is the disappearance of the *chansonniers*, record stars, and theatre entertainers within the popular music sector. Well-known artists such as Max Ehrlich, Kurt Gerron, Willy Rosen, and Otto Wallenburg all died in Auschwitz in 1944. For further background information, see the CD booklet by Chaim Frank and Andreas Koll, *Populäre jüdische Künstler: Berlin— Hamburg— München. Musik & Entertainment* (Trikont US-292, 2001). Particularly concerning art music, the *Exilmusik-AG*, lead by Professor Petersen at Hamburg University, has contributed a large range of rediscoveries of, for instance, forgotten artists, biographies, and publishers.
65. The intention of these *Heimatvereine* was to foster regional traditions until a (still hoped for) return to their former home regions. This, however, opposed the attempts of the two Germanys to integrate into postwar Europe (in the 1950s, the refugee party BHE [Bund der Heimatvertriebenen und Entrechteten] was quite successful during the first elections in West Germany, yet soon, with increasing integration of the refugees, disappeared from the parliament).
66. With 33 percent (856,130 people) of the population being refugees, the present Schleswig-Holstein has become a complete mixture of original inhabitants and immigrants. Even the culture of conservative Bavaria was strongly affected by this change. For further numbers, see Walter Leisering, ed., *Putzger Historischer Weltatlas*. 102nd ed. Berlin: Cornelsen-Verlag, 1992.
67. "Es ist ein Liederbuch für Schleswig-Holstein. Darum ist es gewachsen auf dem Boden der Heimat und aus allem, was sie uns bedeutet, aber es bekennt sich seinem Charakter nach zur großen Gemeinschaft aller Deutschen." Hans Mathiesen and Hannes Schwensen, ed., *Liederbuch für Schleswig-Holstein*, 5th ed. (Wolfenbüttel: Möseler Verlag, 1958).
68. The German National anthem was written by Hoffmann von Fallersleben in his political exile on the then English island Helgoland in 1880 and set to a melody by Joseph Haydn from 1797 (which served as a thematic basis for his string quartet in C major, op. 76, no. 3, Hob. III: 77).
69. In order to indicate a clear break with the past, East Germany decided on a new anthem, "Auferstanden aus Ruinen und der Zukunft zugewandt" ("risen from ruins and turned to the future"), written by Johannes R. Becher and composed by Hanns Eisler in 1949. After the building of the Berlin Wall in 1961, the text, hinting at national unity, "silently" (without official decree) disappeared from the 1970s on—that is, people often just stood up but did not sing any more. Since 1990, the West German version serves as a national anthem for

reunified Germany. See Heike Amos, *Auferstanden aus Ruinen* (Berlin: Dietz Verlag, 1997), for the background of both national anthems.

70. While this may have been correct from an editorial viewpoint, it was regarded as politically insensitive to include the Nazi era text; yet, as Amos, *Auferstanden aus Ruinen* 108–31, demonstrated, especially in the 1950s and '60s, many older Germans still unconsciously lapsed into singing the first verse.

71. These movies are characterized by story lines such as father–son conflict in which the son is accused innocently, has to go into exile, returning unrecognized and redeeming himself. This clearly fits into what Gerhard Schulze, *Die Erlebnisgesellschaft. Kultursoziologie der Gegenwart*, 10th ed. (New York: Campus Verlag, 1997), 150–52, described as the "trivial schemata" in his study of common-day sociocultural aesthetic schemes in (West) Germany. According to Schulze, these images, alongside decoration elements such as garden gnomes, reflect the (lower-class related) yearning for the experience of snugness (*Gemütlichkeit*), which is closely related to the fear of outside threats.

72. Obviously, for similar reasons, many postwar singing clubs continued to be called by the soothing name "Harmonia."

73. Bands such as Wild Silk differ from the British groups only in the use of the language, but not significantly in instruments and the general musical style (this is also true of many northern German groups, such as *Schmelztiegel* who sing in Low German, but arrange their material in a Scottish–Irish folk style).

74. See Spratte, "Die Schulfeier," 143.

75. See also Antholz, *Die (Musik-)Erziehung im Dritten Reich*, 17–32.

76. This corresponds with the observations stated by Neumann in "Musikunterricht und Schulpolitik."

77. As Antholz, *Die (Musik-)Erziehung im Dritten Reich*, 68–81, confirmed, he did not experience any drastic changes at his school in Aurich after 1933; the first new teaching curricula only appeared after 1937 and 1938.

78. Although the "newly rising Germany" is mentioned in the introduction, the song collection is still focused on seafarer romanticism, comprising half-and-half English and German sea shanties.

79. Friedrich Blume, ed., *Die Musik in Geschichte und Gegenwart*, 14 vols. (Kassel: Bärenreiter-Verlag, 1949–1968). Supplements in 2 vols., 1973, 1979. Index, 1986.

80. Karl Michael Komma, "Walther Hensel." In *Die Musik in Geschichte und Gegenwart*, ed. Friedrich Blume (Kassel: Bärenreiter-Verlag, 1949–1968), vol. 6 (1957), 166–68. Much in contrast to Komma, Frey/Siniveer (*Eine Geschichte der Folkmusik*), belonging to the '68 generation, are much sharper with their comments on that era.

81. Spitta, Heinrich, "Heinrich Spitta." In *Die Musik in Geschichte und Gegenwart*, ed. Friedrich Blume (Kassel: Bärenreiter-Verlag, 1949–1968), vol. 12 (1965), 1058.

82. See Fred K. Prieberg, *Musik im NS-Staat* (Frankfurt: Fischer-Verlag, 1982), 242.

83. Antholz, *Die (Musik-)Erziehung im Dritten Reich*, 9–10. This occurred while Antholz was staying at a hotel in Norway. Though it was used extensively by the Nazis, "Alte Kameraden" predated the Nazi era and continued to be performed in the postwar era in other countries as well.

CHAPTER 5

The Making of a National Musical Icon: Xian Xinghai and His *Yellow River Cantata*

Hon-Lun Yang

In the history of music in the People's Republic of China (abbreviated hereafter as the PRC), there is probably no other composer or work so iconic as Xian Xinghai (1905–1945) and his *Yellow River Cantata*. There is also no other work that demonstrates so close a tie between music and political power as Xian's cantata. Although the *Yellow River Cantata* was composed in 1939 as an anti-Japanese protest, it has been willingly adopted by the PRC. As Richard Kraus has pointed out, "Xian embodied all the contradictions that have enveloped Western music in the People's Republic that honours him,"[1] and was both a populist and a cosmopolitan. While Xian wrote a great number of mass songs, he was also one of the first few Chinese composers to write symphonies, orchestral suites, and cantatas.[2] But in the PRC, as Kraus has observed, Xian's populism has been exaggerated and his cosmopolitanism diminished for political reasons.[3] This exaggeration of one side of Xian's image was part of a sanctifying process by which the Chinese Communist Party (abbreviated hereafter as CCP) bestowed iconic power and status upon the composer and his work. Such sanctification was part of the CCP's broader bid for political legitimacy after the founding of the PRC in 1949.[4]

This chapter compares three versions of the *Yellow River Cantata*: Xian's two original versions and the one recomposed collectively by members of the Central Philharmonic and officially adopted in the PRC. Through this comparison, I intend to illustrate how the musical traits of the official version befit socialist ideology and the idolized image of the composer. The creation of the official version of the cantata, I argue, was therefore part of the icon-building process. I then examine when, why, and how Xian and his *Yellow River Cantata* were elevated to an iconic status. I conclude by investigating the relationship between political power and artistic expression in the PRC between 1950 and 1980.

XIAN XINGHAI (1905–1945)

Xian Xinghai was the most revered composer of the PRC, and his *Yellow River Cantata* became his most played and studied composition (see fig. 5.1).[5] Contrary to Xian's eminent posthumous status, his short life was a constant struggle with poverty and despair. His father, a fisherman from Macau, died before he was born, and he took shelter with his mother in his grandfather's home until his death in 1912. The family then moved to Singapore until 1918 where Xian was exposed to various forms of Western music at a local Christian school. When the thirteen-year-old Xian returned to China, he was admitted to the Preparatory Department of the Lingnan College thanks to a recommendation of the Singapore school principal.[6] At Lingnan, Xian learned to play the violin and clarinet from an American teacher who also introduced Xian to Western philosophy and the compositions of Bach, Mozart, Haydn, and Beethoven.[7] Determined to devote himself to music, in the autumn of 1925 Xian enrolled at the music school of the Beijing University, and later transferred to the National Conservatory in Shanghai. However, he was expelled from the conservatory for participating in a radical student movement.[8] In 1930, he left for Paris

Figure 5.1. Xian Xinghai.

where he first studied violin privately with Paul Oberdoeffer. He was then admitted to the Schola Cantorum where he studied theory with Noel Geallon and composition with Vincent D'Indy until his teacher's death in 1931. In 1934, he was admitted to the Paris Conservatory and studied composition with Paul Dukas. But Dukas's death in 1935 prompted Xian to abandon his studies and return to Shanghai.[9] Shanghai did not extend a welcome hand to Xian, though. He was not able to find permanent employment, and the cancellation of a concert of his music with the Shanghai Municipal Symphony Orchestra left him embittered.[10] With the help of his left-wing friends, he wrote songs for the Pathé Record Company and the Motion Picture Company Xinhua Yingye Gongsi. At the same time, he participated in the National Song Salvation Movement,[11] giving free conducting, composition, and singing lessons to the cadets of the Chinese Communist Party.[12] In 1937, Xian followed the communist officials to Wuhan and joined the newly founded Lu Xun Arts Academy at Yan'an (the communist base camp) the following year. It was at Yan'an that Xian composed his *Yellow River Cantata* (1939).[13] In May 1940, he was sent to the Soviet Union by the Central Committee to compose some film music, supposedly. Li Ming raises doubt as to the real purpose of Xian's trip to the USSR, citing Xian's *Composition Notes*,[14] which include no mention of film music.[15] Xian remained in Moscow until his death in 1945, a fact that official histories attribute to the outbreak of World War II. But curiously, while Xian seemed to have lost contact with the CCP, his colleagues were able to return to China safely.[16]

THE THREE VERSIONS OF THE "YELLOW RIVER CANTATA"

Xian Xinghai's *Yellow River Cantata* was an eight-movement choral work composed in 1939. The libretto was a four-hundred-line poem of eight sections by Xian's comrade Guang Weiren (b. 1913).[17] Its text is patriotic and nationalistic, and a rallying call to the Chinese people to defend their land against Japanese invasion.[18] The first three sections of the cantata extol the glory and beauty of the Yellow River, the fourth to sixth sections describe the people's suffering from the Japanese invasion, while the last two are clarion calls to fight the invaders (see table 5.1).[19] Just as the Czech composer Smetana featured the famous river Vltava in his symphonic poem *Ma Vlast*, Xian and Guang used the Yellow River, the cradle of Chinese civilization, to symbolize the spirit of the Chinese people.

The score of the cantata was notated in Chevé notation (see fig. 5.2) as staff paper was in short supply and not many of the cadets at the academy (for whom the cantata was intended) were able to read Western notation.[20]

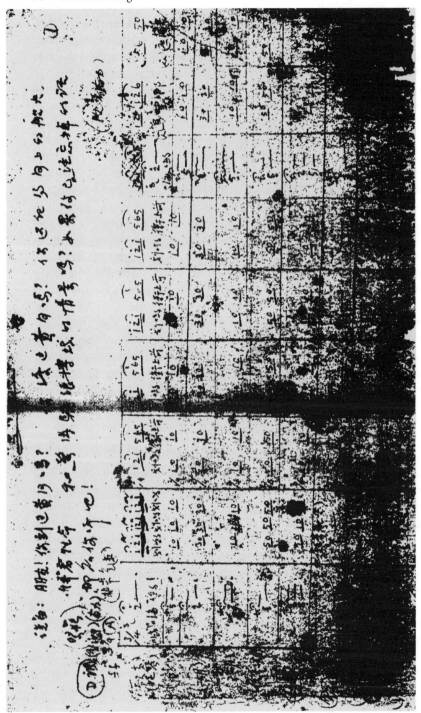

Figure 5.2. Autograph of Xian Xinghai's *Yellow River Cantata* (Yan'an version).

Its instrumentation calls for only *dizi* and harmonica for the wind section, four different types of *huqin* (bow-string Chinese instruments) for the string section, and a handful of Chinese percussion instruments (see table 5.2). In fact, these were instruments available in Yan'an at the time.[21]

The version of the cantata known as the Moscow version was completed in 1941 after Xian had settled in Moscow. He wrote the following in his *Composition Notes*: "I always wanted to compose the *Yellow River Cantata* in Western notation, the singing accompanied by symphonic orchestra. Such is better than using the Chevé notation. But the task was deferred because of teaching duties and other works.... The instrumentation [adopted] is popular in Europe and America. This [version of the cantata] is more international than the one notated in Chevé notation. It is a work in national format but composed with advanced techniques."[22]

A comparison of the two versions shows that Xian made the following changes. First, Xian rewrote the entire score in Western staff notation. Second, Western instrumentation replaced the original Chinese instrumentation. Third, much of the orchestral writing was enhanced with challenging figurations and instrumental techniques. Fourth, new sections of musical passages were added, including an overture, introductions, and bridges to most of the movements, and endings to the second and the seventh movements. Fifth, new music was composed to accompany the original unaccompanied narrations at the beginning of each of the movements. Sixth, the key schemes of movements 2, 4, 5, 6, and 8 were changed. Xian also made embellishments to the vocal line, the melodic contour, and the harmonic language that gave the piece a new harmonic palette (see again table 5.1).

Xian was reported to have proudly expressed the following to a colleague while he was working on the *Yellow River Cantata* in Yan'an: "I'll write a work that represents the grandiosity of our nation. I'll use the cantata format. This will be the first Chinese 'cantata' written in a new format. I'll approach it with national features as well as new techniques."[23] But the limited musical resources in Yan'an prevented Xian from realizing his aspiration in the work. This is especially evident in its instrumentation: The instruments at the academy were limited to two violins, a handful of *erhu* (a bow-stringed instrument), one *sanxian* (a three-stringed pluck instrument), and a few harmonicas, as well as a bass instrument made from an oil can by Xian's colleague.[24] Hence, even if Xian were well-versed in Western orchestration, a scoring of the Moscow version as such would have been unperformable in Yan'an, and, after all, it was a performable version that Xian intended to create.

In many respects, the Moscow version of the cantata was closer to Xian's original conception of the piece. It was a composition much grander in scale than the Yan'an one— much longer, more carefully planned, and its instrumentation and orchestration more complex and firmly ensconced in Western musical tradition. The Moscow version thus elevated the cantata from its humble origins—a piece of anti-Japanese musical propaganda— to a choral composition of international standing. As Xian himself claimed: "The music for this new era had not only to reflect the people's soul and heart, but must also be in a new form with a new harmonic language."[25]

The definitive and official version of the *Yellow River Cantata* was recomposed in 1975 by Yan Liangkun, the conductor, and members of the Central Philharmonic Orchestra. This version is the basis of the published score and the various commercial recordings of the work.[26] Neither Yan Liangkun nor the Central Philharmonic claimed ownership of the work, and their efforts are not acknowledged in any concert programs or recording liner notes. In terms of structure, the official version is closer to the Yan'an version than to the Moscow version (see again tables 5.1 and 5.2). There is no overture and each of the movements has only a brief introduction. Its key schemes are also less complicated than the Moscow version. For instance, the music stays in one key in the movement "Lament of the Yellow River" in the official version, whereas in the Moscow version there are several key changes. In addition, the instrumentation, the harmonic language, and the orchestral writing of the Moscow version and the official version are significantly different. The Moscow version not only asks for a larger orchestra but also displays more complex orchestral writing. The woodwind writing, which is derived from the overture, with its almost clusterlike sound, is a colorful evocation of the raging river (see ex. 5.1). But in the official version, the complex texture is thinned out with a reduced instrumentation and less complicated instrumental writing (see ex. 5.2). The harmonic treatment of the two versions is also different as illustrated by the measure marked X. In the Moscow version, the solo and the choral parts do not seem to stay in the same key, and the G natural and C# interval of the tenor melody outlines a tritone interval (see ex. 5.3). But in the official version, both parts are rooted in *Shang* mode (re mode—re, mi, sol, la, dol) of the pentatonic scale (see ex. 5.4).[27] The vertical sonority in the Moscow version is a dominant eleventh pitch collection, whereas in the official version, the melody is not harmonically supported. In the following measure, marked Y, the Moscow version features a B♭ inflection, which is not found in the official version. Without doubt, the Moscow version is not only more dissonant in sonority and colorful in orchestration, but also more challenging technically. For instance, in the first half, the violins have to play both this almost impossible chord and the harmonics. These are just two of the many examples where the two versions differ.

Table 5.1. Comparison of the three versions of *Yellow River Cantata*.

	Yan'an	Moscow	Yan Liangkun
Overture		F-G-C-D 45mm	
1) Yellow River Boatmen's Song chorus, ABA	D - (end on I + 6) 67mm	D- (end on g mode) 107mm interlude between A, B, postlude	D – (end on I + 6, chord-spelling refined), 130mm
2) Ode to the Yellow River baritone aria	C 92mm	Bb 115mm	C 105mm
3) Water of the Yellow River melodrama	G 320mm	G (opens in Bb signature) 332mm	G 163mm
4) Yellow River Ditty chorus	D 79mm (unison chorus)	C, F (modulation awkward) 109mm (female chorus)	Eb 96mm (female chorus)
5) Dialogue on the Banks of the River male duet and chorus	D 94mm	Eb 119mm	F 69mm
6) Yellow River Lament female aria	A/f# (ambiguous) 102 mm	c, eb, F, Ab, Ab, Db-f, Cb-Eb,G-C 151mm greatly expanded, with new intro, new interlude and postlude	Ab/f 93mm
7) Defend the Yellow River chorus	C 193mm	C 200mm	C,F,Eb 203mm
8) Roar! Yellow River! chorus	F 101	C,E, G,F, F, A, D, Bb 204mm intro shifted place, new interludes	Bb, G, Bb 151mm

Table 5.2. Instrumentation of *Yellow River Cantata's* three versions.

Yan'an version	Moscow version	Yan Liangkun version
Di-zi	Piccolo	Piccolo
Harmonica	Flute (2)	Flute (2)
	Oboe (2)	Oboe (2)
	Cor anglais	
	Clarinet in Bb (2)	Clarinet in Bb (2)
	Bass clarinet in Bb	
	Bassoon (2)	Bassoon (2)
	Contra bassoon	
	Horn (4)	Horn (4)
	Trumpet (3)	Trumpet (3)
	Trombone (3)	Trombone (3)
	Tuba	Tuba
	Timpani	Timpani
	Snare drum	Snare drum
	Tambourine	
	Bass drum	
	Cymbals	Cymbals
	Tam-tam	Tam-tam
	Triangle	
Zhu Ban	*Zhu Ban*	*Zhu Ban*
Gu	*Chinese Xiao Gu*	
Bo, Ling	*Xiao Bo*	*Xiao Bo*
	Xylophone	
		Chinese Da Gu
Luo		*Xiao Tang Gu*
		Diao Bo
		Shao Luo
Mu Yu		*Mu Yu*
	Harp	Harp
Xiao San Xian	Violin	Violin
Da San Xian	Viola	Viola
Er Hu	Cello	Cello
Da Hu	Bass	Bass

Example 5.1. Xian Xinghai's *Yellow River Cantata* (Moscow version), "Yellow River Boatmen's Song," mm.26–28.

Example 5.2. "Yellow River Boatmen's Song" (official version), mm. 56-60.

Example 5.3. "Yellow River Boatmen's Song" (Moscow version), mm. 29-30.

Example 5.4. "Yellow River Boatmen's Song" (official version), mm. 60-61.

THE MAKING OF A SACROSANCT COMPOSER

Why is Xian's Moscow version of the *Yellow River Cantata* suppressed in the PRC and why is Yan Liangkun's version preferred over Xian's Moscow one? A typical Chinese answer to this would be: "The *Yellow River Cantata* was written in the most adverse environment, the composer having no opportunity to carefully work on it. Some of the imperfections in Xian's music lead to better results if fixed."[28] While such "good-will" in order to "improve" a composer's work is readily accountable in the context of Chinese music tradition, its political implications cannot be overlooked.[29] Indeed, I argue that Yan Liangkun's version was created for political reasons and played a part in the process of turning Xian Xinghai into a musical icon of the PRC.

Since its Yan'an premiere on April 13, 1949, the *Yellow River Cantata* was repeatedly associated with the PRC's leadership. Mao himself was present at the second performance on May 11. Xian wrote in his diary: "Mao Zedong, Wang Ming and Cang Shang jumped up and exclaimed 'well done,' I will never forget this evening. I conducted the choir with passion."[30] When Chou Englai donated a piano to the Lu Xun Arts Academy in 1941, Xian's student Li Huanzhi made a piano arrangement of the score. In 1944, Li received an order to convert the piano score into an orchestral one so that the singer, who was leaving Yan'an to join other officials in the so-called *dahuofang*—the hinterland of the CCP—could bring the work along.[31] Upon Xian's death, Mao wrote the dedication, "to mourn the deceased people's composer Xian Xinghai." After the founding of the PRC, The *Yellow River Cantata* immediately became a work of unprecedented political and cultural significance. In 1951, Li Huanzhi made his version of the cantata for the "Chinese Youth Art Club,"[32] an official cultural body founded to attend the Third Word Friendship and Peace Festival held in East Berlin.[33]

In 1955, at the ten-year anniversary of Xian Xinghai's death, the composer was put forward as a model of socialist realism.[34] He was dubbed "the outstanding composer of Socialist Realism,"[35] "one succeeded in developing the revolutionary tradition of realism in [Chinese] national music."[36] In addition to a series of celebratory activities and concerts held to commemorate his death,[37] laudatory articles appeared in abundance. In these writings, Xian was repeatedly portrayed as one whose art was reflective of the reality of the masses and who succeeded in turning art into revolutionary weapons.[38] He was praised for his large output in mass songs. His Moscow works—symphonic and instrumental compositions, of which some were not revolutionary in content—were downplayed, likewise were those works he composed in Paris. His move away from composing mass songs while in the Soviet was explained as "lacking the opportunity to co-operate with poets."[39] In addition, his creativity was described as closely related to his communist worldview—that he was self-conscious as a revolutionary artist, thus able to subordinate music to the service of the revolution.[40] His worldview, regarded as the result of his involvement in the revolution and his interaction with the masses, shaped his music's central message: class struggle. Furthermore, his compositional aesthetics were deemed a manifestation of his patriotic desire to develop national music on the foundation of traditional forms.[41]

Xian Xinghai's elevation to sacrosanct status is illustrated by the Wang Lisan incident. Wang Lisan, a professor at the Shanghai Conservatory, published an article along with two other colleagues on Xian's second symphony ("The Holy War") in April 1957 in *Renmin Yinyue*. The article called for the need to evaluate Xian's music more objectively.[42] According to Wang and his coauthors: "It is a very meaningful task to study and introduce the works of Xian Xinghai to the masses as such an endeavour will not only affect the evaluation of Xian, but also the compositional and theoretical practices of the country.... [But] studies on Xian Xinghai and his works have been lop-sided, [and] all too eager to laud his achievements."[43] They then pointed out what they thought to be the inadequacies of the symphony, such as muddled orchestration, clumsy developmental writing, and overly descriptive programmatic treatment.[44]

Wang's article raised a heated debate in music.[45] Two articles speaking in defense of Xian appeared in the following two issues of *Renmin Yinyue*, and Wang responded in the July issue.[46] In August a number of musicians were reported to have capped "rightist," a conviction resulting in the removal of employment, social and professional rights, and a strong possibility of being sent to a labor camp. Liu Xue'an, for instance, was condemned for raising doubts about musical institutions run by party leaders and not musical specialists, and the validity of applying socialist ideology to the study of musical compositions.[47] He was also attacked for his critique of the practice of idolizing Xian Xinghai.[48] Liu was eventually convicted of attempting to overthrow the party.

It then became clear that the debate on the technical competence of Xian Xinghai had become a political and ideological battle. Those who doubted his sacrosanct status would be deemed disloyal and disobedient to the party, and subsequently purged and persecuted. In the November issue of *Renmin Yinyue*, Wang Lisan and his colleagues were portrayed as enemies of the people, anti-Marxist, anti-Party, and antisocialist, and were also accused of planning to overthrow the cultural policy of the regime.[49] Not surprisingly, Wang's professorship at the conservatory was terminated and he was sent to a labor camp.[50]

After the Wang Lisan incident, Xian Xinghai's sacrosanct position as the nation's musical icon was secured. In 1958, his works were also deemed examples of revolutionary realism and revolutionary romanticism (the PRC's version of socialist realism),[51] and in 1961 a recommendation was made to incorporate his mass songs in the national music curriculum to serve the purpose of "revolutionary traditional education."[52] Such songs, apart from their classroom use, were to be performed in concerts, competitions, and radio broadcasts so as to enhance the appreciation of the composer. Furthermore, aspects of the biography of Xian, such as how he was nurtured by the CCP after joining the Lu Xun Arts Academy, his involvement with the masses, and his devotion to the revolutionary way of life were instructed to be included in the curriculum.[53] In Xian's widow's memoirs (1978), the composer was portrayed with similar traits of self-abnegation as Mao's hero Lei Feng.[54]

Xian's status as a national musical icon was further extended through the *Yellow River Piano Concerto*. The *Yellow River Piano Concerto* was "created" collectively and strictly on ideological lines during the Cultural Revolution in 1970, and is probably more famous than the cantata. It is a four-movement work, each with the title and musical themes taken from the cantata.[55] In 1969, the pianist Yin Chengzhong, knowing how Mao's wife Jiang Qing liked the cantata, proposed the project to Mao. The participants who joined the "composition committee" were carefully vetted for their political background, and the music was scrutinized by party members as well as the public (peasants and workers) to ensure its ideological purity. Consequently, the first movement was originally written in sonata form, but was later replaced by a freer form because choosing a sonata form was considered to be "following the West," and thus not desirable. As recalled by one of the participants in the project, they were put into "study camps" to receive a political education before embarking on the revision process. Jiang Qing was also heavily involved during the later stages of work on the *Yellow River Piano Concerto*. The quotation of motifs from "East Is Red" and "International Anthem" in the final movement of the concerto was her idea, as she thought that the former would allude to Mao's role in the communist victory over the Japanese in the Sino–Japanese War, and the latter to the utopia to which communists aspired.[56]

IDEOLOGY, XIAN XINGHAI, AND *YELLOW RIVER CANTATA*

It is undeniable that Xian was a patriot and the *Yellow River Cantata* a nationalistic work, but Xian's rise to iconic status was steered by the CCP in order to project Xian and his works as embodiments of the CCP's musical ideals. The outer movements of the cantata, for instance, were deemed to have "raised national pride, enhanced . . . the class struggle, and boosted our confidence to fight for our final victory."[57] Likewise, Xian's music encapsulated the musical aspirations of the era and "positively reflected the revolutionary mass and hero, educated the mass and encouraged them to march ahead in their revolutionary journey, and conveyed the party's message in a way easy for the masses to grasp."[58]

Such aspirations also were ideologically rooted in the doctrines of Soviet socialist realism—an ideology first introduced to the PRC in the early thirties, but only hailed extensively in the fifties.[59] As the world's first Communist country, the USSR was then perceived by the PRC, the world's second Communist country, as a kind of helpful big brother whose artistic principles should, naturally, be adopted and provide inspiration and guidance for Chinese artists. Socialist realism was the state-sponsored set of political and aesthetic principles in the USSR to which artists, composers, and writers had to adhere. As described at the First All-Union Congress of Soviet Writers in 1934: "Socialist Realism demands from the author a true and historically concrete depiction of reality in its revolutionary development. Moreover, this true and historically concrete artistic depiction of reality must be combined with the task of educating the workers in the spirit of Communism."[60] As declared later by Gorodinsky, socialist realism directed Soviet composers to "the victorious progressive principles of reality, towards all that is heroic, bright, and beautiful. This . . . must be embodied in musical images full of beauty and strength."[61]

In order for the CCP to establish the ideological legitimacy of socialist realism in the PRC in 1955, composers of the past were sought as models for contemporary musicians to copy. Xian Xinghai, who was a communist and composer of mass songs, was naturally chosen for such a purpose.[62] Yan Linagkun's version of the *Yellow River Cantata*, though recomposed after Sino–Soviet relationship was already strained, was crucial in protecting both Xian's image and his sacrosanct status as a socialist composer. His version, more so than Xian's Moscow one, reflects socialist ideology and has been retained in the repertoire as a model of such principles. It is not only easier to perform, but closer to the musical ideals of the CCP. By contrast, the Moscow version—in terms of its harmonic writing, expansive instrumentation, and complex counterpoint—hardly reflected the CCP's musical doctrines.

If the musical language of the Moscow version was to be judged by the yardstick of socialist realism, it would be branded decadent or formalist because the advanced musical language of twentieth century Western European art music was totally condemned in the PRC and remained banned until the 1980s. As Lü Ji, the PRC's music spokesman, declared in 1957, modernism was viewed as destructive to the art of composition and drove a wedge between audiences and revolutionary reality.[63] It is thus not a surprise that the Moscow version of Xian's *Yellow River Cantata*—its lavish instrumentation and impressionistic harmonic language—was not officially sanctioned in China.

Shortly before Xian Xinghai was crowned composer of socialist realism in 1955, there was already an ideological battle going on in musical circles. He Lüting, the principal of the Shanghai Conservatory, one of the most prominent composers of the PRC, was severely criticized for doubting the wisdom of the CCP's combining Marxism with technical training in music.[64] His plea to party leaders and musicians focused on four areas. He advocated technical and theoretical training, musical exchanges with the West, and toleration and appreciation of the composition of lyrical songs. He also argued that not all complex musical structures deserved the pejorative label "formalism."[65] He was almost denounced as a rightist, but Chen Yi, the vice premier, intervened by making him apologize openly for his "mistakes" at a meeting of the Chinese Musicians Association in 1956.[66]

Had Xian Xinghai lived longer, he might have interfered with the construction of his sacrosanct status. As Kraus has remarked, "Since Xian was dead, his legacy could be bent still further with impunity."[67] After all, Xian had his own vision for the future of Chinese music. Having been a student of D'Indy and Dukas, the so-called French nationalists, it is natural that Xian considered the European nationalistic approach applicable to the development of national Chinese music;[68] however, Xian did not specify in any of his writings on which national schools of the West should Chinese composers base their music. It would be reasonable to assume that he was familiar with the works of the late-nineteenth century national composers as well as those of his contemporaries. In his writings, he also showed indebtedness to Soviet socialist realism, emphasizing the accessibility and educative value of music.[69]

Regarding the future direction of new national Chinese music, he suggested that it: 1) synthesize the good practices of the past and the West; 2) respond to the needs of the nation, 3) be bright, decisive, clear, and simple in format, and 4) be accessible to the masses. But he also argued that it was necessary to raise the masses' cultural standards in order to fend against vulgarity.[70] The means he suggested for these improvements were largely Western and nationalistic, which, if not contradictory to the above ideals, undermined somewhat its significance. His proposals included the improvement and modification of traditional instruments by scientific means so that various Chinese instruments could be utilized in musical works to accompany the advanced Western instruments to produce a more magnificent Chinese sonority. The creation of new Chinese harmonies derived from traditional modes and temperaments was high on Xian's agenda and would, he believed, represent the spirit of the new China. He then recommended the use of advanced Western musical genres such as the symphony, tone poem, tone picture, ballet, and opera as models for comparable Chinese ones. All this could be accomplished by studying the compositions and musical styles of the progressive and nationalist composers of the West and broadening the musical language of the Chinese composers, raising their works to measure up to international standards. Furthermore, he suggested using and developing traditional genres such as regional folk songs and the dance and drum music of China's minorities; all would play a part in the creation of new national musical forms. Last, he mentioned that it was essential to develop the music of the working class.[71]

After all, as Xian repeatedly emphasized, though traditional Chinese musical forms were valuable, they were not necessarily suited to contemporary needs.[72] Xian saw the value in traditional Chinese music, folk songs, and minority dances alike, but only for the purpose of providing the necessary indigenous material for large-scale compositions in a modern Western idiom. It is thus not surprising that he recommended that Chinese composers adopt "advanced" compositional genres such as suites, cantatas, overtures, symphonies, symphonic poems, and tone poems, and cited his own works as examples.[73] In many respects, the Moscow version of *Yellow River Cantata* exemplified his genuine aspiration for "new Chinese music"— one written in Western format but with Chinese content. As he stated, "We could adopt Western compositional formats, but our objective is national, so our works would be different from theirs, but also not the same as the old form of music."[74] Even though Xian acknowledged the populist ideals of socialist realism, his main concern, as David Holm pointed out, was to "win a place in international music."[75]

In fact, not all Xian's musical aspirations were in line with his Communist colleagues. Xian's notion of synthesizing the musical traditions of the East and West was not accepted without question. When he was at the academy, there were objections to his ideas, and his works were criticized by some of the party officials as too complex and Western.[76] Although Xian seemed to have taken the criticisms quite positively and admitted that reading Communist literature helped him develop a new attitude toward life, it's hard to know whether he truly subscribed to this ideology. Besides, Xian was not as beloved as is usually portrayed. As remembered by his Yan'an colleague Li Ling, "Xian was one with a strong personality, quite self-centered. For some one with such a personality trait, an outburst is inevitable when he does not get what he wants."[77]

Xian was hailed in the PRC for his contribution to the repertoire of anti-Japanese songs and had written several articles to promote the cultural thinking of the Communist party. There was no doubt that Xian was patriotic and committed to the idea that music could save the country. But composing mass songs was for him both patriotic and pragmatic, of which the latter was totally denied in the PRC. Xian himself wrote in his *Composition Notes*: "Why did I write the salvation songs? . . . I wanted to write about the country's suffering, so my songs could awake the entire nation to fight against feudalism, imperialism, particularly Japanese imperialism. Besides, I need the money to live. . . . I don't have the luxury of not to write. If I stop . . . I will be in trouble. I can endure material hardship, but my old mother cannot. To give her the comfort she deserves, I work hard to compose those songs."[78] However, he apparently did not take an equal amount of pride in writing mass songs as he did his other works: "The songs I composed in Shanghai belonged to the first stage of my career. I was then still in search of Chinese harmony, form, and style. People welcomed my works with praise. But my heart was tortured. To be honest, I did not compose what I should compose!"[79] When Xian assigned opus numbers to his important works at his deathbed in Moscow, he did not include all his mass songs—an indication of his dissatisfaction with some of them.[80] His Moscow output consisted of no mass songs, but largely orchestral works, including one symphony, two symphonic poems, four suites, and one fantasia for piano and orchestra, as well as several sets of art songs and instrumental chamber works. While it is still a mystery why Xian remained in the Soviet Union and what his relationship was with the CCP during his Moscow years was like, it seems Xian found plenty of musical inspiration while on Soviet soil. He once expressed, "I paid attention to the music around me, and Soviet music had a particularly strong influence on me."[81] Within the span of less than five years, amid material hardship and ill health, he managed to compose over sixteen works of various natures, of which only a few were revolutionary in content. Quite ironic is the fact that his use of postimpressionistic techniques was recognized and praised by Soviet musicians,[82] while his fellow countrymen, even in the most recent studies of his works, did not acknowledge these traits.[83]

Xian was an ambitious artist at heart and aspired to international recognition. His heroes were his teachers Dukas, D'Indy, and Romain Rolland.[84] Regarding the praise heaped on *Yellow River Cantata*, Xian wrote: "Beethoven said on his death bed that all he did was to come up with a few notes . . . Who am I? What good am I? I am far less accomplished than him. So, I have to work harder."[85] In 1945, shortly before his death, he wrote to the Russian composer Rheinhold Gliere and claimed that "for many years I fought for a new Chinese musical scene. The music for this new era not only had to reflect the people's soul and heart, but must also be in a new form [and] written in a new harmonic language."[86] His greatest regret, as he told Gliere, was not having the opportunity to hear his works performed at big European concert halls.[87]

Xian Xinghai in the PRC is comparable to Sibelius in Finland, Liszt and Kodaly in Hungary, and Smetana in the Czech Republic; he is the PRC's musical icon and his *Yellow River Cantata* a national musical epic.[88] In Guang Zhou, Xian's home region, a conservatory and a concert hall are named after him, while he is the only composer to have a small room at the Chinese Research Academy devoted to exhibits of his belongings and manuscripts.[89] Xian is also one of only two PRC composers whose entire output is available in print.[90] Despite these markers of high professional status, this chapter illustrates that Xian's ascension to such an exalted position has a somewhat checkered history, and his creative output and musical ideals have been obscured by political considerations. Xian was made the musical hero of the PRC for political reasons: to bolster respect and reverence for the CCP and help legitimize its authority, both internally and internationally.

Notes

For sources in Chinese, authors' names and titles of articles have been transliterated into *pinyin*, the Romanization of Chinese characters, supplemented by English translation. Chinese names that appear in this chapter are always rendered last name first, as practiced in China.

1. Kraus, "The Ambiguous Legacy of Composer Xian Xinghai," *Pianos and Politics in China: Middle-Class Ambitions and the Struggle over Western Music* (Oxford University Press, 1989), 40. Kraus's article is the only study on Xian Xinghai in English aside from this chapter.
2. Despite his relative short life, Xian Xinghai produced a substantial output, all of which is collected in the ten-volume complete work set *Xian Xinghai Quanji* (Guangdong gaodeng jiaoye chubanshe, 1989–1990).
3. Kraus, "The Ambiguous Legacy," 68.
4. According to the historian David Easton, propagation of appropriate ideology is a means of strengthening legitimacy. While rituals and ceremonies are physical representations of the regime, they are brought into play in varied and numerous occasions, serving to bolster an aura of sanctity, respect, and reverence for the political institutions and reassert the legitimacy of the incumbent authorities. Easton, *A Systems Analysis of Political Life* (Wiley & Sons, 1965), 308–309. In a way, the creation of a musical icon serves the same function as rituals and ceremonies.
5. For biographic information of Xian Xinghai, see Kraus as well as the following Chinese sources. Ma Ke, "Hsien Hsing-hai the Composer," *Chinese Literature* 12 (1965): 110–16. Ma Ke, *Xian Xinghai Zhuan* [Life of Xian Xinghai] (Beijing: Renmin Wenxue Chubanshe, 1980). Qin Qiming, *Xian Xinghai* (Changjiang Wenyi Chubanshe, 1980). Xian's writings are collected in the first volume of *Xian Xinghai Quanji*. For analyses and discussions of the *Yellow River Cantata* [*Huanghe dahechang* as in transliteration], see the following sources. Zhang Xiaohu, "Dui *Huanghe dahechang* geci de yidian ti hui" [Reflections on the text of the *Yellow River Cantata*], *Renmin Yinyue* 6 (1955): 7–9; Guo Naian, "Xian Xinghai zuopin de yinyue xingxiang" [Musical representations in Xian Xinghai's compositions], *Renmin Yinyue* 10 (1955): 14–17; Xie Gongcheng, "Tan 'Huangshuiyao' de yinyue chuli" [The musical treatments in "The Yellow River Ditty"], *Renmin Yinyue* 11–12 (1955): 19–30, 43. The "Yellow River Ditty" is one of the movements in the cantata. Zeng Lizhong, "Dui *Huanghe dahechang* zhong zuoqu jishu yunyong de yixie tihui" [Some thoughts on the compositional techniques of the *Yellow River Cantata*], *Renmin Yinyue* 2 (1957): 29–30, 43. Li Jiti, "Douzhuan xingyi hua Huanghe" [The "Yellow River" revisited], *Yinyue YanJiu* 2 (1995): 3–8. Su Xia, "*Huanghe dahechang* de yishu fenxi" [The artistic value of the *Yellow River Cantata*], *Renmin Yinyue* 8 (1998): 2–5, 9 (1998): 6–10, and 10 (1998): 12–15.
6. Lingnan College was a small American Christian College in China founded by Rev. Andrew

P. Happer in 1888. For history of the college, see Charles. H. Corbett, *Lingnan University* (New York: Trustees of Lingnan University, 1963). When Xian was studying on scholarship at the Lingnan College, his mother worked as a maid.

7. The American professor is only referred to as "Professor B" in Ma Ke's *Xian Xinghai Zhuan*, obviously for political reasons because Ma's biography on Xian was written in the sixties (although it was published in 1980).

8. As revealed by Xian in his autobiography submitted to the CCP along with his application to become a communist, he was responsible for a student strike at the Shanghai Conservatory. *Xian Xinghai Quanji*, 381.

9. When Xian was in Paris, he struggled financially. He described his situation as so desperate as "almost died of hunger." He survived on part-time job and the generosity of his teachers. Xian, "Wo Xuexi yinyue de jingguo" [My training in music], originally published in *Zhongguo Qingnian* 2/8 (1940), now collected in *Xian Xinghai Quanji*, 96–108.

10. The membership of the Shanghai Municipal Orchestra (then led by the Italian pianist and conductor Mario Paci) consisted largely of Westerners residing in Shanghai at the time. Xian befriended the Russian musician A. Avshalomov, who was then the librarian of the symphony.

11. In response to Japan's invasion of China, first started in the Manchuria Region on September 18, 1931, Chinese from various sectors were rallied up to defend their country.

12. He first joined the Song Composers Association, a CCP-led organization consisting of left-wing musicians such as Lü Ji and He Lüting in 1935. Ma Ke, *Xian Xinghai Zhuan*, 126.

13. For discussions on musical activities in Yan'an, see "The Development of a CCP Cultural Policy" in David Holm's *Art and Ideology in Contemporary China* (Oxford: Clarendon Press, 1991).

14. Xian's *Chuangzuo zaji* [Composition notes] was written in 1940 after he had settled down in Moscow. It was written in a notebook using his pseudonym *Huang Xun*. Xian's *Composition Notes* is now collected in volume one of *Xian Xinghai Quanji*.

15. Li Ming, "Xian Xinghai zhi si" [The death of Xian Xinghai], *Tiao Xian Ji* (Haiyin Yishu Xueyuan, 1999), 51–76.

16. It is still an unsolved puzzle as to why Xian was sent to Moscow. In the PRC, the subject is taboo. As related by Xian's wife in her short memoirs about the composer, Xian was sent to Moscow for an unspecified "task" in May 1940. Before the trip, Mao even received Xian and his family at his home. Xian's diary entries stopped after his departure from Yan'an. Between May and November of 1940, Xian wrote to his wife regularly. In the last letter to his wife dated September 18, 1941, he casually wrote the following words: "Perhaps you understand why I haven't written you for such a long time, and now, at last there is this chance, so I just drop in a few lines." Unlike in his other letters, Xian was evasive about his condition in this last letter; aside from telling her that he missed her and their daughter, he merely asked his wife to be strong and said he longed for the time when they would see each other again. More curious is the fact that Xian took up the name Huang Xun after leaving Yan'an.

17. The impetus of the *Yellow River Cantata* was also related to Guang's personal experience. In 1938, along with some other communist officers, he had crossed a treacherous stretch of the Yellow River by a boat steered by forty boatmen to reach an anti-Japanese gorilla point in Jiangxi, the North West of China. During the trip, the poet and his colleagues heard quite some local folk songs, the "Haozi," and there were discussions on different song types. See Yan Gang, "'JuRen' xingxiang de suzao: *Huanghe dahechang* geci de yishu zhengjiu" [The creation of the "giant" image—The artistic accomplishment of the libretto of the *Yellow River Cantata*], *Yinyue Luncong* 1 (May 1978), 56–57. Nevertheless, Guang's decision to write the poem as a cantata libretto only came when Xian Xinghai went to visit him at the hospital, as he was recuperating from a horse accident. Xian mentioned the meeting in his diary dated February 26, 1939. *Xian Xinghai Quanji*, 259. It took Guang only five days to finish the libretto (in largely the present format of the cantata), which was presented to Xian at a gathering on March 11. After receiving the libretto, Xian set out to work immediately, completing the first draft in only six days.

18. The Sino–Japanese war broke out after Japanese armies, using the clash (July 1937) between soldiers of the Japanese garrison at Beijing and Chinese forces at the Marco Polo Bridge as pretext, occupied Beijing and Tianjin. For history of the second Sino–Japanese War, see Hsu Longhsuen and Chang Mingkai compiled, *History of the Sino–Japanese war, 1937–1945*, rev. by Kao Chingchen (Taipei, Chung Wu Pub. Co., 1985) and David P. Barrett and Larry N.

Shyu, eds., *China in the Anti-Japanese War, 1937–1945: Politics, Culture, and Society* (New York: Peter Lang, 2001).

19. For a socialist reading of the libretto, see Yang Gang, "The creation of the 'giant' image: artistic accomplishment of the libretto of the *Yellow River Cantata*" mentioned in note 17.

20. Chevé notation originated in the mid-nineteenth century. The numbers 1 to 7 are used to represent the seven pitches of the diatonic scale. A dot below or above the number indicates an octave lower or higher respectively.

21. Li Huanzhi, "Wo yu *Huanghe* de bujie zhi yuan" [My relationship with the Yellow River], *Renmin Yinyue* 3 (1999), 3.

22. From Xian's *Composition* Notes, in *Xian Xinghai Quanji*, 145.

23. Li Huanzhi, "My relationship," 1.

24. Li Ling, "Guanyu *Huanghe dahechang* de yixie shenke yinxiang" [About some deep impressions of the *Yellow River Cantata*] in Huang Yelu, ed., *Huanghe dehechang zongheng tan* [Yellow River Cantata Miscellaneous] (Xinhua Chubanshe, 1999), 119–120.

25. A letter Xian wrote on his deathbed to the Soviet composer Rheinhold Gliere dated October 2, 1945. Gliere was a well-established Soviet composer who was most remembered for his ballet *Red Puppy*, in which Gliere made use some Chinese elements. *Xian Xinghai Quanji*, 375.

26. Score: *Huanghe Dahechang* [The Yellow River Cantata] (Beijing: Renmin Yinyue Chubanshe, 1978). Recording: Philips: 416 621-2, recorded live August 1985 in Hong Kong; Marco Polo: 8.223613, recorded in Shanghai, 1993.

27. *Shang* mode: a pentatonic scale consisting of a whole tone, a minor third, a whole tone, a minor third, and a whole tone. The *shang* mode is one of five basic modal patterns that govern pentatonic music in China. For theories of traditional Chinese music, see for instance Li Yinghai, *Hanzu diaoshi hesheng* [The harmony of Han scales] (Renmin yinyuechubandshe, 1959), and Fan Zuyin, *Chuantong daxiaodiao wushengxing diaoxinghesheng xiezuo jiaocheng* [Instructions on traditional major and minor tonality, pentatonic and tonal harmony] (Zhongguo renmin daxue chubanshe, 2000).

28. Such were Li Haungzhi's and Yan Liangkun's rationales for the changes they introduced to Xian's original version of the *Yellow River Cantata*. In fact, all Xian's orchestral works now collected in *Xian Xinghai Quanji* were so-called performance versions collectively edited by a panel of Chinese musicians.

29. In traditional Chinese instrumental works, it is not uncommon for the same composition to appear in different versions, each testifying to its own performing tradition.

30. May 11, 1939, *Riji* [Diary] collected in *Xian Xinghai Quanji*, 275.

31. Li Huanzhi, "My relationship," 3.

32. Li Huanzhi's version is supposed to be closer to the Moscow version than the official one.

33. The group also visited Moscow as well as some other major cities in East Germany. The repertoire, aside from the cantata, also included the opera *Bai Mao Nü* [The white-haired girl], as well as Xian's *Zhongguo Kuangxiangqu* [Chinese fantasy].

34. The ideology will be discussed in the following part of this article.

35. Ma Ke, "Xian Xinghai shi woguo jiechu de shehuizhuyi xianshizhuyi yinyuejia: jinian Xian Xinghai shishi shizhounian" [Xian Xinghai is an outstanding socialist realist musician of our nation: To mark the tenth anniversary of Xian Xinghai's death], *Renmin Yinyue* 11/12 (1955): 10–14.

36. Anonymous, "Jicheng Nie Er, Xian Xinghai de yichan: wei shehuizhuyi xianshizhuyi de yinyueyishu de fanrong ernuli" [Continue with the legacy of Nie Er and Xian Xinghai: Work hard for the prosperity of the socialist realist art of music], *Renmin Yinyue* 10 (1955): 2–4.

37. The array of commemorative activities included a commemorative meeting, the opening ceremony of the "Xian Xinghai Memorial Room" at the Chinese Research Academy, the plan to release a movie on the cantata, a commemorative concert, as well as a conference devoted to the study of his compositions. *Renmin Yinyue* 11–12 (1955): 22–24.

38. Anonymous, "Continue with the legacy of Nie'er and Xian Xinghai," 4. Nie'er (1921–1935), the other composer sanctioned by the party, was the composer of national anthem of the PRC. Unlike Xian, Nie'er had no accomplishment in the symphonic repertoire.

39. Ma Ke, "Xian Xinghai," 11.

40. Ma Ke, "Xian Xinghai," 13.

41. Anonymous, "Continue with the legacy of Nie'er and Xian Xinghai," 2–4.

42. Wang Lisan, Liu Shiren, Jiang Zhuxin, "Lun dui Xinghai tongzhi yixie jiaoxiang zuopin de

pingjia wenti" [Reflections on the evaluation of some of Xinghai's symphonic works], *Renmin Yinyue* 4 (1957): 34–40.

43. Wang, "Reflections on the evaluation," 34.

44. Wang, "Reflections on the evaluation," 35–36.

45. Wang Lisan's incident is a case in point of what happened to intellectuals during the period of the *Rectification Campaign* in 1957. The campaign started in 1955 with the good intention allowing intellectuals more freedom in expression, encapsulated in the slogan, "Let a hundred flowers bloom! Let a hundred schools contend!" Intellectuals were first encouraged to speak all they knew with no faults attached to the speakers. But as it turned out, Mao used such an opportunity to purge out those carrying a different worldview—denounced as "rightists"—who were either sent away to labor camp or kept under supervision. See René Goldman, "The Rectification Campaign at Peking University: May–June 1957," *China under Mao: Politics Takes Command*, edited by Roderick MacFarquhar (Massachusetts: The MIT Press, 1966), 255–70.

46. See Han Zhongjie, "Rang Xian Xinghai de jiaoxiangyue genghao de wei renmin fuwu" [Let the symphonic works of Xian Xinghai better serve the people], *Renmin Yinyue* 5 (1957): 17–19; Yao Mu, "Yu Wang Lisan deng tongzhi tan Xinghai de jiaoxiangyue zuopin" [Dialogue with Comrades Wang Lisan, etc. on the symphonic works of Xinghai], *Renmin Yinyue* 6 (1957): 14–17; Wang Lisan, Liu Shiren, and Jiang Zuxin, "Dui yixie wenti de chengqing he dafu" [Clarifications and answers to some of the issues], *Renmin Yinyue* 7 (1957): 32–35. The debate continued as evident in Wang Yunjie, "Bo 'Lun Xinghai tongzhi yixie jiaoxiangyue zuopin de pingjia wenti' " [Against the article "Reflections on the evaluation of some of Xinghai's symphonic works"] in *Renmin Yinyue* 8/9 (1957): 19–23, 18–24 respectively.

47. See Ma Ke, "Liu Xue'an zai da shui de mengun?" [What had Liu Xue'an in mind?], *Renmin Yinyue*, 8 (1957): 3–6.

48. Ma Ke, "Liu Xue'an zai da shui de mengun?" 3–6.

49. Liu Fuan, "Yi Wang Lisan weishou de fandang xiaojituan xi zenyang fandui dang de weiyi fangzhen de" [How Wang Lisan and his anti-party coup attacked the cultural policy of the Party], *Renmin Yinyue* 12 (1957): 15–20.

50. See "Wang Lisan," in Xiang yansheng edited, *Zhongguo Jinxiandai Yinyuejia zhuan* [Biographies of contemporary Chinese composers], vol. 4 (Chunfeng wenyi chubanshe, 1994), 419–20.

51. Revolutionary Romanticism was considered by the writers of PRC to be fundamentally distinct from Romanticism as that term was generally understood in the West. Revolutionary Romanticism demanded that art convey the aspirations of communist ideals while reflecting the reality of socialist life. As they saw it, the PRC was in its socialist stage of revolution, and aspired to progress to the communist stage. Artists and composers were expected to envision the coming, ideal communist world, and depict only the most progressive figures and incidents in their works. Artists thus framed social reality purely in idealized, communist terms. Naturalism, the alternative to Revolutionary Romanticism, was thought to serve no educative purpose and was rejected as an aesthetic doctrine. See for instance, Li Huanzhi, "Tan geming langmanzhuyi" [Discussion on Revolutionary Romanticism], *Renmin Yinyue* 10 (1958): 5, and Gao Feng, "Fanying xianshi zhidao xianshi" [Representation of the reality Instruction on the reality], *Remin Yinyue* 11 (1958): 16.

52. Feng zi, "Zhongshi Nie'er, Xinghai gequ zai qingshaonian yingyue jiaoyuzhong de zuoyong" [Emphasis on the role the songs of Nie'er and Xinghai played in the education of the youth], *Renmin Yinyue* 1 (1961): 15–16.

53. Feng zi, "Zhongshi Nie'er," 16.

54. Qian Yunling, "Yi Xinghai" [Remembering Xinghai], in *Huanghe Dahechang* [The Yellow River Cantata], (Beijing: Renmin Yinyue Chubanshe, 1978), 76.

55. For more information on the *Yellow River Piano Concerto*, see Cheng Shinglih, "The Yellow River Piano Concerto: Politics, Culture, and Style" (D.M.A. Thesis, University of British Columbia, 1996).

56. The composition history of the *Yellow River Cantata* was retold by one of the composers of the work, Xu Wanghua. See "*Huanghe* Gangqin Xiezouqu xi zenyang dansheng de?" [How was the *Yellow River Piano Concerto* created?], *Renmin Yinyue* 5 (1995): 4–8.

57. Editorial board, "Genghao di fayang Nie'er Xian Xinghai geming yingyue de zhandou zhuantong" [To better develop the revolutionary musical tradition of Nie'er and Xian Xinghai],

Renmin Yinyue 10 (1960): 4. "East is Red" is a revolutionary song to glorify Mao, which inspired a number of large-scale compositions during the Cultural Revolution.

58. Ma Ke's "Xian Xinghai shi woguo jiechu de shehuizhuyi xianshizhuyi yinyuejia: jinian Xian Xinghai shishi shizhounian (xu)" [Xian Xinghai is an outstanding socialist realist musician of our nation: To mark the tenth anniversary of Xian Xinghai'd death (continuation of part I)], *Renmin Yinyue* 1 (1956): 10.

59. For discussion on socialism and PRC's musical development, see my forthcoming article, "Socialist Realism and Music in the People's Republic of China" in *Socialist Realism and Music: Anti-Modernisms and Avant-gardes*, Mikulas Beck, ed. (Bärenreiter Praha, forthcoming).

60. C. V. James, *Soviet Socialist Realism* (London: Macmillan Press, 1973), 88.

61. Quoted in B. Schwarz, *Music and Musical Life in Soviet Russia 1917–1970* (London: Barrie and Jenkins, 1972), 114.

62. Xian became a communist on June 14, 1939. In his diary, he wrote, "Today is the most glorious moment of my life." *Xian Xinghai Quanji*, 282.

63. Lü Ji, "Wei sulian shehuizhuyi xianshizhuyi yinyuejjia de shengli er huanhu: qinzhu sulian weidade shiyue shehuizhuyi geming sishi zhounian" [Hail the victory of the socialist and realist musicians in the USSR: To celebrate the fortieth anniversary of the great triumph of the October Socialist Revolution of USSR], *Renmin Yinyue* 10 (1957): 2–3.

64. He Lüting was one of the most prominent composers of the PRC. He became a member of the Communist Party in 1926. In 1934, his piano piece *The Flute of the Buffalo Boy* won first prize in the composition competition for "Chinese piano works" organized by the Russian composer Alexander Tcherepnin. In 1949, he was appointed director of the Shanghai Conservatory. In 1953, he became increasingly concerned about the Party putting politics above professional concerns, and gave a speech outlining his worries at the national meeting of the Chinese Musicians Association. He Lüting's speech "Lun yinyue de chuangzuo yu piping" [On the creativity and criticism of music] was not published until June 1954 because of Lü Ji's opposition to He's point of view. See Li Yedao, *Lü Ji Pingzhuan* [A critical biography of Lü Ji] (Renmin Yinyue Chubanshe, 2001), 121–24.

65. Xia Bai's article represented one of the many that attacked He Lüting. "Lun He Lüting tongzhi dui yinyueyishu jibenwenti de xingshizhuyi guandian" [On Comrade He Lüting's formalistic standpoint on the several fundamental issues regarding the art of music], *Renmin Yinyue* 4 (1955): 11–15.

66. Li Yedao, *Lü Ji Pingzhuan*, 122.

67. Kraus, *The Ambiguous Legacy*, 67.

68. Xian wrote two articles on the subject of Chinese national music. The first one, "Lun zhongguo yinyue de minzu xingshi" [On national forms in Chinese new music], was delivered in October 1938 at a CCP meeting on cultural issues. It was then published in *Wenyi Zhanxian* 5/11 (1939), and is now collected in *Xian Xinghai Quanji*, 48–51. The second article was "Xian jieduan Zhongguo xinyinyue yundong de jige wenti" [Issues concerning the present state of the new Chinese Music Movement]. The article was written in July 1940 when Xian was on his way to Moscow. It originally appeared in *Xinyinyue* 5/3 (1943), now collected in *Xian Xinghai Quanji*, 115–26.

69. Xian, "Xian jieduan Zhongguo xinyinyue yundong de jige wenti," *Xian Xinghai Quanji*, 120.

70. Xian, "Xian jieduan Zhongguo xinyinyue yundong de jige wenti," 120–21.

71. Xian, "Lun zhongguo yinyue de minzu xingshi," *Xian Xinghai Quanji*, 48–49.

72. Xian, "Lun zhongguo yinyue de minzu xingshi," *Xian Xinghai Quanji*, 48.

73. Xian, "Issues concerning the present state," *Xian Xinghai Quanji*, 124–25.

74. Xian, "Issues concerning the present state," *Xian Xinghai Quanji*, 124.

75. Holm, "The Dilemmas of National Form" in *Art and Ideology in Revolutionary China*, 62.

76. Such criticisms are evident in the roundtable discussion on Xian's *Shengchang daheshang* [Production cantata] (1939), which was published in *Wenyi Tuji* 1 (1939). The entire roundtable discussion is reprinted in *Xian Xinghai Quanji*, 138–43.

77. Li Ling, "Xian Xinghai zai Yan'an" [Xian Xinghai in Yan'an]. The article was written and published in 1949, before Xian was sanctified. Article collected in Li Ling, *YueHua* [Musical talks] (Huacheng chubanshe, 1983), quoted in Li Ming, "The Death of Xian Xinghai," *Tiao Xian Ju*, 57.

78. In *Xian Xinghai Quanji*, 129.

79. In *Xian Xinghai Quanji*, 132.

80. Kraus, "The Ambiguous Legacy," 68.

81. Letter to Gliere, *Xian Xinghai Quanji*, 375.

82. When he was in the USSR, Xian was in contact with a number of musicians. In *Composition Notes*, Xian attached the remarks made by two Soviet musicians. On Xian's *Three Chinese Dances*, Maximilian Steinberg (1883–1946) wrote, "The composer adopted very advance composition techniques. He synthesized in his work distinct Chinese musical elements with features of post impressionism." *Xian Xinghai Quanji*, 165. On Xian's *Tone Picture* "Chinese Life," Gavril Popov (1904–1972) wrote, " 'Chinese Life' is a work with its unique features. The composer utilized contemporary Western orchestral techniques—largely French impressionistic techniques—with Chinese modality.... This work, written in a fresh and unique musical language, will no doubt draw the attention of the Soviet musical circle." *Xian Xinghai Quanji*, 167. For information on Soviet composers, see the website "Soviet Composers" compiled by Onno van Rijen, at http://ovar.myweb.nl/sovcom.htm.

83. I am not aware of any articles written in Chinese relating Xian's compositional styles with impressionism.

84. Xian expressed his admiration for teachers Dukas, d'Indy, and Romain Rolland in his notes for *The Yellow River Cantata*. *Xian Xinghai Quanji*, 147–48.

85. *Xian Xinghai Quanji*, 147–48.

86. The letter to Gliere, *Xian Xinghai Quanji*, 375.

87. The letter to Gliere, *Xian Xinghai Quanji*, 375.

88. For performance history of the cantata, see Huang Yelu, *Yellow River Cantata miscellaneous*.

89. Kraus regarded that as a shrine. "The Ambiguous Legacy," 66.

90. The other composer who received the same recognition was Nie'er.

CHAPTER 6

Dancing for the Eternal President

Keith Howard

April 15, 2000. To celebrate the birthday of the "Eternal President," Kim Il Sung, fifty thousand young men and women danced in a Pyongyang square in the capital of the Democratic People's Republic of Korea (North Korea). Each dancer wore a suit and tie or a Korean-style dress. The square was once known as Stalin Square. Now, as Kim Il Sung Square, it is flanked by government ministries, the National History Museum, the National Art Museum and the People's Grand Study House.[1] A portrait of the Eternal President hangs from one ministry; opposite, portraits of Marx and Lenin share a further ministry. Sŭngni Street (Victory Street)[2] bisects the square and because, according to North Korean dogma, the revolution must always continue, it was left open— trolley buses and trucks occasionally trundling across, dividing the crowds of people in two. Across the Taedong River, beyond the square, the Juche Tower was lit up as a backdrop. The tower had been constructed in 1982 to celebrate the seventieth birthday of the Eternal President with 25,550 stone bricks weighing 22,000 tons arranged in 18 layers on two sides and 17 layers on the other two sides.[3]

In the same month, the Mansudae Art Troupe, a large uniformed orchestra and choir raised on a temporary stage, led the proceedings, surrounded on three sides by the massed dancers. "Famous" vocalists offered solo renditions of "favorite" songs.[4] In front of the stage, acrobats and professional dancers performed complex routines. The show was broadcast live on national TV and the recording was destined to become a fill for future broadcasts. The massed dancers performed perfectly synchronized accompaniments to a sequence of songs for almost an hour. A live audience watched the spectacle: approximately two hundred foreign guests—diplomats, dignitaries, aid workers, and musicians and artists in town to participate in the annual Spring Friendship Arts Festival[5]—stood on the steps of the People's Grand Study House. Each guest had been invited individually by the *ch'ŏngsonyŏn*, the young men and women.[6] This was the evening of the day I arrived in Pyongyang. I was met at the airport, given flowers, and driven to a twenty-meter bronze statue of Kim Il Sung in front of the Revolution Museum on Mansu Hill, where a TV camera recorded the moment. I followed instructions to lay the flowers at the base of the statue. If this was a surreal welcome, being one of just a couple of hundred guests watching fifty thousand dancers seemed an illusion. When, at the end of the performance, all the guests were ushered forward to join in the dance, I was completely unnerved.

In this chapter, I explore the context for this event. To do so is problematic: To what extent should we try to appreciate cultural products without evaluating the ideological frame that molds them? My solution is to give only a partial perspective, and to ask you, as readers, to add your own interpretation to the statements I cite from North Korean sources.

LEADERSHIP, IDEOLOGY, AND THE CONTROL OF ARTISTIC PRODUCTION

Mass dances and games are known from many communist states, notably China, and from early-twentieth-century youth celebrations in northern Europe that were appropriated and controlled by the Nazis, but that remain reflected in Rudolf Laban's kinetography and studies of effort.[7] From northern Europe, massed dances and games were appropriated by Stalin's Soviet Union, then imported as a component of Chinese revolutionary display. From China, they were taken up by North Korea where, standing as proof that the populace is like an Engelian cog-in-the-wheel, mass festival performances have been continuously refined. They are used for state celebrations. A Polish TV documentary, *The Parade*, documented one in 1988, performed to mark the fortieth anniversary of the founding of the state and designed to compete with the opening ceremony at the Seoul Olympics. It featured thousands of acrobats and crowds raising placards to create perfectly synchronous human waves the Pyongyang May Day Stadium. Mass performances demonstrate that, to paraphrase state ideologues, the people are in perfect harmony with the state and its leaders; the masses control their own destinies and determine their own cultural production. The genuine creators of good art, said the Eternal President, are always the people, rather than the writers and composers of the educated elite, and art must be both popular and populist. The rhetoric is Soviet socialist realism,[8] filtered through Mao Zedong's talks at the Yan'an forum[9] and observed from a distance by a determined and self-isolated state.

The Eternal President was eighty-eight on April 15, 2000. Born Kim Sŏngju in 1912, Kim Il Sung was officially known later in life as the "Great Wise President-for-life Dearly Beloved and Sagacious Leader." State hagiography ascribes immense personal achievements to Kim. Not that it was always so, but the Communist oligarchy has long since been replaced by personal autocracy. Kim is said, first, to have led a guerrilla army from the mountainous north, effectively expelling the Japanese from Korea. Indeed, he was active through the 1930s, and never submitted to the Japanese, although he moved into the Soviet Far East as Japan sought to control its distant territories (actually, the name "Kim Il Sung" appears in Japanese sources from the early 1920s, but either this is a mythical foe, or Kim Il Sung himself was a truly prodigious child). Second, and as noted above, he is said to have won the Korean civil war, in the process inflicting on America its first foreign defeat.[10] Outside of North Korea, it is generally accepted that Kim Il Sung started the conflagration by invading the South on June 25, 1950, but soon saw his country flattened by a United Nations' bombing campaign. He was saved from defeat only by the involvement of Chinese volunteers. Accounts in the North, of course, say America invaded the North, leading their South Korean "puppets"; the Chinese were advisers rather than front-line troops.[11] Third, Kim is the father of the state. We are told that he built a socialist paradise, overseeing industrial and agricultural reforms that created a prosperous nation looked up to by the rest of the world. He routinely gave on-the-spot guidance, "revolutionizing" industrial and agricultural production through his "inspired" methodologies that allowed ever-greater production.[12] The ongoing political division of Korea after 1945, and particularly following the Korean War, meant the North did develop rapidly, part due to aid and a judicious balancing of Soviet and Chinese interests. Kim, the more closely he was associated with development, the more able he was to strengthen his personal power, casting aside potential competitors for leadership of the state. Eventually, a monolithic system was cemented in place with Kim at the head under the banner of *juche*, a term usually translated as "self-reliance," although somewhat mischievously transliterated by some commentators as "bloody mindedness." Progress, though, went into reverse after the 1973 international oil crisis and, despite interminable "speed campaigns" to increase production, North Korea has never really recovered.[13]

Kim Il Sung died on July 8, 1994. This has not proved to be a major obstacle. At his former palace, now enlarged to create a truly stupendous mausoleum and serviced by a dedicated tram, his body is preserved—in 2000, foreigners could visit it, ferried in convoy from downtown, once a week, early on Thursday morning. His words remain sacrosanct, and his commands are still law. Party members still dutifully wear badges with his image and everybody bows to his many statues. At public events, when his image is projected onto huge video screens, everyone claps. Books continue to open with carefully chosen statements from Kim, and when such statements are read aloud, again, everyone claps. Kim's ideology, developed by sycophants and unconditional loyalists,[14] served to construct a complex political philosophy that mixed and continues to mix the socialism of Stalin and Mao with an isolationist Korean mentality. This explains much of the ossification that has occurred, as state and personal ideology have become frozen, unable to change and respond to challenges.[15] Ideology was reflected in art and artistic policy or, rather, art was to project ideology.

It fell to Kim's son, the "Dear Leader" Kim Jong Il, to energize artistic production. The reason, in essentialist terms, could be interpreted as a solution to the age-old problem faced by dynastic rulers: how to keep an heir-apparent occupied. During the Chosŏn dynasty (1392–1910), several palace coups occurred that illustrate what happens when an heir becomes impatient; elsewhere, many regimes have recognized that nonpolitical activities minimize potential conflict. In North Korea, Kim Jong Il, according to state propaganda, was born on February 16, 1942, in a guerrilla camp on the hallowed White Peak Mountain (Kor: Paektusan; Ch: Changbaishan) near the border between Korea and China,[16] and had to wait a long time to come into his inheritance. He has, then, been kept busy, or so we are informed: he is credited by state publications with overseeing and even creating many artistic productions.

The "Dear Leader's" activities only began to be documented in the 1970s. From 1974 onward, journalists began to use the term "party center," initially without stating Kim's name, in articles about operas, musicals, and films in journals such as the official party organ, *Kullǒja*.[17] Artists were regularly quoted talking about the "party center" as their ever-present advisor. Kim's 1976 birthday marked an important turning point. Posters appeared in factories and mines calling for increased production, with work assignments to be completed on February 16. On the same day, fifteen thousand children and young men participated in a youth festival at Pyongyang Stadium. The posters and those performing at the festival proclaimed loyalty to both the Great Leader and the "party center." We now know that activities were part of a process to prepare the population for the announcement that Kim Jong Il had been chosen as the future ruler. It was only in 1980, following Kim Jong Il's election to high party positions at the Sixth Korean Worker's Party Congress in October, that he began to be openly promoted as heir. It is said that it was the Dear Leader (see fig. 6.1) who designed and oversaw the construction of the Juche Tower, completed in

Figure 6.1. Kim Jong Il offering "on-the-spot guidance" on dance notation.

1982. In the same year, his *On the Juche Idea*, published a month after he was awarded the title "Hero of the Democratic People's Republic of Korea," marked the beginning of his public interpretations of Kim Il Sung's ideology.[18] Today, the Dear Leader's birthday has taken on significance comparable to that of his father. Hence, the Monument to the Party, an edifice standing on the southeastern bank of the Taedong river upstream from the Juche Tower, has a central collar with bronze reliefs of the army, peasants, and writers flanked above and below with 216 white stones.[19] This monument was built in 1994, cementing his position as the successor to his father. Hence, while one geometric axis—the axis utilized in the April 2000 dance performance—runs east–southeast from the People's Grand Study House through Kim Il Sung Square and across the river to the Juche Tower, a second runs east–southeast from the massive bronze statue of Kim Il Sung and, immediately behind it, the Museum of the Revolution, to the Monument to the Party across the river. Both signify the dynasty: father tied to son.[20]

The benefit of hindsight has allowed the deeds of the Dear Leader to be backdated, potentially mundane activities of earlier years now taking on great significance. For example, a plaque at the Pyongyang Film Studios records the many hundreds of times he has offered on-the-spot-guidance, beginning with his appointment as state director of film art in 1968. Kim Il Sung's influential tract from 1973 is titled "On the art of cinema."[21] One room at the Pyongyang Film Studios records how he intervened in the filming of the traditional folktale of Ch'unhyang in the 1970s.[22] A small model of a city gate hung in front of a camera is preserved here. It is said that it allowed a crowd scene beyond the gate to be shot in a small studio, obviating the need to work on a bigger set. It was Kim's idea to do this. Kim is also said to have been involved in the creation of a new opera that premiered in 1971, *P'i pada* ("sea of blood"). This is related to Chinese musicodramatic works promoted during the Cultural Revolution,[23] and in part fuses the then-contemporary Chinese model ballets such as the *White Haired Girl* and model operas such as *The Red Lantern*. *P'i pada* is set during the Japanese colonial period and tells how a mining village hid a nationalist leader; the Japanese police slaughtered villagers in their attempts to find him. The opera *P'i pada* is said to be "revolutionary" because it relates heroic deeds, and "immortal" (or, in some texts, a "masterpiece") because the text was written by (or in association with, or first performed for) Kim Il Sung in the 1930s. Beyond the text, *P'i pada* was written by a collective of composers and performers who, reports tell us, worked under the guidance of Kim Jong Il. A further contribution to opera made by Kim Jong Il is also remembered at the Pyongyang Film Studios: He is credited with developing *pangch'ang*, a chorus sung off-stage to allow—in recognition of the need to project realism within socialist art—the drama to continue on stage.[24] In place of death arias, then, we have a chorus; it is said that experimentation began in the 1950s, but that Kim inspired, perfected, and guided the use of this chorus style in *P'i pada* (Kim Kyŏnghŏi and Rim Sangho 1991a: 121–36). At the studios, his manuscript for a *pangch'ang* is dutifully preserved, together with the desk at which he reputedly wrote it. Kim's discussion of opera was officially given in 1974; this, curiously, is several years after *P'i pada* premiered, and, even more curiously, the discussion was only published in 1990 as "On the Art of Opera." *P'i pada* created a style, and was followed by *Kkŏt panŭn ch'ŏnyŏ* ("the flower girl"), *Tang ŭi ch'amdwin ttal* ("a true daughter of the party"), *Kŭmgangsan ŭi sori* ("song of Mount Kŭmgang"), *Yŏnp'ungho* ("gentle breeze"), and *Millima iyagi hara* ("tell the story, forest"). State catalogues of English-language publications refer to more: The Fate of a Self-defense Corps Man, Heroines of Namgang, Youth Orchard, and Song of Paradise.[25]

All of the above are considered "immortal," but now the association is with either Kim Il Sung or Kim Jong Il.[26] By 1988, revolutionary tales had been joined by "people's operas" (*minjok kagŭk*), the first, *Ch'unhyangjŏn*, based on the Ch'unhyang folktale. No association with creation by the leadership is required of "people's operas," but the Dear Leader was nonetheless closely involved. He issued a decree in August 1988 instructing that the genre should be developed, and the score of *Ch'unhyangjŏn* quotes Kim's words that this truly represents the songs of the people (1991: 3). The Ch'unhyang story is known by all North Koreans and South Koreans alike.

It concerns the secret marriage of Ch'unhyang, the daughter of a courtesan, to Mongnyong, the son of an aristocrat, her imprisonment by a corrupt magistrate after she refuses her advances, his comeuppance, and the reunion of the lovers. To North Korean ideologues, the story symbolizes much that was wrong with feudal Korea and challenges the class hierarchy imposed by Confucianism. The *P'i pada* style is retained in people's operas and has proved immensely popular. In May 2001, the fifteen hundredth performance of the first "revolutionary opera," *P'i pada*, was given.[27] A number of songs from operas are remembered fondly, not only in North Korea but also in China, such as *Haemada pomi omyŏn* (Every Spring [Spring comes every year]), the opening number in *Kkŏt panŭn ch'ŏnyŏ* ("the flower girl").[28] Songs have also been extracted and used as the basis of instrumental compositions, most notably a symphony based on *P'i pada* published in 1975 by a committee of composers.[29] Much the same, incidentally, had happened in China with the *Yellow River Concerto*,[30] a piece rewritten by a committee on the basis of a cantata, and in both China and North Korea, ideology lies behind popularity: Music must be both skillfully crafted but based on the models used by and the products wanted by the proletariat.[31]

DANCE: CREATION, NOTATION, AND PRACTICE

As with music, so, too, with dance, professional execution must be matched to local inspiration. Recent publications tell us that the Dear Leader began to take an interest in dance in the early 1970s when he answered his father's call for a notation system to be established. The new system was to be devised in cognizance of Western practice, but to reflect Korean needs. In keeping with other artistic production, scholars are said to have studied and learnt from other international notations. The resulting Korean system is not unique in its entirety, nor is it meant to be, despite occasional claims to the contrary. A propaganda video about the system briefly shows charts of Labanotation, Benesh notation, and the Eshkol-Wachmann system, with the dates of their creation: 1927, 1956, and 1958.[32] North Korean texts, in both Korean and English, fail to say what was learnt from preexisting systems, although Benesh stage indications seem to be retained, while some ideas of effort—notably the sudden flick of the wrist characteristic of Korean dance—could be suggested to derive from Laban.

We are never told precisely why other notation systems were considered inadequate, though I assume that the use of the latter two notations in the West for ballet would disqualify them in the eyes of North Korean ideologues—classical ballet, because it is elitist and fails to depict reality, is not part of the North's mainstream artistic armory, even though it is still taught and known. Texts talk rather vaguely about other dance notations being "imperfect," so that they "lose valuable heritage" and do not "satisfy the public for want of scientific precision, utility value and popularity." A broad sweep states that other notations "indicate mainly the positions of the parts of the body according to the changing positions and directions in space," but omit features of movement (Yun Yong Ok 1987a: 10). None of the documentation available relates to China even though, as so much North Korean artistic production has tracked Chinese models (see Howard 2001), it is tempting to ask what impetus or influence occurred. Hutchinson Guest mentions a Chinese *wu gao* abstract dance notation system established in 1985 in her *Choreo-Graphics*; and the 1980s saw the publication of a number of works on dance notation in China, including Wu Manying's *Wudao dongzuo suhua fa* ("shorthand sketch method of dance movement"), Long Zhengqiu's *Xin wupu jifa* ("new dance notation method"), and Wu Jimei's and Gao Chunlin's *Dingwei fa wupu* ("fixed position method of dance notation").[33] These, though, are far too late for the official North Korean timeline.

According to Korean publications, the notation system was first displayed in June 1976 using a score read left to right with or without accompanying music staff notation. Kim Jong Il is pictured studying the display charts, offering "on-the-spot guidance," supposedly in 1976. The system, *chamo pyogibŏp* ("chamo system"), uses a complex of symbols assembled from music staff notation and the Korean alphabet, as well as other dance notations. It adds pictograms of movement. The system was first used to notate professional repertory, notably dance in opera and other theatrical forms. By the mid-1980s, a typewriter had been modified to create notations; a computer program was up and running by 1987. Notations could be cheaply printed. It was, in fact, only in the mid-1980s that the system was promoted abroad, notably through a 1987 booklet and then in a 1988 book. A workshop, grandly titled the "First International Congress on the Notation of Movement" was held in August 1984, attracting some two hundred and fifty dancers, notators, teachers and scholars, supposedly from twenty-one nations. A second symposium was organized in April 1988, attended by a UNESCO representative and notators and dance practitioners from ten nations. A larger symposium followed in September 1992, *Research and Work on the Different Fields of Dance*, with broader invitations sent to nations beyond the Communist world.

Kim Jong Il's involvement is claimed as central. According to an English-language account:

> Although dance has a long history, no scientific and easy dance notation has ever been perfected.... The Dear Comrade Kim Jong Il, with a deep insight into this state of affairs, put forward the

idea of creating a new dance notation suited to the specific features and requirements of the art of dance in our time. He said: "We should produce a scientific and popular dance notation of a Juche type consonant with the specific features and requirements of the art of dance." The Dear Leader ... clarified various theoretical and practical problems arising in the creation, use and dissemination of the dance notation including the basic orientation for notating dances in the manner of alphabetic combination, the principles of dance notation, and the question of simplifying the shapes and combinations of dance script. Subsequently, he provided further guidance ... on many occasions (U Chang Sop 1988: 1).

It should strike readers conversant with East Asian history that this sort of credit, although characteristic of today's North Korea, is little different from the credit given Confucian rulers of old for scientific inventions and the composition of poetry and music. Four claims are made for the notation system:

1. It is based on "a scientific analysis of the anatomy and physiology of the human body, all attributes of its movement, specific features of dance actions and all representative elements of the art of dance."
2. It is comprehensive, indicating actions, floor patterns, the relationships between dancers, time, and so on.
3. It uses symbols for shapes and gestures that parallel the function of vowels but "evoke the shapes and rhythmic images of parts of the body." It also uses symbols for positions and directions that parallel the function of consonants. Taken in combination, these symbols "form dance words and dance sentences ... according to definite laws."
4. It is suitable not just for Korean dance "but also the national dances of all other countries, and calisthenics, mass games, and figure skating as well" (extracted from U Chang Sop 1988: 1–2).

Figure 6.2 lists "vowels" and "consonants," the symbols for shapes and gestures and for positions and directions. Figure 6.3 illustrates how these are combined, building a single complex for one carriage position with both arms extended outward.

No published score I have seen predates 1988. In that year, a separate dance score was issued for *P'i pada*, titled, as if the first in a series, *Hyŏngmyŏng kagŭk muyong ch'ongbo 1*. This year also saw the publication of a "people's dance," *Choguk ŭi Chin Tallae* ("the fatherland's Chin Tallae");

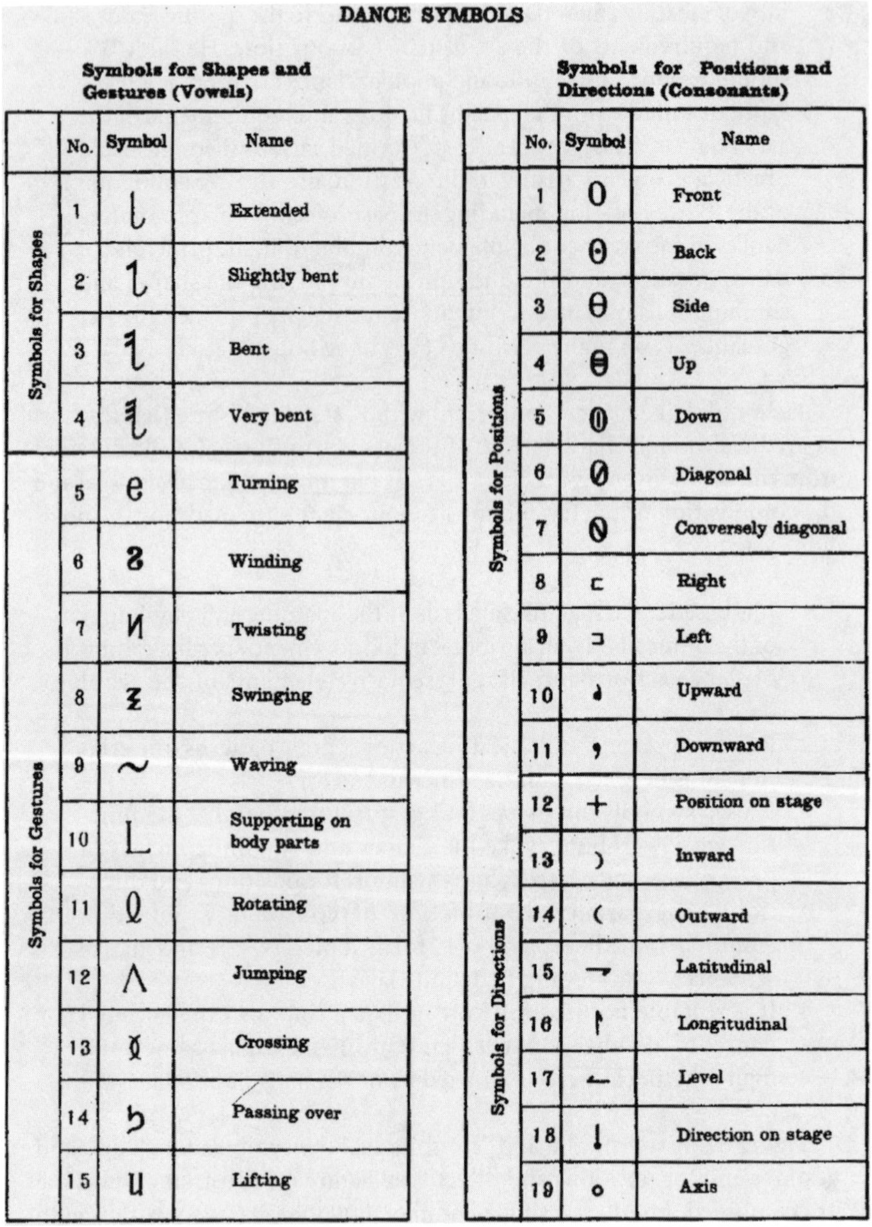

DANCE SYMBOLS

Symbols for Shapes and Gestures (Vowels)				Symbols for Positions and Directions (Consonants)			
	No.	Symbol	Name		No.	Symbol	Name
Symbols for Shapes	1	ι	Extended	Symbols for Positions	1	O	Front
	2	ι	Slightly bent		2	Θ	Back
	3	ι	Bent		3	θ	Side
	4	ι	Very bent		4	θ	Up
Symbols for Gestures	5	e	Turning		5	0	Down
	6	8	Winding		6	0	Diagonal
	7	N	Twisting		7	0	Conversely diagonal
	8	Z	Swinging		8	c	Right
	9	~	Waving		9	⊃	Left
	10	L	Supporting on body parts		10	d	Upward
	11	Q	Rotating		11	,	Downward
	12	∧	Jumping		12	+	Position on stage
	13	ỵ	Crossing		13	)	Inward
	14	b	Passing over	Symbols for Directions	14	(	Outward
	15	U	Lifting		15	→	Latitudinal
					16	↑	Longitudinal
					17	←	Level
					18	↓	Direction on stage
					19	o	Axis

Figure 6.2. Key to dance symbols.

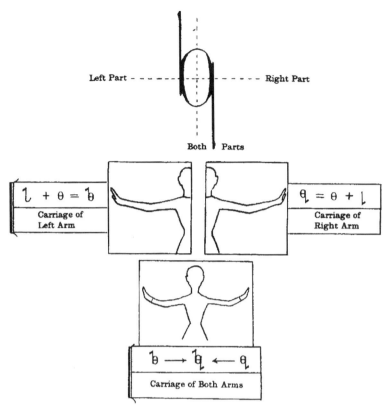

Figure 6.3. Illustration of combined symbols.

this was soon joined by other dance works, the best known being *P'yŏngyangsŏng saramdŭl* ("the people of Pyongyang fortress"). Some opera scores incorporating all the required elements were republished. The score I have for *Ch'unhyangjŏn* is dated 1991, that is, three years after the work premiered. The score is divided into three parts: a full music score (pages 10–496), a section illustrating costumes, props, and stage sets (pages 497–544), and a dance score (pages 545–645).[34]

The opening scene of the fifth act of the "people's opera" *Ch'unhyangjŏn* illustrates the complex mix of notation now available for use. The scene opens with a popular farming song, "Nongbuga," given as Ch'unhyang's lover passes struggling farmers as he journeys back to the city of Namwŏn, disguised as a beggar but in reality a government inspector charged with uncovering misadministration by the local governor. The old story is reinterpreted to better reflect a socialist spirit: This scene is now a farmer's festival. Rather than workers toiling in the fields, we watch a masked dance recognizably adapted from the Korean tradition of Pongsan, a village near Pyongyang, although the farmers here, as in most texts, are from the town of Namwŏn 350 kilometers further south.[35]

The dance score (see fig. 6.4) is divided into four systems; each requires symbol abbreviations or omissions that ensure the score remains readable. The top system comprises music notation—the orchestra is reduced to a piano score—and the bottom gives technical information about staging, lighting, and so on. One line gives the floor pattern for the dancers specified. As an example, this is the point at which the masked dancers come on stage. Above this line the stage positions are prescribed: [come on stage and go to] f2 = right back 2, moving to back [reverse] f8 = left back 8, then center left 7. Below the line the number of dancers, or particular dancers in a group, is given (in this case, eight, dancing together, entering individually in line). The next three bracketed lines offer dance notation, using a tripartite (high, center, low) body division, beginning with an indication of latitudinal direction. Initially, all dancers face across the stage with left arms bent back across the face and back and right arms extended. The head position is given above the top line, the hand property is indicated with a "t" (bent back at the elbow), and a diagonal pose is marked on the middle line. The leg action is marked between the second and third lines, a jump signified by the upturned "v," then a symbol signifying a step with the left foot, front. Both arms and feet have symbols to indicate a shaking action. In summary, then, the eight masked dancers, left arms bent back above their face so that their wide sleeves partially cover their faces, jump and race on from the left, moving to right, then stop center left, their arms and feet held, shaking.

Ideology, however, dictates that dance notation must also serve the needs of the masses. The two functions, for mass training but also for professional staged productions, are not separated within the system itself. The effect is of simplification, represented as abbreviation (as noted above), an aspect that works adequately where dancers are familiar with the movement sequences they are being asked to replicate, and limitation. This would apply not just to Korean dance, but to sequences derived from ballet or Soviet forms. The propaganda video thus claims that the system is sufficiently universal to notate "European" dances, although it in fact illustrates only Russian and East European sample dances. In North Korea, *juche* ideology insists that any creation or replication must meet revolutionary criteria and must be framed by appropriate ideology. This effectively means that free creation is not allowed, and only approved forms and styles of dance may be used; claims of universal applicability may be made, but will never need to be tested.

In 1992, I was told—and print and film propaganda supports this— that both dance and music notation classes were part of middle school and

Figure 6.4. A page of notation from the "people's opera" *Ch'unhyangjŏn*.

high school curricula.[36] As part of lectures on dance notation given to me by scholars at the dedicated institute attached to the Pyongyang Music and Dance University, school children were brought in to the lecture room. "Let's create some notation," said my host, quickly typing a few lines of notation in front of me and printing it out. He handed the sheet of notation to the children, and within a couple of minutes they were dancing the sequence. I was duly impressed—as I am sure I was meant to be. In reality, though, I have no way to verify that what was written really was improvised, nor that all children knew the notation, nor that what was danced faithfully represented what had been written. Ann Hutchinson Guest, in an unpublished report on the 1992 symposium, notes that in a practical demonstration she witnessed, performance subtleties of movement were missed in notation and that, while balletic sequences were simple to write and read back, African movements proved more of a challenge.[37]

The massed forces of dancers celebrating the birthday of the Eternal President in 2000 illustrated the more prosaic use of dance notation. Notation, though, forms but one part of the total strategy. In today's North Korea, each work group in a company, a government office, or a university has artistic functionaries, and time is set aside for group activities before work, after work, or on free days. Each work group is assigned practice space and practice times, if not in the workplace, then in a square in front of public buildings or in a park. Transport, as it is all state owned, is provided as needed. The rubric of such activities insists that participation is "voluntary" but, much as in children's Pioneer groups in other socialist regimes, peer pressure discourages dissent. Artistic activists work with each group on new songs and new dances. They attend organizational meetings and are supported by specialists when needed. In North Korea, artistic production is controlled and rationed. To take one example, the lyrics of songs are considered more important than sonic style—lyrics should be revolutionary, militant, inspirational, and should reflect party policy.[38] Control is top-down, fused by rhetoric into a tight circle of ideologues, creators, and the populace. Control has been extended within the *juche* ideology since the early 1970s—again, Kim Jong Il now takes much of the credit—through two intertwined policies. First, seed theory (*chŏngjaron*) argues that artists can create good art only so far as they are armed with party policy, for the party alone understands the people. Second, collective art (*chipch'e yesul*) demands that groups of artists rather than individuals create new works. As a result of these principles, artistic production is conservative and artistic creators self-censor to conform to ideological guidelines. And the currency of songs, or of dances for songs, remains for many years.

In April 2000, a number of the songs performed and danced to was first recorded a decade or more before (though he writes somewhat inaccurately); "Socialism is Ours" ("Sahoe chuŭi uri kŏya") for example, was a 1992 song that reacted to the collapse of East Germany. Other songs had been dropped because they no longer reflected the dominant ideology; in the early 1990s, songs celebrating bountiful harvests or increased industrial production were the rule, but by 2000, after years of reduced rations caused by natural disasters and economic meltdown, all songs celebrated the revolution, extolled the happiness of the people, or remembered the "Great Leader." Because the repertory changes gradually, only a few new songs/dances need be learned for any given event, the level of change judged sufficient to claim each as new. The massed forces of dancers demanded to demonstrate the people's solidarity with the state present a problem: How can everyone be made to perform adequately irrespective of aptitude? The solution essentially lies in simplicity, tied to the effective transmission of just a few new repertory items for each event. Rehearsals, not just at work places but also in public spaces, began the previous autumn, and although this indicates a long lead-time, it is not so long as might be assumed because there are real difficulties in rehearsing in subzero temperatures in winter.[39]

The complexity of the professional *Ch'unhyangjŏn* was, nonetheless, invoked by such public displays as the one of April 2000. Professional dancers, acrobats, and singers performed in front of the orchestra on the stage in the center of the square. These were a mastery of choreography, as one group seamlessly gave way to another. The contrast with the fifty thousand dancers who fanned out into the far corners of the square, pressing in on the central space, was profound. The choreography for the masses was never complex: forward step-step-step-clap, back step-step-step-clap, forward step-step-step-turn, spot step-step-step-clap. The event's effectiveness came from the relationship between center and periphery, between the professionals and the amateurs. The audience tended to fuse everything together, absorbing the central component but focusing on the periphery. My guide, not surprisingly, insisted I was watching only amateurs, the young men and women who had graciously invited me. They were the people who rushed to the audience at the end of the event, taking us in their arms and coaxing us down to join the dance, while the professionals evaporated away.

Amongst the audience that day was Ermanno Furlanis, a chef working in North Korea to train locals in the art of pizza making. He was duly impressed:

> In the center they set up an immense dais with a band and choir while overhead a board indicated the date and the 'hymn number' on the program. It was the anniversary of some victory. All around the dais, in perfectly regular squares of 300 or 400 people, the population of Pyongyang had dutifully assembled for dance.... And then the dancing began.

First the squares formed into circles and then flared out into stars. I felt a shiver down my spine in front of the precision of their movements: rarely had I experienced such powerful emotions. [We were] invited to join the crowd. We clasped hands with a ring of dancers and had a wonderful time while they playfully reproached us for getting all the steps wrong. It turned out to be an unforgettable evening, historical in every sense of the word.[40]

POSTSCRIPT

In April 2000, as we clapped at the end of the spectacle, our guide turned to us: "Do you have such events in your country?" We wondered whether to be humbled, but then again, we could never envisage circumstances in which so many British people could be coaxed to perform with such synchronicity. Yet, in North Korea, mass spectacles continue. In November 2001, I was told that the young people's groups had begun rehearsing for the dance presentation that observers assumed would be held in April 2002. This would, everyone thought, be an even more massive celebration than the event two years earlier that I have discussed here, since it would mark the "Great Leader's" ninetieth birthday. But it was not to be. Amidst considerable international criticism that North Korea, a receiver of massive international aid, could afford to hold such massive celebrations when it was failing to feed its own people, a smaller presentation was held on February 16: the Dear Leader had assumed greater importance. The Great Leader's birthday was a much quieter affair, and the Spring Friendship Arts Festival passed without mention. I then received an invitation to join the Arirang Festival in Pyongyang, timed to coincide with the lead-up to the 2002 World Cup in South Korea and Japan. I couldn't go, but May saw what a BBC correspondent reckoned was "150,000" people dancing and performing in perfect synchronization. I wonder what the future holds.

Notes

This paper is based on two trips to Pyongyang, in June–July 1992 and April 2000. Earlier versions of my account were presented at the annual conference of the British Forum for Ethnomusicology, Brunel University, in April 2001 and at a study day on North Korean culture at the British Museum in November 2001. I thank those who made suggestions and comments on both occasions. I am also grateful to Ann Hutchinson Guest and Judy Van Zile for their assistance on matters relating to dance. Note that McCune-Reischauer romanization is used throughout, except for Kim Il Sung [Kim Ilsŏng], Kim Jong Il [Kim Chongil], Seoul, and Pyongyang.

1. Effectively, this is the national library.
2. Previously known as Stalin Street. Sŭngni signifies the triumph that official propaganda reminds us the DPRK achieved in defeating the Americans in the Korean War.
3. There were 25,550 bricks because Kim had lived 25,550 days; 22,000 tons because this was the number of days since Kim had supposedly "invented" the *juche* ("self reliance"; *chuch'e*) idea; 18 x 2 + 17 x 2 = 70, as Kim had lived seventy years.

4. "Famous" singers are those such as Jo Chong Mi with the titles "merited artist/artiste" who are featured on individual videos from the state company, Mokran. By "favorite" songs I mean those songs featured on recent CD releases that could be heard repeatedly over the media during my trip to North Korea. Quotation marks reflect the normative way in which specific singers and songs are referred to in North Korea publications.

5. This festival is an annual international event held since 1982 that, in its timing, doubles as a celebration of Kim Il Sung's birthday. International artists are, in keeping with Soviet-style events elsewhere in the recent past, heavily weighted toward participants from the former Communist block. An illustrated account was issued in 1992 to coincide with Kim Il Sung's eightieth birthday celebrations, as "The Song of Independence, Peace, and Friendship" (Pyongyang: Korea Pictorial).

6. The term is typically used for young, unmarried adults. Tickets for the event suggested guests had been invited by an association named after this term, but I noted that many dancers appeared to be in their late twenties and perhaps early thirties, somewhat older than one would expect.

7. Laban organized the dance presentations at the 1936 Berlin Olympic Games, but then left Germany. For an account of German dance, and how it was appropriated by the Nazi regime, see Susan Manning (1993).

8. For a published version of the Soviet policy, see Zhdanov (1950: 7–15). "Socialist realism" first appeared as the title of an essay by Maxim Gorky in 1933. For general discussions of the policy, see for example H. Arvon (1973) and Dave Laing (1978). For the Soviet approach to literature, see Harriet Borland (1950), and for an account of how the policy was applied to music, see Boris Schwarz (1983). For a more comprehensive account of Soviet—and Chinese—approaches to music, see Arnold Perris (1985: 67–121).

9. An English version is published in *Selected Works of Mao Tse-tung* 3: 69–98 (Peking: Foreign Languages Press, 1965). The summary and context of the talks is given in Merle Goldman (1967: 18–50); a more complete discussion is in Bonnie McDougall (1980). Note that the Chinese further developed the concept during the Cultural Revolution, for which see Hua-Yuan Li Mowry (1973). This latter development left an imprint in North Korea, as juche was increasingly applied to art.

10. Actually, American forces had suffered once before at the hands of the North Koreans. An American vessel, the General Sherman, sailed up the Taedong River toward Pyongyang in 1875. It was set on fire and sunk, according to state propaganda, by Kim Il Sung's grandfather. The vessel is said to have tried to escape, and a plaque marks the spot on the river bank where it sank; the spot, conveniently, is immediately adjacent to Kim Il Sung's birthplace at Man'gyŏngdae. Today, a further American trophy is berthed, quietly rusting, at the spot where the General Sherman was set alight: the Pueblo spy ship, captured in the East Sea in the mid 1960s by just three valiant Korean heroes.

11. The building in which the armistice was signed, within North Korean territory, has been preserved. When I photographed it in 1992, three flags were placed on desks for the three armistice signatories: North Korea, China, and the United Nations (South Korea refused to sign, claiming that theirs was the only legitimate government on the peninsula). In 2000, the Chinese flag had been removed, leaving an empty table that my guides told me had merely been used by the aides to the North Korean delegation. In 2000, I was also shown Kim's command headquarters, now protected within a concrete hangar with an adjacent underground complex supplementing the Korean-style house. Off to one side was a small and unpretentious house that my guides said was where the Chinese ambassador had stayed, well away from where planning was taking place.

12. The steel mill at Kangson became closely associated with Kim's post–Korean War reconstruction of heavy industry. Following the December 1959 plenary meeting of the Party Central Committee, Kim spent fifteen days in February 1960 in the farming community of Chongsan-ri to the west of Pyongyang; his "on-the-spot guidance" resulted in the Chongsan-ri Method, still mendaciously promoted today as the only model for collective agriculture. See, for example, New Looks of Chongsan-ri (Pyongyang: Foreign Languages Publication House, 1984). Similarly, an extended trip to the Taean Elec-

trical Machinery Factory in December 1961 led to a collective work system that became the model for industry.

13. See Aidan Foster Carter's reports for detailed discussion (1992, 1994). For a discussion of how *juche* extends to art, see Howard (1997). It is clear that output (and exports) did show a slight recovery in the late 1970s, but never to a great enough extent to avoid the interminable descent that marked the 1990s. "Speed campaigns" included the famous occasion in 1957 when an apartment was constructed in fourteen minutes.

14. Some of whom may in the course of time change their views, as was the case with the primary architect of *juche*, Hwang Jang-Yop, who defected in Beijing in February 1997 and now lives in South Korea.

15. Since Foster-Carter's reports (1992 and 1994), economic, industrial, and agricultural decline has continued. A recent example of policy ossification has been seen in the escalation of tension following North Korea's restart of its nuclear program in December 2002. International observers have noted that the bellicose threats and statements issued by the North closely parallel those made a decade earlier, in 1994, during a previous standoff over nuclear matters. It is as if North Koreans have failed to recognize that international geopolitics—and the American presidency—have changed.

16. Most likely, since the Japanese occupying force had forced most Korean guerrillas to retreat, Kim Jong Il was born in Russian territory; certainly, he had a Russian name, Yura (as discussed, for example, by Suh 1988: 51). His association with the area around Khabarovsk was made clear late in 2001 when, on a long trip on the Trans-Siberian to Moscow, Kim stopped to visit. The date of his birth, 1942, is also disputed by some scholars, as it conveniently falls thirty years after his father's birth.

17. Suh discusses this briefly, citing one particular article by Ch'ŏn Sebong (Suh 1988: 279, and FN24).

18. See Buzo 1999: 105.

19. That is, 2 for February, the second month, and 16 for the sixteenth day of that month: Kim Jong Il's birthday.

20. In fact, on the northwestern bank, a third axis runs between the People's Grand Study House and the Museum of the Revolution, and one can be seen from the other. Similarly, on the southeastern bank, a fourth axis runs from the Juche Tower to the Monument to the Party. The monumental design is deliberate, and extends—but less importantly—to a number of other buildings. For details, see Schinz and Dege 1990, figure 14 (published before the erection of the Monument to the Party).

21. My copy, published in English in 1989, runs to 329 pages.

22. For North Korean films, see Lee 2000. Lee includes a chapter on film adaptations of the Ch'unhyang tale in both North Korea and South Korea (2000: 67–101).

23. See MacKerras 1976 and Howard 2001.

24. As Chŏng Pongsŏk, the director of the Yun Isang ŭmak yŏn'guso (Isang Yun Music Research Institute) in 1992, told me: "[*Pangch'ang*] allows opera to convey an actor's mental state to the audience and, since *pangch'ang* comes from off-stage, it encapsulates the audience reaction to the drama. Consider Verdi's *La Traviata*, where Violetta is expected to sing as she dies on the stage. This may be good music, but the scene has no realism, since nobody can sing when they are dead. *Pangch'ang* allows a chorus to describe what is going on while the character concentrates on acting."

25. I have not found scores or recordings of these other works.

26. A series of children's tales appeared in the mid-1980s (and perhaps before) that were typically said to be authored by Kim Il Sung. One, though, is said to be by Kim Jong Il, "The Rabbit's Pawprint" (*T'okki ŭi paltojang*). Kim, it is said, told this story as a school student to his classmates; the classmates later used it as inspiration for the book (Pyongyang: Kŭmsŏng ch'ŏngnyŏn ch'ulp'ansa, 1988).

27. Reported in *Pyongyang Times*, May 2001.

28. When I played a recording of this song to an international audience at the CHIME conference in Rotterdam in 1995, the Chinese scholar Zhang Boyu told me off for being less than complementary: This was a song, he said, that he remembered with affection from his youth. Zhang is now a professor at the Beijing Chinese Conservatory.

29. No names are given in the published score, although I was told in 1992 that the composers involved included Kim Wŏn'gyun (b. 1917) and others who worked on the opera. Kim Jong Il is again credited with inspiring the composers to arrange the symphony (Kim Kyŏnghŭi and Rim Sangho 1991a: 198).

30. See Hon-Lun Yang's Chapter 5 for a full discussion of *Yellow River Cantata*.
31. Yin Cheng-Chung, on of the committee who created the *Yellow River Concerto*, claimed to have been inspired by spending time with boatmen on the river and argued that the composition played "a militant part in uniting and educating the people and attacking the enemy" (Yin 1974: 97–102).
32. Benesh notation was patented in 1955, but began to be used in teaching at the Royal Ballet in London in 1956. For information on Labanotation, see Hutchinson 1977.
33. I thank Chou Chiener for this information.
34. Eight further pages give an abbreviated explanation of the dance notation.
35. Pongsan masked dance drama is preserved in South Korea as Intangible Cultural Property no. 17. In North Korea, the drama features prominently in picture books on folk culture.
36. Personal interview with U Chang Sop, June 1992, Pyongyang.
37. Ann Hutchinson Guest states:

> The system clearly works at a general practical level. As a tool for elementary and advanced dance education it lacks a sound anatomical movement analysis and the existence of an "alphabet" in the sense of movement verbs, adverbs, nouns, etc, and symbols representing them which are flexible in use—features which in Labanotation have proved so valuable. Much practical inventiveness has been applied in the development of the Chamo system, for example, economy in use of symbols, yet an important question is the range of movement and dance experience of the designers of the system.... Although it serves the needs in the middle range of structured movement description, the freer, general usage needed in education as well as in much avant garde choreography is clearly not taken care of, nor, it would appear, has it been applied to the very advanced level of subtle movement description (unpublished, page 2).

In 1987, Hutchinson Guest requested clarification of a number of symbols she felt were not adequately explained in the documentation she had received. She never received a reply.
38. See Kim Jong Il, "For the Further Development of our Juche Art," a speech originally given in 1975, published in 1992.
39. Reports indicate that heating has not been provided for workplaces or apartment complexes for at least the last six winters; temperatures in Pyongyang plummet to −30 degrees Celsius or lower.
40. "I made pizza for Kim Jong-il, Part 2: Hot ovens at the seaside," *Asia Times* Online, August 11, 2001. *www.atimes.com/koreas/CH11Dg02.html* (accessed on August 17, 2001). Note that the author is unclear about several things. For "victory," for example, read Kim Il Sung's birthday.

References

Speeches and writings by Kim Il Sung and Kim Jong Il and ideological tracts are cited within the text.

Academy of Sciences, eds. 1988. *Chosôn ûi minsok nori.* Seoul: P'urûnsup (Originally published in Pyongyang by the Institute of Archaeology, Academy of Sciences).

Arvon, H. 1973. *Marxist Esthetics.* Trans by H. Lane. Ithaca, N.Y.: Cornell University Press.

Borland, Harriet. 1950. *Soviet Literary Theory and Practice During the First Five-Year Plan, 1928–1932.* New York: Columbia University Press.

Bunge, Frederica M., ed. 1977. *North Korea: A Country Study.* Washington, DC: Foreign Area Studies, The American University.

Buzo, Adrian. 1999. *The Guerilla Dynasty: Politics and Leadership in North Korea.* London: I.B. Tauris.

Foster-Carter, Aidan. 1992. *Korea's Coming Unification: Another East Asian Superpower?* London: The Economist Intelligence Unit.

Foster-Carter, Aidan. 1993. "The Gradualist Pipe Dream: Prospects and Pathways for Korean Reunification." In Andrew Mack, ed., *Asian Flashpoint: Security and the Korean Peninsula.* Sydney: Allen and Unwin and Canberra: Australian National University, pp. 159–75.

Foster-Carter, Aidan. 1994. *North Korea After Kim Il Sung.* London: The Economist Intelligence Unit.

Freeland, Nina, Rinn-Sup Shinn, Peter Just, and Philip W. Moeller. 1976. *Area Handbook for North Korea.* 2nd ed. Washington, DC: Foreign Area Studies, The American University.

Goldman, Merle. 1967. *Literary Dissent in Communist China.* Cambridge, Mass.: Harvard University Press.

Han Chungmo and Chŏng Sŏngmu. 1983. *Chuch'e ŭi munye riron yŏn'gu.* P'yŏngyang: Sahoe kwahak ch'ulp'ansa.

Howard, Keith. 1997. "Juche and Culture: What's new?" In Hazel Smith, Chris Rhodes, Diana Pritchard and Kevin Magill, eds. *North Korea in the New World Order.* Basingstoke: Macmillan, pp. 169–95.

Howard, Keith. 2001. "North Korea: Songs for the Great Leader, with Instructions from the Dear Leader." In Marc Orange et al. eds. *Mélanges offerts a Li Ogg et Daniel Bouchez. Cahiers d'Études Coréennes 7.* Paris: College de France, pp. 103–30.

Hutchinson Guest, Ann. 1977. *Labanotation. The System of Analyzing and Recording Movement.* 3rd ed. New York: Theatre Arts Books.

Hutchinson Guest, Ann. 1989. *Choreo-Graphics: A Comparison of Dance Notations from the Fifteenth Century to the Present.* New York: Gordon and Breach Scientific Publishers.

Hutchinson Guest, Ann. 1992. *The Chamo (Alphabet) System of Dance Notation of North Korea.* Unpublished report.

Kim Kyŏnghŭi and Rim Sangho. 1991a/b. '*P'i pada'-shik hyŏngmyŏng kagŭk* 1 and 2. *Chuch'e ŭmak ch'ongsŏ* 4 and 5. P'yŏngyang: Munye ch'ulp'ansa.

Kim Yol Kyu. 1992. "A Study on the Present Status of Folklore and Folk Arts in North Korea." *Korea Journal* 32, 2: 75–91.

Laing, Dave. 1978. *The Marxist Theory of Art.* Atlantic Highlands, N.J.: Humanities Press.

Lee Hyangjin. 2000. *Contemporary Korean Cinema: Identity, Culture, Politics.* Manchester, UK: Manchester University Press.

Liang Maochun. 1988. '*Dui woguo liuxing yinyue lishi de sikao.*' *Renmin yinyue* 1988/7: 32–34.

Lunacharsky, Anatoly. 1967. *V. I. Lenin: On Literature and Art.* Moscow: Progress Publishers.

MacKerras, Colin. 1976. *China: The Impact of Revolution. A Survey of Twentieth Century China.* New York: Longman.

McDougall, Bonnie. 1980. *Mao Zedong's Talks at the Yan'an Conference on Literature and Art.* Ann Arbor: University of Michigan Press.

Manning, Susan. 1993. *Ecstasy and the Demon: Feminism and Nationalism in the Dances of Mary Wigman.* Los Angeles: University of California Press.

Hua-Yuan Li Mowry. 1973. *Yang-Pan Hsi: New Theatre in China.* Berkeley: Centre for Chinese Studies, University of California Press.

Perris, Arnold. 1985. *Music as Propaganda: Art to Persuade, Art to Control.* Westport, Conn.: Greenwood Publishing.

Scalapino, Robert A., and Chong-Sik Lee. 1972. *Communism in Korea.* Berkeley and Los Angeles: University of California Press.

Schwarz, Boris. 1983. *Music and Musical Life in Soviet Russia, 1917–1981.* Bloomington: Indiana University Press.

Schinz, A., and E. Dege. 1990. "P'yongyang, Ancient and Modern, the Capital of North Korea," *GeoJournal* 22, 1: 21–36 and 121–36.

Suh Dae Sook. 1988. *Kim Il Sung: The North Korean Leader.* New York: Columbia University Press.

U Chang Sop. 1988. *The Chamo System of Dance Notation.* P'yŏngyang: Foreign Languages Publishing House.

Yin Cheng-Chung. 1974. "How the piano concerto 'Yellow River' was composed." *Chinese Literature* 11: 97–102.

Yun Yong Ok. 1987. "A New Dance Notation I & II." *Korea Today* July 1987: 9–11 and August 1987: 25–26.

Zhdanov, Andrei. 1950. *Essays on Literature, Philosophy, and Music.* New York: International Publishers.

CHAPTER 7

The Power of Recently Revitalized Serbian Rural Folk Music in Urban Settings

Jelena Jovanović

This chapter surveys the revitalization of rural folk music in Serbian towns during the 1990s and links its development to post–World War II historical and social conditions in the former Yugoslavia. After discussing the rural songs' key musical features, I examine the music's psychological and physiological effects on performers and listeners in late-twentieth-century Serbia.

HISTORICAL AND SOCIAL BACKGROUND

To grasp the impact of folk music's revival in urban areas of the former Yugoslavia, it is necessary to understand the political, economic, and cultural position of this country in Europe after the Second World War.[1] After the Second World War, there developed an intensive propaganda campaign encouraging urban migration in all parts of Yugoslavia (SFRJ), including Serbia. As in other communist countries, the government instituted policies to foster quick, mass industrialization that created a great population shift from rural to urban areas.[2] New workplaces were created and workers' residences were built all over the country; thousands of village inhabitants decided to move to towns and start families. Once in the towns, this generation of newcomers found it difficult to express their rural identity: they could not communicate with their new neighbors through traditional music because many of them had come from areas with different musical traditions, nor could they easily assimilate elements of urban culture that seemed strange to them.[3] Their music, moreover, was suppressed and the newcomers were thus deprived of their familiar means of spontaneous expression. In time, the migrants from the villages, at first on the level of their own personal and family lives, and later at the community level, adopted the popular urban music genres proffered to them by the mass media of radio and television.

It seems paradoxical that the regime practiced a form of communism that distanced itself from the traditional culture of the common people it was thought to favor. Its leaders preferred that middle class bourgeois (*petit bourgeois*) cultural values define the country's "socialist realism." Folk music was, in fact, regarded as a "primitive" genre. As in other European communist countries, traditional culture was presented in stylized and strictly controlled forms, with few traces of spontaneous expression.[4] Like their music, newcomers to the city were to be "cultivated" according to more "urban" values.

Professional café performers who included popular songs in their repertoire were also important in the transmission of urban genres to newcomers. Cafés have been principal sites for social gatherings throughout the Balkans, so it is unsurprising that they would serve as the main source of entertainment for many newcomers.[5] This new population was thus exposed to the wide range of old and new town songs that prevailed in the second half of the twentieth century.

The predominant popular genres in Serbian mass media at the time included the "new folk song" or "newly composed folk song"[6] and "turbo-folk."[7] These genres were absorbed by the people to such a degree that they seemed to supplant traditional music in the lives of most newcomers.[8] Newly composed folks songs, whose function was entertainment, came to replace the authentic folk songs that had originated in traditional customs and rites.[9] Thus a new cultural model gradually emerged, called the "populist cultural model," which by the 1990s had deeply affected the lives of a significant portion of the Serbian urban population. Milena Dragićević-Šešić describes its proponents as "those from the working class, lower middle class, or the rural population who aspired to higher status" and characterizes consumers within the model as receptive and passive.[10] Andrei Simić defines the consumers as "the peasant urbanites" who formed "a hybrid class halfway on the road from village to city."[11] Clearly, significant music trends in Serbia during the last half of the twentieth century were closely linked to the political climate of the former Yugoslavia.[12]

Even though Serbs were spread widely throughout the country and accounted for the majority of the former Yugoslavia's population, expression of Serbian national identity was extremely problematic.[13] Serbs expressed their national identity during this period in a variety of covert or indirect ways. First, a great many Serbs resolved to be as discreet as possible about their ethnic heritage in order to protect their immediate family and descendants from persecution. This was in response to the slaughter not only of political combatants but also of many innocent and prominent persons following World War II and the parallel civil war in Serbia.[14] Second, they continued to adhere to the Orthodox Church and use the Cyrillic alphabet—basic elements of Serbian national identity. Third, Serbs sought to express their identity through the former Yugoslavia and, of all the peoples living in this country, were the first to declare themselves "Yugoslav." Fourth, though in retrospect it may seem strange, many Serbs displayed national pride by becoming the most faithful bearers of the former Yugoslavia's "invented traditions."[15] These invented traditions served to glorify individuals and concepts that were later overthrown in the course of the 1990s: the ideals of communist revolution, the personality of (the Croat) Josip Broz Tito, and notions of "brotherhood and equality" in a federation composed of many nationalities.

The disintegration of Tito's government, along with several former Yugolav nations' push for independence and recovery of national identities, sparked an identity crisis in many Serbs who had declared themselves Yugoslavs.[16] Given the unstable conditions of the post-Tito period, it is unsurprising that Serbs would look for ways to secure their own identity. During this internal breakdown, enormous external pressure, represented by economic and cultural sanctions[17] against the newly formed Federal Republic of Yugoslavia (SRJ), was exerted by the international public.[18] Economic and cultural isolation followed, then economic decay and poverty, resulting in the so-called "grey economy" and a rise in criminal activity. While moral and other objective social values were thus degraded, the new Yugoslavia was further burdened by a dramatic influx of Serbian refugees from Croatia, Bosnia, and Kosovo who made up ten percent of the population. In sum, daily life in Serbia in the 1990s can be described as unbearable.

Another factor shaped the musical profile of Serbs both in villages and in towns: the decline of singing among families and concomitant spread of the view that singing was a task reserved for specialized individuals and ensembles (*Gesellschaft*). Fieldwork studies reveal that most Serbs today generally sing less than prior generations. Among nonprofessional segments of the population, singing is confined to participation in singing "guilds" or to a shy humming along to the sounds of radio and television.[19]

Professionals, by contrast, play the leading role in socially important concerts and celebrations ("folk spectacles") that have become syncretic substitutions for rituals.[20] The newly composed and turbofolk songs for the occasions of concerts and TV shows appear as syncretic elements— both through the very attractive stage appearance of the singers (in terms of their clothing, make-up, and hairstyles), and through the choreography, lights, and other stage effects. The vocal quality is not always very important, nor is the quality of music or lyrics. The demands of commercialization intrinsically supercede criteria of good taste; everything is subordinated to "a modern ritual—a ritual of show business."[21] Mass communication has been responsible for the diffusion of such programs and government authorities have used them to maintain social control and mold collective tastes and needs.[22]

The features of newly composed and turbofolk songs can be described as follows. Both their subject matter and musical characteristics vary widely and can include (rare) citations of autochthonous folk tunes, melodies in the spirit of folk tunes, and melodies that resemble those found in Western popular music.[23] Songs that borrow from the music of Greece, Romania, or the Near and Middle East are also typical; it is popular to mix these different music styles as well. Arrangements are always vocal–instrumental following the norm of Serbian folk orchestras or Gypsy orchestras, but can also resemble rock arrangements. Despite this genre's great range of musical styles, one feature—the singing style—connects them all to the Balkan rural vocal tradition.[24]

The emergence and flourishing of turbofolk was aided by moves toward democratization at the beginning of 1990s. In contrast to the old communist regime's strict control over the media, democratization brought about reduced media regulation. As a result, many new styles and genres appeared in the media; turbofolk and pornography are just two examples of such new material.

REVIVING THE AUTHENTIC RURAL TRADITION

During the time when newly composed folk songs had primacy in the mass media, authentic Serbian folk songs were all but completely absent.[25] Only music experts had access to the content of sound archives with field recordings of this repertoire.[26] Given the lack of interest, this type of sound seems to have been condemned to oblivion and might have disappeared quietly. However, as Edward Shils has written: "A tradition ... always has the chance of resurgence as long as there is a written record of it or attenuated memories in a small number of adherents."[27] Indeed, the existence of field recordings has made the revitalization of the Serbian rural music tradition possible, and the initial impulse for this rebirth came from younger generations of ethnomusicologists.[28] A parallel phenomenon, spurred by similar conditions, needs, and aims, occurred in other countries of the former Yugoslavia and of the former Soviet Union.[29]

Scholarly engagement with this music led to interest in creating authentic performances and sound recordings of the repertoire. The intention of these efforts has been to present the songs in an authentic manner, without any (intentional) stylization whatsoever; they attempt to recreate authentic tone colour, arrangements, ornaments, and unique rhythms and meters. The aim is to bring to life not only the sounds of past generations, but to evoke the collective experience that accompanied such music making.[30] According to tradition, singers would experience protection from evil, purification by catharsis, and could gain access to inner energies; furthermore, their personal problems and confusions would diminish, and they could establish a healthy relationship with the environment.

The first attempt to revitalize Serbian rural songs began with the founding of *Paganke* (The Pagans), a female vocal group founded in 1983, led by a student of ethnomusicology and supervised by the late ethnomusicologist Petar Vukosavljević. This ensemble did not have great public success. At the same time, the acclaimed singer Svetlana Stević from the region of Homolje, as well as Darko Macura, a player and maker of folk instruments, and Bokan Stanković, a player of folk instruments, were active and did achieve acclaim. Still, it seems clear that there was not much public demand for such a sound at the time. However, ten years later, when the former Yugoslavia had fallen apart and the wars in Croatia and Bosnia were at their climax, *Moba* (Bee, in the sense of a social gathering in order to perform some task), a female vocal ensemble led by young ethnomusicologists, found audiences much more receptive, especially among the young urban public. In later years, other groups and soloists with the same aim followed. Among the most successful ensembles were: *Braća Teofilović* (The Teofilović Brothers), *Drina* (Snezana Spasić), *Belo platno* (White Linen), *Zdravac* (Geranium), and *Ved* (Deep Insight). The Ethnomusicology Department of the Music School *Mokranjac* in Belgrade was also founded during this period.[32] Vocal groups specializing in authentic folk songs were also formed from state amateur ensembles that had formerly cultivated stylized songs and dances. The interest of young people in this genre has been unexpectedly great and indicates that the longing for this sort of authentic music among the young Serbian population is deep.[33] While the worldwide trend toward increased interest in ethnomusicology has contributed to the school's success, native demand for authentic music has been a more significant factor.

MEANINGS FOR PERFORMERS AND LISTENERS

Some devotees of this kind of singing argue for stylization in order to make this type of music more accessible to a wider audience; however, most faithful listeners prefer the "crude," nonstylized sound.[34] In response to a listener survey of 1999, the respondents reported positive feelings: joy, love, a sense of belonging, of feeling relaxed, hope, and optimism. Some mentioned "an amazing sense of calmness" and "a sense of getting back to one's roots, to one's starting point, a sense of something long-lasting, all-embracing." Others said, "These songs do us good, they are 'alive,' they care for us and teach us." Another respondent wrote, "It raises one's thougths and feelings to a higher plane ... puts one in touch with one's roots, with tradition ... [and] evokes a deep sense of fulfilment, calm and meaningfulness." Interestingly, one listener remarked that when he listened to rural folk songs he felt "the absence of any need to bow to anyone's tastes or weaknesses."[35]

Older rural songs are identified as particularly expressive with their narrow, nontempered intervals, chords constructed of seconds, and intensive singing. Rests between phrases, even between words or syllables, seem to be perceived as especially calming psychologically. These are small, short "silences," "stolen" from the throng of the city and from the horrors of lives that are burdened by external pressures and inner anxieties. Moreover, the songs' content and direct lyric expression seem to remind listeners of neglected and almost forgotten "truths of life" or the possibility of comprehending them. These meanings have enormous significance for many Serbs in this specific historic moment of collective and individual intimidation caused by poverty, collective fear and war psychosis. Through ancient phrases and metaphors, our predecessors' view of the world emerges and inspires feelings of collective safety. They can also strengthen performers' and listeners' resolve to meet reality with the courage that their forbears showed in earlier difficult times. The impact of traditional music on our lives can perhaps be explained by the awakening of the "Ur-temperament,"[36] which the outstanding ethnopsychologist Vladimir Dvorniković, describes as "not [an] individual, but [an] ancient communal temperament, hereditary, instinctive and atavistic ... which resonates in us ... [and] becomes accessible to us through introspection ... as individual members of the same ethnic community."[37]

On the physiological level it is possible to speak of the cathartic effect brought about by the sound of the singers' throaty voices and intense delivery (a style that developed because these songs were originally sung, mainly, in the open air) or by the physical closeness of the singers while performing this repertoire. According to tradition, singers of older two-part songs, in order to achieve a specific tonal color, would stand closer together than is common in other styles of singing. The nontempered intervals, especially the prevalent seconds, represent the intimate closeness of the singers and seems to purify, heal, and strengthen them (see musical example on website). The intensely rendered phrases are followed by rests of free duration; their length is determined in proportion to the need for contemplation of the preceding sentiments.[38]

Performers and listeners of rural music in urban Serbian settings seem to have sought out this music partly to help them withstand negative social circumstances. It has also provided a means by which contemporary Serb youth can find and reconnect with one another. The strong demand for this sound may be the result of a rebirth of a collective consciousness among significant numbers of alienated young people.

The revitalization of authentic rural folk song was a spontaneous, intuitive response to the newly composed and turbofolk music genres and the simultaneous suppression of authentic, traditional music. The comeback of traditional music represents resistance to the mass media's tasteless, artificial music, and struggle against the hardship brought about by years of political turmoil. It might be said that it is a "cry for life" that represents a return to tradition as a response to "the sense of suffocation, of the desiccation of vitality under the burden" of problems in everyday life.[39] The movement to revitalize rural sounds has been analyzed in only a few contemporary sociological studies.[40] It has not been steered by any institution (with the exception of the music school); rather, it came about spontaneously, with all its expressive power, at the end of the tumultuous twentieth century, at a time when questions about Serbian ethnic identity were most urgent. While Serbian rural music has helped to address these questions for Serbs themselves, it can also serve as a bridge to listeners, performers, and experts from other countries who seek to understand an important stage in the reassertion of Serbian identity.

Notes

[See website for audio file, musical score, and photos to accompany this chapter.]

1. As historian Predrag Marković wrote, "During the Cold War, the world was divided into two opposing spheres. Yugoslavia was in the peculiar position of being open to the influences of the two quarreling ideologies. These influences were both external and internal; ... we can use the metaphor of a wall, to visualize the divide between the two blocks in the Cold War, the two adversary Empires. Yugoslavia was a tower in the Wall, a tower with a gate inside; both sides monitored each other, traded through this gate, and tried to gain control of it. Dwellers of the tower extorted tolls and taxes from that trade. The tower itself was eclectic; the foundations and the basic construction were eastern but people were allowed to put windows, furniture, wallpapers, in colorful and luxurious western fashion.... Gaining fortune so easily led the leaders and the people of Yugoslavia to the fatal conclusion that they succeeded in combining only good things from both worlds. With the fall of the Wall, this illusion dissapeared, like the country itself." See Предраг Ј. Марковић, *Београд између Истока и Запада 1948–1956* [*Belgrade between East and West*] (Службени лист СРЈ Београд, 1996), 515–524. The author kindly thanks historian Dr. Predrag J. Marković, who suggested especially useful historical and sociological sources, and Dr. Annie Randall for her help in revising the essay.
2. See J. Alcock, *Explaining Yugoslavia* (New York: Columbia University Press, 2000).
3. See Ненад Љубинковић, "Прошлост, садашњост и будућност тзв. новокомпоноване народне музике и турбо фолка" [The Past, Present and Future of "Newly Composed" Folk Music and Turbofolk] in *Расковник* 143 (1999): 95–98.
4. In the former Soviet Union, such activities were called *samodejatelnost* (*самодеятельность*)—literally "self-activity," derived from Marx's term *Selbsttätigkeit*. For the main features of these activities, see Martin Boiko, "The Latvian Folk Music Movement in the 1980s and

1990s: From 'Authenticity' to 'Postfolklore' and Onwards," in *The Word of Music* 43 (Bamberg: Verlag für Wissenschaft und Bildung, 2001), 113–14.

5. See Mark E. Forry, " 'To The Café Every Night': Tamburica Music and Café Life in Vojvodina," in *зборник Матице српске за сценске уметности и музику* [Neofolk Culture—the Audience and Its Stars], vol. 8–9 (Нови Сад Матица српска, 1991), 143–52; Milena Drag-ićević-Šešić, *Neofolk kultura—publika i njene zvezde* (Novi Sad: Sremski Karlovci, Izdavačka knjižarnica Zorana Stojanovića, 1994), 53, 127, and 129.

6. Until the 1990s these terms signified music directed at workers and agricultural laborers. See Јасмина Милојевић *Од народне музике до турбо фолка* [From Folk Music to Turbo Folk], *Политика* 1 (Feb. 6, 2002): 23.

7. "This term appeared at the beginning of the 1990s and signified a music direction, subcultural style and—more widely conceived—a worldview." Cited in Ivana Kronja, *The Fatal Glow: Mass Psychology and Aesthetics of Turbo-Folk Subculture* (Belgrade: Tehnokratia, 2001), 10. This term signifies a belonging to the elite *nouveau riches* of the '90s; it was also "another shock-absorber of social discontent, an amazingly efficient invention of the Serbian media" in the same period. See Јасмина Милојевић, *Од народне музике до турбо фолка* [From Folk Music to Turbo Folk], 23; Ivana Kronja, *The Fatal Glow*, 120.

8. See Dimitrije O. Golemović, "Da li je novokomponovana narodna muzika zaista narodna?" [Is the Newly Composed Folk Music Really Folk Music?], *Etnomuzikološki ogledi* (1997): 175–83; Milena Dragićević-Šešić, *Neofolk kultura*, 57 and 123–25. For many important observations about newly composed folk and turbofolk, see *Antologija turbo folka—Pesme iz stomaka naroda*, eds. Goran Tarlać and Vladimir Đurić Đura (Belgrade, Studentski kulturni centar, 2001).

9. See Dragićević-Šešić, *Neofolk kultura*, 56; Ivan Čolović, *Divlja književnost* [Wild Literature] (Belgrade: Nolit, 1985).

10. For more details about cultural models in Serbia during the '80s and early '90s see Dragićević-Šešić, *Neofolk kultura*, 212–19.

11. See Eric D. Gordy, *The Culture of Power in Serbia: Nationalism and the Destruction of Alternatives* (University Park: Pennsylvania State University Press, 1999), 107.

12. The transformation of Serbian collective musical taste took more than half a century to achieve (see Ненад Љубинковић, "Прошлост, садашњост и будућност тзв новокомпоноване народне музике и турбо фолка"; 141) [The Past, Present and Future of "Newly Composed" Folk Music and Turbofolk], in this chapter I examine only the period after World War II.

13. The beginnings of the Serbian state date from the ninth century. As an independent country and kingdom it existed until the mid-fifteenth century when it was conquered by the Turks. During the period of Turkish rule, mass migrations of Serbs occurred from the south to the north and northwest. A new Serbian state gained autonomy in the first half of nineteenth century. It was again an independent kingdom until 1919 at which time it was incorporated into the Kingdom of Serbs, Croats, and Slovenians, later renamed the Kingdom of Yugoslavia. After the civil war of 1941–1945 a communist government took over and the history of SFRJ began. Good sources for twentieth-century Serbian history are J. Lampe, *Yugoslavia as History: Twice there Was a Country* (Cambridge: Cambridge University Press, 1996, 2000); J. Alcock, *Explaining Yugoslavia* (New York: Columbia University Press, 2000).

14. Belgrade's Council for Democratic Changes began work on this subject recently; results are not yet available. The preliminary investigation first appeared in the paper Наташа Милићевић, "О српском грађанству 1945–50 у мемоаристици с краја XX века," in *Историја XX века* [The Serbian Bourgeoisie 1945–1950 in Late 20th-Century Memoirs," in *20th Century History*], vol. 2 (Belgrade: Institute of the Contemporary History, 2001), 111–27. I thank historian Ranka Gašić for this information.

15. Eric Hobsbawm in *The Invention of Tradition*, eds. Eric Hobsbawm and Terence Ranger (Cambridge: Cambridge University Press, 1989), 1–2.

16. All of them were immediately recognized by the international community (in contrast to the unrecognized, newly formed Federal Republic of Yugoslavia).

17. The sanctions were declared by the European Union in 1991 and then by the United Nations in 1992.

18. This country is a remnant of the former Yugoslavia and is made up of Serbia and Montenegro only.

19. About the passive reception of popular music, see Dragićević-Šešić, *Neofolk kultura*, 41 and 50.

20. For more information on new folk spectacles in Serbia, see Dimitrije O. Golemović, "Narodna pesma: od obreda do spektakla" [Folk Song: From Ritual to Spectacle], in *Opera od obreda do muzičke forme* [Opera From Ritual to Musical Form] (Belgrade: Fakultet muzičke umetnosti, 2001), 21–25.

21. Golemović, "Narodna pesma" [Folk Song: From Ritual to Spectacle], 25.

22. Speaking of the political function of the turbofolk, [Mlađan] Dinkić says: "In all that poverty and misery the people found enough energy to survive. Very often its grief found expression in popular songs. In this it was generously helped by the media, which supported newly composed folk music as a means of suppressing discontent and any thought of revolt." Quoted in Ivana Kronja, *The Fatal Glow*, 121.

23. It may be associated both with rural and urban surroundings, love, patriotism, nostalgia, and the like. For the classification of lyrics, see Ivan Čolović, *Divlja književnost* [Wild Literature], (1985): 150–59.

24. For a more detailed account of these singing styles, see Jelena Gligorijević (Jovanović), "Tri rustikalne pesme iz repertoara Lepe Brene—veza sa tradicijom i odstupanja od nje" [Three *Rustic* "Newly Composed" Folk Songs from the Repertoire of the Singer Lepa Brena] in *Rad XXXVII Kongresa folklorista Jugoslavije, Plitvička jezera 1990* (1991): 203–204.

25. The term "authentic" in this chapter refers to its classic meaning; namely, it signifies music that had been inherited orally from the older generations, with musical features that display its great age. We find this term used also in relation to contemporaneous folk art revitalization movements in Baltic countries. See Martin Boiko, "The Latvian Folk Music Movement in the 1980s and 1990s," 114–15.

26. As A. Simić says, "'authentic' folk ... is a minority music on a level with symphonic music," quoted in Eric Gordy, *The Culture of Power in Serbia*, 129, n. 56.

27. Edward Shiels, *Tradition* (London: Faber & Faber, 1981), 285–86.

28. That is, from representatives of "the elitist cultural model" (the term used according to Milena Dragićević-Šešić), *Neofolk kultura*, 214.

29. See Martin Boiko, "The Latvian Folk Music Movement in the 1980s and 1990s," 114–16.

30. See Јелена Јовановић, *Српска сеоска песма данас—интерференција сеоског и градског културног модела* [Contemporary Serbian Rural Song–Cross-Fertilization of Rural and Urban Cultural Models] in *Pro Musica* 162 (2000): 33; *О (бео)градским покушајима оживљавања сеоског певања и свирања* [Urban attempts in Belgrade to Revitalize Rural Singing and Playing], in *Pro Musica* 163 (2000): 32–33.

31. For more about these ensembles, see Kim Burton, "Feature: The Serbian Singing Scene, New Trad," in *The Singer* (October/November 2001): 18–20.

32. See Сања Ранковић, *Прилог оживљавању српског певања и свирања-Етномузиколошки одсек Музичке школе «Мокрањац» у Београду* [A Contribution to the Revitalization of Serbian Singing and Playing—Department of Ethnomusicology of the "Mokranjac" Music School in Belgrade] in *Pro Musica* 165 (2001): 32.

33. Many of the performers are members of the Serbian Orthodox Church.

34. For more details, see Jelena Jovanović, *Rural Music in Serbian Towns and Two Contrasting Aesthetic Reactions on the Part of the Audience*, in *Man and Music* (Belgrade: Vedes, 2003), 547–552.

35. Гордана Благојевић, *Савремена рецепција традиционалне српске народне музике као елемент етничког идентитета*, диломски рад [Contemporary Reception of Traditional Serbian Folk Music as an Element of Ethnic Identity] (Универзитет у Београду, Филозофски факултет, Одељење за етнологију и антропологију, Београд , 1999), 31–36. Or, as ethnologist Bojan Žikić wrote: "as in myths ... or in practically every form of traditional creation, there is a universal unchangeable message ... that waits for its discovering, receiving and further delivery." Бојан Жикић, *Моба, Вазда жњејеш, Јано, српске традиционалне песме женске певачке групе МОБА, самостално издање МОБЕ, 2001* [Moba, You Just Keep on Reaping: Serbian Traditional Songs of the Female Vocal Group MOBA, an Independent MOBA Edition, 2001], in *Светигора* (Цетиње, 2002), 56 and 127–28.

36. "Not individual, but ancient communal temperament, hereditary, instinctive and atavistic," quoted in Владимир Дворниковић, *Карактерологија Југословена* [The Characterology of the Yugoslavs] (Belgrade: Geca Kon, 1938), 358.

37. Дворниковић, *Карактерологија Југословена* [The Characterology of the Yugoslavs], 358.

38. These general qualities of Serbian and Balkan musical folklore are considered outstanding and important not only for the proponents of the movement under discussion here, but for members of other nations as well. Their significance for Americans is described in Mirjana Laušević, "Biranje nasleđa: zašto Amerikanci pevaju pesme sa Balkana," in *Reč* 65/11 (2002): 391–402, a translation of "Choosing a Heritage: Why Americans Sing Balkan Songs," a paper presented at the Humanistic Studies Center, University in Minnesota, Spring 2002.

39. According to Edward Shils, *Tradition*, 232.

40. Бојан Жикић, *Фолклоризам као концепт и последице његовог деловања на савремену народну културу*, дипломски рад [Folklorism as a Concept and the Consequences of its Impact on Contemporary Folk Culture], (Универзитет у Београду, Филозофски факултет, Одељење за етнологију и антропологију, Београд, 1993); Гордана Благојевић, *Савремена рецепција традиционалне српске народне музике као елемент етничког идентитета* [The Contemporary Reception of Traditional Serbian Folk Music as an Element of Ethnic Identity]. Драгослав Антонијевић, "Фолклоризам—неофолклоризам" [Folklorism—Neofolklorism] in *Сабор народног стваралаштеа Србије, 1, IX* (Топола, 1995): 4–5.

CHAPTER 8

Hands Off My Instrument!

Helen Reddington

> Rock is a pedestal sport, as in being a Monarch—wherever possible
> a boy inherits the throne—females are not thought to be the stuff
> worship/idols are made for/of. Girls are expected to grovel in the
> mezzanine while the stud struts his stuff up there, while a girl with
> the audacity to go on stage is jeered, sneered and leered up to ...
> a guitar in the hands of a man boasts "cock"—the same instrument
> in female hands (to a warped mind) screams "castration."[1]

This chapter focuses on a moment in British rock music history that began
roughly in 1976 when some young women in rock bands, instead of taking
the usual female role of lead singer backed by male instrumentalists, actually picked up electronic instruments, notably guitars, and played them
themselves. This was an unusual phenomenon, almost without precedent
in the fields of rock and pop music.[2] Still considered unusual, especially
in the UK, nearly thirty years later, it is often taken for granted that a
woman's role in a rock or pop band will be that of vocalist. I aim to pinpoint
the reason this phenomenon was so short-lived and why it did not lead to
the revolution in rock music that some of us expected.[3] I explore the female
musicians' participation in the instrumental side of sound creation in
bands, the power this seemed to bestow upon them, and the media's response
to both phenomena. I link the rise of these women instrumentalists both
to the anyone-can-do-it ethic of the punk movement and the Equal Opportunities Act of 1975, and locate their decline in Britain's sociopolitical
atmosphere at the time of the Falklands War in the early 1980s.

FEMININE MUSIC OR FEMALE MUSIC?

Previously, women instrumentalists such as American artists Joni Mitchell or Joan Baez tended to be of the folk rock, singer-songwriter variety.[4] In Britain, this genre was underrepresented; Joan Armatrading was one of the few to provide relief from singers such as Twiggy and Clodagh Rodgers who were promoted wearing frilly shirts with wavy blonde hair and come-hither smiles.[5] The only female rocker in the British charts was bass player Suzi Quatro,[6] yet her "sole purveyor" image gave her a novelty status, which was unfortunate because she was a talented musician with a strong track record in the United States.[7] From its start, the London punk scene prominently featured women instrumentalists, which was almost revolutionary for my generation. Susan McClary placed great faith in what she called "New Wave" music and its openness to female rock instrumentalists: "Its style incorporates other features that qualify as cultural noise: the bizarre visual appearance of many of its proponents, texts with express political content, and deliberate inclusion of blacks and of women (not as the traditional "dumb chicks" singing to attract the libidinous attention of the audience, but—taboo of taboos—as competent musicians playing instruments, even drums).[8]

In the mid 1970s, prog-rock bands (such as Yes, Deep Purple, and Emerson, Lake, and Palmer) seemed to have the music market all sewn up until punk arrived and exposed their innate conservatism and exclusivity. As suddenly as the Sex Pistols appeared, Siouxsie and the Banshees made a mark on the underground music scene; we heard Siouxsie's sessions on John Peel's late-night show and, at the same time, became aware of Gaye Advert, Tina Weymouth, and X-ray Spex. The normally male-centered music press started to review and interview bands playing at punk venues that included women in their instrumental line ups. Just as suddenly, serious opposition to the phenomenon of women in rock bands began to appear in other sections of the press, and every aspect of the female instrumentalist became fair game for criticism, not only her musical skill, but also her appearance, her relationships with the men in the band, and so on.

The first backlash against female instrumentalists appeared in the music media. There was a strong sentiment in rock newspapers (*New Musical Express* [*NME*], *Sounds*, and *Melody Maker*) that female instrumentalists were just a gimmick.[9] The worth of punk rock itself was debated in each paper's editorial meetings. Caroline Coon describes the difficulties she had in persuading her colleagues at *Melody Maker* that something new was happening in music: "Not only I was a woman (and therefore they weren't taking me seriously), but I was telling them there was something quite threatening occurring. I thought this was going to be the new defining counterculture, which was coming after hippies; it was the cultural dialectic, the reaction against the perceived failure of hippiedom."[10]

Within this debate, which essentially reflected the hippie generation's realization that they had now become "the establishment," there was added discomfort about the influx of women into punk and new wave. Sometimes this was manifested in remarks about the incompetence of the musician, as in this review of Talking Heads' Tina Weymouth:

> Tina has short blonde hair and black jeans and looks sexy like a girl on a tennis court. Its only Tina who fills out the sound with her strong bass line. She has a nice new red and white bass and jerks her head with every beat, worriedly checking first her fingering and then making sure she is playing the correct string. Sometimes she glances anxiously over to David to make sure everything's okay.... When Tina left the stage her blouse was sticking to her back—a sign of something.[11]

The "we can tolerate incompetence if the woman is sexy" style of review was very common and was often applied to Gaye Advert, who played bass for The Adverts. Often shown without her bass guitar, her photograph appeared frequently next to small news items or gig dates. She was described as a "pretty bassetist;"[12] indeed, the very diminutive "punkette" was often used to describe not only female band members but also other prominent female participants in the subculture.[13] This could be seen as an attempt to put women in "their place," and editors seemed to go to extreme lengths to undo the appreciation a female artist had earned. For instance, NME included a couscous recipe by respected rock poet Patti Smith (it had never published a recipe before) and finished the feature with the following: "Joe Stevens, our man in New York, pronounced the couscous delicious and added that Patti could roast his raisins anytime."[14] A later NME interview "with Patti Smith" by Paul Morley consisted mainly of quotations from Lenny Kaye about her, her music, and what it was like to be in a band with her.[15] She was, therefore, defined by male journalists, musicians, and editors for the consumption of male readers who could, after reading this article, rest assured that Smith possessed culinary as well as revolutionary skills. As Sally Potter observes:

> Femininity, demands the appearance of lack of skill and emphasises nurturance and appreciation of the skills of men.... Success for women often means gaining the precarious position of token achiever in a male-dominated profession. This position is

circumscribed in such a way that as more women achieve in a given area they are forced to compete with each other for the same space rather than the space itself expanding.[16]

Not all female punk instrumentalists exhibited traditional feminine behavior and appearance; the portrayal of The Slits on one of their album covers (in which they appear naked from the waist up, and covered in mud) serves as an example. Indeed, when rock journalist Viv Goldman proposed writing about the album and showed the cover to her editor, his response was, "Take it away from me. How can they do that? They look so revolting and so fat."[17]

GATEKEEPERS OF THE MOMENT, GATEKEEPERS OF HISTORY

Regardless of how male editors and reviewers felt, the foregrounding of women musicians in the music press provided instant role models for girls who had none beforehand; as a response to this, many other women took to the stage. In Brighton alone there were between fifteen and twenty women playing in various bands. Unlike male performers who, at the beginning of the punk era, tended to draw from genres such as glam rock and heavy metal, many female artists emulated the Velvet Underground and its two female members (extraordinary for the time), drummer Mo Tucker and singer Nico, who later became a solo performer.[18]

Given the great number of women who played in Brighton, England, at this moment in the late 1970s, few female band members are remembered in the male version of punk rock history, and those who are remembered represent only a small minority of the women who were actually involved in the British scene. I speculated that were there other women instrumentalists who had been written out of rock history, and that their erasure served to reinforce the male aura of this type of music. I was interested to find these women and talk to them about their experiences from the time of their first performances to their bands' demise.

In 2000, I distributed questionnaires to three hundred British newspapers in which I asked women rock musicians to respond to questions about their music making between 1976 and 1983.[19]

My request (which was addressed to the Letters editor) appeared in either the letters column or a small feature of its own. It was sometimes situated under a heading that ridiculed the request. For instance, the *Lincolnshire Daily Echo* provided the headline, "Ladies: were you punk rockers?" while the *Newcastle Sunday Sun's* headline read, "Punkette Call." The letter was sometimes rewritten by editors so that it did not specifically refer to women.[20] There were several responses from men wanting to be involved, as well as some anonymous hate mail from northwest England. Of around forty responses I received, I was able to retrieve approximately twenty useful questionnaires. A journalist at *The Independent,* a national broadsheet paper, picked up the story from his local paper and this led to responses from more well-known women such as Poly Styrene, who had fronted X-ray Spex, as well as some interest from tabloid newspapers and from two television documentary companies.[21]

Generally, the questionnaire responses indicated that the less commercial success a band had achieved, the less concerned the band member was about their short shelf life, or the eventual historical suppression of their activity. Members of bands that had had higher profiles, however, identified many ways in which they had been deliberately forgotten. For instance, Enid Williams, whose heavy metal band Girlschool[22] was performing all over Britain at this time, talked to me about the band's absence from retrospective television documentaries:

> One thing that really shocked me ... there was a programme some years ago about Heavy Metal ... and it was an hour long, and they had the Zeppelins and the Deep Purples, but they also had lots of really tiny little bands that most people would never have heard of, and they didn't mention Girlschool once.... By 1981 we had a gold album, got to number 5 in the album charts, and in the singles charts and got a silver record over here, got two thousand people a night, six week tours, you know, things like that.[23]

Christine Robertson, who managed The Slits, found that controversy was much more marketable for male bands than for female bands. Although The Sex Pistols suffered censorship, many other male punk bands did not; the controversial Slits, however, in spite of employing top record pluggers, could not get radio airplay in Britain at all, apart from on John Peel's show.[24] Robertson recalls:

> In this country there was an absolute media block, or brick wall, which could not be penetrated. Because they were girls, and because they were outrageous, because their sexuality was confrontational ... I don't want to get into a syndrome of 'Oh it's all the men's fault, they were threatened by the women,' but I'd have to say that all the media industry, apart from record pluggers, were men. By the time you got to somebody who was gonna make a decision, like a radio producer, it was a man. And I think they threatened men, or their reputation threatened men.[25]

It was not until they played in America and were broadcast on the many small student radio stations that their recordings reached a wider audience.

Other bands experienced different problems with "gatekeepers." For instance, Dollymixture were determined to have some control over their music, and this was not what the record companies expected:

> We signed to Chrysalis quite quickly and did one single with them but the single was crap. After that we nearly signed to A&M. Basically we demanded so much and we were quite stroppy. A lot of people who were interested [were put off because] we were so fussy. We did have managers but we fell foul of them because we wanted to do it all on our own terms. We would insist on going to the record company and saying we want total artistic control, no we're not doing covers, no we don't want our photographs on the front, no.... I think we just blew a lot of things by being like that.[26]

Another form of gatekeeping, violence, was much more direct and was not exclusively targeted toward male punk bands. Lucy O'Brien, keyboard player of the all-women Southampton band The Catholic Girls, describes a gig at a skinhead pub: "We had no idea before we got there that it was a skinhead pub.... Skinheads just hated us; it ended in complete disaster because they were throwing cans and bottles at us when we were on stage and when we came off stage they followed us round to our van where we were loading up instruments and just collectively beat everyone up."[27]

Violence against women by men could also be of a sexual nature. Some informants told of experiences varying in seriousness from blatant public groping to rape. Evidently, the co-option of female-gendered sexual clothing was not always empowering or seen as an ironic statement, particularly in the less sophisticated provinces. Occasionally, threats came from women within the subculture itself; for instance, a local punk woman sprayed a graffiti death threat on a hoarding in Brighton in an attempt to scare me off the stage. Another aggressive activity was spitting, purported to have been started by The Damned's drummer, Rat Scabies. Women were not excused from being the targets of "gobbing."[28]

THATCHERISM AND WOMEN IN PUNK

Early in the 1980s the British punk scene went deep underground. The number of female instrumentalists in bands declined greatly; what Caroline Coon described as a "radical step forward for women in rock 'n' roll"[29] faded from rock consciousness. It is interesting to explore the demise of female intrumentalists within the broader sociopolitical context of Falklands War–era Britain.

During this period of militarism, rock's many similarities to National Service were especially evident: its opportunities for leadership and noise-making; a plentiful supply of desirable, phallic weapons (instruments); male camaraderie; capture of and expansion of (sonic) territory; power struggles; and a distant relationship to the opposite sex (women).[30] Both rock and military life allow *all* young people to express anger, and, as with warfare, the representatives of dissatisfaction are predominantly young men. In rock music young men signify anger and unrest while young women signify peace and tranquility. In Margaret Thatcher's Britain of 1983, the prime minister herself became the Britannia-style figurehead and "the embodiment of the spirit of Britain in travail and then in triumph."[31]

Punk's role in this identification of rock and militarism on the one hand, and the prime minister with Britannia herself on the other, while difficult to gauge, is impossible to dismiss. Did The Sex Pistols clear the way for the anarchic and antiroyalist thought that allowed Margaret Thatcher to take on the iconic role of queen? Though a woman led the charge into war, the Falklands conflict seems to have reinstated traditional maleness—a shift reflected in popular music: as synthesiser pop developed in the early 1980s (albeit a feminized male performance genre, sans phallus), and the Falklands War began, "real men" went off to fight the "Argies." At the same time, the influx of women into rock bands (that had appeared to both terrify and sexually excite male commentators) began to ebb; women returned to their roles as vocalists, allowing men to reclaim their technology and the power that went with it.

In a stroke of genius, Thatcher had already co-opted the entrepreneurial part of punk, detached it from its political meaning, and recreated it as enterprise culture. As Jon Savage observes:

> The Conservatives' victory did mark an end to the period of social unrest which Punk had charted so intimately. The post-war consensus was now over. "Try it": now people had. The very freedom which Punk had not only sung about, but enacted in every possible sense, was now hijacked by the New Right to mean something quite different: an inequality that was not only institutionalized but installed as a ruling cultural and social principle.[32]

The Conservative Party under Thatcher had been changed to appeal to a populace who regarded themselves as estranged individuals rather than a body of the discontented working class.[33] The increasing violence of punk gigs, fueled by tabloid "moral panics,"[34] proved divisive for punk subculture. It became necessary for some bands to rationalize their activities as a small businesses, with self-employed personnel, and as such to focus on moneymaking over communication, on giving pleasure rather than provocation. As Punk became more commercial and less confrontational, women were pushed aside, their disturbing presence almost eradicated from the market. Punk rock, which for many men had been just another development of the rock genre, had provided women unprecedented access to a voice and a platform;[35] it was, however, impossible for women to consolidate their achievements. Burdened by their marginalization and responsibility for social change, the girls who joined bands at this time were unable to "secure the conditions for their own continuance."[36] The boys, meanwhile, could "have a good time," with one eye on a deal. I was told repeatedly of a combination of "burnout" (caused by constant touring and recording schedules), and also a sense of racing against time. In spite of the U.S. female punk stars' relatively advanced years, in Britain women artists had to be young; the cut-off age appeared to be twenty-three.[37] Female intrumentalists' importance in the world of punk did not influence the outside world of marketing and commerce and its obsession with youth.

"EQUAL" OPPORTUNITIES

The influx I have identified in the late 1970s may have been a sort of "equal-ops blip" in the United Kingdom resulting from the 1975 Equal Opportunities Act. Discourse on this topic—both in general and in relation to rock music—often fails to take into account inherent power imbalances between the sexes. As Christine Griffin observes,

> Debates about women's position in non-traditional jobs have been dominated by the ideology of equal opportunities, particularly since the sex discrimination legislation was passed in 1975. In these terms, both women and men can be discriminated against on the grounds of sex, since there is no concept of differential power. Lone "token" women (and men) in non-traditional occupations can then be presented as evidence that particular jobs are equally open to women and men.[38]

This power differential, evidenced by rock culture's predominantly male ethos, is accentuated by the actual *sounds* of rock music, which further limit female participation. Susan McClary, after her initial excitement about New Wave music, modified her opinion of its liberatory potential based on her reading of its characteristic sounds:

> The options available to a woman musician in rock music are especially constrictive, for this musical discourse is typically

characterized by its phallic backbeat. It is possible to try and downplay that beat, to attempt to defuse that energy—but this strategy
often results in music that sounds enervated or stereotypically
"feminine." It is also possible to appropriate the phallic energy of
rock and to demonstrate (as Chrissie Hynde, Joan Jett and Lita
Ford do so well) that boys don't have any corner on that market.
But that beat can always threaten to overwhelm: witness Janet
Jackson's containment by producers Jimmy Jam and Terry Lewis
in (ironically) her song "Control."[39]

Mavis Bayton's studies of women in rock indicate that "the problem was
that so much music had been labelled 'male,' that only the folk area was
considered ideologically safe. Paradoxically, then, the feminist challenge
looked likely to result in retreat from rock and amplified music altogether."[40]
There was, says Bayton, a continuous debate about noisy music and women.
According to Lucy Green, the concepts of rebellion and female sexuality
in the mid-70s were still male-defined; the task of punk was to define these
areas for girls who wanted to join in. Even now, "Girls are . . . seen to avoid
performance on electric or very loud instruments, especially those associated with popular music, most notably electric guitars and drums. By
contrast, boys are depicted as flocking to these instruments, and to active
involvement with popular music.[41]

In critiques such as *The Sex Revolts*, the authors fail to underline the
consequences of the unequal social positions of males (who operate from
positions of power) and females (whose relative power is much less, particularly because the access they have to communication opportunities is
controlled by men). Their disgust at some women's attempts to rework
pop (as opposed to rock) in order to empower themselves within what is
assumed to be the more feminine commercial music form is palpable. For
Reynolds and Press (whose book underscores the rock ethos even in its
aggressive style of writing),[42] there is a "no win situation" for women. Here,
they amplify a comment made by Frith and McRobbie:

> We should probably admit that we don't find representations of
> "strength" in pop particularly compelling. The autonomy of figures
> like Lennox and Joan Armatrading has the reek of mental hygiene
> and health-and-efficiency. As Simon Frith and Angela McRobbie
> wrote of the soft-core feminism of Helen Reddy's "I Am Woman:"
> "What you hear is the voice of the idealized consumer, if the
> commodity for consumption in this instance is a packaged version
> of women's liberation." The posture of tyrannical, marauding
> omnipotence is pure rock 'n' roll; benign self-empowerment isn't.[43]

Thus rock's attitudes have become entrenched and made into rules, making the semantics of rock difficult to revolutionize while, at the same time, rock continues to hanker for revolution. Elizabeth Nelson's study of the underground press in the late 1960s and early 1970s points to a major issue concerning cultural radicalism. In her discussion of the counter-culture's attitudes to women, she remarks that the protagonists basically had a lot in common with mainstream culture, and thus were not challenging hegemony in a very important area: "The question of women's liberation was not only grasped too late and inadequately, but more importantly, women were apparently never considered as suitable candidates in the search for allies.... Even if the countercultural revolution had been 'won,' it would, judging from the evidence presented in the underground press, have been a revolution achieved by and on behalf of men."[44] The countercultural aspect of punk rock in Britain was suppressed gradually by the Queen's Jubilee, the wedding of Charles and Diana, and the Falklands War in a phenomenon described by Iain Chambers as "principled nationalism."[45] In rock, any gains made by women were trampled under the feet of new technology's hold on the imagination of rock and pop audiences; once again, what you could *buy* to make your music cutting edge became rock's ideology.

Thus the flow of women into rock bands as instrumentalists was cut off: first by the gatekeepers in the media and the music business, then by antagonists within the punk subculture itself, and finally by social historians (who, in the early 1980s, delightedly jumped on postmodernism to distract us from the influence of feminist philosophy).[46] Rumsey and Little observe that "feminists know that if rock/pop was really revolutionary, they would be embraced as the greatest rebels of all—real rebels, the genuine article, not just another piece in the jigsaw of popular ephemera."[47] Empirical observation of rock music workshops has shown me the physical domination of young men over young women in the allocation of noise-making instruments. Aided and abetted by the inflexible structures of not only hegemonic culture, but also subculture, the sub-subculture of the female rock "voice" looks likely to be suppressed in Britain for years to come.

Notes

[See website for photo to accompany this chapter.]

1. Julie Burchill and Tony Parsons, *The Boy Looked at Johnny: The Obituary of Rock 'n' Roll* (London: Pluto Press, 1978), 86.
2. A number of women's dance bands, jazz ensembles, and symphony orchestras had, however, flourished earlier in the twentieth century. See Sherrie Tucker's *Swing Shift* (Durham, NC: Duke University Press, 2000); Carol Neuls-Bates' "Women's Orchestras in the United States 1925–45" in Jane Bowers and Judith Tick, eds., *Women Making Music: The Western Art*

Tradition 1150–1950 (Urbana and Chicago: University of Illinois Press, 1987); and Greta Kent's *A View from the Bandstand* (London: Sheba Feminist Publishers, 1983).

3. As a bass guitar player in a mixed-gender punk band in Brighton in 1977 (with a subsequent seven-year career as a bassist and, later, singer/guitarist in my own bands), I shared these expectations. I felt as though I were part of a major change, for it seemed that everywhere I looked bands included female members as equal partners in music making.

4. While their lyrics were pointed, cutting, and, often, aesthetically challenging, their music was rarely "aggressive." The power of noisemaking was not at their disposal.

5. By contrast, Vivienne Westwood's fetishistic clothes designs characterized the genesis of punk in London's Chelsea. (The assistants in her shop, "Sex," Jordan, and Sue Catwoman, were often photographed alongside The Sex Pistols. Jordan later sang and performed with Adam and the Ants.) The women's wearing of fetishistic clothing in public amounted to a sort of "castration of fetishism" according to Caroline Coon; it also underscored the message of their strong and assertive music. Promoter Andy Czesowski put on an evening that featured women bands with this sound and look on the closing night of his club, the Roxy, in 1977.

6. Contrary to what fans may have assumed given Quatro's macho image, her hit material was written by male pop songwriters.

7. Quatro, who claims to have had no role models herself (interview BBC Radio 4 "You and Yours," July 7, 2000), had to work hard to achieve her position; she was not impressed by the quality of musicianship of the new female rockers and must have been irritated to witness the enthusiastic amateurism of some of these musicians. In this assessment she seemed to miss the point that "there was no issue in teenybop of 'paying dues' . . . nor was there in punk rock." Dave Laing, *One Chord Wonders* (Milton Keynes and Philadelphia: Open University Press, 1985), 84.

8. Susan McClary, "Afterword," in Jacques Attali, *Noise: The Political Economy of Music* (Minneapolis: University of Minnesota Press, 1985), 156–57.

9. For an exploration of rock press attitudes toward young women performers see Helen Davies, "All Rock and Roll is Homosocial: The Representation of Women in the British Rock Music Press," *Popular Music* 20/3 (2001): 295–313.

10. Author's interview with Caroline Coon, January 24, 2002.

11. Review of Talking Heads at CBGBs by Miles, *NME*, April 2, 1977.

12. Bad review of the Adverts by Tony Stewart, *NME*, April 16, 1977.

13. See Helen Reddington, *Lady Punks in Bands: A Subculturette?* In Muggleton, *The Post-subcultures Reader* (London: Berg, 2003), 239–251.

14. *NME*, April 16, 1977.

15. *NME*, April 1, 1978.

16. Sally Potter, *On Shows*, in *Framing Feminism*, London: Pandora, 1987, 30.

17. The editor was Richard Williams at *Melody Maker*. From author's interview with Caroline Coon. It is important to note that there was also a strong groundswell of writing that criticized the macho attitudes of rock that were carried into punk music. The Stranglers in particular were singled out for criticism; slightly older than many of the other punk bands, they used misogynistic lyrics—a standard means of expressing rock rebellion—to make their statement. Phil McNeil, for instance, wrote a strongly worded critique of the "Rattus Norvegicus" album's lyrics that alluded to "giving the woman some stick." He went on, however, to remark that the group possesses the aggressive stance that is "today's currency." *NME*, April 30, 1977.

18. Courtney Love describes the Velvet Underground as "a band that only sold 80,000 records, but everyone who bought the record started a band." *The Guardian Guide,* April 29, 2000.

19. Although I concentrated mainly on urban areas (with a distribution of over thirty thousand), I also wrote to papers that served more isolated communities in an attempt to contact "retired" women instrumentalists. Addresses came from the Brad directory, published by EMAP Media, London.

20. I had forgotten the power of the press as gatekeepers. *The Daily Mail* (national UK daily paper), has a large female readership in Britain. When they contacted me for an interview, I agreed, thinking that this would allow me to contact more of the "forgotten" band members throughout the UK. They also asked for contact details of some of the women I had spoken to. Just before publication, I was asked to supply details such as my partner's name, age, and occupation. I refused because I could not see the relevance of this to the research, which I

was undertaking, not my partner. When the interviews were published (using women I had suggested), my name and contact details were omitted, thus rendering the exercise useless.

21. The tabloids and television companies seemed to think they had found another source of "fishnet stocking" stories with which to titillate their audience; this illustrates the double bind of female instrumentalists—they are attractive to both males and females, but for different reasons, yet the titillation factor is stressed almost exclusively by the media. The extraordinary blend of hostility, salaciousness, and patronization toward female punk instrumentalists in the British print media was (and still is) mirrored by television and radio.

22. Although Girlschool is not a punk rock band, they were active within my time parameter and were cited by other musicians as "visible."

23. Author's interview with Enid Williams, November 30, 1999.

24. Peel describes the recorded sessions for his show as "classic." Author's interview with John Peel, October 20, 2001.

25. Author's interview with Christine Robertson, October 9, 2001.

26. Author's interview with Rachel Dollymixture, February 2, 2000.

27. Author's interview with Lucy O'Brien, December 6, 2001.

28. The fanzine *Guttersnipe* reported: "On came the Slits and all the lads were shouting abuse, the wankers were making me sick. The Slits started.... They all started spitting and Ari told the band to stop. She told one of the audience to come and get on stage and when he did she gobbed a greenie right on his face, good one Ari. He almost fell off the stage with shock I don't know what he was expecting." From issue no. 7, undated.

29. Caroline Coon, January 24, 2002.

30. "A lot of people got into it almost like an equivalent of National Service.... Punk as a replacement for National Service! The great things it taught you were petty theft and evasion, so it made you kind of cunning in a way I'd not seen before. I would imagine that being in a band would give you similar skills." Author's interview with John Peel, October 20, 2001.

31. The full quotation reads: "The identification of the Prime Minister with the renewed military grandeur of Great Britain was accomplished in part through the language of female representation; it was natural, as it were, to see Mrs. Thatcher as the spirit of Britain in travail and then triumph, because of the way that spirit of Britain has been characterized, through its famous great queens on one hand, and the convention of Britannia on the other." Quoted in Marina Warner, *Monuments and Maidens: The Allegory of the Female Form* (London: Weidenfeld and Nicholson, 1985), 41.

32. John Savage, *England's Dreaming* (London and Boston: Faber and Faber, 1991), 541.

33. They "appealed not so much to the rich as to those with little or no capital of their own, and who, therefore, were frightened of losing what little they had. It was the small employers and the self-employed ... who saw themselves as the prime victims of 'Edward Heath's economic policies.'" Vernon Bogdanor, *The Fall of Heath and the End of the Postwar Settlement*, in Stuart Ball and Anthony Seldom, eds., *The Heath Government 1970–1974: A Reappraisal* (London and New York: Longman, 1996), 386.

34. See Stanley Cohen, *Folk Devils and Moral Panics: The Creation of the Mods and Rockers* (Oxford: Martin Robertson, Oxford, 1993).

35. See Stanley Cohen, *Folk Devils and Moral Panics*, for an analysis of the relationship between the British tabloid press and youth subcultural activity.

36. Willis observed that the hippies did not "secure the conditions for their own continuance." Paul E. Willis, *Profane Culture* (London: Routledge and Kegan Paul, 1978), 6.

37. A few years after the Dollymixture split up, guitarist Rachel sent some demos to a record company; they telephoned her because they were interested in her material. When they discovered she was almost thirty, they told her that they never signed a woman over the age of twenty-three. Author's interview with Rachel Dollymixture, February 2, 2000.

38. From Griffin's study of career options for adolescent girls. Christine Griffin, *Typical Girls? Young Women from School to the Job Market* (New York: Routledge, 1985), 155.

39. Susan McClary, *Feminine Endings: Music, Gender, and Sexuality* (Minneapolis: University of Minnesota Press, 1991), 154.

40. "This debate, which came to a boil in the early 1980s and still lingers on, is an interesting manifestation of the wider contradiction within feminism of, on the one hand, wanting to do what men do, and, on the other, wanting to create something altogether different, which expresses women's 'femaleness.' This is currently called the 'sameness/difference' or 'equality/difference' debate" (see, for example, Bacchi 1990 and Scott 1990). Mavis Bayton,

Feminist Musical Practice: Problems and Contradictions, in Tony Bennet, Simon Frith, Lawrence Grossberg, John Shepherd, and Graeme Turner, eds., *Rock and Popular Music: Politics, Policies, Institutions* (New York: Routledge, 1993), 185–86. Bayton herself was a member of a punk band called The Mistakes in the late 1970s.

41. Lucy Green, *Music, Gender, Education* (Cambridge: Cambridge University Press, 1997), 176.

42. Simon Reynolds and Joy Press, *The Sex Revolts: Gender, Rebellion, and Rock 'n' Roll* (London: Serpent's Tail, 1995). Underneath the "shouting" text there are some interesting observations about, for instance, the chastity of The Clash's lyrics (p66), the potential implications of which are not explored in any depth, and this is a wasted opportunity; perhaps the volume (sic) of artists they have chosen to cover (sic) prevents them from analyzing them further.

43. Angela McRobbie and Simon Frith, quoted in Simon Frith and Andrew Goodwin, eds., *On Record* (New York: Routledge, 1990), 385.

44. Elizabeth Nelson, *The British Counterculture 1966–1973: A Study of the Underground Press* (Basingstoke and London: Macmillan, 1989), 138–40.

45. Ian Chambers, *Urban Rhythms* (Basingstoke and London: Macmillan, 1985), 185.

46. See, for instance, Doreen Massey's critique of the "ignoring" of feminism by postmodern theorists David Harvey and Emil Soja in the chapter entitled "Flexible Sexism" of her book *Space, Place, and Gender* (London: Polity, 1994), 214ff.

47. Gina Rumsey and Hilary Little, "Women and Pop: A Series of Lost Encounters," in Angela McRobbie, ed., *Zoot Suits and Secondhand Dresses: An Anthology of Fashion and Music* (London: Macmillan, 1989).

CHAPTER 9

Barbadian *Tuk* Music—
A Fusion of Musical Cultures

Sharon Meredith

Unlike the music of other Caribbean countries, such as Jamaican reggae, the music of Barbados is not world famous and has not enjoyed comparable levels of exposure and development for two key reasons. First, the long, unbroken influence of British culture suppressed local musical forms in the face of what some perceived to be superior Western musics. Barbadian musics were often dismissed as being inferior, generally because much of that music was the music of the working classes, who were predominantly black. This contributed to the beliefs, still held by some Barbadians, that if something doesn't come from "outside," it's "no good," and that Barbados does not have its own indigenous music. Both were expressed to me many times during my fieldwork.[1] Second is the heavy influx of North American music during the twentieth century with the advent of radio and television, and the increased availability of recorded music. Greater mobility and movement of people in and out of Barbados also led to wider exposure to different musical cultures. Much of this happened at a time when Barbados was working to achieve independence from Britain and was gradually realizing that the African heritage of the majority of the population had been lost or suppressed during three hundred years of colonialism. After gaining independence in 1966, steps were taken to establish a Barbadian national identity by drawing on this African heritage and reviving aspects of culture that had disappeared or had been kept alive by a small minority.

One such aspect of culture was *tuk*, a fife and drum music. This chapter examines the history of *tuk*, exploring its African and European heritage. I consider the factors that have influenced *tuk*'s status in Barbados today, the issues surrounding its revival and recontextualization as the indigenous music of Barbados, and its role in the country's cultural heritage and national identity.

HISTORICAL BACKGROUND

Barbados is unusual among the colonized territories of the Caribbean region in that it remained in the hands of one colonizer, Britain, from when it was first settled in 1627 until it gained independence.[2] In its early years, London merchants who were influential with the authorities invested vast amounts of money in the island and in trade with the West Indies. This led to the establishment of a permanent military garrison in 1780 to protect the island from potential invasion by other colonizing countries such as France and Spain, and also to provide a British military base in the area.

Early requirements for labor on the plantations were met by importing indentured servants, mainly from England, Scotland, and Ireland. Some of these went voluntarily, others were criminals exported to empty the jails, and some were simply kidnapped off the streets of large cities. During the English Civil War (1642–1652) and Cromwell's regime during the 1650s, many prisoners of war, and those deemed to be unacceptable to the prevailing authorities, were also shipped to the colonies.

During the 1640s, the Barbadian sugar industry developed rapidly, aided by Dutch planters who were leaving Brazil because of civil war there with the Portuguese. The Dutch introduced the Barbadian planters to many aspects of sugar production, including importing African slaves to work the plantations because they were cheaper than indentured servants. By 1700 more than a hundred thousand Africans had been taken to Barbados and, as the number of slaves increased, the number of indentured servants decreased. In an effort to reduce communication and troublemaking among the slaves, African slaves from different regions were purposely mixed together. This mixing was an important part of the creolization process, which contributed to the development of a unique Barbadian culture.

The importation of African slaves continued until 1807 when the Abolition Act was passed, although by that time Barbados was exporting slaves to other colonized territories in the Caribbean and Americas. After complete slave emancipation in 1838, change was slow and many of the former slaves still worked on the plantations, although some left Barbados in search of better opportunities elsewhere. The color and class divisions that had prevailed in Barbadian society from its earliest settlement continued, and it was only in the twentieth century that major changes started taking place. From the 1920s, the influence of Marcus Garvey's black power movement precipitated attempts to gain improved status for the black population.[3]

Many changes followed during the next few decades that put the black majority in control of the government, and independence from Britain was achieved in 1966.

THE DEVELOPMENT OF *TUK*

Before abolition, there was some attempt to ban African instruments on the plantations and prevent slave gatherings. An act passed in 1688 prevented slaves from leaving their plantations without a pass from their owner, particularly on Saturday evenings, Sundays, and other holidays. The use of drums, horns, and other loud instruments was prohibited, and the slave owners were fined if they allowed their slaves to play such instruments.[4] According to Dunn, "The English disliked the racket [the Africans] made with trumpets and African hollow-log drums and banned the drums for another reason, because they could be used to signal island-wide revolts."[5] It was difficult to enforce such bans, however, and the planters gradually accepted that the slaves were less likely to cause trouble if they were allowed some form of entertainment, such as holding a dance. Music was an important pastime for the slaves, and must have been a welcome opportunity to escape the reality of their daily lives and maintain and perpetuate some of their African cultural traditions.

These conditions contributed to the development of a syncretic, Creole, uniquely Barbadian musical tradition. The music played by the slaves could not have been a pure music belonging to the people from one particular region in West Africa because, as noted above, the slaves had been split up. The slaves did draw on the common threads, not just of spoken languages, but also of musical languages, to form a music acceptable to all. There was singing on plantations; work songs probably predominated to ease the burden of field labor. There was certainly music at the weekend dances, as attested by observers such as William Dyott who, in 1796, commented that the "negro dances are most curious and their music still more so."[6] These dances then provided opportunities for performing African music and retaining African traditions.

The history of *tuk* is not documented, and while it seems to have developed from the mid-nineteenth century onward, its roots were formulated in the times of slavery. The name *tuk* derives from an old Scottish word *touk* (or "took") meaning "to beat a drum" or "the beat of a drum."[7] The generally accepted theory about the origins of *tuk* is that it is a fusion of African and European musical elements, an imitation of the fife and drum bands of the British military stationed on the island during the late eighteenth century.[8] The presence of the Celtic population of Scottish and Irish indentured servants, and the long-standing traditions of fife and drum music in both Scotland and Ireland, suggest that these musical traditions also had some influence on this musical fusion in Barbados.

Tuk is performed by a band of four instruments: the kittle (snare drum), the bass drum, the "flute" (in practice, a penny whistle is used, but it is still referred to as a "flute") and the "steel" (a triangle). (See fig. 9.1.)

Tuk bands, or their precursors, seem to have had a variety of formations, often with the fiddle as the melodic instrument. Specific references to flutes or similar instruments do not exist in early texts on Barbados. Indeed, references to aerophones, in general, are rare in these texts. This led anthropologists Jerome Handler and Charlotte Frisbie to conclude that such instruments "played an insignificant role in musical activities."[9] Surely if slaves had been playing flutes, contemporary writers such as Richard Ligon, who lived in Barbados in the mid-seventeenth century, would have commented on it and likened what they saw to practices that were already familiar to them. In 1854, John Davy wrote about the weekly Saturday dances held by the black population and said "their favourite instruments are the fiddle, great drum and triangle," which is the earliest reference to a formation resembling a *tuk* band that I have found.[10] In 1897 the Barbados Agricultural Reporter, in an article about the delivery of the last sugar canes of the harvest to the mill yard, reported that the parade was "accompanied by a band of Negro men and boys playing the violin, the tambourine, the drum, the triangle and the blowing of a horn."[11]

The lack of references to a band resembling a *tuk* band with flute or fife leads me to believe that in fact the *tuk* band, in its modern format, is a late development. The format and musical characteristics of the band may well have been laid down and developed during slavery and the early post-

Figure 9.1. Modern tuk band.

emancipation years, but I believe the band only took on its modern day appearance in the second half of the nineteenth century, and I discuss a further reason for this later. People I have interviewed who grew up in Barbados in the early twentieth century recall the *tuk* band with the flute, so it was certainly in place by then.

Tuk may be an imitation of British military bands, but I believe this imitation could predate the establishment of the island's garrison in 1780. Although there had been visits by the British military before then, the militia could have been a much earlier vehicle for the assimilation of fife and drum music into the African slaves' lives. The militia was created to defend the island in the days before a permanent military presence, and was made up of a mixture of men from different backgrounds, including slaves. Landowners were required to send men to serve in the militia; the more land they owned, the more men they were required to send.[12] Slave musicians were sometimes counted as two slaves when calculating these numbers, and were also counted equally as white men, as Richard Hall noted from muster rolls in the mid-eighteenth century: "the Drummers and Trumpeters (about 100 and all of them Negroes) are included and set down as so many white men."[13] The presence of slaves in the militia from the mid-seventeenth century confirms that they were exposed to military-style music much earlier than the establishment of the British garrison, but exactly when slaves were first used in the militia as musicians is not clear. An early reference to slave involvement in such music is cited by Jerome Handler, who identified an advertisement placed in the *Barbados Gazette* in 1735 that refers to "a young Barbadian Negro-man" who was a "trumpeter in the Life-Guard."[14]

In 1748, Robert Poole wrote that in one of the companies of militia, "the Drum-Major is a black, and all the drummers under him are of that colour."[15] Presumably, the drummers were trained to play in a military style as the militia fulfilled the role of the military in which fife and drum music were prevalent. As in the military, the drum was a key instrument and was used as a signal—to summon parades or to sound an alarm. Thus, precision beating was essential to ensure the correct message was sent, and this could be how *tuk* acquired its name—the beat of a drum. This type of slave involvement in the militia offers a credible explanation for the *tuk* band's similarities to a military band. If slaves were indeed taught to play in a military style, and their masters accepted this, the assimilation of military instruments and musical stylistic features would have been fairly straightforward.

The African link with *tuk* is usually claimed to be a rhythmic one, although the basic drumming patterns appear to be more European in style. However, the improvisatory aspect of the kittle (snare drum) does seem more African in style, and the rhythms are often substantially altered by improvisation. The combination of the two drums and the steel often creates a polyrhythmic effect, which is more evocative of African drumming than European military drumming. Military rhythms were acceptable to the European population, so by adapting and varying these with African features, the slaves were able to continue their own musical traditions to some extent. The syncretization process that blended African and European musical elements created a Creole music that became *tuk*. It was not simply a blend of convenience, but a conscious adoption and adaptation to suit the purpose of the enslaved people, for them to have something that was exclusively their own. As Dick Hebdige says, "By preserving African traditions, by remembering African rhythms, the slaves could keep alive the memory of the freedom they had lost.... At the same time they could adapt European forms of music and dance to suit their needs."[16] Apparently, concealing African forms by blending them with European forms may have given the music a facade that was acceptable to the colonial masters. In reality, the slaves were perpetuating their musical traditions while, in some cases, possibly incorporating an element of mimicry through the use of European-derived musical elements. Musics similar in sound and/or appearance to *tuk* exist in and around the Caribbean region, for example in Mississippi, St. Kitts, and Montserrat.[17] The ready acceptance of this ensemble of instruments (or a very similar one) and style of music suggests that the slave population did not simply imitate the Europeans, but found musical elements with which they could identify—specifically, instruments commonly found in Africa, such as the flute and drum.

THE MUSIC

There is no specific *tuk* music—it is a musical style that can be applied to any tune. Today, music ranging from "The Blue Danube Waltz" by the famous Viennese composer, Johann Strauss II, to the Barbados national anthem can be played by a *tuk* band. *Tuk* has three basic meters: a 2/4 march, also known as *fassie*, a 3/4 waltz, and a 4/4, played at double speed, known as *tuk*. (Examples of each meter can be heard on this volume's accompanying website, played by Ruk-a-Tuk International.[18]) There are standard eight-bar patterns for each meter and each player has his own particular way of playing these. The kittle player is at liberty to improvise on the standard rhythms as much as he wishes, and sometimes totally transforms them.[19] The bass player, however, has an important role to fulfill as the timekeeper of the band. There is, therefore, little opportunity for him to improvise, as this might disguise the pulse of the music. The size of the bass drum also precludes complex rhythms. The steel usually reinforces the pulse played by the bass drum and sometimes adds extra rhythm. The flute player acts as the band leader, often playing a short introduction to the piece before the drummers join in. As the only source of melody in the band, the flute player is at liberty to perform with as much ornamentation and variation as he chooses.

In addition to providing instrumental music, *tuk* bands have also been vehicles for the social commentary song form. The bands played popular tunes and invited their audience "to contribute their own compositions, however innocent or suggestive in lyrics, simple or intricate in melody, as long as they can be fitted to a lively rhythm."[20] The few songs that have survived are documented in Folk Songs of Barbados and are melodically simple and short in length. As *tuk* songs were improvisatory, it is not surprising that few have survived; but few people actually recall sung *tuk*, so it is not possible to be clear about how widespread this aspect of the activity was. I believe this form of *tuk* disappeared when calypso, or *banja*, as it is often known in Barbados, developed in the first half of the twentieth century. Janice Millington has suggested that up to the 1930s, *banja* was practiced by laborers and was only found in villages.[21] In this respect, and in its social commentary and improvisatory aspects, *banja* bears some resemblance to sung *tuk*; in fact, it is possible that the two were the same thing, or at least similar enough that they were interchangeable. The arrival of more varied musical forms through the introduction of modern technology diminished the need for sung *tuk*, which was superseded by other, more high-profile musics and the development of Barbadian calypso.

TUK, THE LANDSHIP, AND THE WORKING CLASSES

Tuk is generally associated with the working classes. During the first half of the twentieth century, the working class played it for their own entertainment on public holidays, at Christmas, and on other special occasions when the *tuk* bands would travel from village to village, playing in return for food or a little money. *Tuk* is especially associated with rum shops, where the band would play and receive payment in rum.[22] *Tuk's* relationship with the working classes is reinforced by its association with the Landship. The origins of the Landship, like those of the *tuk* band, are not documented. The popular account holds that a retired seaman who had served in the British Royal Navy set up the Landship in the 1860s in an effort to recreate some of the discipline of naval life on land.

The Landship is not physically a ship but an organization in which a body of people meet at a "dock," dress in naval style uniform, drill in a pseudo-naval style accompanied by a *tuk* band, and have naval style ranks. Female members, however, are known as nurses and dress accordingly. The

Landship also functions as a friendly society where in return for a small, regular subscription, members are ensured financial support in times of hardship, illness, or death. The organization makes public appearances for ceremonial and official functions, although, like the *tuk* band, the Landship does not have a high profile in Barbados today (see fig. 9.2).

The *tuk* band acts as the "engine" of the Landship, musically driving the crew in their maneuvers, which are dance steps drawn from a variety of sources, such as the sailor's hornpipe and African limbo, fused with military-style drill to produce representations of life at sea. It is generally believed that the Landship and the *tuk* band developed as separate entities and were, subsequently, joined together. However, it is possible that they actually evolved together, with the *tuk* band recreating the musical ensembles found on board British naval vessels of the nineteenth century that provided entertainment during voyages. Such an ensemble is referred to in an account from the vessel *Asia* in 1840: it was noted that fiddlers and a fife and drum band played every night.[23] If the Landship's founder did indeed seek to recreate naval life on land, then it is highly likely that this recreation included the musical aspects of naval life. I have previously suggested that the *tuk* band evolved as a result of slaves trained as musicians in the militia, and there is certainly evidence to corroborate this. What I believe happened is that the musical ensembles that already existed when the Landship was established were incorporated into the Landship as its musical accompaniment because they were the same as those ensembles found on board ships.

Figure 9.2. The Barbados Landship.

TUK IN THE POST-INDEPENDENCE ERA

Along with other traditional forms of entertainment, such as the Landship, *tuk* declined during the twentieth century due to changes in society arising from changes in employment, aspirations for social betterment, and modern technology, with the arrival of radio from the 1930s and television from 1964. This technology brought new and varied forms of entertainment, mainly British and North American, into Barbadian lives, increasingly directly into homes, thus diminishing the need for community music making and entertainment. Even in the rum shops where *tuk* bands had provided entertainment, jukeboxes, radios, and televisions gradually crept in. Thus, by the time of independence, there was little need for live entertainment, little interest in such activity, and, consequently, fewer practitioners of traditional culture. Since then, the efforts of a small number of people, with some government assistance, have ensured the preservation and perpetuation of activities such as *tuk* and the Landship.

A key figure in the revival of *tuk* from the 1980s on has been Wayne "Poonka" Willock. He is well known in Barbados for his efforts to promote *tuk* in all aspects of Barbadian life, and his name is synonymous with *tuk*. He told me that *tuk* players in Barbados are perceived to be of low socioeconomic status and not very well educated. Such perceptions can be refuted today, however, as *tuk* players come from a variety of educational and social backgrounds; for example, Willock himself is a languages teacher. Willock also suggested that *tuk* is often better received outside Barbados, although his efforts have gone some way to redressing that situation, and today *tuk* is officially recognized as part of the country's cultural heritage.[24]

Today, steps are being taken to promote *tuk* in all aspects of Barbadian life, from education to tourism. An important point stressed to me in an interview at the Ministry of Education, Youth Affairs, and Culture is the need to keep outside, notably North American, culture at bay.[25] Younger generations of Barbadians are thought to be easily influenced by the power of American culture and willing to adopt aspects of that culture instead of their own. Like the older generations, they display little interest in preserving their heritage. This may be because what is now considered to be Barbadian culture has only really been promulgated as such since independence; indeed, for people who grew up in the pre-independence era, Barbadian culture reflected the long imposition of European habits and customs rather than the African heritage of the island's majority population.

Tuk is, effectively, drowned out by other musical forms in Barbados and only a small minority appreciate it, or will admit to appreciating it. Barbados hosts many festivals each year but *tuk* only plays a very minor role at some of these, often a seemingly token appearance at an opening ceremony or parade. However, *tuk* plays a more significant role in the annual Crop Over festival, where *tuk* has its own competition, albeit on a very small scale compared to other competitions for genres such as calypso.[26] The *tuk* competition is held on a weekend afternoon as part of an event that includes art and crafts, food and drink, and street entertainment. Unlike other events, such as the Calypso Monarch Competition, which is held at the National Stadium, the *tuk* competition is held on a temporary stage in a field with no proper seating for the audience, usually the band members' families and friends.[27] It is questionable as to why something that is deemed to be part of the cultural heritage of Barbados is relegated to such a back seat in the country's main annual festival—this would seem to send an inconsistent message, both to Barbadians and outsiders. *Tuk*'s relatively low status is further emphasized by the prize money. In 1998, the winning band shared BDS $1,200 (approximately U.S. $600) compared to the Calypso Monarch's prize of BDS $10,000 (approximately U.S. $5,000), plus a luxury car.[28] This reflects the high level of international corporate sponsorship enjoyed by calypso (which attracts the support of companies such as British American Tobacco) and *tuk*'s comparatively meagre support by local companies such as Purity Bakeries and Rotherley Construction.

Today, many performance opportunities for *tuk* bands are connected with tourism. *Tuk* is regularly featured as part of the cultural shows staged in some of the island's larger hotels, alongside steelbands, fire eaters, and limbo dancers. The *tuk* bands are usually accompanied by folk characters said to be of African origin, such as Mother Sally and the Tiltman. Mother Sally dances to the band and is, in fact, a man dressed as a woman, with a well-padded chest and backside, purported to represent the fertility of woman. The Tiltman is a stilt walker who performs some impressive feats. Although stilt walkers are found elsewhere in the Eastern Caribbean, the name and pronunciation of Tiltman is unique to Barbados. Tourists I have interviewed at such shows have generally expressed a positive reaction to *tuk*, saying that they thought it was enjoyable to listen to and some British tourists have likened it to something Scottish or Irish they have heard, such as the fife and drum bands of the Orangemen of Northern Ireland. Some thought they had heard something similar at the annual Edinburgh Tattoo and, given that military corps of drums with fifes do perform at the Tattoo, this is quite likely.[29]

It is understandable that a nation's culture and tourism come together, for as Wallis and Malm say, "The people of any nation feel proud to show off their culture and traditions to the tourists."[30] However as few people in Barbados participate in *tuk*, or will admit to actually liking it, it seems slightly false that *tuk* is paraded as part of the country's culture. However, this is probably no more false than the facets of culture paraded in other countries that few people are actually interested in, for example Morris dancing in England. Perhaps, though, *tuk*'s promotion has been part of the invention of a tradition in postcolonial Barbados; the country, finally independent, has sought to establish its own cultural and national identity, free of the label of being British. Thus, for some, inventing a tradition from the almost forgotten heritage of the African-descended population was seen as a way to move away from British ideals and rediscover, preserve, and perpetuate cultural links with the past.

Not everyone is keen to involve Barbadian traditions in tourism because this may negate the value of those traditions in the minds of some Barbadians. Alissandra Cummins, the director of the Barbados Museum, told me she is "grateful to the tourism industry for ensuring that it [*tuk*] survives because, obviously, it can only survive if the practitioners are in some way supported financially."[31] However, she expressed regret that younger generations might perceive *tuk* to be "simply another colorful aspect of what is offered as entertainment in hotels and not recognize, necessarily, that it is part of their heritage." Whatever doubts exist, tourism has certainly played an important part in preserving this part of the culture, and it seems likely to continue to do so.

Some *tuk* bands now receive corporate sponsorship to enable them to purchase instruments, print promotional material and take part in events that will help them achieve a higher profile. A key example of a sponsor is Rotherley Construction, a major Barbadian building firm, which sponsors Wayne Willock's band, Ruk-a-Tuk International, as their contribution to preserving part of Barbadian heritage. This sponsorship also extends to the running of *tuk* workshops, which have contributed significantly to *tuk*'s promotion among school age children. These proved so popular that an increase in the number of workshops was necessary and, as a result, a number of youth *tuk* bands have been established. The workshops' encouragement of girls to play *tuk* has helped to break down the long-standing "men only" image of *tuk*.

A major initiative to teach all Barbadian children about the cultural heritage of their country has been the government's "Cultural and Historical Exposure for Kids in Schools" program introduced into school curricula in the late 1990s . Coordinated by Wayne Willock, this program started initially in a few schools and has now been extended to include all secondary and primary schools. In ten-week blocks, specialist teachers, traveling from school to school, teach *tuk*, Landship dancing, and stilt walking. So far, the program is highly successful with school principals, teachers, and children alike. However, this is just a beginning; it will take years to ensure that every child has participated. It is, nonetheless, a positive move that gives the up-and-coming generations an opportunity to learn about their cultural heritage in a way that gives it a respected status. Inclusion in the school curriculum signals the government's serious commitment to promoting Barbadian cultural heritage. Though it will be a long time before the results of the scheme can be seen, it is at least helping break down the stigma of *tuk*'s association with rum shops, broaden its appeal to all classes of society, and include women in its performance.

CONCLUSION

Music's important role in establishing individual and group identities is the subject of much current research in musicology and ethnomusicology. Music can create identities recognizable not only to those to whom the music belongs, but also to others. Undoubtedly, reggae and steelband contribute not only to the creation of Caribbean identity, but also to the specific identities of Jamaica and Trinidad, their countries of origin. In Barbados, *tuk* may assume a similar role. Though the majority of *tuk* played today appears to be for the benefit of tourists and other visitors, this music has been chosen above other, more glossy-imaged, money-spinning musics to represent Barbados because it is this unique music that distinguishes Barbados from other Caribbean countries. Visitors who hear *tuk* will not go home thinking, mistakenly, that reggae or steelband is the music of Barbados; rather, they will recognize *tuk* as an identifying feature of Barbadian culture. It is, after all, a fusion of the musics of the cultures that have shaped the Barbados of today and, as such, is a significant representation of Barbadian national identity.

Notes

[See website for audio files to accompany this chapter.]

1. My fieldwork was undertaken in Barbados during November–December 1997, July–August 1998, February 1999, April 2000, and February 2001. The objective of these trips was to provide archival and primary information for my doctoral research. Archival research was undertaken notably at the Barbados Department of Archives, the University of the West Indies Cave Hill Campus Library, and the Library of the Barbados Museum and Historical Society. Observing and interviewing musicians, attending music festivals, and interviewing Barbadians, from government ministers to students, also formed an essential part of this fieldwork.

2. Barbados is the easternmost island in the West Indies archipelago that extends from the Bahamas in the north to Trinidad in the south. Twenty-two kilometers wide and thirty-four kilometers long, Barbados is a coral island and, unlike its volcanic neighbors, is relatively flat. Of the total population (ca. 270,000) more than 70 percent are of African descent. About 20 percent are of mixed African and European descent, and the remainder is made up of white descendants of colonists and indentured servants, more recent immigrants from North America and Britain, and small groups of immigrants from elsewhere. See Trevor G. Marshall, "All O' We Is Bajan" in *Barbados*, ed. Rachel Wilder (London: APA Publications, 1997), 59. The majority of the population lives in and around the major towns of Bridgetown, the capital, and Holetown and Speightstown. Numerous villages, many of which developed around the sugar plantations that dominated the island's economy from the mid-seven-

teenth century to the mid-twentieth century, dot the island. Today, the tourism industry plays a key role in the economy and has grown rapidly since the 1960s, when the introduction of jet aircraft made the Caribbean more easily and economically accessible.

3. Garvey (1887–1940) was a Jamaican political activist and Black Nationalist leader. He led the Universal Negro Improvement Association and advocated the establishment of an African homeland for black Americans.

4. *Acts of Assembly passed in the Island of Barbadoes from 1648 to 1718* (London: John Baskett, 1721), 119.

5. Richard S. Dunn, *Sugar and Slaves: The Rise of the Planter Class in the English West Indies 1624–1713* (London: Jonathan Cape, 1972), 250.

6. *Dyott's Diary 1781–1845: A Selection from the Journal of William Dyott, Sometime General in The British Army and Aide-de-Camp to His Majesty King George III*, ed. Reginald W. Jeffery (London: Archibald, Constable & Co. Ltd., 1907), 94–95.

7. Chambers Scots Dictionary, ed. Alexander Warrack (Edinburgh: W & R Chambers Limited, 1911), 620, 623.

8. For example, see a promotional leaflet written by Wayne Willock, *The History of Tuk Music* (Barbados: Rotherley Construction, 1997).

9. Jerome S. Handler and Charlotte J Frisbie, "Aspects of Slave Life: Music and its Cultural Context," Caribbean Studies 2 (January 1972): 22.

10. John Davy, *The West Indies before and since Slave Emancipation* (London: W. and F. G. Cash, 1854), 102.

11. Barbados Agricultural Reporter, July 23 and 26, 1897. From Research Notes A–H, Barbados Department of Archives.

12. Clause II, "An Act for the Settlement of the Militia in this Island," November 3, 1697, in *Acts of Assembly*, 175–90.

13. Richard Hall, "A General Account of the First Settlement and of the Trade and Constitution of the Island of Barbados" in *George Washington's Visit to Barbados, 1751*, ed. Richard B. Goddard (Wildey, St. Michael, Barbados: Cole's Printery, 1977), 68–9.

14. Jerome S. Handler, "Freedmen and Slaves in the Barbados Militia," *Journal of Caribbean History* 19 (1984): 13.

15. Robert Poole, "The Beneficent Bee or Traveller's Companion," Karl Watson, ed., *Journal of the Barbados Museum and Historical Society* 46 (2000): 237.

16. Dick Hebdige, *Cut 'N' Mix: Culture, Identity, and Caribbean Music* (London: Methuen, 1987; repr. Routledge, 2000), 26.

17. For discussion of these see, for example: David Evans, "Black Fife and Drum Music in Mississippi," Mississippi Folklore Register 6 (1972): 94–107. Frank L. Mills and S. B. Jones-Hendrickson, "Christmas Sports in St. Kitts-Nevis: 'Our Neglected Cultural Tradition'." [n.p., n.d.]. Jay D. Dobbin, *The Jombee Dance of Montserrat* (Columbus: Ohio State University Press, 1986).

18. Reproduced from their album "Indigenous Tuk Band Music of Barbados" (WIRL, WK335, 1991) by kind permission of the band. For further information on Ruk-a-Tuk International, see their website at http://home.caribsurf.com/rukatuk.

19. Throughout this chapter I refer to *tuk* players as "he" because *tuk* has traditionally been a male-dominated musical genre, and continues to be so. There have been a few female practitioners in living memory, though they no longer play and it has not been possible to trace them. Today there are school-age girls participating in *tuk*, which is discussed later in the chapter.

20. Trevor Marshall, Peggy McGeary, and Grace Thompson, *Folk Songs of Barbados* (Kingston, Jamaica: Ian Randle, 1981), 31.

21. Janice Millington, *"Barbados" in South America, Mexico, Central America, and the Caribbean*, eds. Dale A. Olsen and Daniel E. Sheehy, The Garland Encyclopedia of World Music, vol. 2 (New York: Garland Publishing, Inc., 1998), 813–21.

22. There is usually at least one rum shop in each village. They are community gathering places and, traditionally, provided a meeting place for working-class men to drink, talk, and play games. Historically, few women frequented such places and today they are still dominated by men.

23. W. P. Ashcroft, "Reminiscences" in *Naval Review*, 1964, cited in Peter Padfield, *Rule Britannia: The Victorian and Edwardian Navy* (London: Routledge & Kegan Paul, 1981), 34. A further example of this is a photograph taken in 1855 on board H.M.S. *Coquette*, in which three crew

members are shown holding a fiddle, a fife, and a drum. This photograph is reproduced in David Proctor, *Music of the Sea* (London: National Maritime Museum, 1992), 38, and in my doctoral thesis *Tuk in Barbados: The History, Development and Recontextualization of a Musical Genre* (University of Warwick, 2002), 241, by kind permission of the National Maritime Museum.

24. Interview, November 27, 1997.
25. Interview at Ministry of Education, Youth Affairs, and Culture with Ellsworth Young, permanent secretary; Idamay Denny, senior education officer, curriculum; Andrea Gollop-Greenidge, administrative officer, culture, February 18, 1999.
26. Crop Over is Barbados' form of carnival. It takes place over several weeks in July/August, culminating on the Bank Holiday Monday given to commemorate Emancipation Day on August 1.
27. Interview with David Headley, kittle player, August 4, 1998.
28. BDS is the Barbados dollar, fixed against the U.S. dollar at a rate of BDS $1.98 to U.S. $1.
29. Tourists interviewed at Harbourmaster Cruise, April 27, 2000; Accra Beach Hotel, April 27, 2000; Rockley Resort Bajan Floor Show, May 1, 2000.
30. R. Wallis and K. Malm, *Big Sounds from Small People: The Music Industry in Small Countries* (London: Constable & Co., 1984), 292.
31. Interview, February 15, 2001.

Bibliography

Aparicio, Frances R. 1998. *Listening to Salsa: Gender, Latin Popular Music, and Puerto Rican Cultures.* London: University Press of New England.

Ashie-Nikoi, Edwina. 1998. "Cohobblopot: Africanisms in Barbadian Culture through the Lens of Crop-Over." *Journal of Caribbean History* 32: 82–120.

Averill, Gage. 1997. *A Day for the Hunter, a Day for the Prey: Popular Music and Power in Haiti.* Chicago: University of Chicago Press.

Beckles, Hilary. 1990. *A History of Barbados: From Amerindian Settlement to Nation-State.* Cambridge: Cambridge University Press.

Behague, Gerard H., ed. 1994. *Music and Black Ethnicity: The Caribbean and South America.* New Brunswick, N.J.: Transaction Publishers.

Berrian, Brenda F. 2000. *Awakening Spaces: French Caribbean Popular Songs, Music, and Culture.* London: The University of Chicago Press Limited.

Best, Curwen. 1999. *Barbadian Popular Music and the Politics of Caribbean Culture.* Vermont: Schenkman Books, Inc.

Bilby, Kenneth M. 1985. The Caribbean as a Musical Region. Washington, DC: The Woodrow Wilson International Center for Scholars.

Bilby, Kenneth. 1985. "Caribbean Crucible," in *Repercussions*, eds. G. Haydon and D. Marks. London: Century Publishing Co. Ltd., 128–51.

Campbell, P. F. 1997. "The Barbados Militia 1627–1815," in *George Washington's Visit to Barbados 1751*, ed. Richard B. Goddard. Wildey, St. Michael, Barbados: Cole's Printery Ltd., 175–92.

Cowley, John H. 1996. *Carnival, Canboulay and Calypso: Traditions in the Making.* Cambridge: Cambridge University Press.

Downes, Aviston. 2000. "Sailing from Colonial into National Waters: A History of the Barbados Landship." *Journal of the Barbados Museum and Historical Society* 46: 93–122.

Gilmore, John. 1993. *The Barbados Landship Association.* Barbados: The National Cultural Foundation.

Guilbault, Jocelyne. 1993. *Zouk: World Music in the West Indies.* Chicago: University of Chicago Press.

Hagedorn, Katherine J. 2001. *Divine Utterances: The Performance of Afro-Cuban Santeria.* Washington, DC: Smithsonian Institution Press.

Laurie, Peter, and Val McComie. 1989. "Race, Culture, and Barbadian Identity: Our African Heritage in Creole Context." *Banja: A Magazine of Barbadian Life and Culture*, 22–9.

Lewin, Olive. 2000. *Rock It Come Over: The Folk Music of Jamaica.* Kingston, Jamaica: University of the West Indies Press.

Lomax, Alan, J. D. Elder, and Bess Lomax Hawes. 1997. *Brown Girl in the Ring: An Anthology of Song Games from the Eastern Caribbean.* New York: Pantheon Books.

Manuel, Peter, Kenneth M. Bilby, and Michael Largey. 1995. *Caribbean Currents: Caribbean Music from Rumba to Reggae*. Philadelphia, Pa.: Temple University Press.

McAlister, Elizabeth. 2002. *Rara! Vodou, Power, and Performance in Haiti and Its Diaspora*. Berkeley: University of California Press.

McDaniel, Lorna. 1998. *The Big Drum Ritual of Carriacou*. Gainesville: University Press of Florida.

Meredith, Sharon. 2002. "*Tuk* in Barbados: The History, Development, and Recontextualization of a Musical Genre." Doctoral thesis, University of Warwick.

Nunley, John W., and Judith Bettelheim. 1988. *Caribbean Festival Arts*. Seattle: University of Washington Press.

Olsen, Dale A., and Daniel E. Sheehy, eds. 1998. "South America, Mexico, Central America, and the Caribbean," The Garland Encyclopedia of World Music, vol. 2. New York: Garland Publishing, Inc.

Ramnarine, Tina K. 2001. *Creating Their Own Space: The Development of an Indian-Caribbean Musical Tradition*. Kingston, Jamaica: University of the West Indies Press.

CHAPTER **10**

There Goes the Transnational Neighborhood: Calypso Buys a Bungalow

Michael Eldridge

Sly Mongoose ... Wouldn't stop and he reach America.
—Trinidad-born vaudevillian Sam Manning's
1924 version of an old Jamaican mento

I live in a place where, in the early 1900s, the Craftsman ideal took hold as it did in few other places in North America. Today, a good seventy years after its heyday and its eventual eclipse by postwar ticky-tacky, the California Bungalow is still the state's preeminent style of domestic architecture. From one end of California to the other, craftsman cottages blanket the urban and rural landscapes; in Pasadena and the Berkeley Hills, Greene and Greene's showpieces—apotheoses of the genre—have become holy shrines for Arts and Crafts pilgrims; and in my small college town, way up north behind the Redwood Curtain, well-preserved bungalows are so prized by a certain breed of middle-class refugee from the south that they fetch sums well above their already-inflated asking prices. Ever since its inception in William Morris's industrialized England, of course, the Arts and Crafts movement was about nostalgia for a lost organic past; and so the bungalow, avatar of this Arcadian never-neverland, has for several generations symbolized an escape, albeit a rather compromised and disingenuous one, from the depredations of the modern world. Its calculatedly homey appeal may largely explain what my new neighbors (not to mention those legions who were so recently snapping up "Mission Oak" repros everywhere from upmarket Restoration Hardware to downscale K-Mart) are buying into.

Still, the northerly flight of these migrants of means—from something they euphemize vaguely as "congestion," or if pressed, "crime"—points indirectly to another, less homespun, of California's late distinctions: its much-ballyhooed ballot measures of the 1990s restricting immigration, rolling back affirmative action, and (briefly) ending bilingual education. Thus, with the Golden State in the vanguard, did the American nation begin to work through another in a series of demographically inspired identity crises.[1]

The nature of the work carried out here, and the sometimes hysterical tone of its execution, invite us to be careful readers of similar moments in the past. Since the underlying anxieties of this latest crisis are often expressed publicly as concerns over broadening (and, it's implied, divisive) *cultural* differences, for instance, it should be instructive to recall how America's relations with an earlier generation of dark-skinned immigrants were mediated precisely through the transmission and reception of culture—specifically, and surprisingly, through calypso, an urban vernacular performance genre whose sophisticated poetics have not been widely appreciated outside the Caribbean. In this chapter, however, I'm interested not so much in calypso's poetic pedigree as in its elucidation of a forgotten, crosscultural episode, a critical moment in the evolution of modern mass culture when calypso was at the nexus of another odd conjunction of racial tension, immigrant paranoia, and nostalgia for bungalows. I'm concerned, that is, with interpreting calypso's attempted intervention into American pop culture of the 1930s, and with its mixed success in getting a grip on the slippery process by which people—particularly immigrants—of color are assimilated into the American body politic.

In the spring of 1934, two relatively obscure Trinidadian entertainers, who'd come to New York City to put the carnival season's top calypsos on wax for the first time ever, suddenly found themselves flirting with international celebrity. Their cosponsors, a radio and phonograph merchant in Port of Spain and a Trinidadian bandleader based in New York, had formed a long-distance partnership to exploit what they hoped would be a dual audience for recorded calypso: a well-heeled "colored" bourgeoisie back home, and a sizeable pan-Caribbean emigrant class in New York. For its part, the American Record Corporation (soon to become the quasi-independent U.S. arm of British-based Decca), having leapt into the "race" records market just when it and the record trade in general had rather precipitously bottomed out, was attempting to revive sales by focusing on urban styles of black music and by taking risks on other genres with as-yet unknown potential.[2] Calypso, it may have felt, fit both of those strategies. Whatever the reasoning, the experiment was a qualified success: quite by accident (or so the apocryphal story goes), crooner Rudy Vallee overheard the calypsonians—who performed under the sobriquets Atilla [*sic*] the Hun and The Lion—from the studio next door and invited them to appear the following night on his NBC variety show, the most popular network radio program of its day.[3] (By some accounts, they also dined with Lion's idol Bing Crosby at Vallee's Hollywood Cafe, and may even have been enlisted to entertain FDR at the Waldorf Astoria.) Just how their performance registered with the American public isn't known, and it's possible that its effects were felt most strongly back in the Caribbean, where the broadcast had been relayed, weakly, by shortwave. Indeed, Lion and Atilla were greeted on their return to Trinidad as conquering heroes, and local sales of their calypsos (and of gramophones and radios on which they might be heard) helped their shop owner–sponsor expand his chain of "emporiums" considerably over the next several years. For its part, Decca would invite a contingent of calypsonians back to New York annually for most of the next decade, and Vallee booked them again on at least the first of these return trips. The émigré bandleader Gerald Clark, meanwhile, would bolster his local career by accompanying the calypsonians on record, and by taking advantage of their annual junkets to arrange still more radio appearances and club dates for them in the New York area, sometimes for months afterward.[4] It seemed a cozy arrangement, a modest success for all parties concerned.

For Lion and Atilla, though, there was nothing modest, let alone accidental, about any of it. For years afterward, they eulogized their hobnobbing with Vallee as an historic occasion, a glorious vindication: after a long trial run in the provinces before an insufficiently appreciative audience, calypso, as they saw it, had kept its appointment with destiny and arrived to take its place upon the world stage. In a calypso lesson on the "History of Carnival" the following year (1935), Atilla lectured sententiously on the Shrovetide festival's teleology in the Caribbean. In the not-so-distant past, he lamented—pandering to the good burghers of Port of Spain who'd been sounding this same theme for decades—carnival had indeed been a "hideous," scandalous affair, full of half-naked women, drunken masqueraders, obscenity, violence, and lewdness. Today, by contrast, it was wholly and "gloriously" reformed, nothing at all like it had been—perched, in short, at the pinnacle of respectability. The (somewhat elliptical) proof, which Atilla laid forth in the refrain as though it needed no gloss: "Today you can hear our calypso/On the American radio." Calypsonians, naturally, were the Sherpas who had quietly carried Trinidadian culture to such Himalayan heights; but ironically, Atilla adds ruefully, only foreign observers had the acumen to discern their achievement—Trinidadians being too slow-witted or perhaps too prejudiced by tired stereotypes to appreciate their sudden elevation. Back home, a calypsonian might still be treated as a "hooligan," he crows, but "in New York you're an artist and a gentleman,/For instance take the Lion and me,/Having dinner with Rudy Vallee." Henceforth, if New York was, as he insinuated, the crucible of everything splendid and new, the self-evident global standard of *chic,* then certain Trinidadians, at least, were ready to measure up.

Indeed, in Atilla's eyes Vallee had effectively issued Trinidadian culture an overdue invitation to sit at the banquet table of modernity. For the (paradoxically) remarkable thing about Trinidad, went another of his 1935 calypsos, was how much it had changed, changed utterly in recent years, despite the apparent handicap of its insularity: "How different is the island we know/To the Trinidad of long ago," it began.[5] No longer a provincial backwater, Trinidad now had industry and wealth, electric lights and refrigerators, radios and telephones. "With motor-cars runnin' up an' down," Atilla insisted in the refrain (with all the gee-whiz authority of one of Aimé Césaire's "been-to's"), "Trinidad comin' like-a New York town." The tropics, went this thesis, reprising and amplifying Claude McKay and W. A. Domingo's 1920s tagline, were not just in New York; New York and all it represented were in the tropics, too. In fact, one gets the sense that just under the surface of Atilla's simple simile hides an even more hyperbolic promotional claim: that The Tropics *are* New York, that the two places have become virtually interchangeable, that Gotham has been irrevocably inflected with Caribbean culture, and that Trinidad is at the same time thoroughly up to date, happily incorporated into the cultural empire emanating from that North American center. And if the calypsonian is a spurned prophet (as the final stanza of "History" has it), then what his unheeded prophecy foretells is the advent of a rough Trinidadian beast: Despite the fact that the first of Atilla's historical-minded sermons had set out to advertise carnival's alleged gentrification (and the calypsonian's respect for middle-class decorum), both calypsos ultimately slouch toward conclusions that emphasize not cultural decency, but cosmopolitan *currency.* More than anything else, that is, the calypsonian is the herald of Trinidadian modernity.[6]

Atilla could trumpet Trinidad's modernity all he wanted, but the general mood and particular events in New York in 1935 left such an announcement open to severe misinterpretation. To understand the nature and extent of his tactical misstep, though, requires a brief review of the historical context of his proclamation.

To be sure, throughout the 1920s the nascent mass culture industry had succeeded in manufacturing a certain vogue for black culture in the parlors of white America—especially for the culture of the so-called New Negro, the one who wrote distinguished literature, sang venerable spirituals, or performed polite concert music in tie and tails. But toward the culture, especially the musical culture, of the *other* "new" negroes, the faceless masses who had lately swarmed to the northern cities, white America was considerably more ambivalent (though every bit as fascinated). About Afro-Caribbean people there were particular doubts. West Indian emigration to New York had begun in earnest after 1900, and had increased appreciably during the decade following World War I, when Harlem's growing reputation as *the* Black Metropolis made it a cosmopolitan mecca for blacks from across the diaspora.[7] Some decades later, as Malcolm Gladwell (1996) and others have remarked, industrious West Indians might more frequently be held up by whites as exemplars for their shiftless, native-born cousins. But in the twenties, long before that stereotype was fully formed, prominent voices in the xenophobic national debate over immigration policy argued that the country's race problem was already vexed enough without admitting still more unassimilable negroes (some of whom, like the notorious Garvey, might well be troublemakers, to boot). And anyway, relations between native-born and West Indian–born blacks were famously thorny, especially in New York City, which by 1930 had some forty to fifty thousand first-generation Caribbean immigrants—at least 25 percent of the black population of Harlem—and perhaps another eighty thousand or so of the second generation. Culturally, the West Indian presence was not yet so keenly felt: although a handful of émigré bandleaders, vaudevillians, and even one rather second-rate calypsonian had been playing and recording West Indian melodies in New York since about 1915—usually disguising them as "Latin" tunes or as comic novelty songs—their success had mainly been limited to the immigrant and export markets. Yet West Indians' prominence in the business, professional, and political spheres was all out of proportion to their numbers, and this made them the targets of considerable resentment and scorn (bizarrely, one of the taunts hurled at them was "Jewmaican")—as did their reputation for haughtiness and their habitual chafing at the unaccustomed crudeness of American racism. Robert L. Vann, special assistant to the U.S. attorney general and publisher of the (black-owned) *Pittsburgh Courier*, apparently spoke with some authority when he inveighed against West Indians during an address on "The Colored Man and the Administration" at the 135th Street branch of the New York Public Library, just days after Lion and Atilla's arrival in 1934. "If you West Indians don't like how we do things in this country," he allegedly snarled, "you should go back home where you came from. . . . We are good and tired of you. . . . [T]here should be a law deporting the whole gang of you and failing that you should be run out of Harlem."[8]

African American popular music was scarcely kinder. If they were fortunate, West Indians might appear phatically in song titles (cf. Ellington's "West Indies Stomp"), but they were more apt to show up as the butts of ridicule and derision, as in Clarence Williams's "West Indies Blues," a wishful novelty song about a homeward-bound Jamaican immigrant that was covered repeatedly during and after 1924, the peak year of West Indian immigration (and the year in which immigration restrictions were finally imposed). Even well-known vaudevillians and recording stars of the late twenties such as Phil Madison and Sam Manning, who occasionally capitalized on their West Indian provenance, usually did so self-mockingly, performing songs in exaggerated accents that reinforced the popular "monkey-chaser" cliché.[9]

Perennial calls for harmony and solidarity between the two populations had it that if the chasm between them were ever to be bridged, West Indians would have to accept the plain fact that in white America's eyes, a Caribbean Negro was still first and foremost a *Negro*.[10] And an unstated corollary to this axiom, I think (though it was never explicitly voiced in 1935 or at any other time), was that in white America's *ears*, Trinidadians' particular brand of music was liable to be heard first and foremost as *Negro music*—not the dignified concert music and sorrow songs of which the nation had become so anachronistically enamored, but the less sedate forms that had gained ground over the preceding decade: blues and (especially) jazz. By 1935, *pace* Ken Burns, jazz had not yet been wholeheartedly welcomed into the American mainstream: even thrill-seeking white enthusiasts were more likely to imbue it with the wanton and unruly qualities that they associated with the African American masses who, riled by racial injustice and economic desperation, were growing increasingly insurgent in cities throughout the north. On the very heels of the first recording session of Atilla's return visit of March 1935, in fact, rather serious riots and looting broke out in Harlem—alarming enough, for instance, to prompt eight-year-old Harry Belafonte's West Indian mother to move the family to Jamaica for a few years—and white New Yorkers, according to one newspaper account, were "panic-stricken ... as a nightmare of Negro revolt appeared to be a reality" (quoted in Ottley and Weatherby 1967: 275). White America, then, was unlikely to be impressed by the boast of a dark-skinned West Indian (with the sobriquet of a barbarian marauder, yet) that the tropical island whose musical ambassador he claimed to be was "comin' like-a New York town."[11] In the fading light of the Harlem Renaissance, that is, *all* of these so-called modern Negroes appeared to white eyes more shadowy than ever. Pass modernity through a black filter, after all, and it comes out as the "jazz age," with all of that epithet's ambivalent overtones of rampant sensuality and barely-contained pandemonium.

Atilla had unwittingly struck exactly the wrong note, then. According to his wishful thinking, carnival and its music might now be suffused with middle-class virtue—sanitized, as it were, for international consumption.

But for wary American whites, the whole business was liable to reek of the unwashed carnival*esque*: not play-anarchy, but genuine, unreconstructed anarchy. So even though Atilla had clearly meant to pitch Trinidad as a sophisticated center of urbanity, it must have come across the plate as one more urban jungle. Though recorded calypso continued to sell steadily to Trinidadians and West Indian expatriates, it would spend several more years in the wilderness before a larger audience really began to take heed. When they did, it was for reasons that the prophet could never have foreseen.

In 1937 the four calypsonians visiting New York had come, as usual, with several numbers calculated to appeal to North Americans ("The Louis-Schmeling Fight," "Roosevelt in Trinidad"), but it turned out to be a royal theme—the sensational abdication of Britain's Edward VIII for the sake of an American divorcee—that quite unexpectedly caught the prurient imagination of the downtown nightclub set.[12] All four calypsonians composed or improvised on the topic—one reportedly had patrons at the Ruban Bleu standing on their chairs, applauding his *extempo*—but it was the version recorded by The Caresser, with its haunting, dirge-like refrain ("It was love, love alone/That cause King Edward to leave de throne"), that emerged as the popular favorite, eventually becoming the year's top-selling calypso outside Trinidad. By a fluke, Decca suddenly found itself sitting on gold—if not in terms of dollars, then at least in terms of publicity and marketing potential. (The record industry had begun to rebound in 1937, and calypso could conceivably aid its resurgence.) Finally, it seemed, calypso *had* arrived, and calypsonians seized the next opportunity, their recording session of 1938, to resume the public relations campaign they'd had to abort three years earlier. They would be careful not to make the same mistake twice, though: if America was in fact searching for a *new* "New Negro," a less threatening, more assimilable one (one who'd emerged not into jazzy modernity, but into bourgeois respectability), then calypsonians would be happy to assume that role.

"I'm sure you are expecting something will be said by me/About the sweet land of liberty," Atilla and Lion obligingly began their showpiece offering of 1938, "Guests of Rudy Vallee." The duet rosily rehearsed (and embellished) their triumph of four years previous, when America's foremost white-bread entertainer had given them his stamp of approval, and when, in case anyone's memory needed jogging, they had "broadcasted on the WEAF/[and] The American public of their reason was bereft." Caresser, meanwhile, reprising the old "prophet spurned" theme ("So you see my name figures everywhere/I mean in England, New York, don' talk 'bout here") and concluding that living well was nevertheless the best revenge, signified on his own rather more recent celebrity by cataloguing the purported fruits of his newfound fame: fine cigars, tailored suits, luxury sedans, an attractive girlfriend, the latest in electrical lighting ... and a bungalow in suburban Port of Spain ("The More They Try to Do Me Bad"). In contrast to Atilla's up to date inventory of three years before, however, such creature comforts were no longer to be parsed as signs of Trinidad's accession to the modern world. And it's the final item on Caresser's list, which (to American ears) must have seemed an incongruously modest component of an otherwise swank fantasy, that drives this point home.

The bungalow already had a brief history in calypso as a recurring motif: two years earlier, for instance, in the middle of a fairly formulaic *lavway* (a simple, antiphonic form that harkens back to calypso's roots in carnival stickfighting songs, and that typically expresses defiance in the face of aggression—this particular tune, in fact, was the B-side of a calypso castigating Mussolini for his invasion of Ethiopia), Radio and Lion had chanted this throwaway couplet: "I mean to buy a bungalow, we got plenty money/Boy-oy-oy, tell them we ain't 'fraid nobody" ("We Ain't Fraid").[13] As in Caresser's catalogue, the figure makes for a slightly bizarre boast, and since *lavways* aren't noted for their thematic development, it remained for the moment isolated and unelaborated. But once they'd piqued the interest of white New York, calypsonians figured out how to put this folksy trope to work—and in 1938 it was fairly working overtime. Growler opened with "I Want to Rent a Bungalow"; Lion and Caresser upped the ante with separate versions of "I Am Going to Buy a Bungalow"; Atilla demurred ironically with "I Don't Want No Bungalow"; and dance orchestras followed up with instrumental covers. In all of the lyrical versions, the speaker breezily lays forth his ambition to take occupancy of his dream home and install a catalog of standard amenities: a pretty companion, some musical instruments, and plenty of brand name merchandise such as Simmons beds and Zenith radios.

Gordon Rohlehr, who is perhaps the preeminent scholar and historian of calypso, fits this spate of compositions squarely within a tradition of wishful, self-glorifying fantasies, extravagant boasts of the good life accruing to calypsonians as a result of their supposed power, prestige, and material success (Rohlehr 1990: 239–43)[14]—and in the context of a domestic audience in Trinidad, that explanation makes good sense. But something else is clearly going on, as well. For in all of these numbers, the calypsonians take inordinate pains to flaunt their international currency, particularly their experience and familiarity with the United States. (Lion: "I want a trip to America/But me liquor mus' be from the Mermaid Bar.") Heretofore a foreign stamp of approval might have been just one more way of lording it over the clodhopping hicks back home. But in the preceding year, after all, calypsonians had finally hooked a much bigger fish, and this year they'd reeled it in all the way to Trinidad. (In 1938, Decca conde-scended to come to the Trinidadian source—so as to mine more efficiently the raw material to be processed in its U.S. plant, one suspects—and a carpetbagging RCA Victor showed up to stake a claim, as well. The arrival of the American record companies created a local media sensation.) So calypsonians may indeed have been flinging old boasts toward the folks at home—but now, acutely aware of a second, more prestigious, and poten-tially more lucrative audience, they also spun them in a different direction for export consumption.

In this light, their fetishizing of the bungalow was supremely canny, as it couldn't have resonated more deeply with the yearnings of depression-era Americans, who had just concluded a thirty-year-long mania of bungalow-building.[15] Gustav Stickley's *Craftsman* magazine and a slew of house plan books had made "bungalow" a pop culture buzzword by at least 1910 (about the same time that *Good Housekeeping* poetically immortal-ized it in a "Bungal-Ode"), and well before the mid-thirties, its initial incarnation as a leisure-class holiday haven had been thoroughly subur-banized—thanks in large part to developers' well-orchestrated promotional campaigns all across the country. (One of these, in the 1920s, included a catchy jingle declaring California the "land of the bungalow.") Sears, Roebuck and Montgomery Ward, meanwhile, took responsibility for trans-forming bungalows into a truly mass-market phenomenon, shipping hundreds of thousands of them as mail-order kits while pitching them as the repository *cum* proving ground of all of the newfangled consumer goods (sold separately, of course) that must surely fill modern living with ease and contentment. In short, the bungalow embodied America's anxious longing for domestic comfort, security, and seclusion—or at least it cloaked the country's infatuation with machines in a mantle of homespun simplicity. This was just the kind of cozy sentiment that Tin Pan Alley had exploited again and again over the preceding decade or so, most notably in Gene Austin's syrupy 1927 signature tune, "My Blue Heaven," a multi-million-selling hit that was covered throughout the 1930s by popular singers both black and white (including Bing Crosby, a particular idol of The Lion). "Bungalow of Dreams," recorded by Frankie Masters in 1928, paints the picture succinctly: "Our little love nest/Beside a stream/Where red, red roses grow/Our bungalow/Of dreams//Far from the city/Somehow it seems/We're sitting pretty in/Our bungalow/Of dreams."[16]

Against such a backdrop, the calypsonians' seemingly humble desire to settle down and share in this dewy-eyed, apple-pie dream invited a chari-table interpretation: If jazz and the blues were still somewhat unruly and in need of a healthy dose of domestication, then here was evidence that calypso had been domesticated *already*.[17] It could be understood, naturally, that their bourgeois ambitions were being advanced in a fanciful sort of way; if calypsonians had seriously proposed that Afro-Trinidadians integrate Long Island or Westchester County en masse, the conceit would never have flown. Never mind, too, that wholesome romance was undoubtedly the farthest thing from their minds, and that their semitransparent bachelor fantasies of mooching off housebound sugar mamas—far more scandalous than Edward's ultimately boring marriage to Mrs. Simpson—could easily have backfired by playing into white America's more prurient stereotypes about black men. The genius of these calypsos is that they used the coded language of class as a diversionary tactic to draw attention away from race. In this way their composers could and did get away with mimicking a suburban lifestyle to which they weren't necessarily aspiring.

And at any rate, the popular press considerably spread more benign impressions. By August of 1938, calypso had attracted enough attention that *Time* boldly proclaimed a calypso "boom" in New York, noting that records previously found only in the darkest depths of Harlem were now available at four midtown shops. A year later, *Newsweek* reported that sales had reached "fad proportions," and the *New Yorker* and the metropolitan dailies also weighed in on the trend, with *Life, Billboard,* and *Modern Music* bringing up the rear.[18] And if these accounts occasionally tended, unhelpfully, to dredge up the louche image that calypsonians had been simultaneously cultivating and disowning back home, they also graciously seized upon a kind of familiar difference that set calypso apart from any black music known in the States. American journalists were particularly delighted by the "rich British" accent "peculiar to West Indian negroes," which gave them an odd but disarming whiff of gentility. (In particular, one suspects, it provided a comfortingly audible illusion of their obeisance to the civilized authority of the British Empire.) These negroes and their peculiar ditties might be faintly curious, such amused condescension seemed to say, but you had to admit that they possessed at least the trappings of refinement—a quality that could only make them seem all the more nonthreatening, unlikely to stir up the sort of trouble their rawer American cousins had been brewing.[19]

This distinction was crucial—though it had been a close call. A slightly earlier story in *Collier's*, belatedly surveying the "race music" phenomenon just weeks before the calypso "boom" was officially sounded, had quite blithely (and unconventionally, in terms of the orthodox schema of record company segregation) lumped calypso together with other sorts of *domestic* "race" records, categorizing it in passing as an eccentric branch of the same "colored" clan to which all savage peoples (including Cajuns and hillbillies) evidently belonged. The bizarre family tree was elliptically sketched over several paragraphs:

The best colored singer since Bessie Smith is said to be Georgia White, and it is in this field that some of the most remarkable records are made. There are colored numbers so strictly African and special that nobody but a Negro could understand them or appreciate them. When Sleepy John Estes does his own Negro compositions, they seem to be in another language. The melodies are strange, the words are like something out of a voodoo chant and the manner of delivery is such that they make no sense whatever to the untrained white mind....

Among the novelty records are those made by the Calypso people in the West Indies [that primitive tribe!], the Cajuns of Louisiana and Corny Allen Greer and his band. (Crichton 1938: 25)

So if West Indians in general had long resisted the cajoling of their American counterparts to accept their lot as "Negroes"—if they had resolutely ignored, as Malcolm Gladwell has put it, the categories on which American racism depends (Gladwell 1996: 75)—then it was now correspondingly imperative, under the circumstances, for calypsonians to distinguish their musical and poetic production from that of black Americans, in order to dodge the incoherent marketing category "race music." (Never mind the "ethnic" or "foreign" market, which as things then stood occupied a kind of commercial no-man's land.) The events of 1935, if nothing else, had obliquely taught them that they could afford very little blurring of the boundaries, let alone such extreme foreshortening as *Collier's* had done. They couldn't be African-blues-jazz-voodoo-Cajun-hillbilly-negroes; they had to be something else. And luckily the complaisance of the journalistic pack, its smarmy identification of calypsonians as *West Indian* negroes, helped them to become that something else. By embracing calypso, then, mainstream America could temporarily displace its fear of a black planet onto a quaint, exogenous culture that it then saw happily "bungalowed"—suburbanized, domesticated, and contained for mainstream consumption.

And consume, the mainstream did. Beginning in 1938, midtown Manhattan record shops hastily assembled calypso albums for the throngs of bewildered neophytes. (It was still too early—but only by a couple of years—for pseudoauthoritative liner notes by white know-it-alls.) Several new labels mushroomed overnight, scrambling to get into the act both by poaching established calypsonians from Decca and by pawning off inexperienced West Indian expats of questionable talent as authentic calypso stars. One genuine (though derivative) calypsonian, Wilmoth Houdini, who'd been toiling in relative anonymity in Harlem for a dozen years, was profiled in *The New Yorker* (Mitchell 1939) and invited to sing at the opening of the 1939 World's Fair. And finally, in September of that same year, Max

Gordon hesitantly booked a bevy of calypso singers for a short gig at his up-and-coming nightclub, the Village Vanguard. (See Johnson 1940, as well as Hill 1993: 161–62 and Hill 1998: 79–83.) Nightly receipts doubled in ten weeks, and calypso remained a fixture there and in other clubs—uptown, downtown, and out of town—for the next decade. Over the same period, one local calypsonian provided radio commentary for WNYC on the 1940 Democratic convention; Caresser presided over a Caribbean music program for several years on CBS Radio; pop stars like the Andrews Sisters, Ella Fitzgerald, and Louis Jordan all scored huge hits with calypso (or ersatz calypso) covers; two calypso extravaganzas (featuring dancers Pearl Primus and Katherine Dunham, respectively) had short but notable runs on Broadway; and calypsonians played several well-publicized and critically successful dates at Town Hall, Carnegie Hall, and the Brooklyn Academy of Music.[20] By the time calypso finally caught the attention of Hollywood in the early 1940s (Lion's "Ugly Woman," a number he'd sung on the Vallee radio show in 1934, was the first to make it to the screen), the United States was by one estimation the genre's biggest exporter, by another its biggest export market. Either way, it had become the crucible of what Paul Bowles, writing in *Modern Music* in 1940, doubtfully labeled a "hybrid novelty for Pan-American consumption" (154).

While Bowles' sniffiness might be attributed to his well-documented preference for exoticizing his ethnic Others, Calypsonians themselves had reason to be equivocal about attaining such a "hybrid" status. For one thing, some of their initial American reviewers had been taxonomically lax. The same writers who'd been so gratified by the quasi-British accents were often eager to place calypso in a string of interchangeable exotic diversions such as tango, rhumba, hula, or (after Carmen Miranda's celebrated arrival in 1939) samba—a misapprehension that the calypsonians, who ordinarily prided themselves not merely as entertainers but as serious wordsmiths, were for the moment somewhat reluctant to dispel. When they played along, however, it was not entirely under duress: they repeatedly capitalized on cartoonish representations of their country's folkways (in such a way as to clarify how far beyond such backward superstitions they themselves had evolved), and they cheerfully colluded in the production of generic, ideal-ized images of Trinidad aimed squarely at the tourist trade (see, e.g., Rohlehr 1990: 179–82). And no matter how much it may have galled them to be passed off as This Year's Novelty Act, it can only have flattered their self-styled sense of worldliness to be viewed as "Pan-American." Indeed, what Bowles had intended as a lament for a supposedly lost purity in the calypso form (a presumptuous sentiment seconded by Gama Gilbert in the Sunday *New York Times*) ironically echoed a wonderfully baroque and debonair fantasy recently spun by Caresser ("Ruby Canera"). In a mile-high party in a luxury airship, he and his sweetheart would drink champagne in the company of movie stars, nimbly dancing the Continental and the Suzi-Q while being serenaded by the likes of Ellington, Armstrong, and Crosby. An astonished Fred Astaire, meanwhile, would stand agape on the sidelines, while "at las', we'll dance an' sway/Back home in a Pan America airway."

Less than a decade after their initial embarkation in New York, then, calypsonians effortlessly spanned the continent and the hemisphere; and in hindsight, at least, that had been their master plan from the start. The first wave of West Indian migrants had entered America during an era of profound anxiety over race and its role in national identity, a time when anti-immigrant paranoia rose to dizzying heights. But the same era was also marked by the vibrance, visibility, and vitality of black cultures—with whose labor the very notion, not to mention the machinery, of mass culture was being engineered and built. The first cohort of calypsonians, by contrast, arrived just as that cumbersome machinery was in dire need of maintenance and adjustment: when the record industry—especially the "race" record industry—had collapsed, and consequently when all sorts of experiments in the cultivation of audiences, the manipulation of tastes, and the manufacture of markets for new products were conducted in the continental capitals of mass culture, New York and Hollywood. Lion and Atilla, calypso pioneers, had cannily anointed Vallee (who after all had a foot on both coasts) as their shepherd across this parlous terrain. He was, they averred, "so charmed with our ethnic harmony" that "he took us in hand immediately/'You boys are wonderful!' by Rudy Vallee we were told/'You must throw your voice through the radio to the whole wide world.'" They responded to his exhortation, and cleverly. By finding a way to broadcast and capitalize on their "charming" ethnicity,[21] and by simultaneously exploiting a powerful metaphor in America's symbolic lexicon—professing what could at least be mistaken for unobtrusive middle-class aspirations—calypsonians managed to short circuit the cultural machinery by which black people's ambiguous status within the American nation was then being decided.

They were, arguably, victims of their own success. As it happened, almost all of calypso's landmark achievements in the 1940s, in clubs, on screen, on wax, and over the airwaves, were also stages in its makeover for a paler American audience. To fill a sudden overwhelming demand in New York, for instance, the bandleader-entrepreneur Gerald Clark built a stable of local calypsonians who could be on hand full time and year round; they were second-raters for the most part, but most Americans wouldn't be able to tell the difference. This precedent opened a Pandora's box for later generations of promoters and record producers who would take calypso farther and farther away from its geographic roots. One of Clark's creations, moreover (an admittedly sui generis case named Sir Lancelot), influenced Harry Belafonte—who, for better or worse, after 1957 would forever stand in the American mind as calypso incarnate.

From one point of view, then, it might look as though American mass culture unwrapped calypso as flavor-of-the-month, chewed it until the taste was gone, and stuck it to the underside of its chair (or worse, swallowed it whole). But it should be remembered that Lion, Atilla, and the other calypsonians of the 1930s had their own agenda, as well. True, they were out to "get paid," and they were no strangers to the financial perils of migrant labor. But they were also out to finesse the process whereby blacks of all nationalities were warily, selectively, grudgingly, integrated into the American nation. They were jockeying, that is, to position calypso as one of the many (black) genres shaping American culture, all the while charting a course across the somewhat unpredictable racial schemas of the 1930s and steering clear of the problematic status that blacks had been assigned in the United States.

Obviously, there were complex social, cultural, and economic explanations for the fizzling of the Harlem Renaissance and the doldrums in the race records market. But part of the problem, I think, was that culture-industry moguls hadn't quite known how to exploit what was even then shaping up to be a *mixed* black vernacular. What calypsonians did—both as migrant cultural workers and self-professed cosmopolitan (but also "organic") intellectuals—was help American enterprise refine an experiment it had conceived only dimly. The key lay in the Pan-African dimension of the Harlem Renaissance, an idea to which participants and commentators alike had mainly given lip service. Calypsonians' cultivation of a *Caribbean*-American identity, that is, was an ingenious attempt to make good on the "Tropical" assets of New–Negro New York. Ideally their scheme would let them both reinflate the stock of black cultures in general (by diversifying transnationally, as it were), and make an end run around the dead end nativist categories on which the failed—or at least stalled—idea of "race" records had been built. If domestic black vernacular culture was even in the mid-1930s still a trifle too hot for a truly mass market, then calypso (along with other "exotic" imports) might create a sort of international buffer zone.

Granted, as Michael Rogin puts it (in speaking of a rather different group of immigrants), such achievements, far from serving as successful examples of "crossover culture," ordinarily "[move] settlers and ethnics into the melting pot by keeping racial groups out" (quoted in Seymour 1996: 35). But that sober assessment doesn't fully fathom the crosscultural motives of the exceptionally heady affair under consideration here. Calypsonians were not exactly aiming to "cross over," but rather to cross things up. Mainstream America, as I've suggested, may indeed have temporarily adopted a racially different Caribbean cultural form as an anvil on which to hammer out certain unsettled aspects of its national identity. But in turn, calypso's sophisticated class of migrant workers aimed to use their art as cultural capital with which to influence, deflect, and negotiate all such appropriations. By acquiring a small franchise on the cultural kitchen that increasingly set tastes and menus for large chunks of the world, they decisively changed the flavor of its melting-pot stew—however bland and denatured record companies were determined to make things by the late fifties, when even the Norman Luboff Choir had a calypso album or two. That is, they slyly fulfilled Atilla's proleptic tropical prophecy of 1934 by pouring Caribbean culture into the American mix, quietly ensuring that the latter's brand identity thenceforth be relabeled as *Pan*-American. Calypso, moreover, would eventually have to be reckoned as one of a slew of black genres, domestic and foreign, fuelling what had already become a transnational American pop culture. Having briefly but effectively worked the levers of an in-house entertainment machine whose arms extended across the globe, calypso—decades before the coining of the term in the mid-1980s—had the dubious and redoubtable distinction of engineering a commercial market for "world" music.

Such phenomena are of course not immune from questions of power, struggle, and co-optation.[22] Indeed, in view of the history of the intervening years, we can now scarcely utter such hoary terms as "world music" (never mind a mouthful like "transnational American pop culture") without also muttering "cultural imperialism." That calypso underwent its first vogue in the United States at just the moment Roosevelt was scheming to take over Britain's possessions in the Caribbean is a complicating irony that didn't escape calypsonians' notice; and it should remind us once again that the dusky modernity Americans hadn't wanted to hear about from Atilla in 1935 (let alone DuBois in 1900) had always, for peoples of color, marched in lockstep with racism and empire. During and after World War II, in particular, the "world" music that calypso had helped midwife became increasingly complicated by geopolitics. (Calypsonians hadn't exactly crossed any *international* color line, either, as it turned out; they'd merely hashed it up.) In fact, on the political futures charts, calypso was a leading postcolonial indicator. The Andrews Sisters' profitable wartime fencing of stolen calypso goods (not to mention the takeover of Trinidad's economies—fiscal, cultural, and sexual—by resident American G.I.s, a conquest that the original "Rum and Coca Cola" blisteringly lampooned) neatly prefigured a postwar changing-of-the-guard, whereby America would become caretaker of the waning British Empire while Trinidadians would continue to work for the Yankee dollar. Atilla may once have been eager to claim Trinidad's ticket to the modern world, yet at the end of the war it was he who presciently analyzed that world's imminently neocolonial character: The Americans, having traded fifty derelict destroyers for some of the choicest real estate in Trinidad (on which to construct their naval bases), "did as they pleased" for a number of years, then unceremoniously decamped, "[leaving] blue-eyed babies behind." And having thus scored— and scored a bargain—America would thereafter perpetuate not a military but a consumer–cultural hegemony. In retrospect, that is, the soldierly presence was only a crude prototype for the periodic, transitory invasions of *tourists*, often sex-tourists, who were now coming to purchase prepackaged photo- and phonographic fakeways to take back home. Today, Atilla glumly concluded, "we don't know who are masters in this land/If it's the English or the American." In the blank interior of what Gordon Rohlehr (1990) dubs a "transitional space between imperialisms" (360), Atilla's calypso—bleakly entitled "No Nationality"—maps the bumpy terrain of a would-be "post"colonial identity, whose dominant sensibility reads like a migrant, transnational version of DuBois's double consciousness, crafted over more than a decade of sailing back and forth to America, navigating the reefs of its popular and commercial forms with dexterity and versatility.

Now that my story's done, I'm not altogether sure what lessons it offers for the present day; my initial claim that the whole affair would be somehow "instructive" was perhaps just a way of warming up my subject. Yes: migration, as Philip Kasinitz (1992) reminds us, has historically been not just a crucial survival strategy for West Indians, but also a primary means of building a pan-Caribbean social selfhood (19–20). And insofar as entertainers can be counted as "activists" in the public sphere, calypsonians undoubtedly played a vanguard role in articulating, via mass-cultural channels, a usable public identity. But in some ways I think this episode is just as important for how it deepens our understanding of calypso's formal history. Every generation of commentators both in and outside the Caribbean—including present-day scoffers at "world music"—has ritually clucked its tongue over calypso's supposed betrayal of its authentic folk roots, its self-sullying absorption of nonindigenous commercial influences. Yet calypso in its modern incarnation (from roughly the turn of the century onward, that is) has always been commercially oriented, always Creole and cosmopolitan, always "compromised," shaping and reshaping itself according to bourgeois imperatives and market forces; this is in great measure what *made* it "modern" (see especially Cowley 1993). From at least the moment that promoters moved calypsonians out of the streets and barrack-yards of Port of Spain and into admission-charging tents, their emphasis was on exploring and exploiting the commercial possibilities of an erstwhile folk form. Making calypso a "world" music was merely the latest stage in that process. Lion and Atilla (along with King Radio and

Lord Beginner) had first been sent out in search of markets in 1933, touring the Caribbean in what looks, in hindsight, like a warm-up for their foray into America the following year. And as for the U.S. market, calypso had been cultivating it since the first luxury North American liners put into port in Trinidad in the early teens. Since the preceding century, moreover, calypso had casually sopped up all sorts of American musical influences, from spirituals and minstrel tunes to vaudeville, popular song, and jazz. So if, by the end of World War II, calypsonians had figuratively speaking bought the bungalow (as West Indians did quite *literally* two decades later, when they snapped up not only the row houses of Flatbush and Crown Heights, but also the cottages of western Long Island), then buying into a dodgy proposition such as "world music" amounts to just one more mortgage payment.

Such payments, furthermore, needn't come at the expense of structural or formal impoverishment, especially seeing as how calypsonians, adept in the art of the double entendre, routinely played formal device against functional sense. Consider, by way of analogy, that the interior accoutrements of the bungalow, however rustic things might appear from the outside, were in point of fact *très civilisés*; and that like the calypso, the craftsman cottage itself eventually morphed into a craftily designed, mass-market ware. The bungalow might be regarded an ironic talisman of modernity, then, representing that aspect of the modern that is historically, vestigially—perhaps schizophrenically—*anti*-modern. And irony, commercially and poetically speaking, is calypsonians' stock-in-trade. Forswearing his usual role as modernity's cheerleader, Atilla uncharacteristically begins another duet from the late thirties, "Modern Times," as the spokesman for a lost organic past. Trotting out two stanzas' worth of chestnuts about biblical centenarians and the degeneration of the species, he primly ponders whether, all things considered, life wasn't richer when "man lived closer to nature," before the advent of "electricity and trains, radio and aeroplanes." But it's his partner, Lion, who has the last word—or rather, word-from-our-sponsor—with a string of advertisements for ultramodern living that deflates Atilla's solemn hand wringing with plummy, understated wit: "King Solomon in all his glory/Wasn't happier than me/(Why? Because) He couldn't take a diesel truck and travel far,/He couldn't drink at the Railway Bar/There was no new appeal[?] in any serious case/And Green Pastures butter he couldn't taste/So Atilla, say what you may,/But give me the modern times every day!"

Between the two of them, then, Lion and Atilla walked both sides of the street. And to Lion's mind, Trinidad most definitely *was* comin' like a New York town. The tropics really *were* in New York. And welcome or not in this new-fashioned neighborhood (prefabricated in America with the help of migrant labor), they were planning to settle in and stay a while.

Notes

[See website for audio files and photos to accompany this chapter.]

1. Mutatis mutandis: The bungalow's origins are in British Bengal, where colonial officials adapted and expanded on an indigenous style of dwelling, transforming it into a private, single-family retreat where delicate English sensibilities could sequester themselves from the barbarous ways of the very "natives" whose vernacular architecture they'd seen fit to appropriate. And well before its migration across North America, the bungalow stood as a shelter from the adverse circumstances of modern living: the noise, stench, and mechanization—and, of course, the denizens—of the urban metropolis.

   In the wake of 9/11, of course, nativist ire (and Justice Department persecution) has been directed overwhelmingly at Arab nationals and Arab Americans, not Blacks, Asians, or Latinos. It's relevant to recall, however, that in spring of 2001, when census figures confirmed that white Californians now constitute a simple minority of the state's population, many national news stories appeared, expressing thinly veiled alarm that the same trend would soon overtake the country as a whole.

2. See, e.g., Ginell 1989, as well as Oliver 1984, 281. As British Decca had already built an independent empire of international music beginning in the 1920s (consisting of roughly a dozen different genres, precision targeted at as many different colonial markets), U.S. operations may simply have been the next logical step in their imperial plans. Ronald Foreman notes (199–200) that another urban black genre with which Decca had recently begun experimenting, double entendre "erotic blues," had reportedly sold quite well among whites, much to the company's surprise.

3. The anecdote is repeated in many sources; in this instance, as with many other factual details throughout this essay, I'm indebted primarily to the excellent research of Gordon Rohlehr (1990) and Donald R. Hill (1993). (Hill's helpful survey of calypso in mid-century New York, however, appeared in 1998, after this chapter was first drafted and all primary research was complete.)

4. Atilla allocated an effusive stanza to the bandsman in a 1935 calypso, "Sa Gomes' Emporiums," devoted primarily to praising his principal sponsor, Eduardo Sa Gomes: "Our accompany [sic] is a clever lad/Mr. Gerald Clark from Trinidad/Who has organise' an orchestra/That is tearing brass in America."

5. "*Iere* Now and Long Ago." *Iere* is an archaic appellation for Trinidad.

6. From one point of view, Atilla hardly had to insist. Paul Gilroy's well-known argument in *The Black Atlantic* (1993) has it that if alienation and dislocation are the principal features of the modern condition (and slavery and empire, the preconditions of Euro-American modernity), then Africans and their descendents in the Americas have long had an intimate and privileged knowledge of that condition. Others such as Stefano Harney (1996) have gone on to claim that Caribbean nations in particular were "born modern," with migration and displacement as their defining, normative experience. And like so many Creole forms, calypso, the quintessence of Trinidadian culture, is a cultural practice born of continuous circulation—first folk, then urban, then transnational.

7. These facts and many others in this paragraph I've gleaned from Kasinitz 1992 (esp. chapters 1 and 2)—and from Kasinitz's principal source for such material, Reid [1939] 1969. The most thorough study of early Caribbean immigration, and of relations between African Americans and Afro Caribbeans, is Watkins-Owens 1996.

8. The incident was widely reported and bitterly protested; I have relied on the account in the *Philadelphia Tribune* ("West Indians" 1934). Vann flatly denied having made the remarks, and was apparently never reprimanded by his superiors, who said only, in response to formal objections, that he was "one of our best men in this department" and that he had merely been "misunderstood" ("Vann Denies Affront" 1934).

9. This previous generation of tomming West Indian entertainers would have furnished the calypsonians an ambiguous education on how to cash in on their ethnicity in the American market. A more instructive example was provided by an earlier expatriate bandleader, Lionel Belasco. As Hill 1993 makes clear (170ff.), Belasco had a prescient understanding of the promise of mass culture and a well-developed talent for merchandizing Trinidadian folklore—especially for claiming authorship and copyright of what were in fact West Indian folk melodies, and for stealing lyrics and tunes composed by performers less sophisticated than he in business law.

10. See, e.g., Floyd J. Calvin's series of 1928 symposia on West Indian–American relations, begun in the *Pittsburgh Courier* for March 17 and syndicated in all the major black weeklies.

11. Of course, inasmuch as violent labor riots were also flaring up across the West Indies in the mid-thirties, Atilla's refrain had an unintended resonance: New York was, from this perspective, becoming shockingly like Trinidad. The Caribbean strikes were rooted largely in black oilfield workers' poor working conditions and their pointed exclusion from massive oil profits. Yet while Atilla was scarcely unaware, politically or poetically, of either the dark side of modernity (industrial pollution, economic depression, personal alienation) or the inherent ambiguity of his chosen symbols of material progress (even in the triumphalist " *Iere* Now," he notes cryptically that "Pointe-A-Pierre, which is lost in obscurity/Now possesses a giant oil refinery")—and while, moreover, he maintained throughout his career a sharp internationalist sensibility—such issues were scarcely what he wanted to foreground as a savvy international self-promoter.

12. It should be noted in passing that this crowd was no longer composed of the genteel class who had rendezvoused in pre-Prohibition "night-clubs." According to a *New York Times Magazine* story on the remarkable rebirth of nightclubs in the city, patrons now consisted largely of randy businessmen from the sticks whose travel was facilitated by low depression-era train fares, in addition to the "slummers" who had trekked uptown to Harlem for illicit thrills throughout the twenties (Crowther 1937). (Ads in both the New York dailies and the Harlem weeklies confirm that black female burlesque dancers, usually with faux-exotic stage names, featured prominently on the showbills of the new clubs.)

13. Legendary discographer Dick Spottswood (2000) has since borrowed this tune's title for an accounting of calypsos recorded on Decca in the 1930s and '40s.

14. Materially, anyway, such success was almost wholly imaginary, not least because the record shop impresario Sa Gomes retained the royalties from all record sales. Calypsonians did leverage their 1934 record deal into a doubling of tent admission fees in the run up to Carnival, however. And as Rohlehr points out (1990: 123), recording represented (at least in theory) the fulfillment of a kind of American dream for the calypsonian: a dream of at last becoming self-sufficient, of making a living as a professional instead of laying-about and cultivating the image of a hard-living dandy. In this respect, Rohlehr concludes, the role of the calypsonian really was re-orienting itself away from lower-class loyalty towards the bourgeois ideal of individual success.

15. My account of the rise of the bungalow in America owes its details to three fine sources: King 1984, Duchscherer and Keister 1995, and Winter 1980.

16. Jerome Kern had also notched an early hit in 1917 with his improbably-titled showtune "(A Little) Bungalow in Quogue." It's perhaps of passing interest to note that there are striking rhythmic and melodic echoes of "My Blue Heaven" in Lion's "I Am Going to Buy a Bungalow"; the latter, a jaunty foxtrot unlike most Latin-tinged, minor-key calypsos of the day, could almost be sung in counterpoint to the former.

17. That the bungalow stood for the anti-urban was in this instance doubly important because riotous negroes, obviously, were indelibly linked with urban ghettoes.

18. Sales of calypsos reportedly amounted to some thirty thousand for 1938. By any standard (including that of just a few years earlier), this was hardly phenomenal, but in the desperate slump of the late '30s, it was indicative of a hopeful trend. For the articles mentioned, see Bowles 1940, "Calypso Boom" 1938, "Calypsonian Crescendo" 1939, Mitchell 1939, and "Old calypso songs" 1940.

19. One is reminded of an anecdote in Claude McKay's memoir *A Long Way From Home* repeated by Irma Watkins-Owens. Caught in a police dragnet of alleged African American vagrants in Pittsburgh, McKay testifies before a magistrate after a night in jail. Upon hearing that McKay is Jamaican, the judge dismisses all charges and reprimands the arresting officer for his lack of discrimination. Henceforth McKay dryly resolves "to cultivate more my native accent" (quoted in Watkins-Owens 1996: 5).

20. A long-lost recording of one of the Town Hall Concerts, promoted by folksinger Pete Seeger's left-leaning "People's Songs" cooperative, was recently unearthed and issued on CD by Rounder Records ("Calypso at Midnight" and "Calypso After Midnight").

21. Don Hill (1998: 77) hears the line as "rhythmic" rather than "ethnic" harmony, and there is sufficient ambiguity in the somewhat unintelligible phrase to support his version. Obviously, for my purposes, "ethnic" yields the more suggestive reading.

22. For a later variation on a similar theme, see Michelle A. Stephens' illuminating "Natural Mystic" (1998) about the posthumous marketing of Bob Marley. As a "natural mystic," Stephens says, "Marley offers an image of blackness that has helped to preserve a *North American* identity built on the [imagined] integration of racial differences" (142, emphasis in original). "The central thrust of twentieth century American popular music," Stephens quotes the epigrammatic Charles Shaar Murray as saying, is "the need to separate black music (which, by and large, white Americans love) from black people (who, by and large, they don't)" (151).

References

My thanks to the Office of Research and Graduate Study at Humboldt State University and to the National Endowment for the Humanities for funding archival research for this chapter. Earlier versions were presented at the MLA in 1996 and at "XCP/Cross-Cultural Poetics" in 1997, and a later, abbreviated version was adapted for the joint conference of the Center for Black Music Research and the Society for American Music in 2001. I'm grateful to both panelists and audience members at these sessions for their helpful and appreciative comments. Special thanks to the Center for Black Music Research (Columbia College, Chicago) for its support and encouragement.

Bowles, Paul. 1940. "Calypso: Music of the Antilles." *Modern Music* 17, 5 (April–May): 154–59.

Calypso Boom. 1938. *Time* August 29: 21.

Calypsonian Crescendo: Native Trinidad Recordings Attract Much Interest Here. 1939. *Billboard* December 16: 9–10.

Cowley, John. 1996. *Carnival, Canboulay, and Calypso: Traditions in the Making.* Cambridge: Cambridge University Press.

Crichton, Kyle. 1938. "Thar's Gold in them Hillbillies." *Collier's* 101, 24 (April 30): 24–25.

Crowther, Bosley. 1937. "Hi-De-Ho!: The Night Clubs Turn 'Em Away." *New York Times Magazine* March 21: 14–15+.

Duchscherer, Paul, and Douglas Keister. 1995. *The Bungalow: America's Arts & Crafts Home.* New York: Penguin Studio.

Foreman, Jr., Ronald Clifford. 1968. *Jazz and Race Records, 1920–32; Their Origins and Their Significance for the Record Industry and Society.* PhD Thesis. University of Illinois.

Gilbert, Gama. 1940. "Calypso: A Glance at Its Background and Musical Style—Recent Releases." *New York Times* April 7: 8X.

Gilroy, Paul. 1993. *The Black Atlantic: Modernity and Double Consciousness.* Cambridge, Mass,: Harvard University Press.

Ginell, Cary. 1989. "Introduction: The Decca Record Company." *The Decca Hillbilly Discography, 1927–1945.* Comp. Cary Ginell. Westport, Conn.: Greenwood, xi–xvii.

Gladwell, Malcolm. 1996. "Black Like Them." *The New Yorker* 72, 10 (April 29 and May 5): 74–81.

Harney, Stefano. 1996. *Nationalism and Identity: Culture and the Imagination in a Caribbean Diaspora.* Kingston and London: University of West Indies Press/Zed.

Hill, Donald R. 1993. *Calypso Calaloo: Early Carnival Music in Trinidad.* Gainesville: University Press of Florida.

——. 1998. "I Am Happy Just to Be in This Sweet Land of Liberty": The New York City Calypso Craze of the 1930s and 1940s. *Island Sounds in the Global City: Caribbean Popular Music and Identity in New York.* Eds. Ray Allen and Lois Wilcken. New York: New York Folklore Society/Institute for Studies in American Music, Brooklyn College, 74–92.

Johnson, Malcolm. 1940. "Cafe Life in New York: Gerald Clark and His Calypso Artists at the Village Vanguard." *New York Sun* April 5: 27.

Kasinitz, Philip. 1992. *Caribbean New York: Black Immigrants and the Politics of Race.* Ithaca, N.Y.: Cornell University Press.

King, Anthony D. 1984. *The Bungalow: The Production of a Global Culture.* London: Routledge.

Mitchell, Joseph. 1939. "Houdini's Picnic." *The New Yorker,* May 6: 61–71.

"Old calypso Songs from Trinidad Are Now Becoming a New U.S. Fad." 1940. *Life,* April 8.

Oliver, Paul. 1984. *Songsters and Saints: Vocal Traditions on Race Records.* Cambridge: Cambridge University Press.

Ottley, Roi, and William J. Weatherby, eds., 1967. *The Negro in New York: An Informal Social History.* New York: New York Public Library [Federal Writers Program, ca. 1939].

Reid, Ira de A. 1969. *The Negro Immigrant: His Background, Characteristics, and Social Adjustment, 1899–1937.* New York: Columbia University Press, 1939. Reprint, New York: Arno.

Rohlehr, Gordon. 1990. *Calypso and Society in Pre-Independence Trinidad.* Port of Spain: author.

Seymour, Gene. 1996. "Racial Myth and Pop Culture." Review of *Blackface, White Noise: Jewish Immigrants in the Hollywood Melting Pot,* by Michael Rogin. *The Nation* August 12, 19: 34–36.

Spottswood, Dick. 2000. "We Ain't Fraid Nobody: Decca Calypsos in the 1930s." *ARSC Journal* 31, 2: 224–43.

Stephens, Michelle A. 1998. "Babylon's 'Natural Mystic': The North American Music Industry, The Legend of Bob Marley, and the Incorporation of Transnationalism." *Cultural Studies* 12, 2: 139–67.

"Strange Art of Calypso: Topical Songs From Trinidad Become a Record Vogue." 1939. *Newsweek* October 9, 33.

"Vann Denies Affront to N.Y. West Indians." 1934. [Baltimore] *Afro-American* March 24.

Watkins-Owens, Irma. 1996. *Blood Relations: Caribbean Immigrants and the Harlem Community, 1900–1930.* Bloomington: Indiana University Press.

"West Indians Flay Robert L. Vann For New York Insults." 1934. *Philadelphia Tribune,* March 15.

Winter, Robert. 1980. *The California Bungalow.* Los Angeles: Hennessey and Ingalls.

Selected Discography

Atilla the Hun [Raymond Quevedo]. History of Carnival. Rec. March 15, 1935. *History of Carnival: Christmas, Carnival, Calenda, and Calypso from Trinidad, 1929–1939.* Comp. and ann. John Cowley. Matchbox [UK] MBCD 301–2, 1993 [Decca 17253,1935]. Compact Disc.

———. No Nationality. [Unknown mfr., ca. 1946.] (Qtd. in Rohlehr, 359–60.)

———and The Lion [Hubert Raphael Charles]. Guests of Rudy Vallee. Rec. March 10, 1938. *Calypso Breakaway, 1927–1941.* Comp. and transcr. Dick Spottswood and Keith Warner. Rounder CD 1054, 1990 [Decca 17389, 1938]. Compact Disc.

———and Lord Beginner [Egbert Moore]. Iere Now and Long Ago. Rec. March 22, 1935. *Calypsos from Trinidad: Politics, Intrigue, and Violence in the 1930s.* Ed. Dick Spottswood. Arhoolie CD 7004, 1991 [Decca 17264, 1935]. Compact Disc.

Calypso at Midnight and *Calypso After Midnight.* Eds. Donald R. Hill and John Cowley. Fwd. by Steve Shapiro. Rounder CD 11661–1840–2/11661–1841–2, 1999. Compact Disc.

Caresser, The [Rufus Calendar]. Edward VIII. Rec. 1937. *The Real Calypso.* Comp. and ann. Samuel F. Charters. Smithsonian Folkways [RBF Records] RBF 13, 1966 [Decca 17298, 1937]. Compact Disc.

———. The More They Try to Do Me Bad. Rec. February 23, 1938. *Calypso Breakaway, 1927–1941* [Decca 17353, 1938]. Compact Disc.

———and Ruby Canera. Rec. February 25, 1938. *Calypso Ladies, 1926–1941.* Ed. Dick Spottswood. Transcr. Dick Spottswood and Keith Warner. Heritage [UK] HT CD 06, 1991 [Decca 17348, 1938]. Compact Disc.

Keskidee Trio [Atilla the Hun, Lord Beginner, and the Tiger]. Sa Gomes' Emporiums. Rec. March 22, 1935. *Trinidad Loves to Play Carnival: Carnival, Calenda, and Calypso from Trinidad, 1914–1939.* Comp. and ann. John Cowley and Dick Spottswood. Matchbox [UK] MBCD 302–2, 1993 [New York: Decca 17226, 1935]. Compact Disc.

King Radio [Norman Span] and the Lion. We Ain't Fraid Nobody. Rec. April 11, 1936. 78 rpm. Decca 17326, 1936. 78 rpm.

Lion, The. I Am Going to Buy a Bungalow. Rec. February 25, 1938. *Calypso Carnival* 1936–1941. Comp. and ann. Dick Spottswood. Rounder CD 1077, 1993 [Decca 17348, 1938]. Compact Disc.

———and Atilla the Hun. "Modern Times." Rec. February 25, 1937. 78 rpm. Decca 17321, 1937. 78 rpm.

negotiate the fundamental tensions between their positions as rock musicians in the GDR (subject to the restricted discourses of GDR institutions obsessed with security and distanciation toward Western rock) on the one hand, while they contended with the subordination and ultimate incorporation of rock within capitalist discourses outside the country on the other. Discursive negotiations of power refer, therefore, to the bands' attempts to: a) counteract state monopolizing strategies for naming music and circumscribing music behavior; b) develop critical, heterodoxic, and contested reflections on social reality in the country; and c) increase circulation of their music within the domestic and global music industries' prescribed genre discourses. Examining these negotiations contributes to a deeper understanding of how music is used to provide "the social space with material-cultural resources for feeling, being and doing," for structuring "motivation, energy and desire," and material "for action and experience" (DeNora 2000: 125–30).

In my discussion of discursive negotiations of power, I follow Foucault's notions of discourse as "practices which systematically form the objects of which they are speaking,"[1] and that are a result of relations "between institutions, economic and social processes, forms of behavior, systems of norms, techniques, types of classifications, and manners of characterization,"[2] which "offer it the objects of which it speaks."[3] Foucault informs not only my analysis of texts but my examination of naming strategies for music and music behavior. I also employ a modified version of Arjun Appadurai's concept of the circulation of cultural commodities[4] in order to present discursive negotiating strategies as a means of creating and controlling the various institutionalized public spaces in which the bands typically performed. My analysis focuses on the bands' negotiations with the state monopoly record company, the Party-directed and state-operated radio networks,[5] and actors in the highly regulated, politically constrained live performance circuit. These actors comprise what David Bathrick[6] calls the "official" public sphere, which includes the communist Socialist Unity Party (*Sozialistische Einheitspartei*—SED), the agencies of the East German government (primarily the Ministry for Culture but also the police and security service [*Stasi*]), and the regional and local cultural authorities who administered the mandatory licensing of popular musicians. These agencies controlled access to the broadcast media and recording industry by using the *Lektorate* (censorship boards charged with reviewing all music produced in radio, television, and record company studios) and other instruments of discipline. Other participants in constituting the discursive object "popular music" in the GDR[7] were rock bands, vocalists, composers, lyric writers, arrangers, and radio and television station employees—all of whose practices, behaviors, norms, and values were, in part, determined by the global music industry. Within these webs of discourse, GDR rock bands communicated with various audience communities over time as their narratives circulated through different discursive spaces. All three songs reflect the influence of the *Neue Deutsche Welle* or NDW (New German Wave) in different ways and attempt to replace the more romantic and abstract music that characterized GDR rock in the late 1970s with the more concrete and direct lyric aesthetic of the NDW.

"WERKSTATTSONG" (WORKSHOP SONG)

Pankow's "Werkstattsong"[8] formed part of a longer theater piece about a day in the life of a young apprentice named Paule Panke. Panke's unglamorous day in a factory contrasted greatly with the propagandistic heroism attributed to members of the working class by Party ideology in socialist realist literature. The band performed "Werkstattsong" live in late 1981 but only obtained permission to release the complete rock epic on vinyl LP in early 1989,[9] long after interest in the work had subsided and its controversial political orientation (i.e., to effect positive change within the system through critique of its negative phenomenon) was rendered irrelevant by the unfolding crisis culminating in the fall of the Wall.[10]

Lead singer André Herzberg played the part of Paule Panke during the program, and Paule is the object of audience identification. The song was placed in the middle of the program, after the apprentice had grudgingly woken up, eaten breakfast, and ridden in an overcrowded and completely unpleasant bus to the factory at a god-awful hour in the early morning. Paule Panke was bored by his meaningless work (filing down a "bump" on a piece of iron) and mused that spending time with his girlfriend, Mathilde, would be more fun. The work was supervised by Meister Falk, his foreman, who was continually looking over Paule's shoulder to make sure he was accomplishing his task. Finally, the factory radio was turned on, which positively influenced both the tempo of Paule's work and the satisfaction of Meister Falk. The refrain of the song substituted a new person's name ("me," Mathilde, Meister Falk) after each verse and coupled the rhythm of work and personal interactions in the shop with the "electricity" of sexual eroticism that characterized each of Paule's encounters with Mathilde, Meister Falk, himself, and the factory workshop: "Werkstattleben das ist hektisch/das macht mich verrückt elektrisch/es schwingt und scheppert her und hin/da ist irgendwie Leben drin/es schwingt und scheppert her und hin/da ist irgendwie Leben drin."[11]

Instead of politicizing daily life like the songs of the official FDJ-Singebewegung in the late 1960s and 1970s, "Werkstattsong" sexualized and eroticized daily life and personal relations and thus clearly juxtaposed the tedious reality of socialist factory life, and perhaps life in general in the GDR, with enjoyment, fun, and pleasure outside the factory.

Originally, the entire story was criticized by officials for not optimistically depicting the life of apprentices in a socialist factory, where socialist cooperation, optimism, and other working class virtues were, allegedly, evident. Even so, two lines of "Werkstattsong's" third verse were excised from the final production: "Ist die Arbeit noch so seicht, mit Musik da scheint sie leicht ("Be the job ever so banal, with music it appears easy"). After the original song was played on the radio on October 21, 1981, Eberhard Fensch from the SED's Department of Agitation and Propaganda wrote to Heinz Geggel, his superior and chair of that department,[12] that the song "does not promote an attitude of high achievement among young people, but instead, works against that."[13] Fensch insisted that, in the future, songs "with this kind of character" would not be accepted and broadcast at all, because retroactive withdrawal after broadcast "stimulate[d] unnecessary political conflicts"[14]—that is, protests and criticism from the West, who carefully monitored all GDR radio broadcasts.

Initially, *Paule Panke* was approved for public performance only after Gisela Steineckert, the president of the Committee for Entertainment Arts, a supervisory agency of the Ministry for Culture, saw one of the first performances. She changed her initial negative opinion and the band performed the program for two years. A short time later, *Paule Panke* won a prize at a pop music competition; this valuable accolade represented legitimacy and facilitated further live performances and potential radio and record productions. However, after a performance in the city of Leipzig (at which fans, allegedly, fought with one another in front of the stage) the Berlin city administration almost revoked their performance licenses.[15] The attitude of nonconformity prompted the Amiga label to refuse production of *Paule Panke* on an LP even after it was promised by Amiga boss René Büttner. Furthermore, GDR television, which filmed their debut performance, refused to broadcast it. Pankow, however, was not a dissident group, nor were its members intent on a confrontation with the Party or government cultural bureaucracy. In an interview with the author in 1987, lead guitarist Jürgen Ehle stated that the decision by Amiga not to produce an LP with *Paule Panke* merely prompted the band to move away from theater rock and focus more strongly on being a rock band—something they had been planning to do before the ban and that the 1983 *Kille Kille* LP fulfilled.

In the wake of the Amiga refusal[16] the band turned to the state-owned radio station and, later, to the *Lektorat*.[17] As the largest producer of music in the country, the radio network often broadcast its own recordings of bands long before these were released publicly on an Amiga label. As the radio broadcasting networks needed music to fill their increased number of broadcast hours, a recording and airplay for *Paule Panke* seemed likely.[18] Nevertheless, the radio station refused to broadcast *Paule Panke* more than once and the band appealed[19] to the *Lektorat* on July 1, 1982. Denied permission to release *Paule Panke* in its entirety, the band proposed to combine some songs from the program, including "Werkstattsong," with new songs, and to release the resulting LP both in the GDR (on Amiga) and in the West (on RCA). The Amiga LP was eventually released as *Kille Kille* in 1983, while the deal with RCA was squelched by Party bureaucrats. In negotiations with the *Lektorat* of the radio station, Ehle, a former member of the political folklore group "Jahrgang 49,"[20] spoke on behalf of the group and explained that he could speak "functionary German," and thus was able to "speak the language" of the officials, something that singer André Herzberg, on the other hand, intensely loathed.

"DIE GRÄFIN" (THE DUCHESS)

Though Silly's "Die Gräfin" (with text by Werner Karma) was part of the band's live concert performances and was released on the LP *Mont Klamott* in 1983,[21] the song was banned from the radio network after direct intervention by the Central Committee of the Party. *Mont Klamott* was the band's second LP[22] and marked the inclusion of Karma, a lyrics writer, as a full-fledged member of the band; this arrangement continued for their next three productions but ended during the period preceding the fall of the Berlin Wall. It was unusual in that Karma did not play an instrument but still received an equal share of the band's income.

The singer describes a somewhat decrepit old woman, ironically called "the duchess," who lives in the apartment below him in an old apartment building. The duchess belonged to the generation that was expropriated by the Communists after the war and had problems dealing both with her past and with alcohol. The song satirized and belittled her problems and countered her claim to "blaues Blut" ("noble blood") with the remark that she was just "blau" ("blue or drunk"), from "Korn und Kümmel" ("wheat spirits and caraway schnapps"). The woman had "lost everything" and her few remaining possessions included a "small picture of Jesus Christ." The lyrics do not specify whether she lost everything in World War II before the Communists came to power, or if she lost everything because of the Communist expropriations of the nobles who supported the Nazis after the war was over. The singer often invited the "duchess" to her apartment where she offered her guest a grog with double the amount of rum. The song's final verse vacillated between sympathy for the "duchess's" suffering on the one hand, and ironic distance at her apparently ridiculous behavior on the other; the singer compared her own situation with that of the old woman, and laughed not at the old woman's problems, but at her own, indicating that the singer's problems were miniscule in comparison to those of the old woman.[23]

The song was presented by Amiga to the radio editorial board for approval on July 8, 1982, and was rejected.[24] The board objected to the "presentation of an older citizen from the standpoint of youths making music in a band,"[25] and although the depiction of the older woman was subjective, the editorial commission thought its broadcast would encourage one-sided generalizations and "lead to undifferentiated conclusions in the relations between the generations."[26] Instead of informing the band that its song was rejected in July, the band learned about it only in early September by word of mouth. Thomas Fritzsching, a band member, had to first petition the radio station to find out about its fate, and was given the official reason for rejection over two months later. Fritzsching complained[27] that the band was not so much upset that the song was rejected, but that the delay had cost them the opportunity to substitute a different song for that summer's lucrative radio play lists.[28] Fritzsching, who intimated that the rejection by the radio editorial board might be due to jealousy and revenge because of the band's move from the radio station to the Amiga production facilities, vented his frustration that they had lost three months' time in the process. In his answer to Fritzsching's petition, State Radio Committee chief Achim Becker attempted to address Fritzching's concerns, but only offered as recompense the opportunity to submit other songs for approval at the later time.[29]

"HALB UND HALB" (HALF AND HALF)

City's "Halb und Halb" was recorded and released on the LP *Casablanca*[30] in 1987. The LP created a furor when the newspaper of the Free German Youth[31] first published an article in praise of the recording, then reversed its opinion in a subsequent editorial. This prompted a partial, regionally inconsistent radio broadcast ban of "Halb und Halb" and other songs on the LP, but also precipitated a surge in popularity for both the song and the LP, which required multiple pressings to meet demand.

The song is a reference to the incomplete or half-complete nature of human existence, family life, humanity, and a Europe, Germany, and Berlin fractured by Cold War politics. The lead singer reflected about life "being half over," "sitting half full in front of a half-empty glass," and asked rhetorically about life passing by, "what are you waiting for?" In the second verse the singer related that he only "occupies half of a bed," "has only half his hair" on his head, while listening to a "half-loud radio" show informing its listeners that "half of humanity" is dying somewhere.

The first two verses provoked censors because of their rejection of passivity and perceived appeal for sociopolitical change in the deteriorating and stagnant GDR. In contrast to government propaganda that portrayed the GDR's "real existing socialism" as the fulfillment of human destiny and happiness, the song's reference to the half-baked nature of that reality rejected this official discourse. The second verse invokes a biblical image to denote the "half" capitalist world as well as the "half" socialist world—both necessarily incomplete—and concludes with an ambiguous reference to the "demigods that are dancing around a golden calf." This could refer to capitalist consumerism, socialist consumerism, or both.

The song's last three lines proved to be the most provocative: "In half of the country and the cut apart city, halfway satisfied with what you have" ("Im halben Land und der zerschnittenen Stadt/halbwegs zufrieden mit dem, was man hat"). Not only did the authors reject the government's claims to legitimacy, but also the assertion that East Germany and East Berlin were "complete" in either an historical or territorial sense; the country was not, as the leadership claimed, the historic fulfillment of a centuries-long legacy of working class struggle, nor could it claim to be complete while separated from its western half. The GDR leadership had consistently maintained the opposite position as late as 1989, just before the Wall came down.

Despite the censors' objections, the Amiga record label published and released the song along with all the others on the LP because Amiga was one of the few firms supervised by the Ministry for Culture to achieve an economic surplus; its record sales inside the country and to the West helped finance the Ministry for Culture's other, less successful sectors. The popularity of GDR rock had been in precipitous decline ever since the beginning of the 1980s due to its eroding credibility, technical inferiority, inability to address the conditions of reality, and lack of musical risk-taking and experimentation; as a result, the sales of Amiga recordings decreased and created a critical financial situation. In response, recordings such as *Casablanca*, which allowed new lyric and musical risks, were released. After they finished the *Casablanca* LP, the band began a seventy-concert tour but chose to leave "Halb und Halb" and "Gute Gründe" out of the program because of lack of adequate rehearsal time.[32] The band had been too busy to undertake the careful preparations necessary to make these two complex pieces ready for live performance.

DISCURSIVE NEGOTIATIONS OF POWER, PUBLICS, AND MUSICAL PERFORMANCE SPACES

Although the bands were interested in conveying their respective standpoints, neither City nor the other two bands, Pankow and Silly, were willing to engage in a political confrontation with the Party and jeopardize their professional careers for the sake of making a political point. Their primary interest was to maintain or expand their stature within the field of popular music while upholding their political integrity as subaltern participants. Without going into greater detail here, two different types of economic logic underlie these decisions. On the one hand, the bands negotiated for the release of vinyl recordings according to global popular music industry standards by which sales of recordings determine the stature and value of the band. On the other hand, they attempted to accommodate the anomalous situation in the GDR, by which music on vinyl recordings served merely to document a band's live-concert competency. They were therefore trying to negotiate market-based determinations of status with politically determined ones. The pivotal institution in this equation was the radio station, which, as the largest producer of music in the country, supplied both the broadcasting outlets and Amiga with the requisite recording documents.

With the radio station at the center of the discussion, I now consider different types of performative instantiations of the music described above within the framework of discursive negotiations of power. These include 1) live performances, 2) recordings, and 3) radio broadcasts. I explore the means by which authorities controlled the circulation of pop music narratives in the different performative spaces. Each song was performed live and available on an LP-recording, but excluded from radio broadcasting.

What kind of institutional logics shaped these regulatory decisions? They were based only in part on the textual content; clearly, the performative context and its constructed meanings were crucial factors in determining why the same music was subject to different evaluative standards in different performative contexts and institutional configurations. The answer to this question might reveal the extent to which context and social embeddedness affect the discursive construction of the object "popular music" by different agents. If the lyrics were the sole factor regardless of the context, then one might expect a uniform decision to allow performances in either none or all performative situations: a live concert setting, as a vinyl recording, or on the radio station (and also television) airwaves. As Simon Frith emphasizes, a pop song is political not because it stimulates political action, but because it has an impact on how people speak.[33] Each performative context for the lyric message is "an implied narrative" with "a central character, the singer; a character with an attitude, in a situation, talking to someone."[34] Each performative context, whether vinyl recording, live concert, or radio broadcast, entails a differently constructed addressee and audience, and constructs the music differently; indeed, each of the performative contexts for these songs established a unique "communicative situation" for articulating a feeling, for legitimizing the narrative, for setting up different interpretive and situative logics, and for exhibiting the different voices, personalities, and bodies of each band.

Tia DeNora offers a more nuanced view of the impact of restrictions on music's spatial distribution on the development of social subjectivity and identity.[35] She emphasizes that music such as the three recordings analyzed here represents "resources for organizing and elaborating [people's] perceptions of non-musical things," (26) and are "framing devices" that are "projected or mapped onto something else," and "applied to and come to organize something outside themselves" (27). Furthermore, in suggesting that music is both "an instigator and container for feeling" and "a virtual means of expressing or constructing emotion," and thus helps to define its "temporal and qualitative structure" (58), it becomes evident that the discursive negotiations of power relating to the three performance contexts for the songs mentioned above ultimately relate to matters of control over aesthetic agency, time, and subjectivity. The restricted spatial circulation of this music reduces the listeners' opportunity to construct coherent self-identities and insert the music into the full range of human experience so that its meanings might be linked to events unfolding in the listeners' social environment.

Each of the different performance venues constructs a different kind of public with a different political character inherent in the structural logic of that particular performance sphere in GDR society. These performative contexts for rock and pop represent a type of public[36] that it is "self organizing," a "relation among strangers," whose "address of public speech is both personal and interpersonal"; it is "created by the circulation of discourse," and "exist[s] historically according to the temporality of [its] circulation." The Party's cultural bureaucracy preferred live concerts with local publics, or even recordings and their domestic or private publics, because of the spatial and temporal control that could be exerted over both the circulation of the music among these audiences and the bands' narratives. It was much easier to maintain control over live concerts and even vinyl recordings than music over the airwaves. However, contrary to their objectives, Party restrictions on the circulation of GDR rock in East German media had the effect of robbing citizens of the opportunity to establish links between its own GDR-produced music and the GDR environment; as a result, music from the West filled the vacuum and operated as a "device of social ordering" affecting "bodies, hearts, and minds."[37]

Live concerts construct "local publics" consisting of audiences who have invested energy into buying tickets and attending the concert in a local venue, whereby a public community with "local" character is constructed; self-experience, self-performance, and audience community affirmation are values specifically found in such situations. Given their ability to elicit powerful reactions and create communities, it is unsurprising that live concerts were closely regulated in the GDR. Amateur and professional bands were obligated to obtain yearly renewable performance licenses, for which auditions in front of district cultural authorities were required as well as proof of music education and training for amateurs. Repertoire restrictions introduced in 1958 stipulated that 60 percent of all bands, disc jockeys, and radio programming had to be from socialist countries, whereas 40 percent was allowed from Western countries. State-owned, but FDJ-operated youth clubs were subjected to tight control of their programs, and police permits were required for concerts and open air events. In addition to police observation while these events were taking place, attendance was also monitored by the *FDJ-Ordnerdienst*, the in-house security service under the direction of the police and the Stasi.

In spite of these circumstances, a certain degree of autonomy in concert settings could be achieved. Performances only became politicized and embedded within the Cold War confrontation between East and West when certain "deviant" behaviors—such as the 1977 riot on the Alexanderplatz during a Puhdys concert—threatened to become "public,"that is, the object of West German media scrutiny.[38] Drunkenness at open air performances (called "negative-decadent" behavior), rioting against police (called "disruption of order and security"), "special incidents" such as resisting arrest and other acts of opposition against the police, and "anti-state agitation" were usually localized and only became politically significant if the West German media, which always purveyed information suppressed by the GDR media,[39] used it as propaganda to suggest internal opposition to the GDR government.

Performances on vinyl recordings created "private" or "domestic" publics because they relied on specific technological conditions for their realization within certain enclosed spaces such as discos, bedrooms, living rooms, youth clubs, and the like. They became "public" when they were played on the radio, where they were subsumed by the state radio networks' structural hegemony and used as propaganda instruments of the Party. Vinyl recordings in private or domestic spaces help construct a private intimacy in which the private feelings of the performances are foregrounded with respect to the public nature of the performance. When played on the radio, however, these same songs are controlled by the structural hegemony of the state and its propaganda instrument. In this case, private consumption does not become hegemonic when played on the state radio networks, but instead competes and negotiates with it for hegemony in a process that cannot be presented here in greater detail.

With Silverstone and Hirsch we may locate home consumer recording technologies and recordings within the "moral economy of the household," whereby "objects and meanings, in their objectification and incorporation within spaces and practices of domestic life, define a particular semantic universe for the household in relation to that offered in the public world of commodities and ephemeral and instrumental relationships."[40] Sociologist David Chaney emphasizes that social activities of the household, to which listening to the radio belongs, "involve interpersonal relations that are both political and moral": "Political in the sense that power is being deployed to maintain structures of control and freedom, and moral in the sense that some way of justifying a division of labor is, often implicitly, appealed to and confirmed."[41] Chaney also identifies household technologies as "media of political interaction," not on the level of party programs, but rather on the level of the "micro-politics of interpersonal relations." It is understandable, therefore, that the lyrics and music of the three songs under consideration here all feature aspects of the private lives of GDR citizens grappling with what Chaney calls the "irrationality" of everyday normality[42] under the conditions of "real existing socialism." Real existing socialism was more insistent, Manichean, and comprehensive than capitalist society and consumer cultural industries in its assertion that scientific discourse and expertise was the sole source of ultimate truth about society and history in modernity. Therefore, it is not surprising that personal experience and "irrational" representations of these in the form of the three songs presented here "can provide an alternative basis for processes of cultural contestation" and legitimacy.[43] These three songs represent three particular examples of the everyday that help manage cultural change and help people "negotiate their environments in the process of dramatizing identities and subjectivities."[44] These songs are witness to the fact that the household is where the "everyday has become the primary site of cultural participation rather than more public specialized settings such as concert halls, cinemas, auditoria and sports stadia."[45]

Even in the GDR, domestic households created "a spatially and temporally bounded sense of security and trust" in contrast to the extra-domestic sphere. Recordings were a scarce commodity subject to the "politicization of consumption"[46] that "prevented people from consuming by not making goods available." The consumption of records by Western bands in preference to GDR bands "conferred an identity that set you off from socialism," whereas the acquisition of GDR rock music was embedded within the structure of officially sanctioned and distributed music; only when works like "Halb und Halb" or *Paule Panke* were banned on the radio did the songs and bands acquire the "alternative" or "oppositional" status needed to stimulate sales based on this logic.

Radio broadcasts, on the other hand, represented "public" media publics, but positioned within the moral economy of the household. The broadcasts were less tied to spatial demarcations, could traverse East–West borders, and could, therefore, help construct or deconstruct the abstract community and confirm its values, practices, and legitimacy. The broadcast media, according to David Morley and Kevin Robins, serve the dual role of "the political public sphere of the nation-state" on the one hand, and become "the focus for national cultural identification" on the other.[47] Due to the structural deficit of political legitimacy of the GDR government throughout its entire history, as well as the existence of the West German Federal Republic as an alternative "national" society and public—of which most of the GDR population could partake, albeit only as *spectators* (with television) and *listeners* (with radio) and not as active participants—the GDR mass media was unable to construct a true "public" in the Habermasian sense, in which a free exchange of ideas is purportedly at the root of rational and informed political decisions by sovereign citizens in a bourgeois democracy.

The complicated role of the three bands with regard to radio broadcasting coincides with what David Bathrick[48] explains is inherent in the "media public," the second of three different types of "publics" in the GDR, delineated by the media of the Federal Republic. The West German media "played an inestimable role in organizing, creating, orchestrating, and ultimately homogenizing the needs of the two advanced industrial societies," whereby each sphere of "media publics" were subject to each others' radio and television programming. Programming on both sides of the Wall "was carefully structured as systems of debate and rebuttal, persuasion and its counter."

Even popular music programming on both sides of the Wall responded to changes implemented respectively by each side due to the competitive pressure of political conflict during the Cold War.[49] In response to the music programming of the Radio in the American Sector (RIAS) and Sender Free Berlin (SFB) in West Berlin, the GDR State Committee for Radio established the youth radio program "DT 64" in 1964 after an initial period as a ten-day program reporting on the *Deutschlandtreffen der Jugend* ("DT"), a youth festival for both East and West Germans, in 1964. Because of the popularity of the pilot during the festival, featuring popular music along with roving reporters and more spontaneous news reports, the Radio Committee was besieged with requests to continue the program. This became the framework for responding to programming innovations from the West, whereby not only new music styles, but also new types of radio programs could be introduced.[50] The radio *program* DT 64, which started out as a three-and-a-half-hour radio show five days a week, was eventually expanded in 1987 to become its own youth radio *network* broadcasting more than twenty hours a day, seven days a week. This not only brought about a quantitative expansion in the scope of "official" media, but led also to qualitative changes in its programming such that music previously in the "underground,"—that is, promoted by home audiocassette production and clandestine or unofficial performances by bands with no official performing licenses—could be featured in a radio show entitled "*Parocktikum*" and thus become "officialized" and thus co-opted by the state media.[51]

The three rock bands under consideration did not belong to the alternative and independent music scene, part of what Bathrick terms the "third public sphere," in other words, "the various unofficial public enclaves or counterofficial voices that sought to break into or establish dialogue with the officially dominating voices." This third public sphere was not only "literary writers," but also oppositional sectors of the Protestant Church; feminist, peace, and ecology movements; and underground culture and music scenes, including jazz, punk, and rock musicians, that "struggled to establish semi-autonomous terrains of publicness, either within or wholly outside of official institutions." While these musicians also "helped facilitate the development historically of critical discourses,"[52] it is questionable whether, on the basis of their predetermined positions within the cultural hierarchy, they were able to articulate "alternative political views within the larger polity," a quality attributed to the critical intelligentsia, but generally rejected for popular music promoted by the GDR media.

In conclusion, the three bands reviewed here did not belong to the alternative scene, but struggled to dissolve the boundaries between the alternative and independent scene on the one hand, and the range of officially broadcast types of artistic and political expression on the other.

Notes

1. Michel Foucault, *Archäologie des Wissens* (Frankfurt/M: Suhrkamp Taschenbuchverlag, 1981), 74.
2. Foucault, *Archäologie des Wissens*, 68.
3. Foucault, *Archäologie des Wissens*, 69.
4. See Arjun Appadurai, ed., *The Social Life of Things* (Cambridge and New York: Cambridge University Press, 1986), 29, 36ff.
5. That is, at the cabinet-level.
6. David Bathrick, *The Powers of Speech: The Politics of Culture in the GDR* (Lincoln: University of Nebraska Press, 1995), 34ff.
7. Rock, folk, new wave, punk, and Schlager were the GDR's principle rock genre categories at the time. *Schlager* were folk-influenced German popular songs with roots in nineteenth and twentieth-century operetta and ballroom dance.
8. The band's name was a play on at least two different words: the German pronunciation for "punk," and "Pankow," West Germany's Cold War abbreviation for the East German government, which throughout the 1950s they derisively called "the Regime in Pankow." Pankow was a well-to-do East Berlin city district in which many state officials lived.

9. See *Paule Panke. Ein Tag aus dem Leben eines Lehrlings*. Live 1982. Amiga 856 473. This was a recording of a concert on February 2, 1982, in the House of Young Talents in East Berlin. The "Werkstattsong" was released on the *Kille Kille* LP (Amiga 855 994) separately in 1983

10. "Werkstattsong" had, however, appeared on a compilation LP in 1983, which included three others from the *Paule Panke* program.

11. "Factory life is hectic/that makes me crazy electric/there is swinging and clanging back and forth/there is somehow life within/there is swinging and clanging back and forth/there is somehow life within."

12. Letter from Eberhard Fensch to Heinz Geggel, November 2, 1981. BStU DY30 25942.

13. "Dieser Titel fördert nicht die Leistungsbereitschaft junger Menschen, sondern wirkt dem entgegen."

14. "unnötige politische Querelen."

15. The band was held directly responsible for the altercation. This was according to information from an interview with singer André Herzberg in 1995.

16. Amiga's limited resources prevented them from offering recording contracts to all GDR rock bands; however, as a carrot to the band after the *Paule Pankow* ban, Amiga offered to produce one LP a year for the band (an offer that the band was ultimately unable to completely exploit), which was only granted to top bands in the country.

17. All song lyrics had to be reviewed and approved or censored by the *Lektorat*, or editorial board of each institution—television, radio, record company—before it would be produced or broadcast in that medium. This was in addition to the licensing requirement for rock bands before they were even allowed to perform. Licensing auditions were conducted in front of district cultural commission representatives, in the case of amateurs on a yearly basis, in the case of professionals only at serious junctures in their careers, or only once if the band and its musicians are popular and successful.

18. This need was especially acute after 1986 when the DT64 youth radio program (broadcast daily from 4 to 7 p.m. during the week) was expanded into a complete youth broadcasting network with twenty hours of continuous programming each day.

19. Horst Fliegel, Music Director of the State Committee, stated that "the Radio is interested less in the treatment of peripheral problems or critical attitudes toward our social reality. Instead, it is interested in topics which stimulate an optimistic feeling in life." (der Rundfunk [ist] weniger [interessiert] an der Behandlung von Randproblemen oder kritischen Haltungen zu unserer gesellschaftlichen Wirklichkeit, sondern an Themen, die ein optimistisches Lebensgefühl stimulieren). Barch DR6 926.

20. This was one of the two important groups in the *Freie Deutsche Jugend Singebewegung* [Free german youth song movement], the official political folk song movement of the SED youth organization. The other was *Oktoberklub*. J49 was an important incubator for rock bands of the 1970s.

21. See Amiga 855 972.

22. The band's first success was the title song of its first LP *Tanzt keiner Boogie?* ("Does Anyone Dance the Boogie?").

23. The duchess, who was still mourning her losses of decades earlier, had acquired her nondescript apartment just like all the other people in the country, and had to deal with a city housing authority that treated everyone equally (badly).

24. See "Schreiben der Gruppe Silly" September 17, 1982, from Music Editor Klaus Hugo to Music Department Head Horst Fliegel 2pp. Barch DR6 926.

25. "die textliche Darstellung einer älteren Bürgerin aus der Sicht einer für die Jugend musizierenden Gruppe."

26. "erhält aber durch die Sendung im Rundfunk verallgemeinernden Charakter und dürfte zu undifferenzierten Schlußfolgerungen in den Beziehungen der Generationen führen."

27. See Letter from Thomas Fritzsching to Achim Becker September 14, 1982. Barch DR6 926.

28. Summer airplay was lucrative because vacationers inside the country increased their listening time and could become familiar with increased amounts of new music which they would later buy on vinyl recordings.

29. See Letter from Achim Becker to Thomas Fritzsching, September 9, 1982. Barch DR6 926.

30. See Amiga 856 081.

31. The "Free German Youth" was the youth organization of the Socialist Unity Party. It published a daily newspaper called *Junge Welt* (Young World), which usually set the discursive tone and values of youth-related issues, and reflected official Party positions on these issues.

32. During rehearsals, decisions were made as to which tracks of the recording would be left out, and which would be included in the live concert. The band rejected complete computerization of their live performances because it restricted their freedom to respond to variations in the audience's mood from one night to the next. Use of computerized and digital sound equipment (necessary to replicate the polished sound of the recording in a live context) would have required four extra weeks of rehearsal and technical preparation in advance of the live tour.

33. Simon Frith, *Performing Rites* (Cambridge, Mass.: Harvard University Press, 1966), 169.

34. Frith, *Performing Rites*, 169.

35. Tia DeNora, *Music in Everyday Life* (Cambridge: Cambridge University Press, 2000).

36. Michael Warner, quoted in Craig Calhoun, "Constitutional Patriotism and the Public Sphere: Interests, Identity, and Solidarity in the Integration of Europe," in Pablo De Greiff and Ciaran Cronin, eds., *Transnational Politics* (Cambridge Mass.: MIT Press. Forthcoming). Citation in footnote no. 25, p. 22.

37. See DeNora, *Music in Everyday Life*, 129.

38. Contributing to the sense of calamity, scaffolding broke during the incident.

39. See Gunter Holzweissig, "Massenmedien in der DDR," in Jürgen Wilke, ed., *Mediengeschichte der Bundesrepublik Deutschland* (Bonn: Bundeszentrale für politische Bildung, 1999), 574.

40. Roger Silverstone and Eric Hirsch, "Introduction," in Roger Silverstone, Eric Hirsch, eds., *Consuming Technologies: Media and Information in Domestic Spaces* (London: Routledge, 1992).

41. David Chaney, *Cultural Change and Everyday Life* (Palgrave: Basingstoke UK, New York, NY, 2002), 73ff.

42. Chaney, *Cultural Change*, 48.

43. Chaney, *Cultural Change*, 48.

44. Chaney, *Cultural Change*, 55

45. Chaney, *Cultural Change*, 58.

46. See Katherine Verdery, *What Was Socialism and What Comes Next?* (Princeton, N.J.: Princeton University Press, 1996), 28.

47. See David Morley and Kevin Robins, *Spaces of Identity: Global Media, Electronic Landscapes, and Cultural Boundaries* (London: Routledge, 1996), 10.

48. See Bathrick, *The Powers of Speech*, 34ff.

49. See Edward Larkey, "DT 64 und RIAS. Jugendradio, Populäre Musik und Kalter Krieg," *3. Buckower Mediengespräche. Gedanken zur Entwicklung von regionalen Bildstellen und Medienzentren*, Klaus-Dieter Felsmann, ed. (Berlin: Schelsky & Jeep, 1999), 45–50.

50. Larkey, 47.

51. Larkey, 50. For a detailed account of the effects of the co-optation and the symbolic struggles that subsequently ensued, see Ronald Galenza and Heinz Havemeister, eds., *Wir wollen immer artig sein . . . , Punk, New Wave, HipHop, Independent-Szene in der DDR 1980–1990* (Berlin: Schwarzkopf & Schwarzkopf, 1999).

52. Bathrick, *The Powers of Speech*, 35.

CHAPTER 12

Who's Listening?

Bennett Hogg

INTRODUCTION

Audio technology is both a medium and a form of mediation. Its significance as a principal constituent element of our contemporary musical life
has not been achieved through some immanent force of its own, but
rather by the ways in which it has interacted with, and participated in,
relations of power. In this it is not exceptional; all cultural phenomena
depend on their interactions with power in order to become meaningful.
According to Foucault, power, running continuously through society and
occurring in every aspect of a society's activities, "is everywhere, not
because it embraces everything, but because it comes from everywhere"
(Foucault 1984: 93). This chapter on music and power starts from this
position that power is not something that belongs to some and not to
others; rather than something applied *to* it, power is produced *by* society.[1]

One of the most explicit uses of media technologies in the service of
power is surveillance. That surveillance is a concern of power would not
be generally contested; that surveillance can provide models for a
hermeneutics exploring power in recorded music might be. However,
such a speculative, interdisciplinary account is precisely what I concern
myself with in this chapter. Where "traditional" musicology has dealt with
issues of power, it has usually been figured as the power that music has
over us, the bodily or emotional effects of music acting directly upon the
human subject. Those positivist historical discourses concerned with the
ways in which music per se is used in the service of the state or the domi-

nant class only engage the surface of this topic; they tend to operate at the register of empirically observable, explicit "uses" of music, a frequently deterministic discourse of "cause and effect." There is a strong sense in which "traditional" musicology, in its reliance on the ideology of musical autonomy, has tended to distance (and even isolate) music from the social, and thereby from concerns of power.[2]

Causality, if it is allowed as the only meaningful paradigm of discourse, can be a notoriously unreliable mechanism. It is not especially revealing to think about the relations of music and power quite so deterministically. If Foucault's account of power is concerned with more polymorphous operations of power, some of them entangled with other power relations, some of them more embedded or concealed in what we might call the "cultural imagination," if power *does* come "from everywhere," then we might reasonably expect to encounter it "everywhere," in which case we might also expect it to be manifest in a multiplicity of guises whose inter-relationships, in keeping with the Foucauldian terminology, we can figure as "constellations." My account takes the form of a speculative cartography (perhaps astronomy would be a more apt term) of a (constructed and selective, admittedly) constellation of power relations within whose ambit recorded music, surveillance, ideologies about authenticity and authoriality, notions of property, territory, and ownership, and certain culturally embedded ambiguities of the status of the subject located in the "grey area" between listening and being listened to, between observing and being observed, can be positioned.

Perhaps it goes without saying that in such an account, the various relations with power cannot be expected to map neatly or directly onto one another, but I believe that the *process* of attempting such a remapping points toward places where the production practices and public use of music mediated by technology can be revealed as constitutive participants in the constellation of power relations with which this essay is concerned.

Sitting somewhere near the center of all of this are two stories from the war in Bosnia and Hercegovina (1992–1995); it is through trying to arrive at a theoretical interpretation of these stories that I was initially lead to formulate and research the main ideas in this essay. It should be clear that I tend toward an understanding of theory as an investigative tool rather than as an post facto rationalization of positivistically determined patternings, although I doubt whether anyone could ever claim to be able to be entirely consistent in this. To put it another way, this is written in the acknowledgement of the fact that insofar as theory can *proceed from* data, it is also frequently responsible for the *generation of* the same.

SURVEILLANCE AND RECORDED MUSIC:
A PARTIAL HOMOLOGY?

The most immediately apparent connection between music and surveillance concerns the status of technology in the two systems of discourse, specifically what I shall identify as the binarism of perceptibility and imperceptibility. This can supply a conceptual basis from which to begin unearthing medium-specific power relations, insofar as both practices are forms of knowledge, in the Foucauldian sense, mediated through similar technologies that display, to an extent, shared strategies of knowledge.[3] Any links that may be discernable between technological surveillance and technologically mediated music practices might be able to provide a context within which to speculate about the relations between music and power.

It is useful at this point to separate surveillance into two generalized modalities, the visible and the invisible. Visible surveillance includes CCTV cameras, security monitors positioned in shops in full view of the customers, speed cameras, and so on. In this form of surveillance, individuals are aware that they are under observation. The visibility of the technology is usually enough, in and of itself, to regulate or modify behavior. The work that the technology does, its strategy of knowledge, depends on its perception, its presence. Such "visible" operations of technology could be figured as constituting part of "everyday" reality.

Hidden, invisible forms of surveillance include bugging, phone tapping, and plain clothes police cars. Here the individual is not conscious of being observed. Rather than having its effect by being seen, the technology is used to relay information to hidden "specialists" who are concerned with the collation of this information and the subsequent exercise of legality.[4] This is an "expert" form of knowledge, removed from the "everyday"; it is the information itself that is of primary significance rather than any attempt to directly regulate behavior. If the first form of surveillance depends on being perceived as a technology to do its work, the second can only work if it is hidden. In other words, two different strategies of knowledge can be said to be in operation.

What happens if we construct a model of these strategies of surveillance in order to speculate about the possible power relations within recorded music, which is of course another instance of knowledge mediated by technology?

Parallel to the visible and invisible technologies as I have just outlined them, two related models of technologically mediated music practices are possible, similarly defined according to the degree to which they make their technology perceptible; the particular strategies of knowledge with which

I am concerned here are dependent on the perceptibility of the technology, and I am going to attach the labels "hi-fidelity" and "lo-fidelity" to them, terms that also have other resonances and associations.

HIGH FIDELITY

Hi-fidelity *usually* refers to sound quality—a CD player is more "hi-fi" than a transistor radio, and so on. Sound quality is generally taken to refer to the "vertical" aspects of a sound, its timbre, brightness, or ambience, but in the sense that I am using the term, hi-fidelity is also intimately connected to the "horizontal" aspects of sound, to the temporal dimension of music. Although the recording we listen to may, in reality, consist of many different "takes" edited together or superimposed, the listener should not hear the joins. The ideology of "classical" music places one of the primary aspects of the authority of "the work" in the control of the listener's experience of time. Hi-fidelity production practices are particularly vigilant about not interrupting the illusion that the listener is in the presence of "the work" as opposed to being in the presence of "a recording."

Such production practices and values meticulously respect the integrity of musical time and the need for the recording to appear seamless and continuous, not a collage of separately recorded fragments. Ideologically connected to issues of authorship and authority (ideologically as well as etymologically linked terms), such production practices strive to conceal the presence of technology, foregrounding the "work" or the "song" as the object of perception. The medium, in my reading of it, strives to remain faithful to the authoritative "work" (as object and as ideology) and effaces itself, in a sense trying to make itself "inaudible" as a technology. The entire history of commercial sound recording (whether "popular" or "classical") has, until relatively recently, been concerned with developing and improving techniques for the maintenance of this "illusion." Concealment of technology foregrounds "the work" as "pure" information, something that is suggestive of the strategies of knowledge of hidden surveillance, which similarly need to hide themselves to be effective and are also primarily concerned with "information."

It is also possible to trace a quite literal historical development for the self-effacement of the machines of music since the invention of the phonograph to the present day, something that has been paradoxically achieved as those machines have become more and more "hi-tech." In an early essay on domestic audio equipment, "The Curves of the Needle," Adorno ([1927] 1990) mourns the passing of the phonograph with its explicitly technological appearance and its replacement by gramophones, where the characteristic "horn" disappears inside and the machinery is housed inside of a cabinet that looks more like an article of bourgeois furniture than a "modern" technology.[5] With the introduction of stereos, we have a situation where the majority of the sounds are no longer *in* the speakers but are suspended *between* them; the music becomes in a sense separated from the technology (although it isn't actually separated, of course). Headphones complete the process. For the wearer, they are totally invisible and the experience of the sound, like in the real world, is omnidirectional.[6]

In addition, I think it no coincidence that the music industry chose the term "fidelity" (rather than maybe "accuracy" or "clarity"), carrying as it does associations with a "normative" morality. Loyalty, monogamy, patriotism, and even ideas of a transcendental "truth" are ideological configurations invoked by the term "fidelity." One of many pointers to this semiotic slippage can be found in the logo for the HMV Corporation. The Jack Russell terrier remains faithful to the "faithfully" reproduced sound of His Master's Voice, a loyalty, circumscribed by sentimentality, that transcends even His Master's Death.[7] A prototypical "ideal" consumer, Nipper's position as a listening subject is one of subordination in that he listens with performative attention to the direct voice of authority, to his master, not to a technology; such can at least be read into the corporation's claims for its "high-fidelity."

LOW FIDELITY

If I have defined hi-fidelity as a production practice that hides the presence of technology in deference to an imagined original, I will define its opposed correlate, lo-fidelity, as that type of production practice wherein the operation of the technology is actively and intentionally audible, production practices where the audible presence (even the celebration) of the technology is a constitutive element of the musical effect.

I am thinking particularly of sampling, DJ-ing, and other methods of generating sound that do not strive to conceal either the origins of the sound or the means of its production. As with visible surveillance, a great part of the effectiveness of the process is located in the perceptibility of the technology; though the sociological ends are different, the strategies of knowledge are very similar.

Generally used as a critique of sound "quality," I would like to twist the term somewhat; much of the music which I would categorize as lo-fidelity is actually of a very high sound quality. Unlike the ideological conditions under which hi-fidelity operates, with lo-fidelity there is no idealized "work" that could be imagined as existing outside of the operation of the technology. Because we can perceive the technology working, there is a sense that we are privy to the work being constructed. What we hear is not the illusory documentation of some imagined "real" performance—there is a sense in which the operation of the technology constitutes the performance, *the work*—there is nothing beyond this to which it is obliged to be "faithful."

With reference to high fidelity, I discussed the ways in which authority and authoriality are linked to the temporal integrity of the idea of "the work." Sampling and DJ-ing, in the ways that they fracture and reorder other musics, fundamentally violate this aspect of music's authority. At the same time, through representing the creation of "new" music as the re-cycling, re-interpretation and re-contextualization of music we've already heard, lo-fidelity production practices challenge those conceptions of creativity that imagine cultural production as the inspired and unique work of a single author. Although it would be untenably reductive to insist upon any sort of homology between lo-fidelity and visible surveillance, I believe the model has served a useful function in facilitating a train of thought where ideologies of power within discourses of technologically mediated musics begin to touch edges with other discourses of power. At the risk of being overly reductionist, I would like to cautiously suggest that there is a tendency for lo-fidelity production practices to be associated with "alternative" or "subaltern" activities, and for hi-fidelity to be more the concern of established, commercial "mass media," although there are plenty of instances, punk for example, where a "subaltern" ideology is mediated through production practices that, despite their "rawness," are still part of the ideological terrain of "high-fidelity" as I have represented it here.

I'd now like to turn to a second set of issues concerning music and surveillance, those that impinge on the ambiguous status, and the implied positioning within relations of power, of the listening subject.

MICROPHONES AND LOUDSPEAKERS: A "HERMENEUTIC WINDOW?"

Attempts to "make sense" of musical sound and musical practice are, I think, central to recent developments in musicology. Lawrence Kramer speaks of a musical hermeneutics: "In order to practice a musical hermeneutics we must learn first how to open hermeneutic windows on the music we seek to interpret and, second, how to treat works of music as fields of humanly significant action" (Kramer 1990, 6). Hermeneutic windows enable the interpretation of a text "by depreciating what is overtly legible and regarding the text as potentially secretive.... The text ... must be made to yield to understanding. A hermeneutic window must be opened on it through which the discourse of our understanding can pass.... Once that window opens, the text appears, ... not as a grid of assertions ... but as a field of humanly significant actions" (6)

I should like to extend Kramer's notion of "works of music as fields of humanly significant action" to include musical practices as objects of hermeneutics, and to suggest that a particular relationship of technologies, that which exists between microphones and loudspeakers, can be put to use as just such a "hermeneutic window."

Microphones and loudspeakers remain, in essence, almost identical technologies based as they are on the principle of transduction, the technological capability to transform one form of energy into another. The microphone converts the kinetic energy of sound waves into a system of electrical energy; the loudspeaker reverses this process, transforming the encoded electrical signal back into sound.

How might this relationship constitute a "hermeneutic window"? First, the technologies are interdependent, the loudspeaker actualizes the microphone signal and in turn requires a signal to fulfill its function; the microphone completes the loudspeaker and vice versa. Second, loudspeakers can be used in place of microphones. Surveillance systems exist where loudspeakers are used as crude microphones capable of recording speech, something that has been a peripheral phenomenon in sound recording from the preelectrical phase of the Edison phonograph and similar "mechanical" recording systems up to the present day, where "bedroom" techno composers use Walkman headphones to record live sounds when they can't afford recording mikes. The "hermeneutic window" I am proposing lies in this ambiguity between the recording and playback ends of the technology, something that appears in many different guises. It allows for a hermeneutics of the listening subject's relationship with technology in a way that no longer relies on the positivistic, common sense, linearity of cause and effect. I argue that the reciprocity of function inherent in the relationship between microphone and loudspeaker resonates more widely, and implicates the relations of surveillance to propaganda, and the ambiguous position of the listener, in the technological constellation of power.

AMBIGUITY: WHO'S LISTENING?

Michael Chanan, in *Repeated Takes*, his book on the history of sound recording, mentions early uses of the phonograph to "eavesdrop" on courting couples, in one case by the overbearing patriarch keeping tabs on his daughter, in another by a young woman who secretly records words spoken in a moment of passion by her "young man" to push him into marrying her, perhaps one of the earliest uses of recording technology as covert surveillance (Chanan 1995: 40). Edison's original phonograph was a recording and playback device, not a tool for playing commercially produced recordings. With the phonograph, the recording and reproducing technology is identical—horn and stylus working together to inscribe the trace of the sound and play it back. Later, these functions would separate out into the recording and playback devices we know as the microphone and the loudspeaker. Despite the changes of quality and flexibility introduced by electrical recording in 1925 and the availability of tape after World War II, ambiguity remains insofar as recording and playback functions are concerned, something articulated in the "bedroom" recording practices and in the usage of loudspeakers as microphones in certain forms of audio surveillance, which I have already mentioned. That these technological practices inhabit both the private "domestic" space at the same time that they are connected to "state" (or in the case of industrial espionage "quasi-state") forms of surveillance is also significant, something that reappears elsewhere in this chapter.

A less explicit manifestation of this ambiguity between recording and playback crops up in the short story "Goethe Speaks into the Phonograph," written by Salomo Friedlander in 1916 and quoted in full by Friedrich Kittler in "Gramophone—Film—Typewriter" (Kittler 1999: 59–68). In this rather unlikely tale, a certain Professor Pschorr devises a way to record the voice of Goethe, a challenge to the technological capabilities at Pschorr's disposal, as the great man has been dead for more than eighty years. To summarize the main point of the story, Pschorr believes that no sound ever completely dies out, and that in order to hear it, the only thing that needs to be done is to find a way of tuning into it and then amplifying it. To this end, he constructs an accessory for the phonograph that is modeled on the larynx of Goethe (which, in an episode at least as fantastic as his understanding of basic acoustics, he obtains by exhuming the corpse of the great man). The sound vibrations still resounding below the threshold of human perceptibility in the Goethehaus in Weimar resonate perfectly in the replica of the organ that produced them. It is then simply a matter of amplifying and recording them onto a phonograph cylinder.

What this technological fantasy demonstrates, I think, is another instance of ambiguity in the cultural imagination of audio technology. If one was to map audio technologies onto the human body, the ears would surely be microphones and the larynx a loudspeaker; but in this story, it is the speaker, the larynx, that is invoked to function as a microphone, as a point for the collection of information. The same ambiguity we have already seen with microphones and loudspeakers resurfaces. Supplementary to this, the experiment resonates further with the operations of surveillance, inasmuch as technology, as an extension of the human sensorium, gathers apparently inaccessible information much more effectively than the technologically unmediated senses. The knowledge that professor Pschorr collects is already there but not immediately accessible. Like the contemporary sound artist

Scanner, he needs a specific type of surveillance technology to gain access to it.[8] The end result, though, becomes literature, authority, the voice of Goethe.

Although this "hermeneutic window" hardly articulates a causal relationship between the strategies of knowledge of music recording and surveillance, it does allow me to think through the implications of the way that the technology might be doing its work, and to navigate the constellation of technological power relations. Furthermore, the ambiguity between the locations of recording and playback continue to resonate, at the margins, as it were, of the culturally imagined possibilities of audio technology. Though marginal in everyday experience, this very ambiguity resurfaces under certain conditions—in other words, there is sometimes a lack of transparency as to whether we are under surveillance, being listened to, or are ourselves listening. This opacity is not just a theoretical construct but points toward a concrete site for the constellation of power relations that recorded music participates in.

SOUND RECORDING AND SURVEILLANCE: POLITICAL ISSUES

In the constellation I am proposing, power circulates and may be more explicit (surveillance), or less (music), but if power comes *from* the interactivity of technologies, social mores, applications of technology, and so on, then perhaps its explicit articulations can help locate those that are more concealed. Power relations are mediated and transformed as we circumnavigate the constellation in which I have placed audio technology, and it is this transformation of power relations through different medialities that interests me. The microphone is a point for the collection of knowledge, a position that can also be taken by its complementary opposite, the loudspeaker, which completes it. This combination of interdependence and replaceability suggests the possibility of a bidirectionality in the cultural imagination of the system, a nonlinear, circulating flow of power. Might the dissemination of information, recorded music for example, stand in a complementary relationship to its collection—surveillance perhaps?—within this flow of power both as a practical, technological possibility, but also more deeply embedded within the cultural imagination and its attendant sociopolitical mind-set?

The ambiguous position of the listening subject, which mirrors the ambiguities I have discussed in relation to microphones and loudspeakers, appears as a motif in the work of the psychiatrist Jacques Lacan. Ian Biddle has written about "the uncanny reciprocity of looking and listening that so fascinates Lacan" as representing a "curious articulation of the fatal tendency in discourses of the self since Freud for the one looking or listening to readily turn into the one looked at or listened to" (quoted in Clayton, Herbert, and Middleton, 2003: 216).

A similar ambiguity resurfaces under totalitarian political systems, where knowledge of the ubiquity of surveillance is continuous with the presence of explicit propaganda.[9] Hitler is supposed to have given the loudspeaker credit as one of the technologies by which the Nazi party took power, not just the huge public address systems erected for the Nazi rallies at Nuremberg, but more effectively and insidiously the loudspeakers of the radio. In 1934 Goebbels was urging radio announcers to address listeners using casual, *volkstümlich* forms of speech, "The radio speaker must sound like the listener's best friend," he wrote.[10] In other words, the way in which information was to be presented needed to be modulated into a form appropriate for the domestic space in order to be acceptable and believable in this bastion of "the private." Such domestification of media concerned Adorno in his critique of mass culture (see Adorno 1994: 51–52). The parallel domestification of propaganda through technology was clearly part and parcel of the ways in which the Nazis gained such all-pervasive control over the population, one of the factors, according to Max Paddison (1996), that may have contributed to Adorno's profound distrust of mass media.

Although a work of fiction, Orwell's *1984* presents a society where the domestification of technological media, in conjunction with an ambiguity between the collection and the dissemination of information, reaches its logical conclusion. Surveillance and propaganda become ubiquitous and simultaneous in the TV screens pouring out information but through which Big Brother "is watching you." The fact that this is a work of fiction in no way diminishes its effectiveness as an indicator of a subliminal, cultural imagination of audio technology.

With all of this I am not trying to suggest that simply by sharing hardware, music and surveillance are the same thing; rather, I am trying to outline a more generalized picture of the constellation of power that circulates around media technologies, a constellation where music, surveillance and now propaganda are participants whose strategies of knowledge are founded on ambiguity in the functioning of the constitutive elements of the technology, and can represent a contextual ground for a speculative hermeneutics of power relations pertinent to recorded music.

While the simple fact of a shared technology could never be relied on to demonstrate a connection, it does suggest that complete discontinuity is unlikely. The microphone (and by implication, the loudspeaker) has, in our culture, become a metonym for surveillance—the "bug." The poet Tony Harrison foregrounds this attribute of the microphone in his four-line poem, "The Bedbug," set in communist Prague. The microphone here throws into relief another ambiguity; where does the private "real" overlap with the public "performance," where are the protagonists positioned in relation to "surveillance" (the hidden intrusion into the private, domestic space) and "performance" (the recital of sexual noises produced knowingly for the official listening to the microphone, mirroring recording artists, actors)? Around this tiny poem, as around the microphone itself, a veritable whirlwind of power relations circulate. "Comrade, with your finger on the playback switch, /Listen carefully to each love-moan, /And enter in the file which cry is real, and which/A mere performance for your microphone" (Harrison 1984: 54). Surveillance and art here become, as functions of technology, the indivisible, complementary links of a self-supporting chain, or part of a constellation of technologically mediated practices whose gravitational field is power.

SOUND RECORDING AND SURVEILLANCE: SOCIAL ASPECTS

Christopher Dandeker lists three activities, one or more of which are involved in the exercise of surveillance: "(1) the collection and storage of information . . . about people or objects; (2) the supervision of the activities of people or objects through the issuing of instructions . . . ; (3) the application of information gathering activities . . . and, in the case of subject persons, their compliance with instructions." He contextualizes this by saying, "In a general sense, surveillance activities are features of all social relationships" (Dandeker 1990: 37). These activities of surveillance, if mapped onto the use of recorded music in social spaces, uncover further registers where music, surveillance, and power touch edges, other registers of discourse where it becomes possible to further link recorded music and surveillance as participants in a Foucauldian constellation of power.

Within such discourses music recording and surveillance are, as Dandeker has pointed out, collected and stored forms of knowledge "about people and objects," central attributes of the operation of power as surveillance, and powerful forces for the construction and definition of social behaviors and relationships. Social and individual identities, and their constitutive behaviors, form around recorded music. Lawrence Grossberg, for example, describes his concept of the "rock formation" as "a configuration of cultural practices and effects that have been *organized around rock music* [italics mine]" (Grossberg 1997: 16). Our love affairs draw their soundtracks from radios and jukeboxes; Muzak makes us work and shop more efficiently; classical music played over the PA at Gateshead Metro Station on Tyneside (Northern England) is intended to discourage potentially delinquent teenagers from "hanging around" there, a method of social control reported in the British press with increasing regularity. According to experimental research by North, Hargreaves, and McKendrick, different musical styles demonstrably affect customer's choice of what to buy when offered a series of different options. For example, off-license sales of French wines increase when "French" music is played, "Spanish" music increases the sales of Spanish wines, and so on (North, Hargreaves, and McKendrick 1999).

Recorded music is a structured, controlled and controlling form of knowledge produced and regulated within a well-developed system of information (pop charts, PRS/MCPS returns, etc.). It is a site for the socially mediated formation of desire, an object toward which practices of consumption are directed, and frequently the background noise against which such practices of consumption take place. Its "effect" is intended to be more than the simple consumption of an industrial product. This effect of music participates in mythologies that inform our cultural conceptualizations of what music is at many levels. Tropes concerning the affective agency of music are widespread: It "carries us away," we "surrender to the beat," "get into the groove," become "slaves to the rhythm." At the end of the night, when the music stops, we feel suddenly exposed and alone. In Jim Morrison's words, "When the music's over [we] turn out the light."

Numerous registers of discourse are concerned with the power music has over us. In the field of music therapy we find claims for the effects of music on the human psyche and body, claims implying universality and immanence, the highly culture-specific nature of these effects rarely explicitly articulated. However, meanings and effects, so far as we can usefully talk about them in relation to music, are understood in contemporary cultural theory to be determined and maintained culturally and socially, in other words are inextricably entangled with "constellations" of power. Music makes us behave in particular ways, in Dandeker's terms, like surveillance, it "issues instructions." These instructions, however, are not simply the unmediated, autonomous effects of music on the body; they only take effect within a cultural context, which is to say, within the context of power relations that they articulate at the same time that they are subject to them.

Resonances between the operations of recorded music and surveillance activities, between shared technologies and overlapping discourses of power, all point toward a location for media-specific operations of power in recorded music, operations that are closely modeled on surveillance. Ludmila Jordanova has recently spoken of portraiture as doing specific cultural work that other forms of painting do not.[11] Recorded music, similarly, does cultural work that is medium-specific. Music recording inhabits similar places (pragmatic, technological, and ideological) in the cultural imagination to those occupied by surveillance. It occupies a position that exploits the ambiguity of presence, it coerces tastes and the normative reception of cultural products. It is controlled information and a site of power where the stakes include surveillance. In addition, when the music is played in public it physically "occupies" the space that it is heard in, and in doing this engages with yet other tropes of power.

Recorded music is not surveillance per se. If there is a connection between these two discourses, it is a highly entangled, mediated, and more or less illegible one. There is certainly a gap between "real" surveillance and recorded music, but a gap is not necessarily the same thing as an "absence." The issues I have raised so far relate directly to a story from the war in Bosnia and Hercegovina.

RECORDED SOUND, SURVEILLANCE, AND WAR

During the war in Bosnia, Muslim villages and larger multiethnic towns, including the capital, Sarajevo, were isolated and then destroyed in territories claimed by the Četniks (a term used to designate Serbian nationalists, as opposed to "Serbs" in general)[12] in their project to establish an ethnically "clean" Republika Srpska (Serb Republic) on the territory of Bosnia and Hercegovina.[13] Horrific stories abound about the conditions in such places, a litany of abject misery and terror. This terror was compounded when the Četniks would set up loudspeakers and play "turbofolk" at a high volume, sometimes for extended periods of time, before, during, or after shelling.

A relatively recent form of Serbian popular music, turbofolk combines simple techno beats with a melismatic "folk" style of singing.[14] Though seen as a specifically Serbian style of music, similar treatments of folk-type materials are found in Muslim parts of Bosnia, so-called "novokompono-vanje narodne pjesme" (newly composed national songs).[15] Both musics are awowedly nationalistic; in Bosnia, the term "novokomponovanji" is applied to those who have, since the war, embraced Islam with a religiosity that is frequently contradicted by their actions (their relations with alcohol, for example). Such people, representing themselves as Muslims for reasons of political expediency, are termed "novokomponovanji muslimani"— "newly composed Muslims," a derisive terminology appropriated from this Muslim version of turbofolk.[16]

The Milošević regime in Belgrade was intimately connected with the turbofolk industry. Members of his immediate family held significant financial interests in the Serbian record industry, and some still do. Originally a type of Balkanized "Europop" carrying more or less conservative family values, as the nationalist regime of Milošević took hold it became transformed, in the words of Jelena Subotić, a presenter of Belgrade's independent Radio B-92, into "a perfect channel for disseminating the poisonous seeds of hatred" (Collin 2001: 80).

Returning to the besieged villages of Bosnia, what cultural "work" could this "channel ... of hatred" be doing besides providing entertainment for the Četnik troops themselves? I was arrested at a Četnik roadblock at Kasandolska Street on the edge of Sarajevo in 1995 in a confrontation between the UN Security Forces and the notorious "Ilidža Brigade" of Četniks. The contrasts were striking. On one side of the road, French UN troops stood in stony silence stiffly behind an armored personnel carrier, guns at the ready. The Četnik soldiers, however, wandered about waving Kalashnikovs, singing, drinking, and playing loud turbofolk from the car stereo.

Other "work" was being done besides entertainment. A music so intimately connected to a politically radicalized "Serb" identity does not only support that identity; by the very nature of what music is, it projects it outward. This could not have been clearer that day on Kasandolska Street. The same could be said for the situation of the village under siege. Clearly audible in the village, the music projects an identity of dominance onto a space of passivity, telling the story, "We are out here, we are watching you."

Turbofolk, in this specific context, is the simulacrum not of Attali's "ritual violence" (Attali 1985) but a "disciplinary violence" of surveillance. At another level, the music not only simulates surveillance and discipline, obscenely euphemistic terms in such a situation, but also already occupies the space. The message is no longer "we *will* occupy your space," but rather "we're already here."

RECORDED SOUND AND THE OCCUPATION OF SPACE

John Fiske has drawn on the ideas of Michel de Certeau, with resonant echoes of Foucault, to propose the "incarnation" of law and the "intextuation" of the body as sites where "an abstract system of justice [is transformed] into social behaviour.... [P]ower is transformed by an instrumental apparatus onto a body: the law ... is made flesh, is incarnated" (Fiske 1989: 91) In other words, law is "made flesh" by the operation of what Fiske terms "instrumental apparatuses" that occur "not only at the moments of transgression ... ; they are also at work in ordinary, everyday practices. Clothing, cosmetics, slimming, jogging are all means of incarnating rules and intextuating the body" (Fiske 1989: 91–92).

Laws in a society operate far and beyond any obvious exercise of legality, an idea that owes much to Foucault's notion of the ubiquitous and continuous nature of power. I'd add the public use of recorded music to this list of instrumental apparatuses. Recorded music, perhaps because of its explicitly commodified form, carries with it certain features of the idea of property. A CD can be a site of ownership in a way in which a live performance, since the collapse of aristocratic patronage, very rarely is. Recorded music "incarnates" ideologies of property, authority, and exclusivity,[17] and carries these ideologies with it at the same time that it occupies a physical space.

Perhaps most obviously, the recorded material, the "music," is itself owned by someone, it is considered their property, most often a multinational record company. Permission is required for the public presentation of this property. Someone must pay for the sound to enter into their space, whether that space is a club, a bar, or the airwaves. The consumer can buy into this system and possess a copy of this property, though the uses to which this can be legally put are strictly limited.

Second, the recording "incarnates" a two-fold figuration of the idea of "authority"—first, in the sense that the creator of the work claims "authorship," and second, that the "authority" of the recorded work is somehow definitive. Michael Chanan has elaborated on this in detail. In his account, performers' approaches, listeners' conceptualizations, and the "fetishization" of the definitive are all intimately bound up with the authority of the recorded work. As I have mentioned, incarnations of the ideology of authorship and authority, particularly ubiquitous manifestations of power in our culture, are an integral part of most commercial music practices. Third, the public presence of recorded music is frequently "exclusive" in the sense that other musics tend to be excluded. The music fully occupies the space, legislating against opposition, enforcing a social discipline that finds its model and apotheosis in the classical concert.

In typical situations where we might encounter loud music socially, in pubs and nightclubs for example, the power of the music played there to exclude other musics is rarely challenged. Where it is, the exclusive nature of music may actually be reinforced, albeit negatively. I have been in pubs and clubs more times than I care to recall and, in the North of England at least, one striking challenge to the dominance of loud, recorded music is when the local football (soccer) team has won and gangs of drunken fans start singing their team's songs and chants, despite the deafening level of the jukebox or DJ.

At one level, we could say that the fans are asserting an intragroup identity, oblivious to their surroundings, but at another level they could be seen to be continuing the sonic wars that occur between rival fans on the terraces. There is a sense in which they are challenging the dominant soundscape, distancing themselves from it, treating it as an opponent. From the evidence of the physical effort that shows on their faces and in their bodily exertions, there is some evidence to support the idea that they are trying their (vocal) strength against a powerful opposition. This expenditure of effort, the public trial of strength articulating an oppositional, performative agency, throws into stark relief the "normal," passive or participative receptivity of the others in the club. Indeed, their behavior may be read as threatening toward those "passive" others, which it in fact rarely is. In the context of the nightclub, such a musical assertion of group identity could be read as a challenge to, and therefore an acknowledgement of, the exclusivity of recorded music in that space.

Writing on surveillance, Dandeker proposes two strategies around which "a range of sanctions stemming from control of economic, coercive or normative resources" can be "mobilized." The second of these is "to devise mechanisms of excluding potential rule breakers from the opportunity to disobey instructions" (Dandeker 1990: 38–39). Is loud, recorded music such a mechanism? Could this be a function of exclusivity? Do the issues I have just outlined—ownership, authority, exclusivity—point to a connection between ideologies of property, occupation of space, and Dandeker's figurations of surveillance, operating in the public use of recorded music?

Recorded music cannot leave these issues "at the door," so to speak, when it enters into a space. Like the virtual, acoustic space that recorded music imposes onto physical space, traces, encodings of power, are carried within practice. As in its relationship to surveillance, recorded music is positioned within a "constellation" of diverse, culturally embedded power relations. Exclusivity and the ways in which notions of property are carried from what John Fiske calls "an abstract system of justice into social behaviour" (Fiske 1989) offer us opportunities to open more "hermeneutic windows" onto recorded music's "potentially secretive" meanings and associations. As well as carrying these meanings, recorded music acts them out in its ability to define territory, in the way in which it can occupy a space, in its status as commodified property, and in its potential to "police" our behavior as the simulacrum of "disciplinary surveillance." Illustrative of this is a story about the Tabhana in Mostar, the main city of Hercegovina where I lived on and off during the three years immediately after the war in Bosnia and Hercegovina.

When I first entered East Mostar in October 1995, the nearest I had seen to such devastation, despite having spent time in Sarajevo during the war, were photographs of Berlin after World War II. A year after the so-called Ustaša, based in West Mostar, had "officially" ceased hostilities (though sporadic machine-gun fire and grenade explosions could be heard almost every night), there were still no telephones in East Mostar, electricity and water were severely rationed, and there was a strictly enforced curfew at nine o'clock every night. Despite this, a tiny handful of cafes had managed to open among the ruins.

One of these was the "Theatre Bar," alone in the devastated remains of the Tabhana. Built in the sixteenth century as a military barracks for the Ottoman Empire, this square of single storey buildings was a popular tourist site before the outbreak of war. A year after my first visit it had become the center of Mostar's nightlife. Every available space was occupied by small bars, all pumping their different musics out into the central square where, in the oppressive heat, customers would sit, bombarded on all sides by a cacophony of sounds. This in itself is not remarkable, a similar situation can be found in most cities with a warm climate and is a characteristic feature of the sound-scape in most holiday resorts. In this case, though, the sociological context was different, and led me to reflect, for better or for worse, on the situation in a way I would have been unlikely to do had I been in Ibiza.

The sociological context was extreme. Almost no one in Mostar at that time was living in their own house. Displaced persons had taken over those buildings left standing, and the remaining minority of original inhabitants was mostly crowded together with relatives whose property had somehow survived the relentless bombardment. The cafe owners in the Tabhana, similarly, had no legal rights of occupation. Was it because of this that everyone played different music? Was the potential for recorded music to occupy space standing in for the absence of legal occupation, bringing its notions of property, of authority, of exclusivity into the Tabhana? Was the "exclusivity" of music in a social space challenged because the space itself was challenged? Had the ideology of the integrity of authoriality and authority been so profoundly undermined by the experience of war that the illusion of "hi-fidelity" ceased to have any meaning? Had the break-down of social and legislative norms allowed normally hidden power relations to seep through the cracks and onto the surface? Or was it just that cafe owners were too concerned with making ends meet in whatever way possible to worry about aesthetic niceties? In my understanding of the situation, all of the above apply.

Some Bosnian friends of mine, regular customers at Tabhana, asked if I, with my connections in Sarajevo, would be able to organize a PA system to be set up in the middle of the square with a single DJ, so that the chaos of all the conflicting musics could be alleviated. I agreed to do what I could and my friends set off to talk to the various owners about implementing their won-derful new idea, which would of course be to everyone's advantage. None of the owners agreed. "I don't want the same music that he plays next door, I play my own music in my cafe" was the generally aggressive response. My friends soon gave up asking, the cacophony continued, and faced with the choice of having a beer or not having a beer, we got used to it.

Notes

1. See Foucault 1984: 92–97.
2. See, for example, Shepherd 1991: 49–74.
3. I frame recorded music and surveillance as "shared strategies of knowledge" rather than "shared technologies" here, because whereas the technologies of music production and dissemination are exclusively audio, those of surveillance are both audio and visual; it is in

the register of their respective strategies of operation that a useful theoretical model of power relations may be constructed.

4. Or, in the case of military or industrial surveillance, they are concerned with the establishment of a position of advantage over an enemy or rival.

5. See Adorno [1927] 1990: 49–55.

6. Although it is possible to argue that the, at least initial, tactile sensation of wearing headphones, especially those that cover the whole of the ears, stands in for the visual perception of technology at another sensory register.

7. See Tom Gunning's "Doing for the Eye What the Phonograph Does for the Ear," in Abel and Altman 2001: 27–29.

8. Scanner is the alias of Robin Rimbaud, composer and sound artist best known for his use of mobile phone scanning devices to eavesdrop onto mobile users conversations which are then incorporated live into his performances.

9. At The British Forum for Ethnomusicology conference on "Music and Power" in April 2001, Nancy Elizabeth Currey presented a paper on the use of public loudspeakers under the regime of the late President Asad in Syria. The streets of Damascus are lined with literally thousands of loudspeakers giving the regime almost complete control of the soundscape. It is not difficult to imagine how an individual might feel, under conditions where listening is so controlled, as though they were under an almost constant form of surveillance.

10. Quoted in Chanan 1995: 109–110.

11. Unpublished public lecture given at Newcastle University, 2002.

12. Terminologies are difficult here because of the still intensely emotive nature of whatever term is used. I, for personal reasons, will use the same terms that were current during the war in the parts of Bosnia that remained multi-ethnic. Četnik designates someone who identifies themselves as Serb, regardless of where they were born, and who espouses the ideology that Serbs cannot live with other ethnic groups. Similarly Ustaša designates someone who identifies as ethnically Croat with similar xenophobic beliefs. These are terms that originated in World War II and that were revived either as self-proclaimed identities or as political insults, depending on the context of their use.

13. In what was a very complex situation, I have singled out the activities of the so-called Četniks because they illustrate the point I wish to make most vividly. This is not to say that the only victims of the Četnik aggression were Muslims (the Croat people of the Krajina suffered just as much, as did the Serb people when this region returned to Croat jurisdiction) or that the Četniks were the only aggressors in the region. It is generally accepted that paramilitary forces supported by President Tudjman of Croatia were also responsible for aggression against the state of Bosnia and Hercegovina, especially in Western Hercegovina and around the towns of Travnik and Kiseljak. See Malcolm 1996 for a detailed account of this period of Bosnian history.

14. For a brief history of turbofolk in Serbia see Collin 2001: 78–93.

15. More detailed accounts are available by Raljević 1997 and Pettan (ed.) 1998.

16. I learned this term through personal and overheard conversations.

17. Exclusivity in the sense of "excluding . . . rejecting . . . other possibilities [or] events" (Dandeker 1990).

References

Abel, Richard, and Rick Altman, eds. 2001. *Sounds of Early Cinema* (Bloomington: Indiana University Press).

Adorno, Theodor W. 1994 "On Popular Music," in John Storey, ed. *Cultural Theory and Popular Culture: A Reader* (New York, London: Harvester Wheatsheaf).

Adorno, Theodor W. [1927] 1990. "The Curves of the Needle," trans. Thomas Y. Levin, in *October* 55 (Winter 1990).

Attali, Jacques, 1985. *Noise: The Political Economy of Music,* trans. Brian Massumi (Minneapolis: University of Minnesota Press).

Baudrillard, Jean, 1981. *Simulacra and Simulation,* trans. Sheila Faria Glaser (Ann Arbor: University of Michigan Press, 1994; original French publication by Editions Galilee).

Biddle, Ian. Forthcoming 2004. *Listening to Men: Music, Masculinity, and the Austro-German Tradition, 1789–1914* (Berkeley and LA: University of California Press).

Biddle, Ian. 2003. "Of Mice and Dogs: Music, Gender, and Sexuality at the Long Fin de Siecle," in Clayton, Herbert, and Middleton, eds. *The Cultural Study of Music* (New York: Routledge).

Bohlman, Philip V., and Ronald Radano., eds. 2000. *Music and the Racial Imagination* (Chicago: University of Chicago Press).

Born, Georgina, and David Hesmondhalgh. 2000. *Western Music and Its Others* (Berkeley, Los Angeles, London: University of California Press).

Bunt, Leslie. 1994. *Music Therapy: An Art Beyond Words* (New York: Routledge).

Chanan, Michael. 1995. *Repeated Takes: A Short History of Recording and its Effects on Music* (London, New York: Verso).

Clarke, David. 2003. "Musical Autonomy Revisited," in Clayton, Herbert and Middleton, eds. *The Cultural Study of Music* (New York: Routledge) 159–170.

Clayton, M., T. Herbert, and R. Middleton, eds. 2003. *The Cultural Study of Music* (New York: Routledge).

Collin, Matthew. 2001. *This Is Serbia Calling: Rock 'n' Roll Radio and Belgrade's Underground Resistance* (London: Serpent's Tail).

Collins Dictionary of the English Language, 2nd ed. (London, Glasgow: Collins, 1986).

Connor, Steven. 2000. *Dumbstruck: A Cultural History of Ventriloquism* (Oxford: Oxford University Press).

Dandeker, Christopher. 1990. *Surveillance, Power, and Modernity: Bureaucracy and Discipline from 1700 to the Present Day.* (Cambridge: Polity Press).

During, Elie. 2002. "Appropriations: Deaths of the Author in Electronic Music," in *Sonic Process* [published in association with the exhibition "Sonic Process. A New Geography of Sounds" conceived and produced by Centre Pompidou in collaboration with MACBA Barcelona] (Barcelona: Actar) 39–55.

Foucault, Michel. 1984 [1976]. *The History of Sexuality, Volume 1: An Introduction*, trans. Robert Hurley (Harmondsworth: Penguin).

Foucault, Michel. 1991. *Discipline and Punish: The Birth of the Prison*, trans. Alan Sheridan (New York: Pantheon, 1977 reprinted by Penguin).

Foucault, Michel. 1993. "Space, Power, and Knowledge," in S. During, ed. *The Cultural Studies Reader* (London, New York: Routledge).

Fiske, John. 1989. *Understanding Popular Culture* (Boston, Mass.: Unwin Hyman).

Gitelman, Lisa. 1999. *Scripts, Grooves, and Writing Machines: Representing Technology in the Edison Era* (Stanford: Stanford University Press).

Grossberg, Lawrence. 1997. *Dancing in Spite of Myself: Essays on Popular Culture* (Durham, N.C.: Duke University Press).

Gunning, Tom. 2001. "Doing for the eye what the phonograph does for the ear" in Richard Abel and Rick Altman, eds. *The Sounds of Early Cinema* (Bloomington: Indiana University Press).

Harrison, Tony. 1984. *Selected Poems* (Harmondsworth: Penguin).

Kahn, Douglas. 1994 [1992]. "Death in Light of the Phonongraph: Raymond Roussel's *Locus Solus*" in Douglas Kahn and Gregory Whitehead (eds.) *Wireless Imagination: Sound, Radio and the Avant-garde* (Cambridge: MIT Press).

Kittler, Friedrich A. 1999. *Gramophone, Film, Typewriter*, trans. Geoffrey Winthrop-Young and Michael Wutz (Stanford, Calif.: Stanford University Press).

Kramer, Lawrence. 1990. *Music as Cultural Practice, 1800–1900* (Berkeley, Los Angeles, London: University of California Press).

Laing, David. 1991. "A Voice without a Face: Popular Music and the Phonograph in the 1890s," in *Popular Music* 10, 1 (1991).

Leppert, Richard, and Susan McClary, eds. 1987. *Music and Society: The Politics of Composition, Performance, and Reception* (Cambridge, New York: Cambridge University Press).

Little, Alan, and Laura Silber. 1996. *The Death of Yugoslavia* [revised edition with new material] (London: Penguin).

Malcolm, Noel. 1996. *Bosnia: A Short History* (New York: New York University Press).

North, Adrian C., David J. Hargreaves, and Jennifer McKendrick. 1999. "The Influence of In-store Music on Wine Selections," in *Journal of Applied Psychology* 84: 271–76.

Paddison, Max. 1996. *Adorno, Modernism, and Mass Culture* (London: Kahn and Averill).

Pettan, Svanibor, ed. 1998. *Music, Politics, and War: Views from Croatia* (Zagreb, Institute of Ethnology and Folklore Research).

Raljević, Sanja. 1997. "Historical Aspects of the Origins (sic) of the Newly Composed Folk Music in Bosnia-Hercegovina," in *Muzika* 4 (October–December), Sarajevo, Academy of Music.

Rouse, Joseph. 1994. "Power/Knowledge," in G. Gutting, ed. *The Cambridge Companion to Foucault* (Cambridge: Cambridge University Press).

Serageldin, Ismael. 1989. *Space for Freedom: The Search for Architectural Excellence in Muslim Societies* (London: Butterworth Architecture/The Aga Khan Award for Architecture).

Shepherd, John. 1991. *Music as Social Text* (Cambridge: Polity Press).

Thébèrge, Paul. 1997. *Any Sound You Can Imagine* (Hanover, London: Wesleyan University Press).

Waters, Simon. 1997. *Beyond the Acousmatic: Hybrid Tendencies in Electroacoustic Music* (Stockholm: Swedish Section of ICEM).

CHAPTER 13

Subversion and Countersubversion: Power, Control, and Meaning in the New Iranian Pop Music

Laudan Nooshin

INTRODUCTION

On May 23, 1997, a few weeks after Labour's historic election victory in Britain, another historic election—presidential this time—took place in Iran just as the country's Revolution was coming of age. Standing on a platform of greater openness internally and reestablishing Iran's international relations, Hojjatoleslam Mohammad Khatami was swept to power with an overwhelming mandate that gave a real indication of the extent of public support for change.[1] Since 1997, Khatami has initiated a number of reforms in which the most far-reaching have been in the cultural domain. One of the most remarkable developments is that after almost twenty years in which all pop music was officially banned in Iran, there has been a gradual relaxing of government policy in this area, and certain types of pop music have now become legal again.[2] As one of the most prominent signifiers of modernity, the reemergence of pop music into the public domain has sparked a complex and highly emotive debate over Iran's future in an increasingly global world, a debate that draws on a range of discourses, including the role of tradition in modernity and local resistance to global hegemony. This chapter traces the shifting meanings and significance of pop music in Iran over the last twenty-five years, focusing in particular on the implications of the post-1997 changes and the ways in which music and the discourses around music have served as an arena for playing out some of the most contested issues of nationhood, identity, and power. In exploring the various attempts to control pop music and its meanings, the chapter considers the articulation of such meanings through expressions of power and asks how particular types of music acquire subversive potential. In particular, I am interested in what happens when a form of cultural resistance is appropriated by those against whom the resistance was originally directed.[3]

Although never subject to direct colonial rule, from the late nineteenth century onward, Iran experienced repeated intervention from Western powers seeking to secure their own political and economic interests, often with the complicity of the ruling elite.[4] As Ang points out, "The cultural constitution of national identity, as articulated in both official policies and informal popular practices, is a precarious project that can never be isolated from the global, transnational relations in which it takes shape." (1996: 249); in the case of Iran, the deep-rooted legacy of political, economic, and cultural neocolonial influence—and the various forms of resistance to it—has long permeated discourses of national identity. Indeed, as discussed below, the 1979 Iranian Revolution was itself primarily an assertion of national identity and self-determination, and the period that followed was marked by an intense anxiety over questions of nationhood and self-definition symptomatic of people emerging from and coming to terms with the colonial encounter. As such, questions of identity became inextricably bound up with issues of self-determination and empowerment. The post-1979 rejection of Western cultural hegemony led to a decade of partially self-imposed isolation, most notably from the countries of Europe and North America, a period in which Iran attempted to disentangle itself from the web of neocolonial influence and cultural dependency. While many consider the relative isolation of the 1980s to have been a historical necessity, such a position was bound to be untenable in the long-term, and particularly in the global context of the twenty-first century. The gradual process of reestablishing international relations from the early 1990s (which gained momentum after 1997) has sparked an intense debate that draws on contesting visions of nationhood and of Iran's future in the "global village." At the heart of this debate is the central question of how to reestablish international relations without becoming dominated by an outside power, as had been the case for at least a century before the Revolution. Music has provided a public space for playing out such issues. In order to explore the significance of music in the current context, to understand why pop music was banned after 1979 and why certain kinds of pop are now legal again, let us consider the historical context before moving on to more recent events.

HISTORICAL CONTEXT

The history of Iran's political relationship with the countries of Western Europe and the United States is well documented elsewhere, but a brief summary is relevant to the following discussion. Like a number of other countries in the Middle East, it was initially Iran's strategic geographical position and later the discovery of oil that made it a focus of interest for Western countries (Halliday 1996: 22–23; Wright 1991: 22–24). For much of the nineteenth century, Britain and Russia were locked in a power struggle over control of Iranian territories. The legacy of foreign involvement continued through the twentieth century, gradually shifting to encompass cultural as well as political and economic spheres. It was against this backdrop that Reza Shah Pahlavi, and later his son Mohammad Reza Pahlavi, pursued a policy of rapid modernization and Westernization, heavily supported by Western countries for whom Iran represented a ripe market as well as a supplier of oil and a military policeman for the region.[5] The headlong rush toward Westernization, industrialization, and the formation of a largely urban, secular, and capitalist nation state intensified during the 1960s and '70s at a time when any debate concerning the many genuine and urgent issues of development was suppressed in favor of a largely glossy and superficial imitation of the West.[6]

Not only did the processes of modernization take little account of traditional values and ways of life in a country that was still very traditional, but in fact government policies promoted the idea that such traditions were in themselves an obstacle to Iran's development.[7] Nowhere was this more apparent than on the radio and television. Aware of the powerful potential of the broadcast media as a tool in his modernization project, Mohammad Reza Pahlavi brought about a rapid expansion of broadcasting from the late 1950s. Following the so-called "Communications and Development" model put forward by writers such as Daniel Lerner (Sreberny-Mohammadi 1991: 178–79), television in particular became a vehicle for promoting modernization, broadcasting a high percentage of imported (particularly American) programs that were disconnected from the reality of most people's lives (Mohammadi 1995: 371–74). Thus, the idea widely promoted in the 1970s that a single model of development, including the rejection of tradition in favor of modernization, could be applied to all "third world" countries, only served to undermine "the very basis of cultural identity and the traditional values of Iranian society" (Mohammadi 1995: 376). Modernization and Westernization thus became inextricably linked, creating a polarization with repercussions that can still be felt today. By insisting on the incompatibility of modernity and tradition, the Shah foreclosed any avenue of open debate on an issue so fundamental to Iran's future: how to modernize and develop without losing important aspects of national and cultural identity. Many of those with whom I have discussed this issue refer to the 1970s as a period of crisis in Iranian identity, and a number of authors have written about the "intoxication" with the West, which characterized the decade (the most well-known being the essay *Gharbzadegi* by Jalal Al-e Ahmad).[8] Youssefzadeh notes that as far back as 1964: "Ayatollah Khomeini himself had already criticized this Westernization ... [and] denounced the Radio and Television programmes as issuing 'from a colonized culture' (*este'māri*) and producing 'a colonized youth'"(2000: 37).

The whole social arena was dominated by a discourse of "West is best," strongly supported by the government and which allowed little space for cultural or political resistance. The aspirational value that Western products and lifestyle acquired at this time derived from (and further deepened) existing imbalances of power between "first" and "third" worlds, and perpetuated an already deep-rooted colonial mindset in Iran (Sreberny-Mohammadi and Mohammadi 1991a: 55). In considering the impact of global forces in Iran at a time when the country was becoming increasingly cosmopolitan, it's important to bear in mind the complex interweaving of power, and acknowledge the extent to which the discourses that promoted Westernization to the exclusion of tradition were not simply an imposition from above (or from outside), but depended on a certain level of acceptance and complicity. In the words of Martin-Barbero, "We need to recognize that the hegemonic does not [just] dominate us from without but rather penetrates us, and therefore it is not just against it but from within it that we are waging war." (1988, 462, quoted in Ang 1996: 244)

This "westoxication" had a profound impact on all areas of musical life. Alizadeh, for example, discusses the long-term effects on music education of the uncritical imitation of Western models because of their "prestige by association" rather than their relevance or usefulness in the context of Iran (1998: 76–77).[9] As part of Iran's trajectory toward modernization, Western music of various kinds became available from the early 1960s, including a wide range of popular music styles. From the mid-1960s, a new kind of commercial Iranian pop music emerged for the first time, with singers promoted by the government-controlled broadcasting organization. This music was partly rooted in existing urban popular styles and used Persian lyrics and Iranian melodies and rhythms, but also drew heavily on conventions of Western pop music images, fashion, and instruments. Some of the best known singers, including Googoosh, Haydeh, Mahasti, Ebi, and Dariush, attained "pop star" status, and their music was regularly broadcast on radio and television and available through a flourishing commercial recording market.[10] As in many other parts of the "non-western" world:

> Popular music has special importance as a socio-cultural phenomenon, for it embodies and expresses the new social identities which

emerge as products of urbanization and modernization throughout the world.... [M]ost of these [new non-western pop genres], while borrowing Western elements, in their own way affirm modernity and express the contradictions and complexities of modern culture. In doing so, they perform a social function that traditional musics can no longer fulfill. (Manuel 1988: v–vi)

And indeed, it was this music more than any other cultural form that came to represent the modern face of Iran in the 1960s and '70s. In stark contrast to this, and partly in reaction to the fast-growing popularity of pop music, many traditional musicians retrenched into an increasing preoccupation with issues of "preservation" and "authenticity" quite new to this music.[11] Although traditional music was broadcast on radio and television, and recordings were also commercially available, the growing polarization between tradition and modernity meant that this music became more and more removed from the reality of social change in Iran and was increasingly regarded as irrelevant to people's lives.[12]

With the boom in oil prices in the early 1970s, the Shah was encouraged by the United States to increase Iran's military budget (including substantial spending on foreign military advisers). Together with uneven economic development, resentment at decades of external political interference, lack of political freedoms, and a growing gulf between a new elite—reaping the benefits of oil wealth, often educated in the West and aspiring to a Western lifestyle and values—and the majority of the population for whom basic social needs were still not met, this generated the underlying tensions and social unrest that eventually led to the Shah's overthrow in February 1979.[13]

1979 AND ITS AFTERMATH: THE PLAY OF IDENTITIES

One of the most important aspects of the 1979 Iranian Revolution, then, was an assertion of national identity in reaction to the perceived loss of identity during the preceding decades. Brought about by an extraordinary coalition, which included a broad spectrum of political and religious organizations, the Revolution might be regarded as one of the earliest expressions of local resistance against the increasingly global nature of Western cultural, political, and economic hegemony. As such, it shared a great deal with national independence movements in countries emerging from direct colonial rule (Halliday 1996: 73). One of the priorities of the post-1979 revolutionary government was to develop policies that would allow cultural activities to take place within an Islamic framework. However, formulating such policies proved difficult for a number of reasons, particularly because of underlying tensions between religious identity on the one hand and national identity on the other. Iran has been an Islamic country since the 7th century AD, and Islam clearly plays a very important role in Iranian culture and society. At the same time, there is a deep consciousness of a much older national identity that predates Islam by at least a thousand years and to which music and poetry are central. Indeed, it is music and poetry that are often credited with maintaining national identity through a long and turbulent history of invasion and occupation. The profound contradictions in cultural policy during the 1980s were partly the result of a government trying to impose a hegemonic Islamic identity on a people intensely aware of, and unwilling to forfeit, their pre-Islamic heritage.[14]

While national and religious identities are clearly not inherently anti-thetical—indeed, such multiple identities are a normal part of people's lived experiences—where such identities take on particular significance is in relation to issues of power. What is particularly interesting in the case of Iran is the way in which those in power have appealed to one or another of these identities at various times, even setting them off against each other to suit their own political agenda. For example, in trying to build a secular state and at the same time disempower the clergy, whom he regarded as a threat, Mohammad Reza Pahlavi very much played down religious identity, largely misjudging the strength of public feeling on this.[15] At the same time, he sought to validate his own position and legitimize his claim to royalty by appealing to symbols of pre-Islamic power and the ancient Iranian Empire. The lavish celebrations surrounding the Shah's re-coronation in 1972 at the ancient Iranian capital of Persepolis (60 kilometers northeast of Shiraz), attended by dignitaries and heads of state from around the world, were intended to mark 2,500 years of Iranian monarchy, and thereby create a symbolic link between himself and the pre-Islamic kings of Iran.[16] In fact, the Shah was ultimately unable to resolve the inherent contradictions in his own position: on the one hand, he drew on discourses of ancient tradition to counter the power of the clergy; on the other, he undermined the very same discourses when it served the purpose of promoting Westernization and modernization over tradition. In contrast, and partly in reaction to the situation before 1979, the post-1979 regime initially attempted to play down aspects of national identity, appealing instead to a pan-Islamic identity: "Khomeini's relation to nationalism was ambiguous, because in the first period of his rule he virtually never mentioned the word Iran at all, laying stress instead on Islam and on the need to recreate the Islamic 'Universal State'.... The war with Iraq that began in September 1980 forced Khomeini to lay greater explicit stress on nationalist themes" (Halliday 1996: 62–63).[17]

An example of this downplaying of national identity were the initial and unsuccessful attempts by the government to discourage celebration of the Iranian New Year, *no ruz*, an ancient pre-Islamic Zoroastrian tradition that falls on the spring equinox and is the main national holiday in Iran. More recently, Samii refers to an article in the national Iranian press in which the Supreme Leader, Ayatollah Ali Khamenei, criticized Ayatollah Mohajerani (culture minister at the time) for plans to hold *no ruz* celebrations at Persepolis, with all the associations of pre-Islamic heritage (Samii 1999).[18] In fact, as events before and after 1979 have shown, any position that fails to take account of both national and religious identities—or seeks to promote one at the expense of the other—is likely to meet with resistance.

Given the situation in the 1970s, it is hardly surprising that the Revolution itself involved a complex play of identities that in turn reflected contesting visions of what it means to be Iranian. The particular significance of music in this context was that it provided a forum for playing out such visions, most notably because music embodies some of the tensions underlying the political discourses: between national and religious identities, for example, and between tradition and modernity. Although music has long played a central role in Iranian national identity, its status within Islam has been highly ambiguous. The extensive theological debate on the legality of particular kinds of music and musical activities and on the general role of music in an Islamic society is well-documented in the literature, and it is clear that much of this debate rests on a recognition of the power of music on people and the perceived need to control this power.[19] As a result of its ambiguous position in the eyes of the religious authorities, music has rarely occupied an ideologically neutral space in Iran, and has been censored and restricted in various ways over many centuries.[20] In the context of this chapter, it is particularly important to note that both in the symbolic domain and in the domain of practice, such controls have transformed what may originally have been primarily issues of religious doctrine into questions of social and political control. As discussed below, in contemporary Iran at least, what is argued in the name of doctrine is often a facade for specific political positions. Long regarded as somewhat subversive in itself, attempts to control music's power have, ironically, increased its subversive potential and thereby empowered it further. In the post-1979 play of identities, therefore, music occupied an interesting position in relation to a national identity to which music is absolutely central on the one hand, and a religious identity in which its status is highly problematic on the other. In other words, one of the most potent symbols of national consciousness in the 1980s was also one of the most proscribed cultural expressions in Islam, and it was this that precluded the government from appropriating what might have served as a powerful symbol of anti-

Westernization. In the 1980s, then, music became a highly contested issue and presented the government with a dilemma: Aware of the potent force represented by music, and that any government that called itself Islamic must exercise control over it, policy makers were also unable to ignore the strength of popular support for music.

1979 AND ITS AFTERMATH: ON THE GROUND

In seeking to establish control through promoting Islamic values, the theocracy that assumed power in 1979 began life by legislating against a wide range of musical activities, from public concerts to music classes. Certain types of music were officially tolerated: religious music, of course, Iranian "classical" music (known as *musiqi-e assil* or *musiqi-e sonnati*), and regional folk musics. Any music that suggested dance movement or included solo female singing was prohibited.[21] Western popular music in the broadest sense and Iranian pop were also targeted and banned outright immediately after the Revolution, partly because of their associations with the previous regime, but also because of the sensuous dance movements associated with the music and the song lyrics, which the government regarded as crude and explicit. Deemed un-Islamic and potentially corrupting to young people, this music was branded as *musiqi-e mobtazal* ("cheap" or "decadent" music). In short, what had been one of the most prominent symbols of the Shah's modernization project was transformed into *the* symbol of Western cultural hegemony (which later became labeled as *tahājom-e farhangi*: "cultural imperialism" or "cultural invasion"), and the focus of vitriolic rhetoric from the new government. Many of the best-known Iranian pop musicians left Iran after 1979 and Los Angeles eventually became the focal point for an expatriate Iranian pop music industry, the products of which served not only the large market of Iranians outside Iran, but also found their way back to Iran via the black market and later satellite channels.[22]

In order to understand why pop music was banned in 1979, we have to look at what this music had come to mean during the preceding two decades. As Peter Manuel explains:

> In most of the developing world, popular musics cannot be fully understood independent of the legacy of the colonial past and the imperialist present. On the one hand, Western musical styles are often identified, explicitly or not, with progress, technology, modernity, and power. National musics, by contrast, are often seen as quaint and backward [as in 1970s Iran].... On the other hand, a nationalist may well regard the imitation or borrowing of Western

musical features as an illustration of Western hegemony, in the form of an obsequious (and often inept) aping of one's former colonial masters.... [T]he problem of reconciling national and Western cultures can be particularly acute and difficult for the educated middle classes—especially those who have been trained in the West and yet remain loyal to their homelands. (1988: 22)

In the case of Iran, we have seen that the emergence of pop music in the 1960s was closely bound up with the processes of modernization and the values that, through the dominant discourses, came to be associated with them. On the one hand, traditional music was no longer able to meet the needs of an increasingly urbanized and cosmopolitan youth. On the other, Iranian pop (as well as various types of imported Western popular music) became attractive through the aspirational value associated with Western culture. As long as the dominant discourses gave the processes of Westernization positive valence, pop music remained relatively uncontested. But with the reaction against the Shah's policies after 1979, pop music took on the symbolic burden of Western cultural imperialism and became entangled in a web of discourses that impacted significantly on the music's meanings. The post-1979 regime replaced one set of polarized discourses (Westernization at the expense of tradition) with another, which depended on "a growing dislocation" between modernity and tradition (Halliday 1996: 73). Indeed, it is important to note the extent to which the post-1979 period was shaped by, and represented a reaction against, the uncompromising absolutes that had preceded, such that anything supported by the previous regime was dammed by association. And because pop music had been heavily promoted as a (positive) symbol of modernization and Westernization, it was this aspect of the music that eclipsed all other meanings after 1979. Thus, just as Rice (2001) describes the shifting meanings of Bulgarian wedding music during the final years of communism in the late 1980s, so official discourses in Iran after 1979 focused on pop music as a political symbol to the exclusion of other possible meanings such as pop music as entertainment, as aesthetic experience, as commodity or as social behavior, the latter particularly relevant in the context of an emerging youth culture.[23] In failing to take account (or control) of a wide range of meanings, the government was later unable to stop them being used to subvert the dominant discourses.

Of course, Iran is not the only Islamic country in which modernity and Westernization have been contested through the symbolic control of popular music. In the case of Algeria, for example: "Rai has been a particularly problematic idiom for Islamists and secularists alike. Both groups nurture distinct views of the place of Algeria, and Algerians in the world, and the

role of Islam and liberal secularism in Algeria. Rai music constructs its own distinct trajectories linking local and global, 'East' and 'West,' and, in this way, constitutes a distinct problem for Algerians, and indeed other North Africans today" (Langlois 1996: 259).

Where the Algerian situation differs from that of Iran is first that *rai* has gained an international audience that has had significant repercussions for the music's meanings "back home."[24] Second, in taking on a more overtly political role (through its lyrics, for example) than has hitherto been the case with Iranian pop, *rai* has faced a more intense (and at times violent) reaction from its opponents. Nevertheless, there are important parallels in terms of what these musics represent with regard to questions of national identity and each country's relationship with the outside world, particularly with the West.

The 1980s was an extraordinary period with many apparent contradictions. For example, at the same time that the new government was trying to control music making in various ways, the rejection of Western values after 1979 led to a remarkable resurgence of national consciousness and a reclaiming of tradition after decades in which official discourses had presented Iranian culture as the antiquated and backward "other" to the progressive culture of the West, and as having little relevance to modernity. According to Sreberny-Mohammadi and Mohammadi, "the particularly rapid, skewed and over-Westernized pattern of dependent development followed by the Pahlavis provoked the revalidation of a collective identity that had been challenged by the regime-directed path of modernization" (1991b: 217).

Just as "the reaffirmation of cultural 'roots' and the return to orthodoxy has long been one of the most powerful sources of counter-identification amongst many Third World and post-colonial societies and regions" (Hall 1992: 313) where people have felt themselves to be disempowered in some way, so the postrevolutionary period in Iran was marked by "a strengthening of cultural identity and fostering of a positive self-image ..." (Sreberny-Mohammadi and Mohammadi 1991b: 220). According to prominent musician, Shahram Nazeri: "It was as if a nation which had been asleep for centuries had been woken ... as if a fire had suddenly been lit in a reedbed. And each of these reeds, since they are burning, was obliged to think about itself, about its society, about its history.... [P]eople gradually became interested in their own culture, because the reality is that for many years in Iran, really there was a long period of loss of identity (*bihoveiat*) (interview August 21, 1999).[25]

One of the most remarkable manifestations of this heightened awareness of national identity after 1979 was a renaissance of *musiqi-e assil* such as had never been seen before, spearheaded by a new generation of musicians including many of the first generation of university-educated musicians in Iran.[26] Recordings by musicians such as Mohammad Reza Shajarian, Shahram Nazeri, and Mohammad Reza Lotfi provided an emotive focal point for the new mood of political and national consciousness and, most significantly, *musiqi-e assil* started to attract a mass audience for the very first time. As such, discourses about music and national identity became inextricably bound together during this period. The piece *Sepideh* ("dawn"),[27] performed by Shajarian and the Sheyda Ensemble at one of the first concerts permitted after the Revolution (in December 1979), became an unofficial national anthem, particularly after the Iraqi invasion of Iran in September 1980. While detailed discussion of the social history of *musiqi-e assil* during the 1980s lies outside the remit of this chapter, it is important to note that despite severe government restrictions on music making—public concerts were not permitted for many years, for example, and there was little music on radio and television other than revolutionary anthems and military music—unprecedented numbers of people started to learn traditional instruments (Meshkatian 1991: 38). As discussed below, this is something which has proved particularly important in the post-1997 period. Indeed, it was partly because of these restrictions that "Playing and teaching music itself became a kind of resistance and a way of maintaining identity" (Alizadeh 1998: 79), through music's simultaneous affirmation of national belonging and its ambiguous status in the eyes of the religious authorities. Describing the resurgence of interest in *musiqi-e assil*, Alizadeh explains how much music making went underground during this period: "Concerts in homes and private teaching at home became common" (Alizadeh 1998: 79) and Youssefzadeh cites the case of an instrument maker unable to keep up with the demand for new instruments (2000:39). Many musicians I talked to described the early 1980s as a very exciting period for *musiqi-e assil*, the full potential of which, however, was never realized. Shahram Nazeri suggests that one of the most important cultural achievements of the Revolution was that music making (and music as a professional activity) gained much wider social acceptance than before:

> [After the Revolution] people gained a sense of confidence with regard to music. This sense of confidence was never there before, because of our culture, because of religion, since religion never made its position clear with respect to music and regarded it as *haram* ["forbidden"] and consequently this also had an effect on society. Society couldn't decide whether music is *haram* or *halal* ["allowed"], whether it is good or bad, but now this confidence came about and this was a very significant development. (Interview August 21, 1999)

Despite the high level of public support for music, and the fact that *musiqi-e assil* was still legal, the 1980s was a difficult time for musicians, who faced many pressures and were heavily restricted and censored. The government itself was deeply divided on cultural policy generally and many would have liked a complete ban on music making. In the 1980s, music provided a stark forum for the government to impose ideas about permissible (represented as Islamic) and impermissible (represented as un-Islamic) behavior, and as if doctrinal issues were not enough, the war with Iraq (1980–1988) provided yet another pretext to restrict music making. Public musical activity of any kind had to be authorized by the Ministry of Culture and Islamic Guidance (*Vezarat-e Farhang va Ershad-e Eslami*), as it still has to be, and official discourses treated music not as an aesthetic reality, but as a social factor that needed to be controlled. In order to represent themselves as upholders of Islamic values, government officials and clerics would make periodic pronouncements on the Islamic propriety of a particular type of music or music-related activity (making and selling instruments, for instance), such that music became a kind of "political football," a way of scoring points.[28] In fact, there was a great deal of ambiguity, and positions clarified by one religious authority were often overruled by another, creating a situation in which music existed in a liminal space and people were often unsure exactly what was allowed at any particular time. This ambiguity served a purpose for the government, allowing it to change the rules at will or clamp down whenever it was politically expedient to do so; but it made the position of musicians precarious and subject to the vagaries of any religious leader or individual interpretation of Islamic law.[29] At the same time, the lack of clarity created crevices—opportunities for resistance—particularly since many of the laws were effectively unenforceable in the private domain. And it was in the private domain that Iranians, very adept at resistance after centuries of one form of oppression or another, had the greatest opportunity for subversion.[30]

Examining official government policy toward music during the 1980s is important for what it tells us about the political climate of the period, but it should also be understood that this reveals only part of what was happening in Iran at the time. A number of writers have noted the gap between dominant ideologies as expressed through official government policy and the complex reality of people's lives (Youssefzadeh 2000: 38; Sreberny-Mohammadi and Mohammadi 1991a: 34) and this was particularly apparent with pop music. Although officially banned, many people, particularly in the more cosmopolitan and urban areas such as the suburbs of North Tehran,[31] continued to listen to pop music in private. This included a wide range of Western popular music styles, Iranian pop music from before 1979, and imported *los angelesi* pop, all of which were readily available through a flourishing black market that the government was ultimately unable to control (Sreberny-Mohammadi and Mohammadi 1991a: 47–8; During 1992: 140).[32] During the 1980s, revolutionary guards regularly arrested people caught with cassettes of pop music in their cars, or raided homes if they suspected a party was being held. Those arrested were usually brushed up a little and released the next day with a warning or a fine. But it seemed to be a price worth paying. For young people in particular, listening to pop music became a form of resistance—a snub at the government—and the danger a bit of excitement. For example, one young woman to whom I talked about attending mixed-sex parties with pop music, and the risk of being arrested, responded by asking "What's the fun of it without the danger?" Alongside the vibrant resurgence of national consciousness after 1979, then, the deep-rooted cultural legacy of neocolonialism continued to play its part and Western cultural products retained their attraction. Indeed, as in the case of pop music, while the government promoted discourses of local resistance against Western global hegemony, certain aspects of Western culture were used as a means of resisting the government-imposed hegemony.

So how did pop music's meanings change in the 1980s? As we have seen, pop music became illegal after 1979 because of what the musical style as a whole had come to represent before the Revolution. The songs themselves were not particularly subversive or challenging, but by banning this music, the post-1979 government effectively gave pop music its subversive power. By the mid-1980s, pop music had become a symbol of resistance by virtue of being banned: young people wanted to listen to it *because* it was prohibited. Although many people had ambivalent feelings toward pop music—and particularly *los angelesi* pop and the distance of its messages from the reality of life in Iran—to the extent of privately agreeing with at least some of the meanings that the government attempted to assign to it (symbol of cultural dependence, Western decadence, cultural imperialism, and so on), such meanings were simply unable to compete with the quite different meanings many young people in particular assigned to this music: pop as a symbol of social freedoms, of defiance, of youth, and of the outside world. In this way, pop's meanings in the 1980s were largely defined through competing discourses of national belonging versus internationalism on the one hand, and central control versus individual freedom on the other.

In a situation not unlike that described by Rice for wedding music in Bulgaria, so pop music in 1980s Iran became a sign of resistance, of "freedom from totalitarian control, and the state was powerless to control them [it] and their [its] meanings" (Rice 2001: 36). The fact that this was largely a symbolism "by default," following a logic that equated anything that the state opposed as automatically representing freedom, did not diminish its significance. However, what emerged at this time was almost exclusively resistance "by consumption" rather than by creation, in the sense that all of the pop music available either dated from before 1979 or was created outside Iran in very different social and cultural contexts and imported into Iran through the black market.[33] In other words, unlike the case of *rai* or Bulgarian wedding music, there was no active voice of resistance through the *creation* of a local contemporary popular music at grassroots level in Iran itself. As such, any expression of active resistance through music at this time came from *musiqi-e assil*. Indeed, even in the 1960s and '70s when an independent, grassroots popular music might have emerged, most pop music production was centrally controlled, and the music provided little in the way of social comment. Returning to the 1980s, it is interesting to note that this kind of "resistance by dissemblance" has in fact been an important aspect of Iranian culture for centuries, something particularly evident in Persian poetry in which messages are often subtly conveyed using hidden inferences and double meanings.[34] In the same way, the use of pop music created in another time or place—speaking in someone else's voice, as it were—very much followed in this same tradition.

During the 1980s, then, music—and pop music in particular—was a highly contested domain. Used as part of the discourse of social control by official institutions and the government on the one hand, at the same time for many people music came to signify a reclaiming of national culture (through *musiqi-e assil* and regional musics) and of wider social freedoms (through *musiqi-e assil* in the public domain and pop music in the private). While political resistance through cultural expression has a long history in Iranian literature (and particularly poetry), this was the first time that music had taken on this role in such a prominent way.[35] Indeed, what was so interesting about this period was not only that such resistance shifted into a primarily performative and collective mode of cultural expression, providing a potentially more immediate, public, and hard-hitting social impact than previous cultural resistance, but that it involved one of the most religiously contested cultural forms.[36]

Beyond its subversive role, pop music was also important in other ways during the 1980s. For example, it provided a space for celebration (in the private domain) and the expression of happiness, something for which the generally rather austere *musiqi-e assil* was unsuited. Traditionally censured as a sign of disrespect (as well as a sure way to attract the evil eye), the public expression of happiness became even more problematic during the middle and later stages of the war with Iraq, a period of great austerity and perpetual public mourning. Nevertheless, pop music continued to be used for celebrations such as weddings, usually in secure locations such as sound-proof basements. And for many young people—particularly those from the urban middle classes—pop music provided a link with the outside world, a challenge to the isolationist policies of the government and a means of forefronting conflicting visions of Iranian identity and Iran's place in a global environment.

CULTURAL THAW

During the 1980s, the government was able to avoid dealing with fundamental social issues by appealing to national unity against an external aggressor. However, after the ceasefire with Iraq in August 1988 and the death of Ayatollah Khomeini in June the following year, the new president, Hashemi Rafsanjani, began the slow and much-debated process of social reform and reestablishing Iran's international relations.[37] Fully aware of the mood of a nation tired of austerity, Rafsanjani promoted a more open political and cultural atmosphere. As far as music is concerned, a timely statement made by Ayatollah Khomeini soon after the UN ceasefire, sanctioning the use of musical instruments, was used to advantage after his death by those arguing for the legality of music (During 1992: 164; Sreberny-Mohammadi and Mohammadi 1991a: 50; Youssssefzadeh 2000: 39).[38] In line with other changes, the 1990s saw an easing of controls on music making as music classes were permitted again (and the Music Department at Tehran University was reopened) and restrictions were gradually lifted on other musical activities.[39]

However, it was the election of President Khatami in May 1997 and the changes in cultural policy which followed that represented the real watershed. A pivotal figure in these changes was the much respected and liberal-minded head of the Ministry of Culture and Islamic Guidance, Ayatollah Mohajerani, who promoted a new mood of tolerance and open debate, and under whose leadership publishing flourished, with many new books, newspapers, and journals representing a wide range of political views.[40] Music has been an important part of the more liberal atmosphere, and in some respects the changes have been quite dramatic: There is more music on radio and television than before and even a dedicated music channel on radio for the first time in Iran (*Radio Payam*), a flourishing market for cassettes and CDs, and an increasing number of public concerts.[41] Eight *farhangsarā* cultural centers, established by the municipal authority of Tehran and situated in different parts of the city, have been particularly active in promoting concerts and lectures, running music lessons, organizing instrumental and choral groups, and generally providing a focus for cultural activities. News of musical events, articles on music, and reviews of concerts are regularly featured in the national press, and since 1998 there have been three regular publications dedicated to music: *Honar-e Musiqi* ("The Art of Music"), a monthly magazine aimed at the lay reader and readily available in bookshops and even on street newspaper stalls, and two scholarly journals published quarterly: *Faslnameh-*

ye Musiqi-e Mahoor ("Mahoor Musical Quarterly") and *Faslnameh-ye Musiqi-e Maqam*, the latter published by the government organization, Sooreh.[42] Everywhere in Tehran there are posters advertising concerts and music lessons, and the number of young people attending such lessons has increased dramatically in the post-1997 period (Alizadeh 1998: 81). Indeed, despite concerns over the quality of some teaching, many regard this as one of the most positive aspects of music in Iran today and a source of hope for the future: "The limitations which were placed on learning music increased the number of people wanting to learn. When the municipal authorities of Tehran opened cultural centers (*farhangsarā*) all over the city, they started music classes. Now it is really not an exaggeration to say that in every family someone plays an instrument" (Alizadeh 1998: 81). In short, music in Iran is gaining a presence in the public domain never experienced before, not even before 1979.

While support for the more open political and cultural atmosphere is overwhelming,[43] such changes are being contested by a small but powerful conservative clerical lobby, and music continues to provide an emotive arena for this ideological tug of war. Many of the proscriptions put in place in the 1980s still apply: solo female singing is forbidden to male listeners; musical instruments are not shown on television; dancing of any kind is forbidden in public; and on holy days, only religious music is broadcast or allowed in public places. However, inconsistent easing of restrictions on public performance has generated some blatant contradictions and some interesting opportunities for subversion. For example, although musical instruments are still not shown on television, they can be seen quite legally in many other contexts, including live concerts, music lessons, or music shops, a situation that has invited ridicule in articles in the national and music press (for example, see Eftekhari 1999: 8). Similarly, while solo female singing is still prohibited to male audiences, choral singing is not and a number of recent recordings have used this "loophole" to advantage, incorporating a "chorus" of two or three female singers whose solo voices are also heard briefly.[44] In fact, musicians have become skillful at finding creative ways of working around restrictions, subtly pushing at boundaries without appearing to contest them openly and thus averting a reaction from the authorities. In large part, this is made possible by the cleavages opened up by contradictions in cultural policy, which are in turn symptomatic of deep divisions within the government itself.

THE NEW POP ... [45]

One of the most unexpected changes to have come about since 1997 has been a relaxation in government restrictions on certain type of popular music in the public domain for the first time since 1979. The first indication of this came in 1998 when *Seda o Sima* (the government-controlled national radio and television organization) quite unexpectedly started broadcasting a rebranded style of Iranian pop, which soon became known as *pop-e jadid* ("new pop"). Within a short space of time, this music was being broadcast regularly on radio and television, and cassettes and CDs were also freely available on the open market.[46] Mohammad Esfahani, Ali Reza Assar, and Khashayar Etemadi were among the first crop of hitherto unknown singers who were heavily promoted by *Seda o Sima*[47] and who rapidly became household names. Stylistically, this new pop shared a great deal with other kinds of Iranian pop, which were still officially illegal:[48] the formulaic nature of the music, the setting of sentimental love poetry, the dominance of a solo singer (in preference to a group ethos) and an instrumental line-up, usually comprising piano or electronic keyboard(s), acoustic and/or electric guitar(s), and drum kit, and at times other instruments such as saxophone, flute, clarinet, bass guitar, a bowed string section, and Iranian percussion instruments such as *tombak* or *daff*. Moreover, some singers even modeled their vocal style on specific pre-Revolutionary pop musicians. But there were also important differences: first, the absence of any solo female singers; second, the lyrics and subject matter; and finally, as dancing in public is illegal, the new pop was generally at a moderate speed and never fast enough to imply dance (or any erotically suggestive) movement.[49] Indeed, when broadcast on television, singers were required to use minimal body movement.

At least, this is how the new pop started off. Once the processes of change were set in motion, however, the momentum has been hard for the government to control and the centrally promoted singers have been joined by a series of independent singers and groups, some of whom are pushing at the existing boundaries through their music. In particular, the new pop has become increasingly upbeat to the extent that some of the more recent songs are almost indistinguishable from the *los angelesi* pop that is still technically illegal. For example, the 1999 album by new pop singer Shadmehr Aghili—*Dehati*—was authorized for publication despite the speed and dance-like nature of several of the tracks.[50] Also significant is the growing presence of women, initially as backing singers and instrumentalists, but gradually taking on a more prominent role.[51]

Live concerts have presented a particularly important opportunity for musicians to claim greater license in performance. On my first fieldtrip in the summer of 1999, the Ministry of Culture and Islamic Guidance had started to give limited authorization for pop concerts, but these were still infrequent.[52] By the time of my second visit the following year, such concerts had become a fairly regular feature of life in Tehran. As a public expression of the post-1997 changes, and one that symbolically dominates the social space through its volume, these pop concerts have provided a focal point for accusations that moderate factions within the government have sold out to the original aims of the Revolution. In the summer of 2000, the ongoing power struggle over this issue was played out most vividly in the physical disruption of public concerts by the voluntary militia known as *basij*.[53] Even concerts that had official authorization from the Ministry of Culture were often prevented from taking place by key individuals at local level.[54] By the same token, and because they faced such opposition, concerts that did take place became symbolic events and were often used as an arena for challenging imposed limits in a way not always possible on commercial recordings. In order to gain authorization for a concert, musicians were (and still are) required to submit song texts and a concert program in advance of the performance. Unlike a recording, therefore, for which authorization is granted *after* the event (in the sense that the musical product is already complete), in the case of live performance, permission is given *beforehand*, offering musicians the possibility of subsequently altering the agreed program at the actual event—for example, by changing song lyrics or by playing pieces at a faster speed. I heard about several concerts where this had happened. Indeed it was not only musicians who were taking risks. At every pop concert I attended, audience members were visibly moving in their seats and clearly eager to dance as they would in private. On one occasion, some young women got up to dance, but were asked to stop by the event organizers (they could easily have been arrested instead). A similar experience, described by Sohrabi less than two years later, indicates that maintaining central control over such events is proving increasingly problematic. In her review of a concert by the group *Raaz-e Shab* in January 2002, she reports that during the encore "People began standing up, hands clapping towards the stage, singing with the band and moving their bodies. Security people tried to make two screaming girls in the front row sit. But it was no longer orderly as the hall was big, people were coming in, going out, and the band was really rocking" (Sohrabi 2002).

This pushing at boundaries, whether by musicians or by audiences, is part of a wider feeling of empowerment associated with the post-1997 reforms. Pop music in Iran has once again taken on a symbolic role, and for many people this music has become *the* symbol of recent changes. Above all, after so many years of austerity and relative isolation, this music has come to signify a kind of liberation, offering music that is at once contemporary and rooted "at home," and also provides a direct connection with the outside world.[55]

It is difficult to convey quite what an effect the emergence of the new pop music into the public domain has had. Coinciding as it has with so many other reforms, it is not difficult to understand why this music has generally been received with enthusiasm, particularly by young people.

After so many years of pop music being underground, many see the changes as an indication that the government is at last addressing the needs of young people.[56] I talked to a large number of teenagers and young people in their twenties, mainly (but not exclusively) from the middle class suburbs of North Tehran, most of whom still listened to illegal imports of Western popular music (techno and heavy metal appeared to be particularly popular) as well as *los angelesi* pop, and even prerevolutionary pop singers such as Dariush and Ebi. However, many said that they prefer the new local pop to other types of Iranian pop, not so much for dancing as for listening to, and one of the principal reasons that they gave was that the lyrics are more cultured, particularly in comparison with *los angelesi* pop. For example, some of the new pop singers have set the words of medieval mystic poets (such as Mowlana[57]) more usually associated with *musiqi-e assil*. Many of those with whom I talked described the lyrics of imported pop as "cheap" and out of touch with the reality of life in Iran. In short, the young people that I spoke to really saw the new pop as a music with which they could identify. Moreover, alongside the new music, there are signs that a fledgling youth culture is emerging, something that has been given impetus by magazines for young people, such as the weekly *Iran Javan*,[58] and by new television programm aimed at teenagers, including phone-in music request programs such as *Roozha-ye Shafahi*.

Given the backgrounds of the young people that I spoke to, the fairly positive response to the new music was perhaps not unexpected, but Iran is far from a homogenous society and there are significant disparities in income and lifestyle. While the extent to which the responses above might also be found amongst young people of a less affluent and cosmopolitan background isn't clear, anecdotal information, reports in the national and musical press, discussion with a wide range of people, and visits to provincial and rural areas suggest that this music has in fact made significant inroads, particularly through its crucial presence on *Radio Payam*. In the context of the current discussion, what is interesting is the way in which the sanctioning of new pop has served to validate pop music in some of the more traditional areas where this music would previously have met with a great deal of resistance. In a sense, then, the new pop, and its promotion through the national media, is serving as a catalyst for a more unified youth culture, providing a common experience for young people from very different backgrounds.

So how should the change in government policy toward pop music be interpreted? And what impact has this change had on the meanings of pop music itself? The emergence of the new pop, along with the limited legalization of certain other popular music genres, seems to fly in the face of everything that the Islamic Republic has stood for since 1979. Those who spoke out so strongly against cultural invasion and the corruption of the young are now apparently endorsing the very music that once represented the epitome of Western decadence. The decision to ease restrictions on pop music is clearly part of the post-1997 cultural thaw and the more liberal policy toward music generally. Moreover, coming at a time when Iran was in the process of reestablishing diplomatic links with countries such as Britain, with whom normal relations had been suspended since 1979, this might be regarded as being part of a wider indication to the outside world of Iran's readiness to move away from the isolationist policies of the 1980s and to rebuild its international relations: as a way of flagging an emergent liberalism in government policy. The government itself is deeply divided on this issue, and there is little official information on the reasoning behind the decision to sanction pop music. A rare official view on the new pop (and one that presents a very different position with regard to private listening in comparison with government policy in the 1980s) is quoted by Youssefzadeh from a personal interview with Ali Moradkhani, Head of Music at the Ministry of Culture (February 2000): "This kind of music nowadays exists in Iran. It caters to the needs of young people, but does not require our financial or economic aid (*hemāyat*). We have to let it exist, while at the same time preventing it from becoming too repetitive.... As for what people do in private, we are not responsible for it; it's for them to decide what they want to hear" (2000: 40). As Youssefzadeh observes, "Such speeches are a great novelty" (2000: 40).

In direct contrast to government sources, I found a great deal of speculation in my discussions with musicians and others, as well as in the national and music press.[59] Many of those with whom I spoke saw the sanctioning of pop as evidence that after almost two decades of trying unsuccessfully to control the black market in *los angelesi* and other types of pop music, the government had adopted more subtle tactics (more subtle, that is, than simply banning, which rarely proved effective in any case). Certainly, with the increasingly global nature of markets and communications, the government seems to have realized that the cultural imperialism that they are now dealing with is much more complex than the simple "unambiguous domination of one dependent culture by a clearly demarcated other" (Ang 1996: 247), involving more porous and arguably more insidious configurations of power that offer myriad ways of subverting central control. For one thing, many people in Iran now have access to the Internet and can obtain music online from all over the world. If the government was unable to prevent people from listening to pop music, they could at least bring it (or some of it) under their own control. In other words, by creating a local alternative, it seems that the government hoped to attract audiences away from other kinds of pop music and thereby reestablish control over areas that it had relinquished in the 1980s and early 1990s: pop music as entertainment, as commodity, and as social behavior. And to some extent, they are succeeding. The new pop is proving very popular with young people thirsty for a pop music with which they can identify, and Pearl cites the case of one black market cassette dealer whose business has slumped since the emergence of the new pop (2000). Others that I spoke to suggested that there were financial reasons for the changes in government policy, and that the government had finally realized the economic potential of so-called "degenerate" music.

Whether the sanctioning of the new pop was a genuine attempt at liberalization or a cynical gesture aimed at building support (or even simply saving face), something very interesting is happening. For almost twenty years, the government effectively *empowered* pop music—made it subversive—by banning it. Now, by legalizing certain types of pop music, not only has the government blunted the subversive potential of imported pop, but it has done so by appropriating the very form of cultural resistance used against it in the 1980s as its weapon of countersubversion. Moreover, *los angelesi* and pre-1979 pop have perhaps been all the more easy to appropriate because the songs are not directly politically challenging. In extending its control over this music, the government has also changed the meaning of Iranian pop music from a statement of resistance in the 1980s to a symbol of post-1997 liberalism, no longer a subversive threat, but domesticated and rendered safe. As part of this controlling process, the government has sought to insert pop music into an official establishment framework, as seen, for example, in the inclusion of a pop music section as part of the Fajr festival, from 2000 onward.[60] Once again, there are interesting parallels with the situation of Bulgarian wedding music in the 1980s, as described by Rice, when "The state tried to control these new musics and meanings through state-sponsored festivals of wedding music" (2001: 36).[61] This "domestication" clearly strips pop music of its power to question and challenge.

What is also interesting is that while the new pop singers are readily distinguished from pre-1979 and *los angelesi* singers, as discussed earlier, the musical style has become increasingly similar to these other kinds of Iranian pop, which are still officially illegal. In other words, while the text itself has not changed greatly, its meanings have. As mentioned above, the most significant differences are in the song lyrics and subject matter, with new pop composers often choosing to set mystical poetry or use religious symbolism (which a number of my informants suggested was a means of avoiding censorship). An example of this can be seen on Ali Reza Assar's first album, *Kooch-e Asheqaneh* (1999), in which the tracks "Ghodsian-e Aseman," "Ensanam Orezoost," and "Koo-ye Eshq" are all set to the poetry of Mowlana. The first track of the album, "Ghodsian-e Aseman," in particular was heavily promoted and regularly aired by *Radio Payam* in the summer of 1999.[62] The religious and mystical ambience of this album is further reinforced by the use of the *daff* frame drum (which originates in the Sufi *khanegah* of Iranian Kurdistan), and also by the cover, which presents the bearded profile of Assar thrown into partial silhouette by a distant light toward which he is looking. In contrast, the cover of Shadmehr Aghili's album *Dehati* (1999; referred to earlier) presents a very different image. (See these images on the book's website.) Also looking to the side (and thereby avoiding direct eye contact with the viewer), Aghili's clean shaven face, prominent bare arms, and slicked-back hair present an image of modern, urban youth, publicly challenging the accepted dress code for men, which includes covered arms and legs, but which has been relaxed somewhat since 1997.[63] Even before the listener gets to the music, then, the visual message represents a challenge in a way that is not the case on *Kooch-e Asheqaneh.* While a detailed analysis of album covers lies outside the remit of this chapter, it is important to recognize their semiotic significance and note that such images are subject to as much government scrutiny as the music itself. What is also noticeable about the new pop is that musicians now have access to a much broader range of musical styles than previously and are drawing on these in their compositions. One example of this is the clear South African influence that can be heard in the song "Delkhoshi" on Aghili's album *Dehati.*[64]

It is worth noting that this is not the first time that the government has employed a strategy of offering a local alternative to imported Western cultural products. As discussed earlier, Iranian cinema (like pop music) also became a target of anti-Western feeling at the time of the Revolution. However, from 1983 on there was a drive to encourage domestic film-making, which had a profound impact at home, providing a local alternative to the Hollywood blockbusters available through the black market. Although initially aimed at a domestic market, the ensuing international success of Iranian filmmakers from the early 1990s clearly highlighted the potential influence of such cultural products abroad. A growing awareness of this influence is revealed in the following extraordinary statement by Hashemi Rafsanjani, the then Speaker of the Parliament (and who later became president) at the Fifth Islamic Film Festival in Tehran (date not stated): "In order to export the Islamic Revolution, we have to make effective films and not let Hollywood be the dominant influence. We have to change the attitudes of people. Instead of giving grants for building mosques, they should give grants for building cinemas and making films!" (quoted in Sreberny-Mohammadi and Mohammadi 1991a: 46).

Coming from a senior cleric, this bold suggestion highlights the remarkable transformation of cinema from a symbol of foreign cultural domination to one of resistance against Western cultural hegemony. In fact, Iranian cinema has proved to be a double-edged sword for the government in the international arena. On the one hand, the success enjoyed by Iranian filmmakers brings with it a certain prestige and a positive image for Iran on the world stage; on the other, film is often used as an avenue for social and political critique, which the government is unable to control outside Iran. While filmmakers inside Iran continue to face restrictions, they are able to make direct social comment in a way that was previously unthinkable. What is particularly interesting is the extent to which film as a cultural medium has shed its previous associations with Western culture and come to be regarded as a local cultural expression.[65] Whether Iranian pop music can achieve the same remains to be seen. Certainly, as will be discussed below, music continues to engender quasi-moralistic discourses of authenticity, high and low culture, and national belonging, all of which film is relatively unfettered by.

...AND BEYOND

In fact, the new pop music is just one aspect of the changing public "soundscapes" of Iran, as a wider range of musics have become permitted in public and indeed, certain (limited) kinds of Western popular music now receive government authorization. Perusing commercially available recordings in the summer of 2002, a range of musical styles was available, including jazz, flamenco, certain kinds of rock,[66] and Latin music, and musicians such as Kenny G. and the Gypsy Kings appeared to be particularly popular. Sheet music of a few Western popular "classics"—for example, Pink Floyd's "The Wall"—was also on sale in several bookshops. Moreover, beyond the still fairly limited public presence of Western popular music itself, upbeat music composed in the style of Western pop was used regularly on television commercials and program credits, as well as in other public spaces. For example, the open-air children's skating rink in *park-e qeytarieh* (a regularly frequented park in North Tehran), regularly broadcast techno-style music from its loudspeakers. Ironically, although dancing to this music would not be permitted in public, skating to it is legal. Particularly significant in this respect is *Radio Payam*, the first (and so far only) radio channel in Iran specifically dedicated to music. *Radio Payam* was established two years before Khatami's presidential election victory, indicating the extent to which the events of 1997 represented something akin to an avalanche following a long period of thaw. Essentially an easy listening channel, *Radio Payam* broadcasts an eclectic mix of new pop, *musiqi-e assil*, Western classical, rather bland "ambient" arrangements of tunes, and even instrumental arrangements of Western pop music, including songs by Madonna, Rod

Stewart, and the Rolling Stones, none of whose original songs are autho-rized for commercial sale in Iran.[67] As on all other channels, the *azan* (call to prayer) is broadcast three times a day: at dawn, at midday, and at dusk. The music is interspersed with the recitation of poetry and philosophical reflections, and none of the music is identified unless a particularly well-known musician (usually a singer) is featured. There is a strong tradition of listening to the radio in Iran, and the immense audience that *Radio Payam* has attracted points to its significance in filling a vacuum in music broadcasting.[68] Even so, *Seda o Sima* is still going to great lengths to promote this radio station, and one of the few advertising hoardings to be seen alongside the ubiquitous murals of religious figures and martyrs of the Iran–Iraq war on the recently built by-pass highways of Tehran is for *Radio Payam*. Like the new pop music, *Radio Payam* has for many people also become a symbol of the changing cultural climate.

Perhaps the government thought that such concessions might be enough to satisfy demands for greater openness. But by the summer of 2000, it was quite clear that having tasted freedom, many (particularly young) people were testing the water to see how far they could go. In a myriad of ways, and taking cues from one another, people pushed at the boundaries, for example, by playing loud Western pop music (still banned) while driving or even from parked cars. One could hear loud rock music coming from apartment blocks (something that would have been inconceivable even a year before) and people no longer made much effort to hide satellite dishes, which were still officially banned (but unofficially tolerated; people previ-ously went to elaborate lengths to hide or camouflage dishes).[69] And in the communal taxis that provide such a rich source of information in Tehran, drivers openly played cassettes of the popular pre-revolutionary female singer, Googoosh. Despite increasing skepticism over Khatami's power to effect genuine reform in other spheres—the government has even been accused of using the cultural changes as a facade to mask the country's serious economic and social problems—people were still seizing the oppor-tunity offered by changes in the cultural domain, and there was a mood of optimism, even courage. Everywhere, music was used as an avenue for exploring how far the boundaries of the permissible could be pushed.

One thing seems fairly certain in the current climate: the tide of change will be hard to reverse. For one thing, music is finally emerging from its liminal position and assuming a more central and active role in Iranian society. One indicator of this is the extent to which the debate over music's legality has lost much of its potency over the last two decades (and partic-ularly since 1997). Although music continues to be used as part of the rhetoric of Islamic propriety, particularly by those opposed to the recent changes, the evidence suggests that for most people this issue is more or less resolved. A new organization, *Khaneh-ye Musiqi-e Iran*, combining the roles of professional body, trade union, and a public voice for music and musicians, was established in 1999, following the formation of similar organizations in other artistic fields and very much in accordance with the emergence of a Civil Society discourse in Iran.[70] More recently, the government has made moves toward reintroducing music and other creative arts subjects into the school curriculum.[71] Each of these ostensibly minor changes forms part of a larger picture in which the significance of music's new-found position has yet to be fully realized.

THE DEBATE: NEW POP AS CULTURAL IMPERIALISM OR EMPOWERMENT?

Beyond the predictable objections of traditionalists, what is most interesting is that, of all the changes to have come about since 1997, none has provoked such an intense and public debate as the emergence of the new pop music. Lines clearly demarcated since the Revolution have been thrown into disarray, and musicians who worked together for many years toward a common aim of establishing an unambiguous position for music in Iranian society now find themselves divided on this issue. The debate focuses on questions of national identity—about what is and isn't Iranian and who holds the franchise on Iran's future—and what the role of pop music should be in contemporary Iran. Of particular interest is the way in which this debate brings together two sets of dualistic discourses, which have become inextricably linked. On the hand, there is what might loosely be called the "popular music as hegemony versus popular music as empowerment" debate: to what extent is the new pop truly an expression of the people as opposed to a tool of hegemonic control imposed from above? On the other, there is the long-standing debate over questions of Western global hegemony versus national identity: is the new pop truly "Iranian" or simply an imitation of the West, using the language of the oppressor, so to speak? And if so, does it matter?

This is an issue that has polarized feelings, and many of the musicians and others I talked to had strong views on the subject. Much of this debate has been aired in public, particularly in the national and musical press, where a plethora of articles have been published since 1998 defending or criticizing first the legalization of the new pop and other kinds of popular music, and second the new pop as a musical genre. Most criticism has come from the musical establishment: both from traditional musicians and also from those trained as Western classical musicians (composers, conductors, and performers). While many welcome music's greater public presence, they criticize *Seda o Sima* in particular for promoting new pop almost to the exclusion of other musical styles, and for supporting pop musicians, whom they largely regard as opportunists with little musical skill or training, in preference to traditional musicians. Among the latter, the legalization of pop and its promotion by *Seda o Sima* are generally viewed as a "dumbing down" of the culture, and they claim that the recent changes are ideologically and populist driven (and also possibly commercially driven) rather than being based on aesthetic values. In other words, critics of the new pop counter the newly ascribed meanings of pop music as entertainment and commodity (alongside the continuing pop music as political symbol) by appealing to music as art and to discourses of high and low culture in which the new pop is definitely low. At the same time, critics validate their position by warning against the dangers of slipping back to the identity crisis of the 1970s and drawing on discourses of national identity and cultural imperialism in which the new pop lies firmly with the latter. For example, the following quotation from an article by prominent musician Kambeez Roshanravan is fairly typical: "Not only is this music not based on the *radif* but it is solely a simplistic imitation of music from outside this country without maintaining any of its cultural identity" (2000: 5).[72] Another musician, Dariush Pirniakan, also focuses on national identity in an article titled "The Current Pop Music Has No Identity" (2000), in which he claims that a few untalented musicians have taken advantage of the absence of any coherent cultural planning on the part of the government. Similarly, "Pop Music Is Not the People's Music" is the title of an article by well-known traditional singer Mohammad Noori (1999), in which he argues that the new pop has neither artistic value, nor is it truly "popular" in the sense of being "of the people." These are just a few of the many hundreds of articles that have been published on this topic.[73]

What is significant for the purposes of this discussion is the way in which critics focus on questions of national identity in order to validate what are largely aesthetic objections. This is particularly revealing, given that some of the most outspoken critics are themselves trained primarily as Western classical musicians: for these musicians, it seems, Western classical music doesn't represent a threat to notions of identity in the way that pop music does.[74] Moreover, in a rather odd twist, those musicians who oppose the new pop music find themselves in an awkward position. Having worked throughout the difficult period of the 1980s to establish a secure position for music in Iranian society—at a time when their very right to make music was in question—they now find themselves on the same side of the battlelines, even using some of the same arguments and appealing to the same discourses, as those who oppose music altogether. Inadvertently or otherwise, this has been a clear case of divide and rule.

In response to such criticisms, a great deal has been published in defense of the recent changes. Commentators argue that the emergence of the new pop was inevitable and that traditional music is no longer able to fulfill the needs of young people increasingly in touch with the outside world.[75] "You Can't Stop This Type of Music" (author unknown, 2000a) is a review of one of the earliest pop and rock concerts held at the Andisheh Cultural Centre in Tehran and asserts the right of young people to listen to popular music as well as arguing for a more realistic view that doesn't automatically reject everything that comes from the West. Similar articles include "Pop Music, A Necessity" (Javidfar 1999) and "The Guitar Is Not Western, Honest!," an interview with two pop musicians, the brothers Dariush and Mohammad Ali Khajenoori, which challenges critics to define exactly what is and isn't Iranian in the contemporary context (author unknown, 2000b). These and many other articles point out that pop music is a reality of the modern world and the global environment, from which Iran can no longer afford to be isolated. In particular, the monthly magazine, *Honar-e Musiqi*, promotes pop music, profiling musicians, reporting on concerts and new recordings, and even including posters of both Iranian and Western pop musicians (two issues have featured pictures of Eric Clapton on the back cover).[76] Then there are those who support the spirit of the changes, but who are concerned about how they have been implemented and about the lack of clear government policy on cultural matters generally. Above all, *Seda o Sima* is criticized for abandoning the best traditional musicians and for failing, with all its resources, to play a positive educational role.

Significantly, those writing in support of the changes have drawn on similar kinds of discourses as those used by Khatami in his time as president. First, such writers invoke notions of civil liberty that resonate strongly with current debates on the role of Civil Society in Iran. Second, these articles appeal less to discourses of national identity and more to a new kind of internationalism, also a central pillar of Khatami's 1997 election campaign that he has continued to use as a hallmark of his vision for Iran's future. Central to this has been the replacement of discourses of "cultural invasion" with talk of "dialogue between civilizations."[77] What I found particularly interesting was the stark contrast between concerns about national identity raised in the press and by the (mainly) older traditional musicians who I spoke to, and the ways in which others spoke about the new pop. While many of the latter complained about issues such as poor facilities for music performance or the growing vested financial interests of promoters,[78] most were simply pleased that pop music was legal again and few regarded it as a threat to their national identity. As Alizadeh observes, people have been denied music for so long that they will welcome almost anything: "Maybe we can assess this general tendency to support any kind of music as a form of resistance against those who oppose music altogether" (1998, 80). Moreover, because music itself came to represent a kind of resistance during the 1980s and '90s, opposing any kind of music now becomes problematic. Whilst identity—*hoveiat*—is still an important issue (and people talk about it a great deal), so is normalizing relations with the outside world, and many therefore welcome the new pop as a music that symbolizes such relations, but which is at the same time controlled from inside Iran, not from outside.

TOWARD EMPOWERMENT?

This brings us back to the central underlying questions regarding Iran's future, as set out at the opening: how to forge that future in the global environment without subsuming its identity, as happened in the 1970s; how to accommodate modernity without losing its traditions; and how to move beyond the neocolonial inheritance and two decades of relative isolation in order to normalize relations. As we have seen, the extreme reaction against decades of external influence resulted in post-1979 official discourses that rejected much of Western culture and which made little distinction between the remnants of cultural imperialism and what Ahdaf Soueif calls "the legitimate commerce of humanity" (1999: 484). At the same time, there remains a persistent colonial mentality that has survived the period of isolation and militates against a normalized relationship. While the 1980s was in many ways a difficult decade, it was at least marked by a pride in self-determination and independence. The anxiety over pop music's recent legalization, as illustrated above, suggests that issues of cultural dependency are far from resolved in Iran, and there are genuine concerns about a possible return to the situation of the 1960s and '70s. As Khatami himself suggests, this is something that can only be changed from within, as a more mature understanding of the West develops: "One of the biggest intellectual problems that societies like ours face ... is lack of adequate understanding of Western political thought, which is itself a result of our historical ignorance ... getting to know the culture and society of the West is an intellectual and historical necessity ... (Khatami 1997: 14, quoted in Kamrava 2001: 177).

Khatami warns against "either complete avoidance or uncritical admiration [of the West] ..." (Kamrava 2001: 177), something which certainly continues to characterize the ways in which many Iranian musicians approach Western music and which itself perpetuates the colonial mindset.[79] In order to transcend this, musicians need to develop an understanding of Western music as one musical system among many. While Kamrava suggests that the profound current cultural crisis in Iran is partly rooted in "a chronic stalemate between traditional and Western values" (2001: 182), he also shows that as the mood of anti-Westernism in the country has subsided, people have become more willing to examine Western concepts such as modernity (and even postmodernity).

To the extent that the new pop is an important symbol of the post-1997 changes, it is widely seen as a sign of empowerment, particularly for Iran's youth. At the same time, as much of the music is still centrally controlled, it could be argued (and many do) that the new pop simply represents cultural hegemony in a new guise. By the time of my third visit in 2002, it was clear that the initial shock and excitement at the changes had become somewhat subdued, partly because of what many perceived to be Khatami's lack of power to make real changes in areas outside the cultural domain. The changes had become an accepted part of life in Iran, and the number of pop musicians producing commercial recordings had soared since my visit in 2000. Underneath the apparent calm, however, something very interesting was happening. The new pop, it seems, has acted as a catalyst for the emergence of a grassroots popular music for the very first time in Iran, where pop has generally either been produced centrally or outside the country. Now, alongside the centrally promoted new pop music, a growing number of young people have become involved in creating and performing their own music, drawing on a range of influences and popular styles that they have hitherto only been consumers of. I had initially become aware of this during my first visit in 1999. Many of the young people I spoke to at that time had formed their own bands, were writing their own music, and rehearsing in private. A few had even performed in public.[80] By 2002, the number of independent bands has risen and many have been given permission to perform in public and to release albums.[81] While some bands perform cover versions of pieces in a variety of Western popular styles, others perform original compositions, both in a broadly "pop" idiom and incorporating ideas from a wide range of styles such as jazz, progressive rock, heavy metal, and other experimental and avant-garde idioms.[82] For example, a concert by the group Imaj, which I attended in July 2000 at the Ebn Sina Cultural Centre in West Tehran, was billed as a "jazz" concert but the group performed instrumental arrangements of pieces by Paul Simon, John Lennon (including "Imagine"), and Kenny G., all under the watchful eyes of authority symbolized by the photographs of Ayatollahs Khomeini and Khamenei above the stage. The audience of young people was ecstatically enthusiastic. Kasraie recently reported on what he claimed to be the "first state-authorized Rock concert" in Iran (in May 2002) by the group Pedjvak, whose music he describes as "Sometimes jazz, sometimes Frank Zappa, sometimes Dream Theater, their music was a mix of their inspirations and creations. Their talent was unquestionable." (2002) "New age music" is how Pedjvak describe their first album, *Bar Bastar-e*

Laghzan-e Zaman ("On the Slippery Shores of Time"), which was released in the United States in 1999 and has only recently received authorization for sale in Iran itself, even though this is where the band is based.[83] By the summer of 2002, bands such as Raaz-e Shab, Arian, and O-Hum had started to make a name for themselves, even though gaining authorization for public performance and for releasing commercial recordings was still problematic. For example, O-Hum (formed in 1998) was refused official authorization three times for the release of its 1999 debut album *Nahal'e Heirat* ("Sapling of Wonder"), and the group has been unable to secure government authorization for public performance.[84]

What has come to be known as "underground rock" or "alternative music" is characterized by a group ethos that contrasts strongly with the solo singer "star" cult of the centrally promoted pop (and other kinds of Iranian pop). Something else that is quite new is the prominence of instruments in a musical culture that has hitherto been largely dominated by the voice. Like the centrally promoted new pop, underground rock has so far received little scholarly attention, partly because the phenomenon is so new. In contrast, Iranian magazines, newspapers, and websites are full of debate, commentary, and reports on these groups, their recordings, and their concerts. One of the best sources of information on current developments in this area is the website www.tehranavenue.com, which promotes the music of independent bands and includes interviews with musicians and reports on their activities. This website hosted the first online festival of underground Iranian rock music in the autumn of 2002, when bands were invited to submit recordings, of which nineteen were selected for the festival competition and available online for listeners to access and vote.[85] The UMC (Underground Music Competition) clearly demonstrates the opportunities that global technologies offer musicians to enable them to circumvent government censorship and control. I was able to listen to and discuss a number of the pieces submitted for the competition when I visited the studio of one of competition organizers in August 2002. A number of these songs highlighted what appears to be a trend toward increasingly socially engaged subject matter, either using modern lyrics or drawing on the hidden and double meanings of medieval mystic poets (already seen in the context of the new pop). For example, all of the songs on the O-Hum album *Nahal'e Heirat* are set to words by Hafez and a recent album entitled *Zibazi* with music by Ramin Behna includes a number of tracks that use the poetry of Mowlana.[86] Another group that has recently received a great deal of public attention is Arian, a pop band of eleven musicians, eight men and three women, that was formed in 1999. Arian has published two albums to date: *Gol-e Aftabgardoon* ("The Sunflower," 2000) and *Arian II—Va Amma Eshgh . . .* ("Arian II—And Now Love," 2001).[87] While their music is somewhat less experimental and challenging than some of the groups mentioned above, Arian is interesting for a number of reasons, including the role of the three women musicians in the group and the large following the group has attracted. According to Taqizadeh (2002), a week of concert performances (with two performances each night) in Tehran in October and November 2002 were sold out within hours of tickets going on sale. While none of the lyrics are overtly political, a number of Arian's songs contain veiled references to current social issues and the final track of the 2000 album—"Farda Mal-e Mast" ("Tomorrow is Ours")—is an optimistic statement of youth power.[88]

While it is still too soon to draw conclusions about the long-term implications of the most recent changes, one thing is clear: For the very first time in Iran, young people are creating a grassroots popular music through which they can address current social issues, speaking with their own voice rather than using someone else's music as an indirect statement of resistance. Ironically, this growth in grassroots popular music would not have been possible had the initial legalization of new pop not paved the way. Nor would it have been possible without the 1980s renaissance in *musiqi-e assil* and the resulting widespread culture of music making, as well as the availability of music education. In seeking to appropriate and take control of the pop music market by legalizing it and thereby blunting its symbolic subversive potential, it seems that the government has inadvertently opened the way for this new kind of actively engaged popular music. While detailed discussion of the new underground rock music lies outside the scope of this chapter, such recent developments have clear implications for musical meaning. By taking control of the music, musicians have once again transformed the meaning of popular music in Iran, or at least added another layer of meaning: music as active engagement. What we see now is perhaps the beginning of a process described back in 1991 by Sreberny-Mohammadi and Mohammadi in which the creation of a "more diverse and less controlled cultural space ... offers the possibility for the articulation of other identities and other ideas, which might eventually be translated into more specifically political discourses, demands, and organizational structures (1991a: 57).

Moreover, much of the music that is emerging clearly goes beyond a mere imitation of Western models, but represents a fusion of styles based both on a greater understanding of those styles and clearer reasons for choosing to use them. While the West still holds a powerful fascination for many people, what is interesting is the way in which many bands are transcending what might be regarded as the "aping of one's former colonial masters" (Manuel 1988: 22) and developing a new sound in which Iranian melodies and rhythms meet the sounds of jazz, progressive rock, heavy metal, and so on. In this way, the emergence of a grassroots popular music in Iran relates directly to current debates both about notions of Civil Society (through a diverse cultural space) and universalism. The direct involvement of young people in music making is one of the most exciting consequences of the post-1997 changes and indeed, it seems likely that the long-term consequences of this development will prove to be more significant and far-reaching than the emergence of new pop itself. Certainly, talking to young people, particularly young musicians, one gets an overwhelming sense of confidence. This, I believe, is where the real empowerment will lie.

Conclusion

In exploring the changing meanings of Iranian popular music since 1979, this chapter has sought to illustrate the extent to which music and its discourses are intimately bound up with notions of national belonging in Iran. From the banning of pop music in 1979 through to its legalization in 1998, the use of this music as a form of subversion and later counter-subversion is indicative of a struggle to control both the music and its meanings. Popular music's affirmation of modernity serves to position music at the center of debates concerning the place of tradition in modernity and the assertion of national identity in an increasingly global environment. What makes this such a fascinating area of study is music's semiotic complexity and semantic richness, its capacity to simultaneously symbolize many things and to embody different meanings. This mercurial quality clearly enables musicians and others to choose between a wide range of possible meanings; by the same token, the fluidity of those meanings militates against any attempt to fix and thereby control them. The recent emergence of local grassroots popular music in Iran has provided a space for the creation of music that is rooted at home, but also engages with modernity and the outside world. Not only does this allow for the symbolic expression of a particular vision of and claim on Iran's future, but through the act of performance, such a vision becomes a possible reality.

Notes

[See website for audio files and photos to accompany this chapter.]
1. An estimated 20 million people (70 percent of the electorate) voted for Khatami (Kamrava 2001: 170).
2. The term "pop," when applied to Iranian music in this chapter, refers to the Western-style genre that emerged in 1960s Iran and the production of which continued outside Iran after 1979. Previous local popular musical styles were partly eclipsed by the arrival of Westernized pop, but such styles did survive and are still performed. In this chapter, I use the broader

term "popular" to refer to a range of musical styles that go beyond "pop" in its restricted sense, including jazz, rock, heavy metal, and so on. It should be noted that in Iran itself, while such categories are recognized and distinguished, the term "pop" is in fact used in an analogous way to "popular" in the West, as a broad term to refer to popular music in the widest sense.

3. Much of the discussion in this chapter is based on material collected during three periods of fieldwork in Iran in the summers of 1999, 2000, and 2002, when I interviewed and talked informally with a great many people, including musicians and others, attended concerts, and followed what was happening on the broadcast media and in relevant debates in the national and musical press. I took every opportunity to observe and discuss these issues with people. My thanks are due to the many individuals who gave freely of their time to talk to me and to help me in countless ways during my visits to Iran. I also acknowledge support for these trips provided by Brunel University and by the British Institute of Persian Studies (Travel Fellowship Scheme).

    As it was not possible to undertake fieldwork in Iran during the 1980s, primary source information from this period is largely based on the many discussions I had with musicians and others visiting from Iran, as well as correspondence and relevant literature.

4. See Kazemzadeh (1968), Halliday (1979), Katouzian (1981, 2003a), Keddie (1981, 1995), Abrahamian (1982), Martin (1989, 2000), Hunter (1990), and Cronin (2003), among others, for further information on the history of Iran since the nineteenth century.

5. Reza Shah Pahlavi was an army general who led a coup d'etat in 1921, became Prime Minister of Iran in 1923, and eventually Shah in December 1925, replacing the last of the Qajar monarchs. In 1941, he was forced by Allied Powers to abdicate in favor of his son, Mohammad Reza Pahlavi, who reigned until the 1979 Revolution. See Katouzian (2003b).

6. See Katouzian (1981) and Mohammadi (1995), among others. As a socio-political/geograph-ical category that glosses over many differences and that depends on dualistic notions, the term "West" is problematic. At the same time, the countries usually included in this category share a recent history of colonial and neocolonial power that has served to link them, both in their own discourses and in the eyes of the countries that have come under their influence. As such, it is useful to retain the category (however provisionally) for the purposes of discussion at this particular historical juncture. Moreover, while not wishing to perpetuate categories that have become increasingly questioned in a globalizing world, the equivalent Persian term—*qarb*—is used regularly in Iran, particularly to refer to those countries whose involvement in Iran has been most marked. As such, this term has highly emotive associations of direct relevance to the current discussion.

7. As evidenced, for example, by the banning of the veil in 1936 (see Parsa [1989], 36 and Chehabi [2003]) and the gradual disempowering of the clergy between 1925 and 1979 (see Akhavi [1980], Fischer [1980], and Keddie [1980]).

8. Written in 1341 (1962), *Gharbzadegi* translates as "Westoxication" as "Fascination with the West."

9. Another example is the common use of expressions such as *musiqi-e 'elmi* ("scientific music") and *musiqi-e benolmelali* ("international music") to refer to Western classical music. The first in particular rests on an implied dualistic division in which Iranian music was (and still is) often represented as the implied opposite or "other" of "scientific." There are many examples of this terminology in the literature, for example see Alizadeh 1998, 76 and Eftekhari 2000: 5.

10. Relatively little has been published on Iranian pop music of the 1960s and '70s other than a brief article by Nettl 1972 and similarly brief references in Nettl (1987, 126–280) and Manuel (1988: 167–69). See also Shay (2000), who includes discussion of traditional styles of popular music.

11. Fayaz charts the growing concern with *essalat* ("authenticity"/"purity") among traditional musicians in the 1960s and '70s and the role of Western musicologists in promoting such ideas (1998: 97–98). He describes how many musicians in the 1970s became more concerned with establishing a relationship with the past than with the present (1998: 105–6). Miller (1999: 29–46) discusses the crucial role of the Centre for the Preservation and Propagation of Iranian Music (*Markaz-e Hefz-o Eshaeh-ye Musiqi-e Irani*) in supporting the documentation and study of traditional music during the 1970s.

12. For further discussion of the impact of modernization/westernization on music in Iran, the reader is referred to Nettl (1978 and 1985: for example, pages 40–3, amongst numerous references to Iran in this book).

13. For detailed information on the background to, course of events, and the aftermath of the 1979 uprising, see (among others) Keddie (1981, 1995), Bakhash (1985), Parsa (1989), Farhi (1990), Wright (1991), Halliday (1996: 42–75), Katouzian (1981, 2003a), Martin (2000).

14. It is necessary to clarify two points here. First, I use the term "cultural policy" to refer to decisions pertaining to cultural activities, particularly regarding what was permitted in the public domain, that were made and implemented by the government (and organizations attached to the government). It should be understood that there was little in the way of coherent forward planning, which the term might imply. Secondly, as discussed below, while I generally refer to the government as one body when discussing such policies, the government in fact comprised different factions with a range of viewpoints on cultural matters, including music.

15. As Hall observes, the Revolution was, in part "a reaction to the 'forced' character of Western modernization; certainly, Iranian fundamentalism was a direct response to the efforts of the Shah in the 1970s to adopt Western models and cultural values wholesale" (1992: 313).

16. Interestingly, this event was staged by a Hollywood film director (Shaw 2002).

17. At the same time, it should be noted that Shi'ism, the branch of Islam practiced in Iran, became established as the state religion as part of a nationalist movement in the sixteenth century (Halliday 1996: 59–60). Regarded with some suspicion by Sunni Muslims, Shi'ism thus serves a partly nationalist agenda in distinguishing between Islam as practiced predominantly in Iran with most of the rest of the Islamic world.

18. A similar situation in Egypt is reported in "*Musiqi va aqaz-e hezareh-ye sevvom*" ("Music and the Beginning of the Third Millenium") in *Faslnameh-ye Musiqi-e Mahoor* 6 (*Mahoor Music Quarterly*, Winter 2000): 193–97 (author not stated, but the article is reproduced from the newspaper *Asr-e Azadegan*, Dey 12, 14, and 21, 1378 (January 2000), where fundamentalists opposed Jean Michel Jarre's Millenium concert at the pyramids on the basis that celebration of the Pharonic past is incompatible with the Islamic present.

19. For further discussion of the theological debate surrounding music in Islamic societies, see al-Faruqi 1985, Shiloah 1995, Doubleday (1999: 111–13) and Youssefzadeh (2000: 40–41), among others.

20. Youssefzadeh presents a number of interesting recent quotations from religious and government officials that illustrate this ambiguity (2000: 40–42).

21. In the case of solo female singing, the prohibition applied to any contexts where the singing might be heard by men.

22. See Anquetil (1980), During (1984, 1992), Adelkhah (1991) and Youssefzadeh (2000: 38–39) for further discussion of the situation of music in Iran during the 1980s in writings published outside Iran. In Iran itself, relatively little was published until the following decade, when musicians and other commentators started to publish articles in the national press and in the growing number of cultural and artistic magazines and journals (see Meshkatian [1991] and Alizadeh [1998], for example). Relatively little has been written on what came to be known as *los angelesi* pop, but the reader is referred to a series of radio programmes written and presented by Niloofar Mina and available at www.radioazadi.org (accessed 3/16/2003). See also Mina (2001).

23. These metaphoric categories are based on Rice's work (see in particular 2001: 22–29).

24. As has also been the case with the Iranian film industry. See Shaw (2002) and Tapper (2002).

25. Unless stated otherwise, all translations from Persian in this chapter are by the author.

26. Iran's first university Music Department, at the University of Tehran, was opened in 1969.

27. With music by Mohammad Reza Lotfi and words by the contemporary Iranian poet, H. A. Sayeh. *Sepideh* was first published on *Chavosh no. 6* (cassette) in 1980 by the Chavosh Cultural and Artistic Institute, Tehran, and later reissued on CD as *Sepideh, Concert-e Goroohe Shaida* (no date; Avaye Shaida Cultural and Artistic Institute, Tehran).

28. Something that continues today. Take the case of bagpipe music (found only in the Southern Gulf region of Iran), the religious legality of which has become strongly contested in recent years. Local bagpipe player Mohsen Sharifian describes how a former member of his own ensemble in the town of Bushehr was standing for election to parliament and sought to increase his vote by speaking out against this music, music that he himself used to perform (Moshtagh 1999: 172).

One could draw direct parallels with the ways in which issues such as Law and Order or asylum laws, for example, are currently used by politicians in the UK to gain votes by being seen to be "tough." An analogy even closer to home might be the implications of the 1994

Criminal Justice and Public Order Act on certain kinds of music making in the UK. Available at www.hmso.gov.uk /acts/acts1994/Ukpga_19940033_en_6.htm#mdiv63 (accessed 6/29/2002).

29. Samii notes a similar situation more recently with press laws, under which journalists are censored for crossing the so-called "red line," although this line remains largely undefined (1999).
30. The distinction between private and public domains remains an important one in Iranian society.
31. And therefore continuing the association of pop music with privilege established before 1979.
32. Or perhaps unwilling to control. A number of my interviewees suggested that the government was fully aware that music served as an outlet—a kind of safety valve—for social grievances and was therefore reluctant to control the black market. At the same time, they needed to be seen to be attempting to control it.
33. Sreberny-Mohammadi and Mohammadi write about "passive resistance" (1991a: 47), but I prefer to avoid the implications of submission and acquiescence suggested by this expression.
34. For example, see De Bruijn (1997).
35. As far as popular music is concerned, with the exception of a few songs dating from the time of the 1906 Constitutional Revolution (particularly those of Aref Ghazvini, 1880–1933), there is little evidence of it being used as a form of active resistance (see Chehabi [1999]). During the 1970s, a handful of independent singers provided social commentary, but few of these gained wide popularity. The best-known was Farhad, whose song *Jomeh* ("Friday") was a critique of the Shah's repression of political opposition.
36. Film is another example of a previously contested cultural form that has flourished since the mid-1980s and has in recent years served as a candid forum for social criticism. The comparison with music is particularly apt because, like pop music, film was also targeted as a symbol of Westernization after the Revolution. Indeed, the extent of religious and popular opposition to film was such that cinemas became the target for arson attacks in the immediate pre-Revolutionary period: a hundred and eighty cinemas were destroyed in Iran between August 1978 and February 1979 (Naficy 1999: 19). The gradual post-Revolutionary recovery and eventual transformation of the Iranian film industry is one of the most remarkable stories of recent cultural history in Iran. See Tapper (2002).
37. For further information on this period, see Wells (1999: 31–4) and Ehteshami (1995).
38. Throughout this chapter, the term "sanction" is used in a positive sense to indicate permission or approval (as opposed to indicating a threatened penalty).
39. During, for example, notes the overwhelming demand for concert tickets when restrictions on public concerts eventually eased in the late 1980s (1992: 142–43).
40. See Samii (1999), Wells (1999), and Kamrava (2001) for further details of changes that have come about under Khatami. Mohajerani was forced to resign by conservative elements in the government in December 2000, but his work has nevertheless been continued by his successor, Ahmad Masjed Jamei.
41. A point of clarification regarding the term "liberal," which is used in this chapter to refer both to government policies and to a social environment characterized by a willingness to tolerate difference, be open to new ideas, and accept freedom of choice for individuals.
42. *Honar-e Musiqi*, ISSN 1560–196X; *Faslnameh-ye Musiqi-e Mahoor*, ISSN 1561–1469; Faslnameh-ye Musiqi-e Maqam (no ISSN number).
43. As evidenced by the decisive majority gained by Khatami's supporters in the parliamentary elections of February 1999 (Ehteshami 1999: 206) and by Khatami's own reelection as president in June 2001.
44. An example of this is *Razé No* ("A New Secret"), by Hossein Alizadeh, which includes a "chorus" of three singers: two women and one man. One musician with whom I discussed this piece described the male singer as being there "for decorative purposes only," in other words, solely to legitimize the female singers. A commercial recording of *Razé No* was released in the summer of 1998, following public performances in Tehran's Vahdat Hall in March of the same year (*Razé No*, music by Hossein Alizadeh, performed by the Hamavayan ensemble. Mahour Institute of Culture and Art. M.CD—38). More recently (January 2002), the Irani Ensemble has used a similarly strategy, performing in public with a chorus which included a prominent female vocalist (see Taqizadeh 2002b).

45. Much of the information in this section is based on my three periods of fieldwork in the summers of 1999, 2000, and 2002, mainly in Tehran, but also in the provincial towns of Bandar, Anzali, and Saari (in the northern provinces of Gilan and Mazandaran, respectively). Primary source material includes interviews with musicians and others, the latter including a large number of teenagers and young people in their twenties. Most of my informants were middle class, educated, and urban and (to varying degrees) cosmopolitan in outlook. Musicians interviewed included Shahram Nazeri, Kayhan Kalhor, Ramin Behna, and Hamid Reza Dibazar. In addition, I was able to talk to a number of individuals involved in teaching music at higher education level and visit music studios, arts centers, and other establishments where music is taught. I also attended a number of concerts and rehearsals, including several pop concerts, both by established singers such as Khashayar Etemadi, and by less well-known musicians, such as the group Imaj, and followed the broadcast media and the national and musical press, the latter including reports and reviews of concerts, as well as relevant debates.

46. As is often the case in Iran, no specific law was passed "legalizing" pop music, but it seems unlikely that *Seda o Sima* would have taken such a step without endorsement from elsewhere within the state apparatus. The action of *Seda o Sima* effectively rendered this music "not illegal" (and by implication "legal"). It is important to note therefore that the term "legalization" as used in this chapter refers not to the passing of a particular law, but to the fact that by virtue of being broadcast, this music became permissible again in the public domain. Everyone that I spoke to used the term "qanooni" ("legal") to refer to the status of the new pop (in contrast to the still "qeir-e qanooni" ["illegal"] status of other kinds of pop music). It should be noted that *Seda o Sima* is one of three primary state institutions dealing with music in Iran, the other two being *Vezarat-e Ershad* and *Hoze Honari* (see Youssefzadeh 2000:43–58), which are independent of one another and which in fact represent competing power bases. There is some evidence that the more conservative institutions of *Seda o Sima* and *Hoze Honari* (the latter under the direct auspices of the Supreme Leader, Ali Khamenei) have been attempting in recent years to present themselves in a more liberal light, something which may have been a factor in the decision to initiate a new kind of pop music.

47. Particularly through the regular broadcasting of their songs on Radio Payam.

48. But were still available through the black market, satellite channels, and the Internet.

49. While I refer to some reference to aspects of musical style, the main aim of this chapter is not to present analytical discussion of specific new pop songs, but rather to explore the broader social implications of the emergence of this music and the impact of recent changes on the music's meanings.

50. Shadmehr Aghili, *Dehati* (Farsnava, 1999). During my summer 2000 trip, there was a great deal of speculation as to how this album had managed to gain authorization. According to Pearl, within a few months of its release, *Dehati* had sold more than a million copies (2000).

    Unlike the broadcast media (where there are no independent radio or television channels), the commercial recording sector in Iran is not under direct government control. However, central control is maintained by the Ministry of Culture and Islamic Guidance that, since 1986, has been responsible for granting permits for recordings destined for sale (Youssefzadeh 2000: 44–7 provides a useful overview of this process) and for authorizing all public performance of music. No recordings can be published or public performances take place without permission from this ministry. In June 2000, the government published a list of musicians who no longer required a permit for performances or for recordings. This list comprised the most prominent classical and folk musicians in Iran, but no pop musicians were included.

51. See Sohrabi (2002), for discussion and images of female backing singers in a concert by the band Raaz-e Shab. It is important to note that the gradually increasing role of women in the new pop music is both a symbolic challenge to existing boundaries and an indication of further concessions to liberalization.

52. Even in the initial stages, such concerts were by no means limited to Tehran. I heard reports of a pop concert held in Saari, a provincial town in northern Iran, and I also attended a street theatre performance in Bandar Anzali (on the Caspian coast), which was preceded by a performance given by a local pop band.

53. This happened on several occasions during my summer 2000 trip.

54. One pop concert I tried to attend was cancelled without notice; obtaining tickets for another proved to be a bureaucratic obstacle course. This is not just the case with pop music; such

disruptions and cancellations are often as much to do with local power struggles (for example, between local religious leaders and provincial representatives of the Ministry of Culture, representing central power) as between different factions of central government. Take the recent example of bagpipe music in Bushehr and other towns in the southern region of Iran (see note 28). Although technically legal, local opposition to this music, fuelled by statements by local religious leaders, have led in some cases to concerts being physically, even violently, disrupted (see Moshtagh 1999). This level of physical obstruction to music performance gives some indication of how emotive the issues are.

55. Relatively little has been written about the new pop in the scholarly literature, either in Iran or outside (Youssefzadeh mentions it briefly, 2000: 39–40). In contrast, there has been a great deal of journalistic attention and media-based debate in Iran on this issue, some of which I discuss below.

56. In a country where an estimated 70 percent of the population is under the age of thirty. According to the *Statistical Centre of Iran*, at the time of the last Iranian census in 1996, just under 68 percent of the population was below the age of thirty (available at www.sci. org.ir/english/sel/f2/ [accessed 4/14/2004]). The most recently available United Nations statistics (for 2000) give a figure of 36 percent of the population under the age of 15 (available at http://cyberschoolbus.un.org/infonation3/basic.asp [accessed 4/14/2004]). This demographic imbalance, caused by official policy in the early years after the Revolution, is a serious issue for the country and is now being tackled by the government (see http://news.bbc.co.uk/ 1/hi/world/middle_east/ 1949068.stm).

57. Generally known in the West as Rumi (1207–73).

58. ISSN 1029–2586.

59. Most of the information in this section is based on the "demotic" (Baumann 1996) discourses gathered in the course of my research. I found a vacuum in official government discourses on this subject, but Pearl (2000) claims that even before 1997, Ayatollah Khamenei's "cultural advisers convinced him that if Iran didn't produce its own pop, music from abroad would corrupt Iran's youth and undermine Islamic values." However, neither the source of this statement, nor that of Pearl's suggestion that much of the pop music is in fact being promoted by conservative factions within the government, are clear.

60. A major annual arts festival held in February of each year on the anniversary of the Revolution. For further information on this and other festivals, see Youssefzadeh (2000: 49–54).

61. Youssefzadeh discusses the impact of government-sponsored festivals—particularly those with a competitive element—in imposing central control and "standards" on regional musics (2000: 49–54).

62. Ali Reza Assar, *Kooch-e Asheqaneh* (Avay-e Barg, 1999). According to Pearl, this album exceeded all expectations by selling an estimated three hundred thousand copies (2000).

63. To quote from www.iranian.com/Music/AghiliS/index.html (accessed 7/15/2002), "If he sings like a Pop star, looks like a Pop star and has millions of teenage fans like a Pop star, he IS a Pop star." Aghili left Iran in 2002 and soon after released his first album abroad, Khiali Nist (2003, Nava Media Co., CD-126).

64. Music by Shadmehr Aghili, words by Mohammad Ali Bahmani.

65. See Naficy 2002.

66. For example, I purchased a compilation cassette titled "Asar-e Bargozideh-ye Rock" ("The Best of Rock"), published by Arqanoon (no catalogue number or date) and featuring tracks by musicians such as Carlos Santana, Joe Satriani, and Brian May, including a number of pieces with references to the "East," such as Camel's "Sahara."

67. The removal of lyrics is important. Besides the obvious reduction of impact these songs can have without their (usually English) words, there is also a symbolic "disempowering" of the songs by removing the words and rearranging the music, particularly because words are perceived to have such power in Iran. Without their words, the songs become just another instrumental piece for Iranian audiences. Or, at least, that would seem to be the intention. In reality, many people do recognize the songs, even if they don't know or remember the words.

68. The popularity of Radio Payam became very clear to me through my interviews, discussions, and observations.

69. On the issue of satellite broadcasting see Barraclough 2001 and Naficy 2002: 54–5.

70. *Faslnameh-ye Musiqi-e Mahoor* 9 (2000), 160–62 published a statement issued by the Management Committee of this organization on the first anniversary of its establishment and also reported on an event held to mark the anniversary. There is an increasing literature on the

subject of Civil Society in Iran. See, for example, Banuazizi (1995), Amirahmadi (1996), Kamali (1998), Bashiriyeh (2001), Gheytanchi (2001), Kamrava (2001), and Chaichian (2003). The question of Civil Society will be considered briefly below.

71. As reported in *Honar-e Musiqi* 33 (Dey and Bahman 1380/January and February 2002): 25.
72. The *radif* is the traditional canonic repertoire of *musiqi-e assil*.
73. The issues raised by my collection of some two hundred such articles will be discussed in greater detail at a later date.
74. Indeed, it is interesting to note that Western classical music has remained a relatively uncontested domain in the post-Revolutionary period, despite the connection with Western culture. This can be partly explained by its "high art" associations, which have served to ensure that the music's meanings are defined primarily through discourses of "music as art"—perhaps partly drawing on the dominance of this discourse in the West—thereby overshadowing other possible meanings of Western classical music in Iran. Moreover, as the association between music, movement, and the body are less explicit in Western classical music than in pop (particularly in the eighteenth- and nineteenth-century mainstream which is the repertoire predominantly available in Iran), this music has generally been regarded as fairly innocuous by the government. As such, the exclusive focus on "music as art" has meant that Western classical music was never targeted in the way that pop music was. However, in attempting to apply the same discourses to pop music, many classically trained musicians have failed to understand the significance of other dimensions of meaning in this music.
75. Particularly as many traditional musicians have once again retrenched into notions of "purity" and "authenticity" in the face of recent changes.
76. *Honar-e Musiqi* 14 (Azar and Dey 1378/December and January 1999–2000) and 25, Bahman 1379 (February 2001).
77. See Ehteshami (1999: 216). Khatami's inaugural speech of August 1997 is printed in *Civil Society* 6, 69 (1997): 7–9. Indeed, it was at the suggestion of President Khatami that 2001 was declared as the "United Nations Year of Dialogue among Civilizations." Available at www.unesco.org/dialogue2001/en/annan.htm (accessed 6/2/2002).
78. See Sohrabi (2002) for an example of this.
79. As seen, for example, in the continued use of the terms *musiqi-e 'elmi* ("scientific music") and *musiqi-e benolmelali* ("international music") to refer to Western classical music. See note 9.
80. Avizheh, a group that mixes Iranian music with elements of jazz and progressive rock, gave its first concert in November 1998 at the Arasbaran Culture Centre in Tehran. One young man that I spoke to in 2000 described how his band had been given permission to present a pop concert at school, but that a screen had been erected in front of the performers to hide the instruments from the audience, to the amusement of performers and audience alike. Friedman (2002) also writes about the emergence of grassroots pop music into the public domain: "When I was last here, six years ago, a friend took me to see an Iranian guitarist who had an electric guitar but could only play songs in his bedroom, because pop music had been banned. Today he is giving public concerts of Iranian pop songs and cutting CDs." There is some evidence that a small number of grassroots bands did exist in the late 1980s and early to mid-1990s, but their activities were extremely limited and such bands certainly didn't comprise a broad movement on a scale that one sees emerging today.
81. Although not without the usual contestation, official difficulties, and constant threat of last minute cancellation. A series of concerts by the rock band Meera, scheduled for the Simorgh Hall in Tehran in July 2002, was cancelled after "the band's representative was politely asked by authorities in the Office of Leasehold (Amaken) not to perform music at this particular time and place. This in spite of the fact that Meera had full permission from the Ministry of Guidance." Available at www.tehranavenue.com/bulletin_board.htm (accessed 12/2/2002).
82. According to Shadi Vatanparast, "Alternative music has gained its ardent followers in the Islamic Republic and the summer time is high season for rock groups to reach out to their fans." Available at www.tehranavenue.com/bulletin_board.htm (accessed 7/3/2002).

In July 2000, I attended a concert by the Fouzhan Ensemble, performing *Jazireh-ye Parvaz* ("The Isle of Flight") by composer Hamid Reza Dibazar, at the Niavaran Cultural Centre in North Tehran. Using both Iranian and Western instruments as well as a mixed choir, the music drew on a wide range of styles, including *musiqi-e assil* and Iranian folk musics, as well as progressive rock, jazz, and Western classical music. The highlight of the performance for me was what can only be described as a virtuosic rock *kamāncheh* (Iranian spike-fiddle) solo that received a rapturous response from the audience. *Jazireh-ye Parvaz* is published on CD by the Bonyaad-e Afarinesh-haye Honari-e Niavaran (2002).

83. Published by Shahram Music Books, SITC-438.
84. However, some of O-Hum's music is available through their website www.o-hum.com (accessed 4/16/2002), and I had no difficulty in purchasing a copy of *Nahal'e Heirat* from a music shop in Tehran, even without government authorization. O-Hum disbanded in 2001 when two members of the group emigrated to Canada. It seems unlikely that the group will reform, despite the return of one of these musicians to Iran.

In general, the current situation is very much one of flux and uncertainty. Many musicians are still cautiously "feeling their way," and it is not uncommon for individuals to work with more than one group or for groups to form, disband, and reform on a regular basis, particularly as a result of musicians emigrating to the West.

85. Available at www.tehran360.com/ (accessed 11/11/2003). A second festival—Tehran Avenue Music Open (TAMO)—was held in the autumn of 2003.
86. See Vatanparast 2002.
87. Both published by Tarane Sharghee Cultural & Artistic Company.
88. For further information on this band, see www.arianmusic.com (accessed 11/11/2003).

References

Abrahamian, Ervand. 1982. *Iran Between Two Revolutions*. Princeton, N.J.: Princeton University Press.

Adelkhah, F. 1991. "Michael Jackson ne Peut Absolument Rien Faire—Les Pratiques Musicales en République Islamique d'Iran," *Cahiers d'études sur la Méditeranée orientale et le monde turco-iranien*, 11.

Akhavi, Shahrough. 1980. *Religion and Politics in Contemporary Iran: Clergy-State Relations in the Pahlavi Period*. State University of New York Press.

Al-e Ahmad, Jalal. 1973. *Gharbzadegi*. 2nd edition. Tehran: Ravagh Publishers.

Alizadeh, Hossein. 1998. "Negahi Gozara be Amuzesh-e Musiqi dar Iran" [A Brief Survey of Music Education in Iran], *Faslnameh-ye Musiqi-e Mahoor* 1 (*Mahoor Music Quarterly*, Fall 1998), 73–83.

Al-Faruqi, Lois Ibsen. 1985. "Music, Musicians, and Muslim Law," *Asian Music* 17: 3–36.

Amirahmadi, Hooshang. 1996. "Emerging Civil Society in Iran," *SAIS Review* 16 (2): 87–107.

Anquetil, P. 1980. "Iran: Silence! On Islamise," *Le monde de la musique* 24 (June).

Ang, Ien. 1996. "Culture and Communication: Towards an Ethnographic Critique of Media Consumption in the Transitional Media System," in *What Is Cultural Studies? A Reader*. Ed. J. Storey. London: Arnold Press, 237–54.

Bakhash, Shaul. 1985. *The Reign of the Ayatollahs*. London: I.B. Tauris.

Banuazizi, Ali. 1995. "Faltering Legitimacy: The Ruling Clerics and Civil Society in Contemporary Iran," *International Journal of Politics, Culture and Society* 8(4): 563–78.

Barraclough, Steven. 2001. "Satellite Television in Iran: Prohibition, Imitation and Reform," *Middle Eastern Studies* 37(3): 25–48.

Bashiriyeh, Hossein. 2001. "Civil Society and Democratisation during Khatami's First Term," *Global Dialogue* 3(2/3): 19–26.

Baumann, Gerd. 1996. *Contesting Culture: Discourses of Identity in Multi-ethnic London*. Cambridge: Cambridge University Press.

Chaichian, M.A. 2003. "Structural Impediments of the Civil Society Project in Iran. National and Global Dimensions," *International Journal of Comparative Sociology*, 44(1): 19–50.

Chehabi, Houshang. 1999. "From Revolutionary *Tasnif* to Patriotic *Sorūd*: Music and Nation-Building in Pre-World War II Iran," *Iran* 37: 143–154.

_____ (2003) "The Banning of the Veil and its Consequences," in *The Making of Modern Iran. State and Society under Riza Shah, 1921–1941*. ed. Stephanie Cronin. London: Routledge Curzon, 99–119.

Cronin, Stephanie, ed. 2003. *The Making of Modern Iran. State and Society under Riza Shah, 1921–1941*. London: Routledge Curzon.

De Bruijn, J. T .P. 1997. *Persian Sufi Poetry. An Introduction to the Mystical Use of Classical Persian Poems*. London: Curzon Press.

Doubleday, Veronica. 1999. "The Frame Drum in the Middle East: Women, Musical Instruments and Power," *Ethnomusicology* 43, 1: 101–34.

During, Jean. 1984. "La Musique Traditionelle Iranienne en 1983," *Asian Music* 15, 2: 11–31.

———. 1992. "L'Oreille Islamique. Dix Années Capitales de la Vie Musicale en Iran: 1980–1990," *Asian Music* 23, 2: 135–64.

Eftekhari, Mohammad. 1999. "*Ata-ye Andak va Jafa-ye Besiar*" [Little Presentation and Injustice Galore, editorial], *Faslnameh-ye Musiqi-e Mahoor* 3: 5–8 (*Mahoor Music Quarterly*, Spring 1999).

———. 2000. "*Jay-e Pahlevanan dar Resane-ye Melli-e Shoma Kojast?*" [Where do Heroes Stand in Your National Television? editorial], *Faslnameh-ye Musiqi-e Mahoor*, 6 (*Mahoor Music Quarterly*, Winter 2000): 5–8.

Ehteshami, Anoushiravan. 1995. *After Khomeini: The Iranian Second Republic.* London: Routledge.

———. 1999. "Is the Middle East Democratizing?" *British Journal of Middle Eastern Studies* 26, 2: 199–217.

Farhi, Farideh. 1990. *States and Urban-Based Revolutions: Iran and Nicaragua.* Urbana: University of Illinois Press.

Fayaz, Mohammad Reza. 1998. "*Bazkhani-e Esalat*" [A Look at the Notion of Originality in Iranian Music], *Faslnameh-ye Musiqi-e Mahoor* 1 (*Mahoor Music Quarterly*, Fall 1998): 93–112.

———. 1999. "*Dood-e Een Atash*" [The Smoke of this Fire], *Faslnameh-ye Musiqi-e Mahoor* 5 (*Mahoor Music Quarterly*, Autumn 1999): 49–56.

Fischer, Michael M. J. 1980. *Iran: From Religious Dispute to Revolution.* Cambridge: Harvard University Press.

Friedman, Thomas. 2002. "Iran's Third Wave," *The New York Times on the Web*, June 16, 2002. Available on www.hvk.org/articles/0602/160.html (accessed 3/12/04).

Gheytanchi, Elham. 2001. "Civil Society in Iran. Politics of Motherhood and the Public Sphere," *International Sociology* 16(4): 557–76.

Hall, Stuart. 1992. "The Question of Cultural Identity," in *Modernity and Its Futures.* Eds. S. Hall, D. Held, and T. McGrew. Cambridge: Polity Press, 273–325.

Halliday, Fred. 1979. *Iran: Dictatorship and Development.* Harmondsworth: Penguin.

———. 1996. *Islam and the Myth of Confrontation: Religion and Politics in the Middle East.* London: I.B. Tauris.

Hunter, Shireen T. 1990. *Iran and the World. Continuity in a Revolutionary Decade.* Indiana University Press.

Javidfar. 1999. "*Musiqi-e Pop, Yek Zaroorat*" [Pop Music, a Necessity], *Sobh-e Emrooz* (daily newspaper), 27 Esfand 1377 (March 18, 1999).

Kamali, Masoud. 1998. *Revolutionary Iran: Civil Society and State in the Modernisation Process.* Aldershot: Ashgate Press.

Kamrava, Mehran. 2001. "The Civil Society Discourse in Iran," *British Journal of Middle Eastern Studies* 28, 2: 165–85.

Kasraie, Nima. 2002. "Iran Rocks: *Honar Nazd-e Iranian Ast o Bas*, Even If That Honar Belongs to the West." June 17, 2002. Available at www.iranian.com/Music/2002/June/Rock/index.html (accessed 7/15/02).

Katouzian, Homa. 1981. *The Political Economy of Modern Iran. Despotism and Pseudo-modernism, 1926–1979.* London: Macmillan.

———. 2003a. *Iranian History and Politics. The Dialectic of State and Society.* London: Routledge Curzon.

———. 2003b. "Riza Shah's Political Legitimacy and Social Base, 1921–1941," in *The Making of Modern Iran. State and Society under Riza Shah, 1921–1941.* ed. Stephanie Cronin. 15–36. London: Routledge Curzon.

Kazemzadeh, Firuz. 1968. *Russia and Britain in Persia, 1864–1914: A Study in Imperialism.* New Haven, Conn.: Yale University Press.

Keddie, Nicki R. 1980. *Iran: Religion, Politics, and Society. Collected Essays.* London: Cass.

———. 1981. *Roots of Revolution. An Interpretive History of Modern Iran.* With a section by Richard Yann. New Haven, Conn.: Yale University Press.

———. 1995. *Iran and the Muslim World. Resistance and Revolution.* Basingstoke: Macmillan.

Langlois, Tony. 1996. "The Local and Global in North African Popular Music," *Popular Music* 15, 3: 259–73.

Manuel, Peter. 1988. *Popular Musics of the Non-Western World.* Oxford: Oxford University Press.

Martin, Vanessa. 1989. *Islam and Modernism: The Iranian Revolution of 1906.* London: I.B.Tauris.
————. 2000. *Creating an Islamic State. Khomeini and the Making of a New Iran.* London: I.B. Tauris.
Meshkatian, Parviz. 1991. *"Musiqi-e Melli dar Barabar-e Musiqi-e Sonati"* [National Music in the Face of Traditional Music], *Adineh* 55/56: 34–38.
Miller, Lloyd Clifton. 1999. *Music and Song in Persia. The Art of Avaz.* London: Curzon Press.
Mina, Niloofar. 2001. "Political Islam and Iranian Exiles' Changing Views of Iranian Popular Music." Paper presented at the 46th Annual Meeting of the Society for Ethnomusicology, Southfield, Michigan.
Mohammadi, Ali. 1995. "Cultural Imperialism and Cultural Identity." In *Questioning the Media: A Critical Introduction,* 2nd ed. Eds. A. Mohammadi and A. Sreberny-Mohammadi. London: Sage, 362–78.
Moshtagh, Zahra. 1999. *" 'Nay Anban' Tahajom-e Farhangi Ast!"* [The Bagpipe is Cultural Invasion!]. Interviews by Zahra Moshtagh originally published in the daily newspaper *Aftab-e Emrooz,* 15th Mehr 1378 [7th October 1999], plus material originally published in *Aftab-e Emrooz,* 8th Azar 1378 [29th November 1999], *Faslnameh-ye Musiqi-e Mahoor* 5 (*Mahoor Music Quarterly,* Autumn 1999), 169–81.
Naficy, Hamid. 1999. "Iranian Cinema." In *Life and Art: The New Iranian Cinema.* Eds. Rose Issa and Shiela Whitaker. London: The National Film Theatre, 13–25.
————. 2002. "Islamizing Film Culture in Iran: A Post-Khatami Update" in *The New Iranian Cinema. Politics, Representation and Identity,* ed. Richard Tapper. 26–65. London: I.B. Tauris.
Nettl, Bruno. 1972. "Persian Popular Music in 1969," *Ethnomusicology* 16, 2: 218–39.
————. 1978. "Persian Classical Music in Tehran: The Processes of Change." In *Eight Urban Musical Cultures. Tradition and Change.* Ed. B. Nettl. Urbana: University of Illinois Press, 146–85.
————. 1985. *The Western Impact on World Music. Change, Adaptation, and Survival.* New York: Schirmer Books.
————. 1987. *The Radif of Persian Music—Studies of Structure and Cultural Context.* Champaign: Elephant and Cat.
Noori, Mohammad. 1999. *"Musiqi-e Pop, Mardomi Nist"* [Pop Music Is Not the People's Music], *Iran* (daily newspaper), 1st Mordad 1378 (August 1, 1999), 12.
Parsa, Misagh. 1989. *Social Origins of the Iranian Revolution.* New Brunswick, N.J.: Rutgers University Press.
Pearl, Daniel. 2000. *Rock Rolls Once More in Iran: As Hard-Liners Back Pop Revival.* June 2, 2000. Available at www.iranian.com/News/2002/June/rock.html (accessed 7/15/2002).
Pirniakan, Dariush. 2000. *"Musiqi-e Pop-e Rayej, Bihoveiat Ast"* [The current pop music has no identity]. *Hayat-e No* (daily newspaper), 1st Shahrivar 1379 (August 22, 2000), 1.
Rice, Timothy. 2001. "Reflections on Music and Meaning: Metaphor, Signification and Control in the Bulgarian Case." *British Journal of Ethnomusicology* 10, 1: 19–38 (Special issue on Music and Meaning).
Roshanravan, Kambeez. 2000. *"Musiqi-e Pop-e Emrooz-e Ma, Hoveiat-e Irani Nadarad"* [Our Contemporary Pop Music has no Iranian Identity], in *The 15th Fadjr Music Festival Brochure, February 2000* (Tehran), 4–5.
Samii, A. W. 1999. "The Contemporary Iranian News Media, 1998–1999." *Middle East Review of International Affairs* 3, 4 (December 1999), available at www.biu.ac.il/SOC/besa/meria /journal/1999/issue4/jv3n4al.htlm (accessed 7/15/2002).
Shaw, Susan. 2002. *Cinema of Fire.* Documentary on Iranian cinema broadcast on the South Bank Show, London Weekend Television (UK), 30th June 2002. Produced and directed by Susan Shaw, edited and presented by Melvyn Bragg.
Shay, Anthony. 2000. "The 6/8 Beat Goes On: Persian Popular Music from *Bazm-e Qajariyyeh* to Beverley Hills Garden Parties," in *Mass Mediations. New Approaches to Popular Culture in the Middle East and Beyond,* ed. Walter Ambrust. 61–87. Berkeley: University of California Press.
Shiloah, Amnon. 1995. *Music in the World of Islam: A Sociocultural Study.* Scolar Press.
Sohrabi, Naghmeh. 2002. *Just a Concert: Still, It Was an Incredibly Surreal Experience in Iran.* January 4, 2002, available at www.iranian.com/NaghmehSohrabi/2002/January/ Concert/ index.html (accessed 7/7/2002).
Soueif, Adhaf. 1999. *The Map of Love.* London: Bloomsbury.
Sreberny-Mohammadi, Annnabelle. 1991. "The Global and the Local in International Commu-

nications." *Mass Media and Society*. Eds. J. Curran and M. Gurevitch. London: Edward Arnold, 177–203.

Sreberny-Mohammadi, Annabelle, and Ali Mohammadi. 1991a. "Hegemony and Resistance: Media Politics in the Islamic Republic of Iran." *Quarterly Review of Film and Video* 12, 4: 33–59.

———. 1991b. "Iranian Exiles as Opposition: Some Theses on the Dilemmas of Political Communication Inside and Outside Iran." In *Iranian Refugees and Exiles Since Khomeini*. Ed. A. Fathi. Costa Mesa: Mazda Publishers, 205–27.

Tapper, Richard, ed. 2002. *The New Iranian Cinema: Politics, Representation, and Identity*. London: I.B. Tauris.

Taqizadeh, Naghmeh. 2002a. "How Precious Can a Concert Be?" Available at www.tehranavenue.com/at_city_queue.htm (accessed 11/12/2002).

———. 2002b. "The Irani Ensemble." Available at www.tehranavenue.com/ec_interview.htm (accessed 12/11/2002).

Vatanparast, Shadi. 2002. "Neither Formal nor Cheap Stuff." Available at www.tehranavenue.com/ec_feature_zibazi.htm (accessed 12/14/2002).

Wells, Matthew C. 1999. "Thermidor in the Islamic Republic of Iran: The Rise of Muhammad Khatami." *British Journal of Middle Eastern Studies* 26, 1: 27–39.

Wright, Robin. 1991. *In the Name of God: The Khoneini Decade*. London: Bloomsbury.

Youssefzadeh, Ameneh. 2000. "The Situation of Music in Iran since the Revolution: The Role of Official Organizations." *British Journal of Ethnomusicology* 9, 2: 35–61.

Author unknown. 2000a. "*Jelo-e Voorood-e Een No Musiqi ra Nemitavan Gereft*" [You Can't Stop This Type of Music], *Sobh-e Emrooz* (daily newspaper), 20th Farvardin 1375 (April 8, 2000), 8.

Author unknown. 2000b. "*Be Khoda Guitar Qarbi Nist*" [The Guitar is not Western, Honest!], Interview with Dariush and Mohammad Ali Khajenoori, *Iran Javan* (magazine), 5th Khordad 1379 (May 25, 2000), 20–22.

Contributors

Michael Eldridge is an associate professor of English literature at Humboldt State University in Arcata, CA. His interview with Harry Belafonte appeared in *Transition: An International Review* (Summer 2002). Past publications include "The Rise and Fall of Black Britain," also in *Transition* (Fall 1998), and "Out of the Closet: Nuruddin Farrah's *Secrets* and the American Press" in *World Literature Today* 72: 4 (Fall 1998).

Ruth Hellier-Tinoco is a scholar and performer who currently teaches in the School of Community and Performing Arts, University College Winchester, UK. Her research areas include Mexican performance practice with a focus on politics, ideology and tourism; arts and disability; arts in education and radical performance practices. Her publications include "La Danza de los Viejitos de Jarácuaro: La tradición sigue evolucionando" in *Piel de Tierra, Journal of the Instituto Michoacano de Cultura* (1998), and "Experiencing People: Relationships, Responsibility and Reciprocity," *British Journal of Ethnomusicology* (2003).

Bennett Hogg is a composer and lecturer at University of Newcastle-upon-Tyne and Edinburgh College of Art, UK. His dissertation " The Cultural Imagination of Musics Mediated by Technology" centers on the voice in early sound technology, and focuses on early twentieth-century ideas about writing, memory and anxieties surrounding mechanization, in partic-ular, the ways such phenomena are encountered in psychoanalysis, surrealism and the writings of Walter Benjamin. He has written for the

Times Higher Education Supplement (London) and will soon publish "High Fidelity, Low Fidelity: Technological Paradigms for the Ideologies of Power" in the British, refereed on-line journal *ARiADA text.*

Keith Howard is reader in music at the School of Oriental and African Studies, University of London, UK, and director of the AHRB Research Centre for Cross-Cultural Music and Dance Performance. He is the author or editor of ten books and approximately 100 articles and 100 reviews. These include *Bands, Songs, and Shamanistic Rituals: Folk Music in Korean Society* (Seoul: Royal Asiatic Society, 1989), *Korean Musical Instruments* (Hong Kong: Oxford University Press, 1995), *True Stories of the Korean Comfort Women* (London: Cassell, 1995), *Korean Shamanism: Revivals, Survivals and Change* (Seoul: Seoul Press, 1998), *Korean Music: A Listening Guide* (Seoul: National Center for Korean Traditional Performing Arts, 1999). His new book, *Preserving Korean Music, Creating Korean Music,* is forthcoming.

Jelena Jovanović is an ethnomusicologist currently affiliated with the Institute of Musicology in Belgrade. Most of her research and publications concern Serbian traditional folk singing. She is one of the founders and artistic directors of the female singing group Moba, which specializes in rural traditional Serbian songs. Moba has released two CDs: *Grow Up, Grow Up, You Green Pine* (Boxpocks, Paris, 2001) and *Vazda znjejes, Jano: Srpske tradicionalne pesme/Serbian traditional songs* (Sokoj/Biem, Belgrade, 2001) and has performed in Greece, France, Lithuania, and Germany. She is also a principal contributor to the book *Hey Rudnik, You Old Mountain! Traditional Singing and Playing of the Crnucanka Group, Central Serbia* (Belgrade, 2003).

Edward Larkey is an associate professor of German Studies and Intercultural Communication at University of Maryland, Baltimore, USA, where he is currently director of the M.A. program in Intercultural Communication. His many publications on rock music in the former East Germany include "Contested Spaces: GDR Rock Between Western Influence and Party Control" in his edited volume *A Sound Legacy: Music and Politics in East Germany* (Washington, DC: American Institute for Contemporary German Studies, 2000).

Sharon Meredith completed her Ph.D. in ethnomusicology and Caribbean studies at Warwick University, UK with the dissertation "Tuk in Barbados: The History, Development and Recontextualisation of a Musical Genre." Articles include "Tuk Music: Its Role in Defining Barbadian Cultural Identity" in *European Meetings in Ethnomusicology* (vol. 8, 2000), and "Barbadian Tuk Music: Colonial Development and Post-Independence Recontextualization," in *British Journal of Ethnomusicology* (vol. 12/2, 2003). Current research interests include fife and drum musics in former colonial countries and Caribbean popular culture.

Laudan Nooshin is a senior lecturer in ethnomusicology in the Music Department at City University, UK. Recent and forthcoming articles include "Improvisation as 'Other': Creativity, Knowledge and Power. The Case of Iranian Classical Music," *Journal of the Royal Musical Association* (2003); and "Circumnavigation with a Difference? Music, Representation and the Disney Experience: *It's a Small, Small World,*" *Ethnomusicology Forum* (2004). Two books are forthcoming from Ashgate Press in 2005: *Iranian Classical Music: The Discourse and Practice of Creativity* and *Music and the Play of Power: Music, Politics and Ideology in the Middle East, North Africa and Central Asia.*

Grant Olwage is a research fellow at the Wits School of Arts, University of the Witwatersrand, South Africa. His essays "Hym(n)ing: Music and Masculinity in the Early Victorian Church" and "The Colour and Class of Tone" appear, respectively, in *Nineteenth-Century British Music Studies*, vol. 3, edited by Bennett Zon and Peter Horton (Ashgate Press, 2003), and *Ethnomusicology Forum*, vol. 13/2 (2004). Current projects include editing a monograph titled *Composing Apartheid*, and work on "the voice" and club/dance music. He performs as a DJ under the name of Dr. G.

Annie J. Randall is an associate professor of musicology at Bucknell University in Lewisburg, PA. She has published several journal articles and book chapters on late eighteenth and early nineteenth-century German music and is coauthor of the book *Puccini and 'The Girl,' History and Reception of* The Girl of the Golden West (University of Chicago Press, 2004). She is currently collaborating on a collection of essays, *She's So Fine: Whiteness, Femininity, Adolescence, and Class in 1960s Music*, edited by Laurie Stras.

Helen Reddington is a senior lecturer in the Commercial Music Department of University of Westminster, UK. Her Ph.D. dissertation, "An Analysis of the Role of Female Instrumentalists in Punk and Rock Bands in the 'Moment' of Socio-Political Change in Great Britain, ca. 1976 to ca. 1982," was partly based on her experiences as a bass player for Joby and the Hooligans, "the worst band in Brighton." Her "Lady Punks in Bands: A Subculturette?" appears in *The Post Subcultures Reader* edited by David Muggleton and Rupert Weinzerl (Berg, 2003). In 2001 she toured the UK with her song-cycle "Voxpop Puella," and in 2004 Near Shore Records released the CD "Helen and the Horns" under Reddington's *nom de chanson* Helen McCookerybook.

Britta Sweers is junior professor in ethnomusicology at the Hochschule für Musik und Theater in Rostock, Germany. Recent publications include "Das Andere im Eigenen entdecken—musikethnologisches Denken in der historischen Musikwissenschaft" [Discovering the Other in One's Self: Ethnomusicological Thinking in Historical Musicology] in *Hamburger Jahrbuch für Musikwissenschaften*, vol. 15 (Peter Lang, 1998), and "Die Fusion von traditioneller Musik, Folk und Rock—Berührungspunkte zwischen Popularmusikforschung und Ethnomusikologie" [The Fusion of Traditional, Folk, and Rock Music—Popular Music Research Meets Ethnomusicology] in *Dreißig Jahre Popularmusikforschung: Konzepte Ergebnisse, Perspektiven. Hamburger Jahrbuch für Musikwissenschaft* vol. 19 (Peter Lang, 2002). Her book *Electric Folk: The Changing Face of English Traditional Music* is forthcoming from Oxford University Press.

Hon-Lun Yang is an assistant professor of musicology at Hong Kong Baptist University, Hong Kong, PRC. Publications include "Nationality versus Universality: The Identity of George W. Chadwick's Symphonic Poems" in *American Music* 2003/21; "Politics, Identity, and Reception: Composers of the Second New England School" in *Past in the Present*, Conference Proceedings of the 16th Congress of the IMS, 2000; "The Chinese Piano Tradition and Liszt" in *The Liszt Society Journal* 2001/21; "Socialist Realism and Chinese Music" in *Socialist Realism and Music: Anti-Modernisms and Avant-gardes*, ed. M. Bek (Bärenreiter; forthcoming); "Globalization and Western Music Historiography in the PRC, Taiwan, and Hong Kong" in the Conference Proceedings of the Musicological Society of Japan International Congress in Shizuoka in Celebration of the 50th Anniversary (2004).

Index